Nietzsche and Modern German Thought

Edited by
Keith Ansell-Pearson

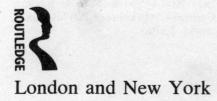

London and New York

First published 1991
by Routledge
11 New Fetter Lane, London EC4P 4EE

Simultaneously published in the USA and Canada
by Routledge
a division of Routledge, Chapman and Hall, Inc.
29 West 35th Street, New York, NY 10001

Typeset in 10/12 pt Times by
Columns Design and Production Services Limited, Reading
Printed in Great Britain by
Biddles Limited, Guildford, Surrey

British Library Catagloguing in Publication Data
Nietzsche and modern German thought.
1. German philosophy. Nietzsche, Friedrich 1844–1900
I. Ansell-Pearson. Keith
193

Library of Congress Cataloging in Publication Data
Nietzsche and modern German thought / [edited by] Keith Ansell-Pearson
    p.   cm.
    Includes bibliographical references and index.
    1. Nietzsche. Friedrich Wilhelm. 1844–1900—Contributions in modern
German philosophy.   2. Philosophy, German—19th century. 3. Philosophy,
German—20th century.   I. Ansell-Pearson, Keith.
B3317.N485   1991
193--dc20 ·   90–48665
                                                                            CIP

ISBN 0–415–04442–1

Contents

Contributors

Keith Ansell-Pearson is lecturer in political theory at Queen Mary & Westfield College, University of London, having previously taught philosophy at the University of Malawi. He has published essays on Nietzsche, Kant, Marxism, Foucault, and African thought. His study of Rousseau and Nietzsche will be published later this year by Cambridge University Press, and he is currently preparing a new edition of Nietzsche's 'On the Genealogy of Morals' for the Cambridge University Press series *Texts in the History of Political Thought*.

Jay Bernstein is reader in philosophy at the University of Essex. He was educated at Trinity College, Connecticut, and Edinburgh University. He is the author of *The Philosophy of the Novel: Lukács, Marxism, and the Dialectics of Form* (Harvester: Minnesota University Press, 1984), *Art, Metaphysics, and Modernity: Aesthetic Alienation from Kant to Derrida and Adorno* (Polity). He has also edited a selection of Adorno's essays on mass culture published by Routledge. At present he is engaged on a study of Rousseau's critique on liberalism.

Howard Caygill lectures in the School of Economic & Social Studies at the University of East Anglia. He was educated at the universities of Bristol and Sussex and has held research posts in Sociology and Philosophy at Balliol College and Wolfson College, Oxford. He is the author of *Art of Judgement* (Blackwell, 1989).

Nicholas Davey studied the history of ideas and philosophy at the universities of York, Sussex, and Tübingen, and has undertaken research in Berlin and Weimar. Since 1976 he has lectured in philosophy at the City University, London, Manchester University, and South Glamorgan Institute of Higher Education, Cardiff. He has published essays on Baumgarten's aesthetics, Hume, Heidegger's aesthetics, Gadamer, Habermas, and Nietzsche's contribution to aesthetics and hermeneutics.

Ian Forbes has been a lecturer in politics at Southampton University since 1983. His prize-winning Ph.D. thesis, *Marx and the New Individual*, is published by Unwin Hyman. He has co-edited a book on human nature, and published essays on Nietzsche, feminist thought, rights, and socialism. For three years he was director of the Socialist Philosophy Group, and edited the influential pamphlet *Market Socialism: Whose Choice?*.

Christopher Janaway graduated from Oxford in philosophy and German and went on to do a D.Phil. on Schopenhauer. Since 1981 he has been lecturer in philosophy at Birkbeck College, University of London. He is the author of *Self and World in Schopenhauer's Philosophy* (Oxford, Clarendon Press, 1989).

Nick Land studied philosophy at the universities of Sussex and Essex and is currently lecturer in philosophy at the University of Warwick, where he specializes in mass materialism. He has published essays on Blanchot, Kant, and de Sade, and is currently completing a book on Bataille.

Michael Newman is an art critic and is currently writing a Ph.D. at Essex University on Nietzsche and Walter Benjamin. He lectures in art history and theory at various art schools and universities. His publications include 'Revising Modernism, Representing Post-modernism' in *Postmodernism*, ed. Lisa Appignanesi, London, Free Association Books (1989), and essays and catalogue books on modern and contemporary art.

Robert B. Pippin is professor of philosophy at the University of California, San Diego. He was educated at Trinity College, Connecticut, and Pennsylvania State University. He is the author of *Kant's Theory of Form* (Yale University Press, 1982), *Hegel's Idealism: The Satisfactions of Self-Consciousness* (Cambridge University Press, 1989), and numerous articles on the history of the modern philosophical tradition. His most recent book is *Modernity as a Philosophical Problem: On the Dissatisfactions of European High Culture* (Basil Blackwell).

Robert Rethy is currently associate professor of philosophy at Xavier University. He was educated at Trinity College, and Pennsylvania State University. During 1989–90 he was visiting professor at the University of Essex. He is the author of numerous articles and reviews on Heraclitus, Descartes, Nietzsche, Schopenhauer, and modern German philosophy.

George J. Stack is professor of philosophy at the State University of New York, Brockport College. Amongst his books are *On Kierkegaard: Philosophical Fragments* (Humanities Press, 1976), *Kierkegaard's Existential Ethics* (University of Alabama Press, 1976), *Sartre's Philosophy of Social Existence* (Warren H. Green Inc., 1978), and *Lange and Nietzsche* (Walter de Gruyter, 1983). He is currently completing a study of Nietzsche and Emerson.

John Walker was educated at Queen's College, Cambridge, and has studied at the University of Tübingen. He has been a research fellow at Wolfson College, Oxford, and at the University of Liverpool. Since 1988 he has been fellow and director of studies in German at Selwyn College, Cambridge. He is currently completing a book on Hegel.

Introduction

Keith Ansell-Pearson

> Almost every important German thinker, even if he has not remained a Kantian, has at least started out from Kant and from the need clearly to define his position with respect to Kant's ideas.
>
> Lucien Goldmann, *Immanuel Kant*

Recent years have seen an astonishing array of studies on Nietzsche's philosophy reflecting the emergence of a serious and scholarly interest in Nietzsche's writings amongst Anglo-American philosophers, sociologists, and political theorists. This volume sets out to make a contribution to the current revaluation of Nietzsche's philosophy. All of the essays have been specially written at the request of the editor and have not appeared before. The aim is to examine in a critical and illuminating way Nietzsche's relation to Kant and the post-Kantian tradition of modern German thought. The volume taken as a whole is designed to cast light on the chief areas of Nietzsche's relation to the Kantian heritage that encompasses the domains of knowledge, ethics, and art as articulated in Kant's three major critiques of pure reason, of practical reason, and of judgement.

Some grandiose claims have been made on behalf of Nietzsche's writings in recent years – that he brings about the end of the western philosophical tradition, that he overcomes metaphysics, that he inaugurates a post-philosophical style of thinking, that he is the first postmodernist, and so on. But the claim that Nietzsche breaks with the philosophical tradition neglects the fact that his innermost thinking is born out of a 'confrontation' (the German is *Auseinandersetzung*, denoting a settlement, an exchange) with the modern philosophical tradition. By emphasizing the importance of situating Nietzsche's ideas in the context of the modern philosophical tradition it is not the intention of the volume to undermine the radical nature of his thought; rather, it has to be the case that the originality and radicalness of any thinker can only be fully appreciated when his or her ideas are situated in the context of the tradition that the particular thinker was seeking to overcome. In several ways the essays which make up this volume can be taken to constitute exercises in what Nietzsche called philosophical labouring (a kind of labour that he himself was fairly industrious at). This does not reflect an impotence of the intellect, or a failure to take risks and experiment, but the belief shared by a number of the contributors is that the task of philosophical legislation has become increasingly problematic in recent years with the advent of what, for the sake of shorthand, can be called the 'post-modern condition' – a condition which is neither regressive nor progressive, but which simply denotes a difficulty and a problem concerning the actualization of philosophy and the status of modern forms of knowledge and truth.

In the essay on 'Nietzsche, Christianity, and the legitimacy of tradition' which opens the volume, John Walker examines Nietzsche's appraisal of the significance of Kant's critique of metaphysics. Kant's critique of metaphysics undoubtedly constituted the most important and lasting influence on Nietzsche's education as a philosopher. In his philosophical notebooks of 1872–3, for example, he is preoccupied with what he regards as the fundamental revolution in thought brought about by Kant's philosophy: 'The altered position of philosophy since Kant. Metaphysics impossible. Self-castration. Tragic resignation, the end of philosophy. Only art has the capacity to save us' (Kritische Gesamtausgabe: Werke III, 4, 19 [319]). Walker draws on the insights of Alasdair MacIntyre in order to show that Nietzsche's attempt to inaugurate a new style of philosophy has to be understood in the context of a tradition, in this case that of European Christianity and its philosophical inheritance in Kant and Hegel. Despite its claim to have established the possibility of a new kind of philosophy, Nietzsche's thought, Walker maintains, remains inextricably tied to the philosophical tradition in so far as it retains what are essentially Kantian premises. Walker shows that Nietzsche wished to cultivate a specifically existential reading of the meaning and significance of Kant's critique of metaphysics, so that it becomes, as it had been for Kleist, an existential experience. Thus he is less concerned with the validity of the conclusions arrived at about truth and knowledge by Kant from a critique of reason than with the existential conclusions we need to draw from our reading of that critique about the activity of philosophy itself. However, Walker argues that Nietzsche's critique of metaphysics is ultimately self-contradictory in that it attempts to establish a philosophy that will be life-affirming and life-enhancing but which, in its claim that thought must serve existential and practical needs, cannot demonstrate the legitimacy of its own mode of philosophical argument and reasoning. Walker finds Hegel's attempt to overcome metaphysics a more coherent enterprise since, unlike Nietzsche's critique, it does not separate the epistemological and existential aspects of philosophical argumentation. Walker is adamant that his reading of Nietzsche is not a reactionary one but a concrete one which situates the 'text' of Nietzsche's philosophy in an appropriate and illuminating 'context'.

In his essay on 'Kant, Lange, and Nietzsche', George Stack sets out to show the importance of a book which Nietzsche read avidly on its publication in 1866, namely, F. A. Lange's *History of Materialism*, and which served to mediate his reading and appropriation of Kant. Stack shows that Nietzsche's preoccupation with Kantian themes extends from the philosophical notebooks of 1872 to the late 1880s, a longevity which reveals Nietzsche's intense concern with epistemological questions and issues. Nietzsche's critical analyses of truth, knowledge, belief, and scientific concepts are essential, Stack argues, to his attempt to articulate a post-metaphysical and post-epistemological conception of philosophy. Stack's essay illuminates for us the philosophical context in which Nietzsche sought to formulate a new mythopoetic and existential conception of philosophy.

In his essay entitled '*Schein* in Nietzsche's philosophy', Robert Rethy examines the extent to which Nietzsche's attempt to overcome metaphysics still operates within metaphysical oppositions, notably Kant's distinction between appearance and the thing-in-itself. What concerns Rethy is the use of the distinction between *Schein* (semblance) and *Erscheinung* (appearance) in Nietzsche's early writings and the way in which his later work is characterized by the opposition between *Schein* and the will to power. In the *Birth of Tragedy* semblance is conceived by Nietzsche to be the power that is constitutive of visibility, whereas *Erscheinung* is conceived as mere appearance. Turning to the works of Nietzsche's so-called middle period (1878–82), Rethy contends that here we find an elimination of the duality between appearance and a deeper level of reality such as the thing-in-itself, and in its place the triumph of the notion of *Schein* as a notion which contains its opposite within itself.

Art is celebrated by Nietzsche precisely because it affirms the 'good will to semblance'. The rest of his essay is devoted to examining the implications of the fascinating relationship between *Schein* and will to power as it appears in Nietzsche's later works. Throughout, Rethy's analysis is guided by the question to what extent Nietzsche's thinking remains determined by metaphysical oppositions in spite of its radical pretensions.

In his essay on 'Hermeneutics and Nietzsche's early thought', Nicholas Davey sets out to show that Nietzsche's early thought is best understood as a hermeneutic project. Davey argues that Nietzsche's place in this important tradition of modern European thought rests not so much on his posthumous influence on thinkers as diverse as Heidegger, Derrida, and Foucault, but on the rigour and independence of his attempt to develop a radical style of hermeneutic philosophizing that is attuned to the existential needs of modern European culture. His essay contains a reassessment of Nietzsche's early philological output in order to show that for Nietzsche hermeneutics did not constitute a distinct branch of philosophical criticism but an integral part of his classical interests. Davey shows that Nietzsche's appreciation of hermeneutic thought arises out of a critique of the tradition of *Sach-Philologie* which ignored the existential context of learning and culture. This leads him to the major argument that the *Birth of Tragedy* is not simply an essay on Greek art and literature, but a dual response to the crisis within the discipline of philology and within European culture. However, Davey argues that Nietzsche aimed not to simply destroy philology but to reform it by showing how it could become culturally and existentially relevant. Thus, it is mistaken to view Nietzsche's relationship to the philosophical tradition either in terms of a revolutionary break or in terms of an eccentric decentring.

When Nietzsche is celebrated today as a deconstructionist *avant la lettre* it is usually for what is widely regarded as his destruction of the notion of the rational, unified, self-conscious, autonomous self or subject. In his essay on 'Nietzsche, the self, and Schopenhauer', Christopher Janaway critically examines Nietzsche's critique of the idea of the self from the perspective of Schopenhauer's understanding of the will. His major contention is that despite claims to the contrary Nietzsche does not fully overcome the problems and tensions which result from any attempt to abandon or deconstruct a notion of the self. Janaway argues that a great deal of the undermining of the notion of the wholly rational, self-conscious subject had already been performed by Nietzsche by his great mentor Schopenhauer. However, unlike Kant and Schopenhauer, both of whom attacked the notion of the soul conceived as substance, Nietzsche does not wish to hold on to the notion of the subject as a single, united entity which claims to be an 'I'. Nietzsche sets out to discredit both the notion that there is a single subject and the notion that there is a single entity called the 'will'. If in the end a notion of the subject is indispensable this is not because of an epistemological a priori but a psychological one, that is, such a notion does not serve the purpose of grounding the truth or falsity of objective knowledge of 'reality', but that of enhancing or depressing the will to power. In an intriguing concluding assessment of Nietzsche's relation to Schopenhauer, Janaway aims to show that Nietzsche's celebration of multiplicity and heterogeneity (of impulses, drives, affects, even subjects) must still rely on a notion of the self as agent since there must exist 'something' which gives style to character and controls the drives and affects necessary for there to be a coherent sense of selfhood (the way in which, as Nietzsche teaches, 'one becomes what one is').

In his essay on 'Marx and Nietzsche: the individual in history', Ian Forbes sets out to show that although Marx and Nietzsche cannot be compressed into the same theoretical mould it can be demonstrated that their achievements as two great 'masters of suspicion' have been formative influences in the development of western perceptions of self and change in society. Despite the fact that the political and economic order of western societies confirms narrow, 'bourgeois' assumptions about the individual, Forbes insists that it is a concept that is always open to contestation. What Forbes shows through a careful reading of the two thinkers is that a concern with the possibilities for effective autonomous action is fundamental to both. Against any easy categorization of Marx's thought as the pinnacle of Enlightenment modernism and Nietzsche's thought as the expression of an irrationalist counter-Enlightenment, Forbes argues that it is more accurate to describe their contributions to the development of a radical conception of individuality by seeing Nietzsche as the Dionysus to Marx's Apollo. Despite their different valuations of consciousness and rationality, the political vision of both is of a polity in which individuals who are the product of a certain social and historical evolution learn how to preside over a personal re-creation, that is, how individuals learn to become self-determining, in a word, 'autonomous'.

In his essay on 'Nietzsche and the problem of the will in modernity', Ansell-Pearson situates Nietzsche's notion of will to power in the context of Hegel's recognition of the autonomous will as a defining moment of the modern, in order to illuminate its status as a metaphor of self-legislation. Viewed as a problem of politics, the question of the will, as it is posed by the modern tradition deriving from Rousseau, is a question about the nature of law and sovereignty (political legitimacy). In Rousseau, for example, it is the authentic self-legislation of the individual will which provides the only legitimate ground of political authority: 'I submit only to the law I myself have given', as Nietzsche puts it in a passage in *Daybreak*. Nietzsche departs from Rousseau and Kant, however, in positing the relationship between autonomy and morality (universality) as mutually exclusive. The crucial question for Nietzsche about politics in the modern period is that concerning the value-basis on which sovereign individuals – individuals emancipated from the morality of custom and proud possessors of free will – are to enter into social relationships and construct their ethico-political identities. Ansell-Pearson is sceptical, however, about recent claims that Nietzsche's doctrine of will to power is capable of providing the basis for developing a postmodern conception of human agency, since the question about the relationship between the particular and the universal which runs through the modern tradition is not resolved in Nietzsche but revealed in all its tension and difficulty.

In the context of a discussion of Kant's attempt to establish autonomy as the supreme principle of morality in the form of the categorical imperative, Jay Bernstein's essay on 'Autonomy and solitude' examines how Nietzsche's non-moral conception of autonomy partakes of the aporia characteristic of modernity. The key contrast to be drawn is that between autonomy and heteronomy, that is, between what the will determines for itself and what determines the will, while the crucial question concerns how it is possible to distinguish between the autonomous and heteronomous aspects of our being, of locating precisely where the 'freedom' of the will lies. Bernstein contends that unless it is possible to provide the self or subject with any essential determination then the project of autonomy must collapse. His essay contains a novel and suggestive reading of the relationshp between the doctrine of eternal return and that of will to power. The thought of eternal return is designed, Bernstein contends, to illuminate the relation of the self to itself, in the sense that it poses the question, what relation must there be between a self and its ruling thought if that thought is to be autonomous? What concerns Nietzsche is not the universality of the will which wills itself (is autonomous), but rather the attitudinal relation between the self and its will. But, considered as a categorical imperative, the eternal return immediately cancels itself out when it is commanded because it becomes something unconditional and dogmatic. It is within the paradoxes of the thought of eternal return that Bernstein instinctively locates the source of Nietzsche's interrogation and dissolution of the modern project of autonomy.

In his essay on 'Affirmation and eternal return in the Free-Spirit Trilogy', Howard Caygill performs a major reassessment of the place of the doctrine of eternal return in Nietzsche's thought. Through a reading of Nietzsche's Free-Spirit Trilogy (the works written between 1872 and 1882), Caygill sets out to show that the true significance of the thought of eternal return is best appreciated in the context of Nietzsche's confrontation with the 'crisis of judgement' experienced in post-Kantian thought. Jürgen Habermas, for example, traces the 'philosophical discourse of modernity' to the problem of validating discrimination, and sees Nietzsche's will to power as the source of recent anti-Enlightenment tendencies in French thought. The legitimacy for his own reading, Caygill insists, is to be found in Nietzsche himself, notably in *Ecce Homo* where eternal return is construed neither in terms of its systematic relationship to the notions of will to power and the overman nor as a solution to the problem of liberation from *ressentiment*, but as an aporia or puzzle which opens up new philosophical spaces. The thought of eternal return, Caygill sets out to show, is 'beyond' the yes and no of judgement. Consequently, it is argued, the thought should not be construed, as is commonly the case, in terms of its relationship to the doctrine of will to power since the thought is beyond the judgement contained in will to power (its yes and no, its active and reactive nature). Here Caygill departs radically from the interpretations put forward in the essays by Ansell-Pearson and Bernstein in which will to power itself is seen as the major principle of Nietzsche's philosophy beyond good and evil. To include eternal return within the teaching of will to power, however, Caygill argues, is to subject it to the oppositions of metaphysical thinking. The affirmation contained in eternal return precludes and exceeds the judgemental willing of the subject.

In his essay entitled 'Art as insurrection: the question of aesthetics in Kant, Schopenhauer, and Nietzsche', Nick Land develops a challenging reading of Nietzsche's radicalization of aesthetics in the context of a discussion of Kant's third critique on judgement, arguing that Kant's thought on art is a symptom of a

deep trauma afflicting the critical enterprise, and in the context of
Schopenhauer's discovery of the unconscious basis of drives and his
radicalization of desire. Land reads the figure of Dionysus in
Nietzsche as an exacerbation of the radical tendencies of the
tradition in that it conceives desire as the collective liquidation of
institutions, in which art and desire are utterly fused. He further
contends that the problem of desire finds a materialist displacement
in Nietzsche, in that it is affirmed as recurrent excitation and freed
from any redemptive metaphysics. Land sees the significance of
Nietzsche's aesthetic practice in the way in which it refuses
philosophy's attempt to rationalize, normalize, and limit the
unconscious, imagination, and genius. It is art which exceeds and
resists the policing of the unconscious by philosophy and the
attempt to control and limit libidinal energy. Contra the bureaucrats
of pure reason Nietzsche celebrates the madness of art.

In 'Reading the future of genealogy: Kant, Nietzsche, Plato',
Michael Newman addresses the problem of reading as an explicit
theme of Nietzsche's writing. In aphorism 137 of his *Mixed Opinions
and Maxims* (1879) Nietzsche writes that the worst readers are the
ones 'who proceed like plundering soldiers'. In the preface to the
Genealogy of Morals he argues that in order to understand his texts
there needs to be cultivated 'an art of exegesis', an art which
requires not the plundering of soldiers but the 'rumination' of a
cow. Newman explores the implications of Nietzsche's demand for
an art of exegesis in the context of the 'future', the fate, of a
genealogy of morals where the emphasis is on effecting a self-
overcoming of modernity. The fate of Nietzsche's *Genealogy of
Morals* must reside in the future as his project is unreadable by
'modern men' who are unskilled in the art of exegesis. Nietzsche's
text is thus composed for the benefit of a future humanity that is in
some sense 'beyond' (*über*) man, that is, *over*-man. Newman's focus
on the problem of reading in Nietzsche has the effect of showing
that questions about Nietzsche's importance and about the significance of his thought are inseparable from questions of how we
are to read him and about how his experimental texts are designed
to serve as mediums of philosophical education. Newman attempts
to illuminate the problem of reading (in) Nietzsche by relating
Nietzsche's concerns with those of Plato in the *Phaedrus* on love,
reading, writing, and speech, and with those of Kant on art and
genius in the *Critique of Judgement*.

Finally, in the essay on 'Nietzsche, Heidegger, and the metaphysics of modernity' which concludes the volume, Robert Pippin

sets out to raise a number of important questions concerning the radical turn philosophy takes in Nietzsche by considering Heidegger's influential reading of him as the last metaphysician of the west whose thought completes the modern metaphysics of subjectivity. For Pippin the key question to be asked of Nietzsche's philosophy is quite simple: how are we to understand it? It is especially important to ask this and related questions if we are to comprehend the grip Nietzsche continues to hold over our current imagination. Heidegger's great claim is that despite its radical pretensions Nietzsche's thought remains inextricably linked to metaphysics (not only in its Cartesian sense but also its Platonic one) in that it shares certain assumptions about subjectivity that are common to the tradition. Pippin's essay, however, has wider ambitions than merely assessing Heidegger's controversial reading of Nietzsche. He also wants to challenge the way in which Heidegger develops an intellectual history through a history of philosophy. What needs to be considered, Pippin argues, is the Nietzschean counter-charge to a Heideggerian nostalgia for the experience of Being. Such a change would amount to the claim that the disclosure of the contingent, social and psychological origins of metaphysical beliefs discredits any romantic yearning for the kind of experience of Being which prevails in Heidegger's work.

It is hoped that the essays in this volume will serve to inspire further research into the area of Nietzsche's relation to the modern philosophical tradition. No attempt has been made to impose a unity on the collection. Indeed, a number of essays clash on how we are to interpret fundamental aspects of Nietzsche's thought. But this conflict of interpretation seems to me to represent a more healthy and appropriate response to the challenge of Nietzsche's legacy than any spurious unanimity of what that legacy amounts to.

1 Nietzsche, Christianity, and the legitimacy of tradition

John Walker

There seems to be a dilemma: either we anachronistically impose enough of our problems and vocabulary on the dead to make them conversational partners, or we confine our interpretive activity to making their falsehoods look less silly by placing them in the context of the benighted times in which they were written.

Richard Rorty[1]

Self-understanding is more than just self-observation: we need to study history, because the stream of the past flows through us in a thousand waves; we ourselves are nothing but our constant experience of the motion of the stream.

Friedrich Nietzsche[2]

I want in this essay to argue that Nietzsche's thought can best be understood as part of a tradition; and that the decisive element in the tradition is the interaction of philosophy with European Christianity. My point is not that Nietzsche was a crypto-Christian or that we should read him as a theologian rather than a philosopher. I want rather to argue that Nietzsche's engagement with Christianity is relevant precisely to our assessment of his philosophical achievement. This reading of Nietzsche, I believe, bears directly both on our understanding of Nietzsche's reaction against his predecessors in German philosophy – specifically Kant and Hegel – and on some of the most important issues raised by the modern reception of Nietzsche's thought.

My account will be divided into three parts. In the first section I will argue that there is an ahistorical emphasis in much modern Nietzsche criticism which, although it appears to be licensed by Nietzsche's rhetoric, cannot be supported by the logic of his actual texts. Nietzsche's rhetoric proclaims that he intends to create an absolutely new kind of philosophy: one which will be free of the inherited conceptual vocabulary of the European philosophical tradition based upon metaphysical beliefs. But the dialectic of Nietzsche's actual arguments reveals that his thought is still inextricably connected to that tradition. This ambivalence is made manifest in Nietzsche's engagement with Kant. Nietzsche's attack on metaphysics, I will suggest, retains essentially Kantian premisses although it makes systematic misuse of Kant's arguments.

In the second section I will maintain that the systematic ambivalence in Nietzsche's critique of metaphysics is also present in his attempt to give his thought a historical legitimation. For Nietzsche the intellectual culture of European Christianity is the objective form of life in which his own thought, like that of his philosophical predecessors, inheres. Nietzsche's philosophical ambition is to create a post-Christian as well as post-metaphysical philosophy. But just as his critique of metaphysics presupposes a metaphysical conception of the activity of philosophical thought itself, his critique of Christianity presupposes the Christian culture against which it reacts. Comparing Nietzsche's account of the relationship between philosophy and Christianity to that of Hegel, I will argue that Nietzsche's critique of Christian thought is connected to Christian culture in a way which the conceptual apparatus of his thought makes it impossible for him to articulate or to describe.

In the third section, drawing on the work of Alasdair MacIntyre, I will argue for the relevance of the idea of *tradition* to the defence of Nietzsche in modern philosophical debate. I will suggest that Nietzsche's account of the relationship of his own thought to Christianity is coherent only if we read his thought as part of the tradition of Christian thought and Christian experience.

I

Much of the modern reception of Nietzsche outside the German-speaking world seems to have been written as if we could talk about the contemporary relevance of Nietzsche only by taking Nietzsche's thought out of its historical context. For French-speaking commentators such as Deleuze, Foucault, and Derrida it is above all the stubbornness with which Nietzsche's texts resist dialectical integration into the history of philosophy – the impossibility of interpreting those texts *in relation to* the metaphysical tradition against which they react – which is the source of their appeal. On this reading Nietzsche is an ally of the deconstructionist project because he has turned philosophy into a kind of negative hermeneutics: because there is nothing to interpret except 'interpretation' itself.[3] For Deleuze it is this which makes Nietzsche's mode of thought the necessary antidote to the false consciousness of the Hegelian dialectics;[4] for

Foucault one of the intellectual fathers of the archaeology of know-ledge;[5] and for Derrida the paradigm of the deconstructionist style.[6] But it is just this feature of Nietzsche's thought which is responsible for its neglect by the analytic tradition of the English-speaking world. Arthur Danto, for example, makes the astonishingly parochial claim that 'Nietzsche has seldom been treated as a philosopher at all', and urges that 'Nietzsche's language would have been more colourful had he known what he was trying to say'.[7] From this perspective, a philosopher whose arguments cannot objectively be assessed is a philosopher who does not know what he means and hence not a philosopher at all: a literary man, perhaps, but not a philosopher, a writer whose statements have to be translated in order to be intelligibly discussed.[8]

The ahistorical tendency of much Nietzsche criticism and exegesis is, of course, not without warrant in Nietzsche's texts themselves. Nietzsche does indeed assert that the significance of a philosophy is nothing other than the meaning of the life of the philosopher who has written it.[9] He conceives of a philosophical book as a literary text in which 'style' is indissociable from substance.[10] He tells us that the abstract philosophical vocabulary he has inherited from his predecessors is built upon manifold psychological deception, and that he has had to invent a new 'aesthetic' philosophical discourse of his own.[11]

In the very possibility of philosophy as Nietzsche conceives it there is an existential paradox. Philosophy, for Nietzsche, is a product of the immediate energy of life, but it is also a most potent instrument which can be turned against life. Philosophy can be a form of life at war with itself. Nietzsche in the 1880s described the whole history of philosophy as a 'secret raging against the presuppositions and instinctual values of life' (*ein heimliches Wüten gegen die Voraussetzungen des Lebens, gegen die Wertgefühle des Lebens*).[12] Whether Nietzsche really considers all philosophy to be the enemy of life – as he says in the posthumously published fragment just quoted – or just some philosophy, as he says in the preface to *The Gay Science*,[13] is unclear. What does seem clear is that Nietzsche wishes to offer us a discourse which will not be divided against life in this way: a philosophy for 'free spirits' which will contribute to the affirmation of life, which for Nietzsche is the affirmation of the will to power.

The name Nietzsche most consistently gives to the kind of philosophy he is seeking to oppose or overcome is 'metaphysics'. Metaphysics is a form of thought which is divided against life because it seeks to compensate for a failure of life; it is a product of 'creative resentment against the real'.[14] Nietzsche's critique of metaphysical reasoning is in the first place a critique of the existential and not of the intellectual dishonesty of those who engage in such reasoning: people whose dominant motives, he thinks, are resentment and fear.[15]

It is crucially relevant that by 'metaphysics' Nietzsche (unlike many other thinkers) means something more than a particular branch of the philosophical discipline, or indeed any body of argument or doctrine as such. He means a mental activity and a network of beliefs which support personal commitments springing from an experience and a need: the same experience and the same need which gives rise to religion. The experience in question is one of fear and self-division. The original religious experience, according to Nietzsche, is the experience of the human will that it is subject to an overwhelming power other than itself, a power which is nevertheless manifest within itself. This is man's experience of the alienation of his essential powers:

> *In summa*: the origin of religion lies in man's experience of a great power, strange to himself, which overwhelms him. Like the invalid, who has an unusual sensation of heaviness in one of his limbs and concludes that another man is lying on top of him, so the naïve religious man becomes divided against himself [*legt sich der naïve homo religiosus in mehrere Personen auseinander*].[16]

This experience, according to Nietzsche, gives rise to a need for compensation: a need to compensate for an actual experience of weakness with an imagined or projected experience of power. Religion, therefore, responds to this need by a morbid self-division of the personality, in which man's vital powers are projected on to a deity.[17]

This experience and need, according to Nietzsche, belong in the first place to the will and only secondarily to the intellect. But it is clear that Nietzsche's account of the origin of religion is closely related to his account of the origin of metaphysics. Both religion and metaphysics, on Nietzsche's account, arise from the division of the personality and the existential need to which that division gives rise. Both religion and metaphysics respond to this need: neither is identical with it. But religion, for Nietzsche, is primary in relation to metaphysics in two senses. First, religion is historically prior to metaphysics; it is religion which first responds to the need, and metaphysics which comes to the aid of religion when religious belief is threatened by a culture of rational critique:

> For every religion is born of fear and of need: they have all crept into being when reason has been led astray. Perhaps when religion has been threatened by learning it has fraudulently incorporated

some philosophical doctrine into its system, which one discovers later on; but this is a theologian's trick, which arises when a religion has already begun to lose faith in itself.[18]

Second, what Nietzsche calls the metaphysical need (*das meta-physische Bedürfnis*) is not, in his conception, the origin of religious belief. Rather the reverse is the case. The metaphysical need is a product of the decay of religious life: of man's inability to satisfy the existential need which gives rise to religion by religious means alone.[19] Metaphysics does not produce religions; for religions are born of a real, if also a destructive, need of the human will. But metaphysical thought is a product of that search for certainty which derives from an instinctual weakness of the will (*Instinkt der Schwäche*). Metaphysics cannot produce religions; it can only preserve them.[20]

Nietzsche's attack on what he calls 'metaphysics', then, cannot be dissociated from his attack on religion and the moral and cultural imperatives to which religion gives rise. Indeed Nietzsche explicitly casts his critique of his predecessors in the German philosophical tradition as a critique of the Christian ethical consciousness which he sees as the motive force behind that tradition's modern history. Hence Nietzsche characterizes modern German philosophy as a kind of Christian romanticism and homesickness,[21] and describes the critical and historical philosophies of Kant and Hegel as having a moral and ultimately a theological motivation.[22] In particular, he characterizes the movement from Kant to Hegel as the eclipse of the critical spirit in German philosophy and its replacement by an apologetic metaphysic of Revelation.[23]

But if the self-consciousness of philosophy serves what are at root always existential imperatives and needs, how is Nietzsche to *argue* against the philosophers he wants to undermine?

Our metaphysical beliefs, according to Nietzsche, are essentially practical rather than intellectual in character. We have taken them up less because they are true than because they enable us to live; and we will abandon them only if we can be persuaded that we will live better if we let them go. The task of the philosopher, therefore, is to 'create new values'[24] which will enable us to do so by replacing the old values which spring from the religious need and sustain its metaphysical justification. How can a philosopher create new values? Only by undermining our *belief* in the capacity of the old values to sustain and further what Nietzsche calls 'life'; but such belief, if it is not the product of philosophical argument, cannot be destroyed by philosophical argument alone. Nietzsche's use of argument, for this reason, has to be something other than a strictly rational one; for the very point of his mode of argument is to necessitate the will by making people aware of the divorce between their self-understanding and their life.

It is for this reason that the divorce between the rhetorical claims of Nietzsche's writing and the actual content of his arguments is more than a rhetorical matter; it is implicit in the very idea of a post-metaphysical mode of thought as Nietzsche conceives it. The rhetorical force of Nietzsche's psychological critique of metaphysics depends upon his ability to show that the arguments of the philosophers, whatever their philosophical logic, derive from an existential need, and that the need in question stands in no necessary relationship with the ideal of intellectual truth. In *Human, All Too Human*, for example, Nietzsche defines his programme as follows:

> all that has made metaphysical assumptions *valuable*, *terrible*, pleasurable to people, all that has produced such assumptions is passion, error, and self-deception; the worst possible, not the best possible methods have led us to believe in them. To refute every existing religion and metaphysical system one has only to show that they have such methods as their basis.[25]

But the *coherence* of Nietzsche's critique of metaphysics cannot depend upon arguments like this. For Nietzsche's central contention is that *all* philosophical arguments derive from existential needs of this kind, indeed that we should judge the worth of a philosophy not by its argumentative coherence but by its existential effect: by whether or not its discourse contributes to the affirmation of the human will. If we take Nietzsche on his own terms, then his claim that it is possible to refute metaphysical beliefs by demonstrating that they originate in 'passion, error, and self-deception' is either incoherent or at best irrelevant.

This ambivalence in Nietzsche's project is intimately bound up with his reading of Kant. The significance of Kant's thought, for Nietzsche, lies in its critical achievement: its exposure of the limits of speculation in relation to experience,[26] and so of the impossibility of any positive metaphysics or natural theology.[27] Nietzsche sees as the primary consequence of Kant's achievement an undermining of that optimistic confidence in the power of the theoretical intellect which is at the root of the modern metaphysical alienation from life.[28] For Nietzsche, the real relevance of the Kantian philosophy lies in the cultural relevance of its critique of knowledge. Kant's positive ethic and constructive epistemology Nietzsche sees as theology in disguise, and utterly rejects.[29] But Nietzsche's unwillingness to endorse Kant's movement from critical procedure to constructive affirmation derives less from a failure to be convinced by Kant's epistemological arguments than from Nietzsche's own conception, which is radically different from that of Kant, of the existential significance of philosophy itself. Nietzsche is concerned less with whether or not Kant's critique of knowledge leads to philosophically valid conclusions than he is with the conclusions we draw from our reading of that critique about the point of doing philosophy at all.

Nietzsche makes the remarkable claim that hardly anyone has ever understood what Kant meant.[30] He wants reading Kant to be for his contemporaries what it was for Kleist: an existential experience.[31] Reading Kant should have that effect on us, Nietzsche argues, because the result of the Kantian critique is to show that our discursive intellect, like all our immediate knowledge, is irrevocably tied to the existence of the self in space and time. In his engagement with Kant, as indeed in his engagement with the whole philosophical tradition, Nietzsche deliberately exploits and yet also blurs the distinction between epistemological and existential modes of argument. Nietzsche cannot conceive of an epistemological circle which is not vicious: of a critique of knowledge which is immanent to rather than in abstraction from the actually existing faculty of cognition which it articulates and describes.[32] But his argument to this effect, when it is explicit, is that the critical philosopher is the same *person* as the self which is immediately involved in experience: and that the philosophers have consistently concealed this fact by disguising their own self-investigation as an academic discipline which can be safely isolated from the remainder of their experience.[33] For this reason Nietzsche sees as the inevitable consequence of the Kantian critique 'gnawing scepticism and relativism': those very things which Kant was most concerned to counter and to overcome in the philosophical culture of his own time.[34]

Nietzsche similarly exploits and yet deliberately misconstrues the idea of the thing-in-itself. In a crucial passage in the *Will to Power* Nietzsche rejects the idea of a sphere of things-in-themselves, intrinsically beyond the scope of possible knowledge, for the very reason that Kant had to postulate that idea: because all knowledge conditions and mediates its object, and so what is absolutely unconditional (*unbedingt*) can never be known:

> The greatest fable is the one about knowledge. We want to know how the things-in-themselves are constituted: but behold, there are no things-in-themselves. But let us suppose there was something 'in itself', something unconditional; then that would be the very reason why that something could not be known. Something unconditional cannot be known; otherwise it would *not* be something unconditional. To know means to put oneself into a conditional relationship to something [*sich irgendwo in Bedingung setzen*].[35]

Nietzsche rejects the Kantian doctrine of the thing-in-itself because it posits the ultimate object of thought as a reality intrinsically removed from the self and its desire to know, which for Nietzsche is the inescapable condition of all human knowledge:

Someone who wants to know unconditionally desires that what he knows should not affect him at all [*da das, was er erkennen will, ihn nichts angeht*] and that it should not affect anyone else: but there is a contradiction in his *wanting* to know and at the same time wanting not to be affected by what is known, for what then is the point of wanting to know? [*wozu doch dann Erkennen?*].[36]

The apparently anti-Kantian thrust of Nietzsche's argument is, in fact, profoundly misleading. Nietzsche's argument about the thing-in-itself, like his argument about the self, produces an existential critique of what was intended only as an epistemological argument. His real target is not the content of Kant's epistemological theory, but Kant's confidence in the general relevance of epistemological argument. Nietzsche's real thesis is that the idea of objective truth is untenable because of the connection of knowledge to the self and so to the will. But it is not by accident that the idea of the thing-in-itself is the starting point of Nietzsche's own argument. Nietzsche needs things-in-themselves because the idea of a divorce between an immediate and therefore absolute truth and the mediating faculty of the discursive intellect is the very basis of Nietzsche's own thought. Nietzsche's thing-in-itself is the existential opposite of discursive thought: 'life', 'the Will', or whatever other category he chooses to employ at a particular point in his argument.

Nietzsche indebtedness to the Kantian critique and his misreading of Kant's arguments have, I believe, a common origin. Both stem from a central contradiction in Nietzsche's very idea of what 'metaphysics' means. By metaphysics Nietzsche means both a body of philosophical doctrines and a mode of being: an existential attitude which we can choose to adopt or not to adopt in relation to our experience as a whole. Nietzsche's critique of all hitherto existing philosophy relies for its rhetorical force upon an attack on metaphysics in the second sense. But it relies for many of its arguments on Kant's critique of metaphysics in the first sense. The problem is that Nietzsche's arguments are at odds with his rhetoric, and his rhetoric at odds with his arguments. Nietzsche's thought, for all the force of its critique of metaphysical *doctrines*, in fact lacks a non-metaphysical conception of the *activity* of philosophical thought itself. Nietzsche conceives of speculative thought as necessarily the opposite of 'life', of intellectual mediation as necessarily destructive of the immediacy of experience. What Nietzsche's thought most lacks is what its own logic most requires that it should possess: an articulate doctrine of the activity of philosophy as embodied in and giving expression to the existential reality which he calls 'life'. This is so because Nietzsche's way of doing philosophy is in a radical sense a way of negation. However persuasively he can tell us what the new and post-metaphysical mode of truth is *not*, he can never, by any process of argument, tell us determinately what that truth *is*. For if he ever did tell us that, his arguments would become part of the common philosophical conversation of mankind, capable of objective comparison with the arguments of his predecessors. And it is the very possibility of such rational comparison – of a coherent regulative idea of Reason informing the history of philosophical debate – which Nietzsche is most concerned to deny.

II

It is this difficulty in the legitimation of Nietzsche's thought which gives rise to the historical form of the contradication in Nietzsche's critique of metaphysical argument. Nietzsche hopes to derive from an historical critique of metaphysical beliefs a dialectical and a practical effect on his readers which a merely speculative critique could not achieve. The new philosophy of the future which he is proposing is not, in Nietzsche's conception, the manifestation of a timeless truth, but rather one which is made necessary by the unresolved conflicts in the experience of his own age. Nietzsche has to claim this because, if the truth of his philosophy could in fact be grasped in abstraction from the experience of his own time, it would be a metaphysical kind of truth just like the truth he considers to be at odds with the needs of the human will. Hence in his proposal for a *Gay Science*, where he speaks about himself and his disciples as the authors of a new ethical code, he also says that their task is to become the people they already potentially are: to remove from an inauthentic into an authentic mode of being.[37] But this implies that his task is to give his disciples a certain kind of practical knowledge: not just intellectual knowledge which will make them know about the gap between the inauthentic and the authentic mode of their own being, but existential knowledge which will impel them to want to close it. Since (despite Nietzsche's rhetorical idiom) it is not to single individuals but to a whole culture that his writing is addressed, the knowledge in question will have to be able to relate to the historical and cultural self-consciousness of his age.

Nietzsche's historical critique of metaphysics, however, is shot through by the same paradox which belongs to his psychological and existential critique. The greatest danger of historical knowledge, in Nietzsche's judgement, is that it can paralyse the springs of action of a culture with collective self-knowledge. It can lead us to use our knowledge of ourselves as an excuse for failing to become ourselves or, as Nietzsche puts it, to become mature.[38]

Yet Nietzsche more than any other thinker is aware that knowledge, once attained, cannot without existential danger as well as intellectual dishonesty by suppressed. He knows himself to be addressing a historically self-conscious age, and the insight he is seeking to communicate is likely to intensify that self-consciousness to the highest degree. Nietzsche's purpose is to make his age conscious of the meaning of its own self-consciousness, to make his readers aware that the kind of critical and comparative knowledge their culture is able to give them is at odds with the needs of life. In his historical as in his metaphysical argument Nietzsche is proposing to give his readers intellectual knowledge in the service of the principle of life: a principle which, in Nietzsche's understanding, is necessarily at odds with the values implicit in discursive argument. The intellectual equivalent of Nietzsche's injunction that the will should overcome itself is the demand his philosophy makes that his readers should be able to overcome the effects of the kind of insight he is proposing to give them.

This dialectic in Nietzsche's philosophical attitude to the culture of his own age can only be understood in the context of his account of the relationship of his own thought to the philosophical history of Christianity.

Throughout Nietzsche's critique of Christianity there is a radical distinction between the teachings of Christ and the historical phenomenon of Christianity (*das Christentum*). Nietzsche considers 'Christianity' (*das Christentum*) to be an existentially dishonest mode of life because it tries to make the absolute ascetic renunciation of the world – which Nietzsche takes to be the teaching of Christ – into a historically successful way of life. In Nietzsche's understanding an authentically Christian way of life is intrinsically negative in character. Spirituality, he tells us in *The Antichrist*, cannot give rise to action (*der ganze Begriff geistiger Ursächlichkeit ist falsch*) and so Christianity is defined less by 'doing' than by 'not doing a great deal' (*ein Vieles-nicht-tun*).[39] There can, for Nietzsche, be no Christian culture, no Christian politics, no Christian philosophy; all are contradictions in terms.[40] The history of European Christendom is the history of the creation of those fictions; and the life of the Christian who tries to be a European citizen, soldier, business man and so on is the very kind of life from which Christ preached redemption (*genau das Leben, von dem Christus die Loslösung predigte*).[41]

This is why Nietzsche says that Christianity is born of a spirit of resentment and that the moral code of Christianity (*die Moral des Christentums*) is a capital crime against life.[42] The Christian *religion*, for Nietzsche, is the negation of life pretending to be life; it is life divided against itself. The Christian religion, on Nietzsche's account, is intrinsically a destructive rather than a creative movement: a movement which by its very nature reacts against something (*eine Gegenbewegung ihrem Wesen nach*).[43]

It is clear that Nietzsche's critique of Christianity is closely related to his critique of metaphysics. Both Christianity and metaphysics are forms of consciousness which are at war with life. They are antithetical to the instinctual affirmation of the will and promise a release from the contingent necessity of being into a sphere of eternal and purely spiritual truth. But Nietzsche's argument about Christianity is different from his argument about metaphysics because Christianity is an objectively existing form of life. Nietzsche attributes the origin and the success of the Christian religion not to the intellectual appeal of its dogmatic theology, but to its ability to respond to and to satisfy instinctual needs. Nietzsche's critique of Christianity centres upon the contention that the Christian religion, quite apart from the theology and the philosophy which it generates, is itself a 'metaphysical religion'. That is so because Christianity remains connected, however vicariously and paradoxically, to the authentic teaching of Christ. Because the Christian ideal, in Nietzsche's understanding, is the absolute negation of the worldly experience, Christian belief is not *intellectually* at odds with negative knowledge about itself; for the core of Christianity is the insight that spiritual truth is 'not of this world' and can never be so. The impossibility of positive Christianity, Nietzsche insists, consists not in the intellectual dishonesty of its intention, but in the existential dishonesty of its practice: in the fact that a religion with this pure ascetic ideal must destroy itself as soon as it tries to constitute itself as an objective form of life. Historic Christianity is a way of life which is condemned to be sincere without being authentic, to be *wahrhaftig* and never *wahr*.[44]

The transcendental meaning of his own age, in Nietzsche's view, is that in it the cultural conditions are given for philosophy to emancipate itself from the Christian religion and so to contribute to overcoming the divorce between human self-awareness and the energy of the will which Nietzsche sees as the historical consequence of Christian culture. Nietzsche holds that view because he thinks that the European metaphysical tradition which has grown up in conjunction with Christianity has developed to such a point that it can be turned against Christianity itself. In the preface to *Beyond Good and Evil* Nietzsche in one of his most famous metaphors speaks of his own thinking as an arrow released from a bow. The tension in the bow is the history of European philosophy in the Christian era, and the progressive estrangement of philosophy from the life of that era which Nietzsche considers to have come to a head in his own time:

> But the fight against Plato (or, to put it the way the people understand, the fight against the Christian-clerical oppression of millennia – for Christianity is Platonism for the people), has given rise to a splendid tension of Spirit in Europe, such as the world has

never seen before. With a bow as tight as that one can shoot at the furthest possible targets.[45]

Nietzsche goes on to say that modernity has tried desperately to loosen the bow: first by means of the 'democratic enlightenment' – the attempt to divert the spiritual energy of Christianity in ideologies of secular progress, and second by means of 'Jesuitism'. He characterizes himself and his disciples as 'neither Jesuits nor democrats' but as free spirits, who carry with them 'the whole need of the spirit and all the force in its bow' (*die ganze Not des Geistes und die ganze Spannung seines Bogens*).[46]

What Nietzsche is concerned to do is not to propose a 'solution' to the problem manifest in the situation of his age, but to make explicit and so to bring to a head the unresolved contradication in the experience of that age. For the problem in question, in Nietzsche's understanding, is a product of the needs of the human will, needs which Nietzsche knows can never be supplied by dialectic. He wishes to intensify the need of the will in order that the orientation of the will might be changed, not by an argument but by an experience: an experience which his philosophy will contribute to creating.

On one level at least, Nietzsche's critique of the cultural situation of his age faces the same problem as his purely philosophical critique of metaphysics. Because it is the *will* of his age he is seeking to influence, and because of what he conceives the relationship of the will to the discursive intellect to be, he cannot achieve the effect he desires by the coherence of his arguments alone. He must therefore in his critique of his age, as in his purely philosophical critique, use an ironic and self-negating kind of discourse, a discourse the object of which is not to convince the intellect but to solicit the action of the will. But there is a crucial difference as well as a crucial connection between the two kinds of argument. The core of Nietzsche's argument about the relationship between Christianity and European thought in his age is the thesis that there is, in that age, a condition of human experience which mirrors in reality the antithesis between his own mode of thought and the metaphysical mode he is seeking to overcome. Nietzsche's critique of his age amounts to the claim that his critique of metaphysics is not just an argument, but the articulate form of an actually existing need of the human will.

Given Nietzsche's concept of the existential status of philosophical argument, his historical critique of his age has the potential to have a more profound effect on his readers in the sense he intends than his existential and psychological critique of metaphysical reasoning. For this reason an assessment of Nietzsche's engagement with the European Christian tradition has to be central to our assessment of his thought as a whole.

To understand the logic of that claim is to understand that the tension Nietzsche discerns between the clashing and converging histories of Christianity and philosophy is also a tension which is present in his own thought. Nietzsche aspires to write a kind of philosophy which will make an absolutely new beginning in the history of European thought. But the attempt to overcome metaphysical or 'Christian' philosophy which is the core of his own thought is conceived by Nietzsche as an articulation of the *experience* of his own age: an experience which is permeated by the self-consciousness of European Christianity. Like an arrow shot from a bow Nietzsche's argument will only go as far as the tension which has given rise to it will allow. Nietzsche's critique of the Christian consciousness is only as strong as the strength of its *reaction* against that consciousness; it is *eine Gegenbewegung ihrem Wesen nach*.

Indeed, Nietzsche's historical critique of Christianity reveals an ambivalent relationship not only to Christian culture, but also to the philosophical heritage which he is seeking to overcome. The major target in Nietzsche's attack on the idea of a Christian philosophy of history is Hegel. Nietzsche attacks Hegel with much greater vehemence than he attacks Kant because he reads Hegel's philosophy as what Hegel explicitly declares it to be: a philosophy of history which is also a theodicy and a philosophy of the Christian Revelation.[47] He sees the development from Kant to Hegel as a philosophical regression because it means that the critical power of the Kantian philosophy has been neutralized, its intellectual resources put in the service of an ethical and theological imperative.[48]

Hegel is as concerned as Nietzsche was to attack and to overcome what Nietzsche calls metaphysics. But metaphysics, for Hegel, is a descriptive and not automatically a pejorative term. By metaphysics Hegel means both the belief that the ultimate structure of reality can be articulated by reason,[49] and the mode of thought which is concerned with 'absolute' or speculative objects: the soul, the world, God and so on.[50] In this sense Hegel considers metaphysics to be both a possible and a valuable mode of thought. Hegel uses Kantian terminology to define the object of his attack, which is not metaphysics as such but a particular conception of metaphysical thought, one which ignores the difference between the way the understanding thinks about objects of experience and the way reason thinks about speculative or metaphysical objects.[51] What Hegel is most concerned to attack is the belief that speculative thought can relate to its objects as if they are 'things' which can be conceived of in abstraction from the activity of thought itself:[52] that substance and subject are absolutely different spheres of existence.[53] In this sense Hegel, like Nietzsche, is seeking to overcome both a body of philosophical doctrine and a conception of the activity of speculative thought itself. His arguments are directed as much against the belief that speculative thought can meaningfully be conceived of in this way as they are against the particular metaphysical doctrines which flow from that belief.

Hegel's critique of metaphysics does, however, differ profoundly from that of Nietzsche. Nietzsche's epistemological arguments against metaphysical doctrines, as we have seen, are utterly different in character from the existential arguments which he directs against the metaphysical conception of the activity of philosophy itself. But Hegel's arguments are epistemological and existential at once. Hegel's most important epistemological arguments are that reason has to be understood as the immanent form of experience itself,[54] and that the purpose of philosophy is nothing other than to make articulate the truth which is implicit in human experience as a whole.[55] If thought and being are not categorical opposites, and if reason is not just our thinking about our experience but the rationality which is present in that experience itself, then it follows that philosophy as the vehicle of reason cannot relate to human experience as a whole merely by making this or that part of human experience into its object. Philosophy has to be concerned with the whole of human experience because the whole of experience has reason in it; and the way philosophy is connected to the whole of experience has as much to do with the logic of experience as it has to do with the logic of philosophy. The point of Hegel's doctrine of historically actual Spirit is to show how human experience as a whole makes the enterprise of philosophical thought necessary and relevant.

Only in this context can the differences between Hegel's and Nietzsche's views about the philosophical significance of Christianity in relation to their own thought be understood. For Nietzsche, Christianity is the metaphysical religion because it turns the separation of reflection from life into an objective form of life. For Hegel, Christianity is a religion which is profoundly anti-metaphysical in the Nietzschean sense. That is so because Christianity proclaims that the truth which is spiritual is also the truth which is actual. As soon as human history becomes the history of Christianity, Hegel says, we cannot construct any absolute antithesis between the truth we apprehend in religion, or articulate in philosophy, and the actual and determinate kind of truth which is the truth of our historical experience. For both kinds of truth are but different modes of the one truth which is the truth of Spirit;[56] and the history of the Christian era is the history of the revelation of Spirit.[57] For Hegel, the very possibility of his own philosophy – a philosophy which *says* explicitly and articulately that human history is the history of Spirit – means that Spirit is now philosophically revealed; or, what is the same thing, that there is now a fully Christian philosophy.[58]

Hegel's connection of his own thought to the cultural history of Europe, therefore, does not detract from the originality of his critique of metaphysics. On the contrary, his critique of metaphysics can only be understood in relation to his account of the historical significance of his own thought, which is also an account of the relationship of his thought to Christianity.

It is for this reason above all that Hegel's historical as well as his metaphysical arguments are relevant to our understanding of Nietzsche. Nietzsche, of course, does not believe in the truth of the Christian revelation; indeed he considers the very concept of revelation to be the product of a psychologically motivated self-deception.[59] But it is clear from his argument about Christianity and philosophy that he thinks that the history of his own time itself independently 'reveals' the truth which it is the task of his philosophy to expound. The real difference between Nietzsche's and Hegel's conception of the relationship between philosophy and history is this: Hegel's understanding of the significance of his own thought means that his philosophy has articulately to acknowledge the fact that it is made possible by the culture of his age and the way that age is connected to human history as a whole. But Nietzsche's understanding of the purpose of his own thought means that his philosophy has to know about, but can never explicitly acknowledge or articulate, its connection to the culture of his age.

By reading Nietzsche in relation to Hegel we will not necessarily be persuaded to accept Hegel's account of the relationship between philosophy and Christianity in preference to Nietzsche's own. But what such a reading can do, I suggest, is to explain why the rhetoric of Nietzsche's claims about the absolute novelty of his own thought is so much at odds with the logic of his real account of the significance of his own thought in the history of Christian Europe. Nietzsche, like Hegel, believes that the history of Christianity itself discloses the truth which it is the task of his philosophy to proclaim. But, unlike Hegel, he cannot philosophically *say* that this is the case without abandoning his claim to inaugurate a post-metaphysical mode of thought.

Nietzsche is one of the most acute exponents of the way thought implies the human context from which it derives. But as far as his own thought is concerned he is compelled to treat this connection with irony, to affirm it and to retract the affirmation at the same time; for to do otherwise would be to acknowledge the sovereignty over his thought of a reality other than the infinite play of his own dialectic.[60] The cultural source of the radical irony of Nietzsche's writing is the fact that his very intention to overcome the metaphysical mode in philosophy makes it necessary for him to define his own thought in relation to the intellectual history of European Christianity.

III

It is in this sense that I want to propose that we should read Nietzsche's thought as part of a tradition. I use the term 'tradition' broadly in the sense outlined by Alasdair MacIntyre in *After Virtue* and later in *Whose Justice? Which Rationality?* Central to MacIntyre's concept of tradition are the ideas of *givenness* and *open-endedness*. In *After Virtue* MacIntyre characterizes our experience of being in a tradition like this:

> What I am . . . is in key part what I inherit, a specific past that is present to some degree in my present. I find myself part of a history and that is generally to say, whether I like it or not, whether I recognize it or not, one of the bearers of a tradition.[61]

I think it is meaningful to describe Nietzsche's work as part of a Christian tradition in this sense. To claim this is not to claim that Nietzsche had anything approaching a belief in any of the dogmas of Christianity or even that his own existential critique of Christianity would be recognized by an orthodox Christian as an intelligible or a coherent one. As MacIntyre and other writers[62] have shown, adherence to a tradition does not consist in acceptance of a body of doctrine whether philosophical, theological, or otherwise, but in a shared and continuing conception of what 'doctrine' means and of how doctrines can appropriately be extended and discussed. This is what MacIntyre means by saying that the kind of 'rational justification' the first principles of a tradition receive is 'at once dialectical and historical'.[63]

I hope to have shown that Nietzsche's concept of the validation of philosophical argument is not only an existential one, but also one which is, precisely, 'dialectical and historical at once'. Nietzsche addresses his arguments to a philosophical audience who find themselves at a particular point in the intellectual history of Christian Europe. Indeed, the claim Nietzsche makes is that his philosophy articulates his readers' experience of themselves in that history: that their experience, which he himself shares, solicits and requires the new kind of philosophy he proposes to them.

One of the most important questions the modern reception of Nietzsche has to ask, therefore, is whether or not this claim is justified. Is Nietzsche's account of the significance of his own thought in relation to the history of European philosophy and of Christianity a credible one? Is the account Nietzsche gives of the connection between Christianity and metaphysics a tenable one, and does his critique of metaphysics have the consequences for our understanding of Christianity he says it has? Does the history of thought since Nietzsche suggest that he should be read as closing a tradition, or rather as engendering a crisis for a tradition which continues, at least in part, on the strength of his insights?

To be sure, the reading of Nietzsche I have proposed means that we have to 'read in' to Nietzsche's text a context such as I have outlined. That is so because Nietzsche's mode of thought makes it impossible for him explicitly to acknowledge that his thought has any context at all. The pervasive tension between the mode and the actual content of Nietzsche's arguments – the fact that his arguments consistently reveal the connection of his thought to a history and a culture, although the mode of his writing is intended to nullify any such connection – derives above all from the fact that Nietzsche's mode of thought is intrinsically incapable of coming to terms with the fact that it is embedded within what MacIntyre calls the narrative of a tradition.[64]

If we read Nietzsche only on his own terms, then we are forced to choose between accepting him on those terms and not accepting him at all; and this has to be an irrational choice. But if we try to abstract a set of arguments from his philosophy and to assess them on some neutral or disengaged basis we do not read what he has to say. To read Nietzsche in terms of his problematic relation to a tradition is to steer a middle course between these two alternatives. This reading offers the possibility of both a relevant critique and a relevant defence of Nietzsche's achievement: a critique and a defence which do justice to what Nietzsche conceives philosophy to be, and yet do not allow him unilaterally to determine the rules of philosophical debate.

The relevant defence of Nietzsche's thought is that we do *not* have to take or leave Nietzsche solely on his own terms; Nietzsche's arguments can become part of a philosophical debate because they have a context and 'so a structure of justification'.[65] Nietzsche's mode of argument is that which belongs to participation in – or reaction against – a tradition, and as such has a rationality different from, but no less coherent than, that of modern analytic philosophy. The relevant critique of Nietzsche's thought is that we can only make sense of it in terms of an idea which his rhetoric insistently denies: the idea of tradition. Whether or not we think Nietzsche's thought represents an epistemological crisis from which metaphysics or Christianity have never recovered will depend upon an assessment of the content of his particular arguments. But the contradiction between the form and the content of his arguments should be enough to engender such a crisis for any mode of thought which claims to be absolutely new in the way Nietzsche's does. For Nietzsche's critique of philosophical tradition reveals by its very dialectical success the power of the tradition against which it reacts.

Nietzsche's account of the relationship of his own thought to the philosophical history of Christianity does not allow us to read his philosophy, as does Habermas, as an absolute critique of the idea that value-judgements can or should be legitimated by reference to a normative criterion of rational validity.[66] For the central argument in Nietzsche's critique of ethics – the thesis that value-judgements are grounded ultimately only in the will to power – is intelligible only by reference to the context from which the concept of the 'will to power' derives: Nietzsche's rejection of the Christian ethical tradition which he considers to be the manifestation of a will to weakness. We cannot read Nietzsche's critique of metaphysics, as does Deleuze, as a critique which is absolute or historically unique.[67] For the logic of that critique is a logic which grounds critique in a context. The logic of Nietzsche's critique of metaphysics is also the logic of Nietzsche's paradoxical and self-divided relationship to the Christian philosophical tradition which he is trying to end and so to overcome.

This is, I believe, not a reactionary but a concrete reading of Nietzsche. To see Nietzsche in this context is to bring out the full force of Nietzsche's critique of metaphysical abstraction, of his exposure of the historically, culturally, and linguistically contingent presuppositions of all philosophical arguments. These arguments become all the more powerful if we are prepared to apply them to Nietzsche's own thought, and if we recognize why they necessarily undermine Nietzsche's rhetoric. One of the greatest obstacles to the modern reception of Nietzsche has been the assumption that we have to understand the significance of his thought in philosophical and cultural history in the way which his rhetoric tells us we should, as a discourse without a history and a context, a 'text' rather than a debate.

Nietzsche's deconstructionist disciples and his analytic critics alike have been guilty of *abstraction* in their conception of what Nietzsche actually has to say: of the assumption that he has to speak to us now either immediately or not at all. But the antithesis between originality and tradition – between immediacy and mediation – is a false one, even if our belief in it would appear to be licensed by Nietzsche's own most powerful appeals. We do not have to choose between the horns of Rorty's dilemma, because the dilemma is not real. We do not have to choose between reducing our reading of Nietzsche to an exercise in the history of ideas and reading him only in the light of the concerns of the last two decades. As Nietzsche knew, history *can* be in the service of life. We need a historical reading of Nietzsche in order to find out what Nietzsche is telling us about ourselves.

NOTES

As there is no English edition of the whole of Nietzsche's works I have used throughout Karl Schlechta's edition *Friedrich Nietzsche: Werke in drei Bänden*, Munich, Hanser Verlag, 1954–6. The translations are my own. To enable cross-referencing with other editions each reference includes the English title, a volume and page reference to the Schlechta edition, followed in brackets (where possible) by the corrsponding paragraph or aphorism number from Nietzsche's own text. Nietzsche's posthumously published writings which Schlechta refers to as *Aus dem Nachlass der Achtziger Jahre* I refer to by the more common title of *The Will to Power*.

1 Richard Rorty, 'The Historiography of Philosophy: Four Genres', in Rorty (ed.) *Philosophy in History*, Cambridge, Schneewind & Skinner, 1984, 51.
2 Friedrich Nietzsche, *Human, All Too Human*, Werke I, 823 (223).
3 See e.g. Jacques Derrida, *Spurs: Nietzsche's Styles*, Chicago, Chicago University Press, 1979, 73.
4 Gilles Deleuze, *Nietzsche et la Philosophie*, Paris, Presses Universitaires de France, 1962, 180–3.
5 Michel Foucault, *The Archaeology of Knowledge*, trans. A. M. Sheridan, London, Tavistock, 13–14.
6 See Derrida, op. cit., especially 119–43.
7 Arthur C. Danto, *Nietzsche as Philosopher*, New York, Macmillan, 1965, 13.
8 See the discussion of the difference between the 'elucidation' and the 'translation' of a philosophical text in Michael Rosen, *Hegel's Dialectic and its Criticism*, Cambridge, Cambridge University Press, 1982, 3.
9 Nietzsche, *The Gay Science*, Werke II, 12–13 (3).
10 Nietzsche, *Ecce Homo*, Werke II, 1104 (4), cf. *Aurora*, Werke I, 1209 (375).
11 Nietzsche, *On Truth and Falsehood in an Extramoral Sense*, Werke III, 313–22.
12 Nietzsche, *The Will to Power*, Werke III, 736.
13 Nietzsche, *The Gay Science*, Werke II, 10 (2).
14 Nietzsche, *The Will to Power*, Werke III, 883.
15 Ibid., 912.
16 Ibid., 747.
17 Ibid., 748.
18 Nietzsche, *Human, All Too Human*, Werke I, 519–20 (110).
19 Nietzsche, *The Gay Science*, Werke II, 138–9 (151).
20 Ibid., 212 (347).
21 Nietzsche, *The Will to Power*, Werke III, 464.
22 Ibid., 479.
23 Ibid., 902–3.
24 Nietzsche, *The Genealogy of Morals*, Werke II, 798 (17).
25 Nietzsche, *Human, All Too Human*, Werke I, 452 (9).
26 Nietzsche, *The Gay Science*, Werke II, 226 (357). See also the critique of Kant in *The Will to Power*, Werke III, 863.
27 Nietzsche, *The Genealogy of Morals*, Werke II, 894 (25).
28 Nietzsche, *The Birth of Tragedy*, Werke I, 101.
29 Nietzsche, *The Antichrist*, Werke II, 1171–2 (11).
30 Nietzsche, *Schopenhauer as Educator*, Werke I, 302.
31 Ibid., 303.
32 See e.g. Nietzsche, *The Will to Power*, Werke III, 884–5.
33 Nietzsche, *The Gay Science*, Werke II, 10–12 (2).
34 Nietzsche, *Schopenhauer as Educator*, Werke I, 303.
35 Nietzsche, *The Will to Power*, Werke III, 386.

36 Ibid., 387.
37 Nietzsche, *The Gay Science*, Werke II, 197 (335).
38 Nietzsche, *On the Use and Disadvantage of History for Life*, Werke I, 232 (4).
39 Nietzsche, *The Antichrist*, Werke II, 1200–1 (39).
40 See the remarkable passage in Nietzsche, *The Will to Power*, Werke III, 639–40.
41 Ibid., 641.
42 Ibid., 826.
43 Nietzsche, *Ecce Homo*, Werke II, 1143.
44 Nietzsche, *Aurora*, Werke I, 1061 (73). Lionel Trilling's distinction between 'sincerity' and 'authenticity' is, I believe, analogous to Nietzsche's own. See Trilling, *Sincerity and Authenticity*, Oxford, 1972.
45 Nietzsche, *Beyond Good and Evil*, (Preface), Werke II, 566.
46 Ibid.
47 Nietzsche, *The Will to Power*, Werke III, 496.
48 Ibid., 902–3.
49 See Hegel, *Lesser Logic*, trans. William Wallace, Oxford, 1975, 47 (paras 26–7).
50 Ibid., 50–1 (para. 30).
51 Ibid., 47–8 (paras 27–8).
52 See e.g. ibid., 53–4 (para. 34).
53 Cf. Hegel, *Phenomenology of Mind*, trans. A. V. Miller, Oxford, 1971, 9–10 (para. 17): 'In my view, which can be justified only by the exposition of the system itself, everything turns on grasping and expressing the True, not only as Substance, but equally as Subject.'
54 Hegel, *Philosophy of Mind*, trans. Wallace and Miller, Oxford, 1971, 226 (para. 467, Zusatz): 'The following distinction must be firmly established between Understanding and Reason . . .'
55 Hegel, *Philosophy of Right*, trans. T. M. Knox, Oxford, 1952, 11: 'To comprehend what is, this is the task of philosophy, because what is, is reason. Whatever happens, every individual is a child of his time; so philosophy too is its own time apprehended in thoughts.'
56 Hegel, *Philosophy of Mind*, 13 (para. 381, Zusatz).
57 See Hegel, *Philosophy of History*, trans. J. Sibree, ed. C. J. Friedrich, New York, Dover Publications, 1956, 319ff.
58 See Hegel, *Lectures on the History of Philosophy*, 3 vols, trans. Haldane & Simon, London, 1986, vol. 3, 551–2.
59 See e.g. Nietzsche, *Aurora*, Werke I, 1053.
60 The consequences of this for the status of philosophical argument in Nietzsche are well brought out by Alasdair MacIntyre: see his *Whose Justice? Which Rationality?* London, Duckworth, 1988, 368.
61 Alasdair MacIntyre, *After Virtue. A Study in Moral Theory*, London, Duckworth, 1985, 221ff.
62 See Edward Shils, *Tradition*, London, Faber, 1981, especially 12–33.
63 MacIntyre, *Whose Justice? Which Rationality?*, 360.
64 MacIntyre, *After Virtue*, 216.
65 MacIntyre, *Whose Justice? Which Rationality?*, 363.
66 See Jürgen Habermas, 'The Entwinement of Myth and Enlightenment', in *New German Critique*, 26, 23–8.
67 See Deleuze, op. cit., especially the concluding chapter.

2 Kant, Lange, and Nietzsche: critique of knowledge

George J. Stack

Henceforth . . . let us be on guard against the dangerous old conceptual fiction that posited a 'pure, will-less, painless, timeless knowing subject'; let us guard against the snares of such contradictory concepts as 'pure reason', 'absolute spirituality', 'knowledge in itself': these always demand that we should think of an eye that is completely unthinkable, an eye turned in no particular direction, in which the active and interpreting forces, through which alone seeing becomes seeing *something*, are supposed to be lacking; these always demand of the eye an absurdity and a nonsense.

On the Genealogy of Morals, III: 12

Even though Nietzsche lamented the obsession with theory of knowledge in modern philosophy and considered it a sign of philosophical dissolution, he found it necessary, ironically, to create a radical and critical analysis of knowledge and truth in order to clear a path to a new way of thinking and existing. Fortunately, he did not have to carry out this self-imposed and demanding task of the dismantling of previous conceptions of knowledge and truth unarmed. For his subterranean work of undermining the foundations of knowledge and truth had already been started by Kant, F. A. Lange, and a host of neo-Kantian scientists of the nineteenth century. It is with a genealogical tracing of the origins of Nietzsche's critical reflections on knowledge and truth that I will primarily be concerned.

Although Nietzsche did not have a deep understanding of the complex details of Kant's *Kritik der reinen Vernunft*, he had a profound understanding of the implications of Kant's agnosticism. As his notes in the *Nachlass* indicate, he was brooding over the destructive, anti-metaphysical implications of Kant's critical philosophy as early as 1872, the same year in which his Schopenhauerian-inspired 'artist's metaphysics' was expressed in *The Birth of Tragedy*. Even then, he later suggests, scepticism had already taken root in his mind in so far as he tells us that he practised a form of 'Jesuitism' in his 'first period'. That is, 'consciously holding fast to illusion and compulsorily incorporating it as the *basis of culture*.'[1]

In notes from 1872 we find frequent references to the *agon* between art and knowledge against the background of Kant's exposure of the 'anthropomorphic' nature of all knowledge. Nietzsche even uncovers a circularity in Kant's enterprise in the first *Critique*: that is, if the sciences are right (that is, if they give us objective knowledge of the constituents of the natural world), then Kant's theoretical critique gives them no support; if Kant is right (about the constitution of objects of knowledge by virtue of the a priori intuitions of space and time, the receptivity of man's specific mode of 'sensibility', and the application of categories of the understanding to experience), then the sciences are mistaken in holding that they acquire genuine, objective knowledge.[2] Much later he refines earlier reflections on the *Critique of Pure Reason* and argues that Kant's work proceeds on the assumption of the possession of knowledge about knowledge.

It is true that Kant is optimistic about his knowledge of the extent and limits of human knowledge, as well as about his knowledge of cognitive functions and the conditions of knowledge. He says that 'I am concerned with nothing except reason itself and its pure thinking; and to gain complete knowledge of these, there is no need to go far afield, since I come upon them in my own self.'[3] Nietzsche sees that Kant seems to assume that his account of knowledge has an a priori validity, especially since Kant explicitly denies that he is presenting a mere 'hypothesis'. He maintains that

> Any knowledge that professes to hold *a priori* makes a claim to be regarded as absolutely necessary. This applies *a fortiori* to any *determination* of all pure *a priori* knowledge, since such determination has to serve as the measure and, therefore, as the example of all apodictic philosophical certainty.[4]

Nietzsche considers such a claim to rest upon a belief in so far as judgements are primitive expressions of belief. The 'determination of knowledge' cannot be based upon presumed 'knowledge' without circularity. Nietzsche suggests that the *Critique* rests upon 'regulative principles'. When he refers to the categories as 'regulative' concepts or as 'regulative articles of belief', he is not misinterpreting Kant. He is denying their 'constitutive' function against Kant. In effect, he is suggesting that the conception of categories of the understanding is not itself a constitutive mode of knowledge. Kant cannot consistently claim that his statements about knowledge are 'constitutive' claims because what would be constituted in this case would be knowledge claims about the conditions for the possibility of knowledge! If his analysis of the conditions for human knowledge is a priori, this means that it is based upon a transcendental use of reason made possible by the surreptitious use of regulative principles or regulative concepts. The a priori categories of the understanding, on the other hand, are meaningful and not 'empty' because they are applied to appearances encountered by our sensibility. But the supposed a priori structures of knowledge themselves cannot be objects of the understanding. Therefore they must be known by reason itself. If the categories themselves are known by reason, then they are postulates that function as regulative concepts. Hence, the basic principles of the condition for knowledge cannot be demonstrated to be 'absolutely necessary' in so far as they must be construed as derived from a transcendental use of reason. Kant practically acknowledges this in the *Prolegomena to Any Future Metaphysics* when he maintains that

> reason has the sources of its knowledge in itself, not in objects and their observation. . . . When . . . it has exhibited the fundamental laws of its faculty completely and so definitely as to avoid all misunderstanding, there remains nothing for pure reason to cognise *a priori*, nay, there is no ground to raise further questions.[5]

Nietzsche criticizes Kant for assuming the necessary a priori validity or 'truth' of the content of his theory of knowledge. For the idea of pure knowledge or a pure, knowing subject is, for him, an absurdity. He agrees, though, with Kant's view that knowing is a form-giving, constructive activity. If 'regulative principles of belief' were to replace 'pure forms of knowledge', he would be willing to give Kant his due.[6]

If in this reconstruction of Nietzsche's critique of Kant I've run somewhat ahead of my theme, it nevertheless serves a purpose. It shows that Nietzsche's *Auseinandersetzung* with Kant extends from 1872 (and, if we include his youthful, unpublished reflections on 'Teleology since Kant', even from 1868) to 1887/8. Moreover, it reveals the longevity of his intense concern with epistemological questions and issues. Rather than being occasional or incidental, his radical and critical analyses of knowledge, truth, common-sense beliefs, language, and scientific concepts and theories were essential to his polemical philosophical projects and to his experimental, mythopoetic post-metaphysical and post-epistemological vision of a Dionysian world and his correlative ethico-cultural ideals.

KANT AND LANGE: INITIAL REACTIONS

Aside from Schopenhauer's *The World as Will and Idea*, Nietzsche's earliest contact with epistemic problems (both in the domain of philosophical claims to truth and knowledge and in early versions of the philosophy of science) was in his study of F. A. Lange's *History of Materialism and Criticism of Its Present Meaning* (1866). In this remarkable work he found the ingredients for his two global philosophical orientations: the development of a radical, critical, and sceptical phenomenalism and the projection of personal and cultural ideals from what Lange called 'the standpoint of the ideal'. Lange provided Nietzsche with the essential conceptual weapons which he would later use in his battle against metaphysics, an optimistic teleology, and the rationalistic conception of the world and man.

Summarizing Lange's conclusions in a letter to his friend von Gersdorff,[7] Nietzsche explains that, for Lange, we cannot know 'the true essence of things' and that the conception of the thing-in-itself is the result of an antithesis that is conditioned by 'our organization'. Despite his critical analysis of knowledge, Nietzsche continues, Lange believes that philosophers should be free to project ideals, provided they are edifying. Nietzsche asks, 'Who would refute a phrase of Beethoven, and who would find error in Raphael's *Madonna*?' What he does not tell his friend is that he is quoting Lange verbatim. And, of course, he has no inkling of the profound and long-lasting effect that the Kant–Langean agnosticism will have on his thought.

In *The Birth of Tragedy* Nietzsche suppressed his burgeoning scepticism and seemed to share Schopenhauer's view that the secret identity of the 'thing-in-itself' was a cosmic 'primal Will'. In his unpublished essay of 1873 'On Truth and Lying in an Extra-Moral Sense', however, his scepticism comes to full growth. In the preface to the second part of *Human, All Too Human* (1886) he calls attention to this ultra-sceptical essay and tells us that it was written in a period in which he 'believed in nothing'.[8] The basis of this scepticism is the disrelationship between our most common judgements and the experience to which they refer. Perhaps for dialectical purposes he still retains the notion of 'things-in-themselves' and emphasizes their inaccessibility and incomprehensibility. In point of fact, his scepticism is twofold. Not only can we not know things-in-themselves, but the process of expressing judgements about what we perceive is a simplification and metaphorical transformation of our immediate experience of unique particulars.

The analysis of language in 'On Truth and Lying' proceeds on the basis of an earlier presupposition: 'There is no "genuine" expression and *no authentic knowledge without metaphor.*'[9] This assumption is derived from earlier reflections on the nature of language which were reinforced by Lange's repeated uncovering of the use of metaphors in philosophy and the frequent reliance on anthropomorphic projection and transference in scientific language.[10] Nietzsche combines the idea of the metaphorical nature of language with the physiological studies discussed in Lange's *History of Materialism* in such a way as to argue that language cannot be said to picture actuality.

In 'On Truth and Lying' Nietzsche argues that words are copies in sound of nerve stimuli. The words we use in judgements are arbitrary signs that do not accurately represent the phenomena of our experience. The gender we apply to certain entities is purely arbitrary. Moreover, certain words, such as 'snake', are derived from a single trait of the entity we perceive. That is, a snake or *Schlange* is something which twists or winds (*schlingen*). This word, then, is not only a vague designation of the being we perceive, but it is a falsifying simplification of it. Although Nietzsche doesn't mention it, the German word for snake is not merely metaphorical, but is actually a synecdoche. Of course, this would only strengthen his case. For it suggests that our ordinary language is permeated with tropes.

The outcome of 'On Truth and Lying' owes a great deal to Lange's sceptical interpretation of Kant's agnosticism, his denial that we have access to the nature of actuality as it is in itself. What was only implicit in Kant's *Critique of Pure Reason* is amplified by Lange's disclosure of the anthropomorphic nature of truth. With the addition of his theory of the metaphorical nature of language

Nietzsche undermines the traditional conception of truth or the correspondence theory of truth. Thus, truth is defined as:

A mobile army of metaphors, metonyms, and anthropomorphisms: in short, a sum of human relations which have been poetically and rhetorically intensified, transferred, and embellished, and which seem to a people, after long usage, to be fixed canonical, and binding. Truths are . . . metaphors that have become worn out and drained of sensuous force, coins that have lost their embossing and are now considered as mere metal and no longer coins.[11]

The abbreviated account of language and conceptualization presented in this unpublished essay was an exponential increase of the scepticism Nietzsche found in Kant's analysis of knowledge.

Nietzsche kept in mind Lange's insistence that Kant showed that the objects of experience are 'our' objects, conditioned by our senses and our conceptual 'apparatus', that the absolute nature of things is hidden behind the impenetrable veil of the phenomenal world that exists for us.[12] What particularly impressed Nietzsche was that Lange held that the agnosticism of numerous nineteenth-century scientists seemed to confirm Kant's theory of knowledge. Then current physiological theories lent support to the view that our senses determine, in a restricted way, the nature of appearances for us. Combining this with the Kantian analysis of the conceptual scheme that we impose on our experience, Nietzsche plausibly concluded that our sensory-cognitive 'organization' conditions the phenomena we know in such a way that we cannot know whether the objects of our knowledge correspond to any objective entities or relations between such entities. Ordinary language and philosophical language are not genuine representations of actuality but are means by which we impose order on the presumed chaotic 'manifold' of sensory impressions that are themselves, Nietzsche believed, already the result of a selective, possibly unconscious, primitive synthesis. Our conceptual, sensory, and linguistic framework enables us to create a 'world' that is intelligible to us, a humanized world in which we can function effectively and preserve ourselves in existence.

Kant's notion that experience and understanding, as well as the a priori intuitions of space and time (which yields a constituted world of phenomena but provides no access to the true essence of things), meant to Nietzsche that there is an asymptotic relation between conceptualization (and language) and actuality. Even as he later jettisons the idea of things-in-themselves this postulate deeply influences and shapes his radical critiques of knowledge and truth. If our linguistic-conceptual framework does not provide us with an accurate or authentic representation of the 'truth' of things, Nietzsche reasoned, then it generates a false world-picture or produces a systematic 'falsification' of actuality which is a thoroughly anthropomorphic world or a world, as he says in the *Nachlass* from the late 1880s, that is 'true for us'. If 'knowledge' (as delimited by Kant) pertains to a sensory, conceptual world which is not actuality-in-itself then the only truths we can know are 'conditional truths'. In the wake of his study of Kant and Lange, and in association with his conception of language, Nietzsche drew out of the *Critique of Pure Reason*, before F. C. S. Schiller and C. S. Peirce, a pragmatic theory of truth. There is no doubt that Nietzsche's critical analyses of language, knowledge, and truth – which run through his writings from the early 1870s to the late 1880s – owed their inspiration, at least initially, to his understanding of the implications of Kant's epistemology. Nietzsche's sceptical reactions to Kant's thought and Lange's interpretation of it metastasized in his later thought.

AN EVOLUTIONARY EPISTEMOLOGY

It is ironic that in the rash of recent work on evolutionary epistemology Nietzsche's name is conspicuously absent. For he is a forerunner of this interpretation of the development of knowledge who anticipated many aspects of this orientation. Once again, it is Lange's *History of Materialism* which provided the elements out of which Nietzsche constructed a fairly sophisticated account of the evolutionary basis of knowledge. What complicates matters is that his theory is an amalgam of Kant's cursory speculations on human evolution and the role of reason in it, Lange's remarks on man's 'apparatus' for knowledge, and Darwin's theory of natural selection. It is not only Lange's discussions in 'Darwinism and Teleology' that inform Nietzsche's reflections on the philosophical significance of the naturalistic origin of conceptualization. From a single reference that he makes we may infer that he was familiar with an atypical work of Kant's, *Anthropologie in Pragmatischer Hinsicht* (1798). Although the specific reference to this work that Nietzsche makes seems, on the surface, inconsequential, it touches upon a question that haunted his thought until he found his solution to 'the riddle of existence' in the idea of the will to power. Kant speculates in a footnote (which Nietzsche refers to) on the reason why organic beings propagate by means of the union of two sexes. While Kant doesn't try to answer his question, he remarks that 'human reason gets lost when it tries to probe the source' of such natural phenomena.[13] Not only is Nietzsche curious about the confession, on Kant's part, that the ultimate source of natural phenomena is unknown, but he undoubtedly noticed what occasioned Kant's question. What probably struck Nietzsche was something that Lange stressed in his critical exposition of Kant's thought. That is, the observation that

> Understanding and sensibility, for all their similarity, join together spontaneously to produce knowledge, as intimately as if one had its source in the other, or both originated from a common root. But . . . we cannot conceive how heterogeneous things could sprout from one and the same root.[14]

In his *History of Materialism* Lange calls attention to Kant's admission of the imagined, but unknown, root or origin of sensibility and understanding. If we join this to Lange's psychologistic view that these processes are expressions of our 'psycho-physical organization', and if, in turn, we relate this to his sympathetic understanding of the Darwinian emphasis upon the priority of life and the struggle for existence over theoretical knowledge or an 'Alexandrine' culture (a culture of knowledge), we can discern the beginnings of Nietzsche's search for the organic basis of sensory experience and thought. And later, of course, he traces the source and dynamism of life to a hypothetical *Wille zur Macht*.

Since Lange cites passages from Kant's *Anthropology* in a chapter on 'The Relation of Man to the Animal World', and given Nietzsche's reference to this work, we have reason to believe that he was familiar with Kant's rudimentary speculations on evolution. Given the background of the first *Critique*, it is surprising to hear Kant say that 'man, as an animal endowed with the *capacity for reason*, can make of himself a *rational animal* – and as such he first *preserves* himself and his species'.[15] Elsewhere reason is referred to as a 'weapon' in the service of survival. In the same vein Kant imagines that infants, in earlier stages of development, must not have cried at birth because, in a crude state of nature, this would render them vulnerable to prey. And in the same context he further assumes that 'the Orang-Utang or the Chimpanzee would develop the organs for walking, manipulating objects and speaking, until it had a human form'.[16]

Given Kant's speculations on evolution, in co-ordination with Lange's insinuation of the naturalistic origin and function of the intellect and reason, we need not look too far for the source of Nietzsche's conviction that the drive for knowledge, as well as the categories of the understanding and our selective mode of perception ('the perspectival optics of life'), have their origin in the struggle for existence and have as their function the preservation of the species. When Nietzsche seeks to go behind the scenes of Kant's analysis of the functions of sensibility and understanding (or, for that matter, of reason) and tries to ferret out the organic and species needs that such functions serve, he is *not* abusing Kant's thought or distorting his philosophy: he is completing it along the lines suggested by Kant himself.

Most of the other aspects of Nietzsche's evolutionary epistemology were elaborations on ideas suggested by Lange, Darwin, and, to a lesser extent, Schopenhauer. While Kant held that objects of knowledge were conceived of in terms of the application of the category of unity, Lange argues that there are no pure unities in the natural world. For Lange, 'the assumption of absolute unities' is fictitious.[17] At best unity is a relative concept, one that has practical use but which does not pertain to the complexity of material or organic multiplicities. Lange speculates that we derive the concept of unity from our fallacious notion that we are a unified 'ego'. Although Nietzsche sporadically refers to the falsity of our belief in unities and in the unity of the ego in his published works, it is in his unpublished notes that he reveals his indebtedness to Lange quite clearly.

> We have need of unities in order to be able to reckon: that doesn't mean that we must assume that such unities exist. We have borrowed the concept of unity from our 'ego'-concept – our oldest article of faith. We would never have formed the concept 'thing' if we did not take ourselves to be unities. At present . . . we are firmly convinced that our I-concept does not guarantee any real unity.[18]

What Lange insinuated in Nietzsche's mind was the idea that categories such as unity, substance, being, object, cause, etc., were basically convenient hypothetical notions that have practical value but no ontological reference. A conventionalist in regard to scientific conceptions, Lange continually suggests the pragmatic utility of a host of categories and often refers to their 'anthropomorphic origin'.[19] If we superimpose this orientation on the discussion of evolution by means of natural selection, we can see how Nietzsche arrived at the idea of the evolutionary development of some of our most basic concepts. That is, the foundation of logical thinking emerged out of the non-logical nature of ways of perceiving the world that were selected out in the long evolutionary process. Thus, 'numerous beings who reasoned otherwise than we do at present, perished'.[20] Whoever, in the remote past, was unable to discern 'the like' frequently enough in regard to food or dangerous animals decreased his or her ability to survive. The inclination, in such primitive times, to see the similar as the equal was 'illogical' and erroneous. However, this simplifying and falsifying way of understanding things in one's environment proved highly valuable for survival. Moreover, this fusion of similarity and equality becomes the primitive origin of logic.[21]

Nietzsche contends that a certain inaccurate sensory-cognitive mode of apprehension proved to have life-preserving utility. Hence, this pattern of apprehension eventually generated the concept of self-identical entities and, by way of abstraction, the 'self-identical A' or the principle of identity. Presumably, these modes of thinking, through simplification and falsification, proved so serviceable for human survival that they were perpetuated and valued long before they were transposed from their practical use in experience to a purely formal codification in logic. The intellectual practice of falsification by means of simplification proved so valuable, in a utilitarian sense, that it became a canon of reason and reached its apogee in scientific understanding.

This aspect of Nietzsche's thought resembles the sociobiological theory of the development of primary and secondary epigenetic rules that are conceived of as biological constraints on man's development and capacity for acquiring knowledge. Certainly he would agree with the sociobiologists that the sensory information we acquire by means of the primary epigenetic rules is then organized, structured, and evaluated by the secondary cognitive rules.[22]

In his discussion of the specificity of human perception Lange speculates that organic beings with different modes of 'organization' than our own would perceive the world differently – would, in effect, live in different worlds. It may be supposed, he remarks, that a 'whole infinity of different interpretations is possible for all these different modes of apprehension of differently organized beings'.[23] This is undoubtedly one of the primary sources of Nietzsche's notion that the 'perspectival optics of life' generates a plurality of interpretations of the 'world'. But this perspective is not only that of the organic individual. For Nietzsche avers that entire species come to share *concealed* customs, habits, ways of seeing'. And these are adopted because they are 'propitious to the conditions of existence of such beings'.[24]

It is Lange's insistence that the common root of sensibility and cognitive understanding is the 'physico-psychological organization' of an organic individual that led him to argue that what Kant considers a priori is derived from experience, is, in effect, a posteriori. Lange held that even our most rudimentary sensory experience is pervaded by cognitive, logical connections that correspond to the activity of 'conscious thought'.[25] Nietzsche basically accepts this physiological and psychological interpretation of the ground of human knowledge and carries it one step further by suggesting that what Kant considers a priori concepts have *evolved*. And when, in *Beyond Good and Evil*, he argues that 'the most diverse philosophers again and again fill in a basic schema of *possible* philosophies' and relates this phenomenon to a 'similarity of languages', 'a common philosophy of grammar', he anticipates the French structuralists even to the extent of suggesting the evolution of an unconscious a priori in peoples affected by 'the unconscious domination and guidance' of 'similar grammatical functions'.[26] Because he emphasizes not only the selective and genetic features of evolution, but the power of language and culture in shaping man's ways of thinking and being, Nietzsche clearly adopts a co-evolutionary theory of human development.

Looking backward, Nietzsche postulates a long evolutionary selective process by which certain types of human beings survived and transmitted their cognitive-linguistic framework to modern man. The cognitive-linguistic schema that has been inherited and culturally transmitted has been formalized and codified in philosophical discourse. Despite his critical stance towards Kant, Nietzsche treats his table of the categories as if it were a sedimentation and formal presentation of a conceptual schema that has undergone an extensive evolutionary development. In fact he never really denies the heuristic and pragmatic value of Kant's categories of the understanding.

Nietzsche speculates that many exceptions who, in the past, did not perceive and think as others did 'perished'. In this sense, our culture, including what he considers our knowledge-culture, rests upon a 'terrible foundation'. For those who perceived differently than others, who discerned differentiation missed by others, who thought differently than others, were eliminated in the long natural history of man. Those whose perceptions were 'coarse' and those whose thinking involved a reductive simplification and a proclivity to conceive of the similar as the equal survived and propagated themselves even though their ways of perceiving and thinking were fallacious. That is, their percepts and concepts were functionally useful but ontologically false. This is what Nietzsche is thinking of when he asserts that 'truth' (inherited and culturally transmitted 'truth') is that kind of 'error' without which a certain species could not have survived. Here he is attempting to explain the origin of what Lange, *en passant*, calls 'errors a priori'.

Having absorbed and appropriated the emphasis on process or 'becoming' he found in the writings of Heraclitus, Emerson, Lange, and Buddhism, Nietzsche embraces a theory of universal flux. This plays a central role in his retrospective understanding of the opposite orientation towards actuality. Thus he maintains that 'for a long time the changing process in things had to be overlooked, and remain unperceived; the beings not seeing correctly had an advantage over those who saw everything "in flux" '.[27]

Nietzsche's claim that our knowledge of the external world is a co-evolutionary transmission of earlier modes of perception and thought seems to emerge out of a creative amalgam of the ideas of Kant, Lange, and Darwin. His generalization that the 'knowledge' expressed in ordinary language judgements and philosophical discourse involves a systematic falsification of actuality has sometimes been looked upon as peculiar. Ironically, however, it has been defended, in less dramatic language, by a number of recent and contemporary philosophers.

W. V. O. Quine has argued that our 'subjective speaking of qualities' seems to accord with our ability to understand and predict natural events. He surmises that our spacing of qualities is 'a gene-linked trait' that has proven successful in our inductions because it has become dominant by means of the process of 'natural selection'. Without Nietzsche's sympathy with unfortunate 'exceptions', he avers that 'Creatures inveterately wrong in their inductions have a pathetic but praiseworthy tendency to die before reproducing their kind.'[28] If we join to such observations Quine's claim that the idea of 'physical objects' is a 'cultural posit' or 'myth',[29] we are not far removed from Nietzsche's similar judgement concerning the ideas of 'thing', 'object', 'substance', 'being', etc. A more recent admission of the limits of scientific (and, hence, *a fortiori*, common-sense) knowledge of reality virtually replicates Nietzsche's standpoint. In his study of empirical inquiry, Rescher states that

> We have no decisive way of discriminating real from apparent truth, of distinguishing between *our* truth and *the* truth . . . . Once we acknowledge that a prospect of incompleteness and a presumption of . . . incorrectness attaches to our present picture of the world, we can no longer subscribe to the idea that the world really exists as we conceive of it. And . . . we can no longer adopt the view that . . . our world-picture depicts 'the real world' – the world as it actually is.[30]

What is often overlooked in accounts of Nietzsche's epistemology is that it is not only his adoption of a process theory of actuality derived from others and coincident with his own intuitions that is informing his thought. For the theories of the natural scientists that are discussed at length in Lange's *History of Materialism* encouraged him to appreciate what he later called 'the indescribable complexity' of the natural world. When he characterizes nature as a 'chaos', he is expressing a philosophical response to the immensely complicated 'relations-world' that Lange and nineteenth-century scientists disclosed. What may have sounded strange – even to the scientists from whom he derived this impression of the natural world – does not sound strange in a time which has seen the emergence of 'chaos theory' in science. What has been said about this very recent study of 'the irregular side of nature, the discontinuous side' would have pleased Nietzsche in so far as chaos theory is described as 'a science of process rather than state, of becoming rather than being'.[31]

Throughout the natural history of man specific types of psychological individuals with similar patterns of perception and cognition have been selected out by the winnowing process of natural selection. We have inherited these highly effective, but ontologically erroneous, ways of perceiving and thinking. The cultivation of the rational mode of thinking which was the precursor of the scientific mentality required the control of contrary inclinations or tendencies of thought in our pre-scientific ancestors.

> The course of logical thought and reasoning in our modern brain corresponds to a process and struggle of impulses, which singly and in themselves are all very illogical and unjust; we usually experience only the result of the struggle, so rapidly and secretly does this primitive mechanism now operate in us.[32]

The practically useful conceptual-linguistic schema that modern man had inherited from his ancestors reaches its fulfilment, Nietzsche suggests, in the Kantian synthetic theory of knowledge. However, the 'categories' that have served man so well for so long are being undermined (as Lange reiterates) by the burgeoning scientific conception of reality. What had previously been a powerful, practically valuable, conceptual system is being eroded by the exact sciences and their more precise methods. Hence the serious modern thinker, whether philosopher or scientist, finds himself or herself in a bifurcated world or, in fact, in two competitive cognitive 'worlds'.

What Nietzsche saw emerging in his time was what A. N. Whitehead later called 'the bifurcation of nature'. That is, he was concerned (among other things) with the problem of reconciling the qualitative phenomenological nature of our experience with the complex, quantitative scientific world-picture. The deanthropomorphic world disclosed by the sciences violates what he characterizes, in *The Gay Science*, as our 'aesthetic humanities'. And the mechanistic world-interpretation proffers an image of reality that is 'senseless'. Or, expressed in the language of his later notes, he was beginning to discern the 'nihilistic consequence of contemporary science' a theme forcefully reiterated in *On the Genealogy of Morals*.

Despite his foreboding concerning the powerful and rising scientific culture, Nietzsche was nonetheless impressed by the 'small, unapparent truths' discovered in the exact sciences. In fact, it is the small 'fragments of truth' (as Lange had called them) to which he appeals in order to undermine confidence in previously regnant philosophical categories. The cultural evolution of the scientific way of perceiving and thinking has given us a radical, new way of interpreting 'the world'. Thus, for example, 'thanks to the sharpening of the senses and the attention entailed in the conflicts and developments of exceedingly complex forms of life, cases of identity or likeness are admitted ever more rarely'.[33] This evolved correction of earlier, more imprecise, assumptions about 'identity' or 'similarity' is specifically cultivated in the exact sciences. In his notes he reminds himself that we should say that phenomena have 'similar qualities' not 'the same' qualities, even in chemistry. And these qualities are similar 'for us'.[34]

Many of Nietzsche's criticisms of Kant's conception of knowledge are based upon the Langean inspired appeal to then-contemporary scientific theories and philosophies of science. That the sciences conceive of the natural world (especially at microphysical levels) as in a state of 'absolute flux' complements his intuitive view of actuality as a dynamic process of becoming. This indicates the dialectical nature of the epistemological positions he adopts. For, as we shall see, he also argues in defence of the conventionalist nature of scientific theories, principles, and concepts. Nietzsche not only argues for a 'perspectival theory of knowledge', but displays perspectival approaches to the problem of knowledge in his own philosophical discourse.

The psycho-social evolution of the scientific interpretation of nature has produced a sea change in the way we understand the circumambient world. It has dethroned a multiplicity of common-sense beliefs (which for thousands of years have proven serviceable for life), and it has undermined the Kantian account of the nature of phenomena. With the development of more refined modes of observation and thought our understanding of the natural world has changed. Nietzsche tells us that

> Little by little, the external world is . . . differentiated; but for incalculable periods of time on earth a thing was thought of as identical and consubstantial with a single one of its qualities, its colour, for example. Only very gradually have the many distinct qualities pertaining to a single thing been granted; even the history of human language betrays a resistance to the multiplication of names.[35]

Here evolutionary speculation about the advancement in the ability to make finer distinctions among entities is supported by a philosophical point: that the diachronic development of natural languages reveals a resistance to increasing the number of names used to characterize individual entities. Not only have beings been identified with their colour-quality, but our colour perceptions are permeated with evolved valuations. Each colour is an 'expression of value' or signifies the useful or the harmful, the pleasant or the unpleasant. We are, in fact, responsive only to a relatively limited range of phenomena, especially to those having value for our organic processes.[36] Such primary epigenetic rules (as socio-biologists call them) are intimately associated with our natural history. This notion of inherited patterns of perception is one of the primary bases of the concept of the 'perspectival optics of life', a conception derived from Lange's discussions of the multiplicity of 'interpretations' of phenomena inferred from the variety of sensory systems in different organic beings.

As early as 1874 Nietzsche was brooding over the theoretical implications of the scientific world-interpretation in 'Schopenhauer as Educator'. He was cognizant of the fact that the physical sciences disclose a neutral, colourless world of atoms in motion, an 'atomistic chaos'. He lamented the scientifically revealed grey visage of nature. What he saw clearly was that the evolved scientific understanding of the natural world deleted the cognitive value of the full, rich colourful, emotion-charged, aesthetic world of human experience and replaced it with a cold, grey, senseless world of constantly moving atoms.

Nietzsche's conception of nature, his critical epistemology, and his experimental (and consciously anthropomorphic) interpretation of the underlying basis of actuality as 'will to power' (or, to be more precise, wills to power) were all profoundly conditioned by the image of actuality he found in the writings of Lange, Boscovich, and a host of nineteenth-century natural scientists. His variation on Spinoza's formula, 'God or nature', *Chaos sive Natura*,[37] was not derived from the ancient Greek mythical image of Chaos, but from the complex, dynamic, process theory of nature emerging in the natural sciences. Thus, for example, his repeated comments on our 'coarse senses' are based upon his acceptance of the physical theoretical conception of the constituents of material entities. So he tells us that if our senses were more acute, if their functioning were more rapid, we would perceive a massive cliff as a moving, vibrating chaos.[38] In numerous other instances he marshals information garnered from the theories of natural scientists to undermine our faith in common-sense beliefs and categories and to question the validity of Kantian categories of the understanding. Even though science had originally developed out of common-sense beliefs and conceptions of the world, its further advance undermined the validity of precisely those beliefs and conceptions.

Nietzsche is alert to the crisis that this clash between common-sense beliefs and scientific knowledge generates. For now these new, scientific 'cognitions and those primeval, fundamental errors' clash with each other 'even in the same person'. 'The thinker', he tells us, 'is now the being in whom the impulse to truth [the drive for scientific truth] and life-preserving errors [inherited from our remote ancestors] wage their first conflict, now that the impulse to truth [i.e. scientific truth] has also *proved* itself to be a life-preserving power.'[39] What has been disclosed here is the conflict between two practical, pragmatic ways of perceiving and thinking, both of which serve to preserve the species in existence. However, Nietzsche discerns the enormous power of the scientific perspective, its capacity to provide a strong sub-structure for a life-enhancing cultural ideal. Through the pragmatic power of scientific knowledge man is able to gain power over nature and then he can employ this power to develop himself freely, to augment his strength and enhance his life.[40]

As early as 1872 he saw that the point is not to try to negate the dynamic 'knowledge-drive' in science, but to master it, control it, guide it, give it an aesthetico-philosophical meaning and goal.[41] He views science as an enormously powerful instrumental good for mankind and not an end in itself, because he is convinced, with good reason, that its theoretical consequences tend to nullify the aesthetic and humanistic values, the 'illusions', that have previously made existence endurable and meaningful. 'Ever since Copernicus', he tells us in *On the Genealogy of Morals*, 'man finds himself on an inclined plane – now he is slipping faster and faster away from the centre into – what? Into nothingness? Into a *"penetrating sense* of his nothingness"?'[42]

Aside from his purpose of attaining a Hegelian *Aufhebung* of the scientific world-interpretation (that is, a suppression of it as 'the truth' and a preservation of it as a means to the enhancement of life), Nietzsche undertakes a behind-the-scenes epistemic critique of scientific theories, principles, and concepts in his notes. Although he uses some of the material he stores in his notes sporadically (notably in *The Gay Science*), most of it remained unpublished. In these notes he relies upon the suggestions he found in Kant, Lange, and the agnostic neo-Kantian scientists of the nineteenth century for his critique of scientific 'truth'.

KANT, LANGE, AND SCIENCE

In his *History of Materialism* F. A. Lange associated the growing agnosticism about the ultimate constituents of the world – Emil DuBois-Reymond's slogan, 'we are ignorant', expressed what many other nineteenth-century scientists were thinking – with Kant's restriction of knowledge to constituted phenomena. He called attention to a remark in the *Prolegomena* that coincided with the theme of the limits of the natural sciences. That is, that the 'natural sciences will never discover the inner nature of things' or any other ultimate ground of explanation that transcends sensory experience.[43] In addition, focus is placed on Kant's assertion that every cognition of things that is based upon 'pure understanding' is nothing but appearance and that 'truth is in experience only'.[44] Although neither Lange nor Nietzsche express it in quite this way, what this implies is a doctrine of two modes of truth. There are the truths of experience and there is the truth of 'things-in-themselves'. Since Kant insists that truths of experience are constituted phenomenal truths, and since he claims that the natural sciences cannot have genuine knowledge of what goes beyond the bounds of sense, then science cannot attain genuine objective truth. It is clear that the germination of the conventionalist theories of science we find in Lange and Nietzsche began with Kant's first *Critique*.

Paradoxically, Kant's endeavour to provide a philosophical justification for the scientific interpretation of nature led to a scepticism about that interpretation. At one point he maintains that 'the order and regularity in the appearance, which we entitle *nature*, we ourselves introduce. We could never find them in appearance had not we ourselves, or the nature of our mind, originally set them there.'[45] If we add to this projection of order and regularity into nature the unknowability of 'things-in-themselves', then we have an exacerbated scepticism. Kant himself admits that it is 'strange and absurd' to say that the natural world 'should direct itself according to our subjective ground or apperception, and should . . . depend upon it in respect of its conformity to law'. We are asked to

consider that this nature is not a thing-in-itself, but is merely an aggregate of appearance, so many representations of the mind, we shall not be surprised that we can discover it only in the radical faculty of all our knowledge; namely, in transcendental apperception, in the unity by virtue of which alone it can be called object of all possible experience, that is, nature. Nor shall we be surprised, for just this very reason, that this unity can be known *a priori* and, therefore, as necessary.[46]

Here we can see why Nietzsche responds critically to the idea of 'nature as representation'. For just as there are 'objects in general' for Kant, so, too, is there a 'nature in general', a domain constituted by our sensibility, our intuitions of space and time, and our a priori categories of the understanding. Precisely because the natural order is an elaborate construction, things-in-themselves, as well as what may be called 'nature in itself', transcend our knowledge.

Lange calls attention, in his critical interpretation of Kant, to the admission of the unknown origin of sensory experience that one finds in his *Prolegomena* and his *Anthropology*. The objects of sensation are apprehensible 'by means of the quality of our senses'. However, Kant tells us, our senses 'are affected in a particular manner by objects that are unknown in themselves'.[47] Since our sensibility has an 'unknown root' and 'objects' of our senses are unknown, we have an agnosticism at the subjective and the objective pole of our sensory experience. Aside from criticizing the very notion of things-in-themselves (which he advises us not to concern ourselves with at all), Lange probes a weakness in Kant's carefully wrought theoretical structure, a weakness which he himself suggested to Lange (and hence to Nietzsche): the question of the unknown common root of sensibility and understanding. For a time Nietzsche adopts a Lange-cum-Darwinian account of the evolution throughout man's natural history of specific modes of sensibility and understanding that are grounded in the being of psycho-physical organic individuals. Later, he will propose his imaginative interpretation of energistic wills to power as the hypothetical origin of human psychology, sensibility, and conceptualization. But he does so by completing the anthropomorphic circle that had begun with Kant's theory of knowledge in so far as this elaborate interpretation of a will to power (or wills to power) acting through all beings is explicitly based upon 'human analogy'.

Summarizing a rather lengthy story, Nietzsche understood that Kant's account of knowledge led to the view that our comprehension of nature is that of a representation-world, that man does not discover laws of nature, but projects them into the natural world. In 'On Truth and Lying' he contended that 'all we actually know about . . . laws of nature is what we ourselves bring to them – time and space, and therefore relationships of succession and number . . . everything marvellous about the laws of nature . . . is . . . contained within the . . . inviolability of our representations of time and space'. And, of course, these are *our* forms of intuition. 'All that conformity to law which impresses us so much . . . coincides . . . with these properties that we bring to things.'[48]

The subjective determinations of phenomena stressed in the first edition of the *Critique* aggravate the problem of our (genuine) knowledge of the external world. If 'experience' is a synthesis of the receptivity of sensibility and the spontaneity of understanding, and if phenomena are 'representations of the mind', then we can have no knowledge of an independent actuality. What is the case for knowledge in general is *a fortiori* the case for scientific knowledge. The scientist, too, imposes 'form' on the manifold of sensory impressions that is manifested in space and time.

In terms of Kant's account of knowledge, the transphenomenal constituents of the natural world elude our comprehension. The world we know in ordinary experience or in scientific inquiry is an already constructed world in terms of its origins. Kant informs us that nature is known solely as the 'sum-total of phenomena, the sum-total of representations in our mind'. The mind does not 'derive its a priori laws from nature, but prescribes them to nature'.[49] In *Human, All Too Human* Nietzsche quotes this remark with approval and adds that our conception of nature yields a *Welt als Vorstellung*, a 'world as representation'.

Despite his frequent references to things-in-themselves, Kant is unable to offer a coherent account of such 'transcendental objects'. The inapplicability of categories of the understanding to noumena leads to an extreme agnosticism about actuality. If the categories are subjective determinations of objects, then the presumed independent reality of things-in-themselves can neither be designated as one nor many. For the categories of unity and plurality are inapplicable to it. There are neither things nor things-in-themselves nor a thing-in-itself. For the former imply plurality and the latter implies a single unity. Cause and effect also cannot be applied to a supposed transphenomenal actuality and, therefore, Kant cannot consistently suggest (as he does) that our sensations are 'caused' by unknowable 'objects'. The domain of things-in-themselves cannot even be designated as real or unreal in so far as these (reality and negation) are inapplicable categories. If the presumed realm of things-in-themselves cannot be referred to intelligibly then it is clear that the sciences deal with a constructed nature, a nature for us. The empirical elements of the natural world are conditioned by our specific (evolved) sensibility and the lawful aspects of nature are conditioned by a priori principles that are legislated by human understanding. All in all, Nietzsche concludes, the common-sense conception of the world, the philosophical (Kantian) conception of the world, *and* the scientific understanding of nature entail the 'humanization of nature'.

Nietzsche was impressed by the neo-Kantian conventionalism he found virtually throughout Lange's *History of Materialism*. An agnosticism supported by neo-Kantian scientists and amplified by what may rightfully be called Lange's philosophy of science, provided Nietzsche with the means by which he sought to show that the independent sciences, despite their astonishing accomplishments, do not give us access to actuality or truth. Although, then as now, they provide us with a bewildering variety and multiplicity of truths, they do not present us with a unified truth about nature or *Wirklichkeit*. The radical agnosticism concerning scientific principles, theories, and concepts propounded by Nietzsche was a consequence of his accurate synthesis of the sceptical implications of Kant's analysis of knowledge, the sceptical views of nineteenth-century neo-Kantian scientists, and Lange's sceptical phenomenalism.

Among many similar references, Lange cites the physicist Lichtenberg's assertion (later restated and rephrased by Heisenberg in another context) that 'We can properly speaking know nothing of anything in the world except ourselves and the changes that take place in us.' When something acts upon us, the effect not only depends upon its original cause, but upon the observer as well.[50] Helmholtz's views are shown to continue in the same spirit. He insisted that we are acquainted with the 'effects' of things only and we have no genuine knowledge concerning 'matter-in-itself'. He also maintained that the notion of an enduring 'substance' is an assumption, a 'hypothesis' that satisfies the demands of thought, but corresponds to no known feature of actual entities. Helmholtz, Lichtenberg, and other scientists are cited by Lange in order to substantiate Emil DuBois-Reymond's thesis: that nineteenth-century scientists have confronted the limits of natural-scientific knowledge.

Lange sought to create a synthesis of Kant's general conception of knowledge and the agnostic views of nineteenth-century scientists who either supported it or amplified its sceptical tendencies. He reinterprets Kant's theory concerning the conditions for knowledge in a radical (and Darwinian) way by arguing that all knowledge is conditioned by our dynamic psycho-physical 'organization'. The sciences of the day support Kant's belief that we have no access to the ultimate constituents of the natural world. Lange contends that the more we think of the idea of things-in-themselves (even as a limit-concept), the more we are persuaded that the phenomenal world embraces all that we can consider as 'real'.[51] Nietzsche virtually appropriates Lange's phenomenalism and augments his suggestions concerning the practical or pragmatic function and value of knowledge. By presenting a decidedly psychologistic version of Kant's theory of knowledge, and by referring to the basic concepts in the natural sciences (i.e., matter, force, atoms) as hypothetical constructs, Lange laid the groundwork for Nietzsche's conventionalist understanding of science and his construal of the principles and concepts employed in the sciences as 'regulative principles' or 'useful fictions'. The instrumentalist interpretation of scientific principles and concepts that was later presented by the pragmatists had already been anticipated first by Lange and then by Nietzsche.[52]

Nietzsche's conception of the principles and basic constructs of the sciences as regulative, heuristic, provisional presuppositions and as 'conventional fictions' was directly derived from a creative completion of Lange's suggestions and from aspects of Kant's critical philosophy. The postulation of 'ideals of reason' as if they were 'true' provided a model for a conventionalist approach to scientific knowledge. In his *Prolegomena* Kant postulated the existence of God in terms of a 'symbolic anthropomorphism' that was solely concerned with language, with a *façon de parler*. Interpolating his treatment of Kant's critical thought, what Nietzsche seems to have done was to have superimposed this mode of 'regulative' thinking on *all* of Kant's claims to knowledge. We have already seen that this is not a 'misunderstanding' of Kant's philosophy but an insight into the 'regulative' nature of the framework of Kant's analysis of knowledge.

Nietzsche correctly points out that the content of the *Critique of Pure Reason* is a 'knowledge about knowledge'. Assuming such knowledge about knowledge, what is its source? It cannot be a priori knowledge in so far as Kant is concerned with establishing the a priori dimension of human knowledge; hence, this would involve circularity. It cannot be a posteriori knowledge since such knowledge, of course, is derived from experience. It cannot be synthetic a priori knowledge since neither the a priori nor the synthetic foundation for such knowledge has been (or can be) established except (if we follow Kant) in terms of the presuppositions of the *Critique* itself. Therefore, Nietzsche seemed to have reasoned, the entire content of the first *Critique* (in Kant's terms) would have to be comprised of regulative principles of reason or regulative ideas of reason. Despite Kant's disclaimer, the *Critique* itself is a hypothetical use of reason (which seeks to establish the conditions for the possibility of knowledge and to determine the extent and limits of knowledge). And, as Kant points out, 'a hypothetical employment of reason is regulative only'.

The scientific interpretation of the natural world and of man-in-nature operates, Nietzsche maintains, on the basis of 'regulative principles of method', 'conventional fictions', 'provisional assumptions', 'working hypotheses', 'heuristic fictions', and 'regulative fictions'.[53] Although he is cognizant of the immense value of the growth of scientific knowledge, he insists upon the instrumental and conventionalist nature of scientific conceptual schemata. He conceives of the scientific world-interpretation as an elaborate and sophisticated 'symbolization of nature'. Once again, Kant prepared the way for this mode of thinking when, in the *Critique*, he held that the problematical use of concepts of reason functioned as *heuristische Fiktionen* or 'heuristic fictions'.[54] Although he never denies the reality of the process of becoming and therefore never embraces a form of idealism, Nietzsche's approach to scientific knowledge of 'reality' is clearly anti-realist or, at least, allied with phenomenalistic and instrumentalist approaches to science. This, in a sense, may be seen as the final twist in his meandering stream of epistemological analyses. He has cut off all access roads to pure, objective knowledge, absolute knowledge, apodictic knowledge, or holistic 'truth'.

The perspectival theory of knowledge that Nietzsche developed was indirectly transmitted to him by his studies of Boscovich, Lange, and a number of nineteenth-century scientists whose theories and philosophical reflections on them revealed fragmentary empirical truths and agnosticism about the ultimate ground of natural phenomena. Although, after Boscovich's eighteenth-century theory of nature, he extends perspectival awareness to each hypothetical 'centre of force', each posited 'power-quantum', Nietzsche is also concerned with describing the 'pluralility of interpretations' of the world in the sciences. Unfortunately he often intermixes these two levels of discourse in his notes.

The problem of the relation between phenomena and things-in-themselves found in Kant's thought is replicated in the various scientific interpretations of the world. In order for our intellect to grasp the distinction between the essence of things (according to the sciences) and the phenomenal world we experience, he observes, it would need to have a 'contradictory character'. That is, it would have to be

> designed to see from a perspective (after the manner required of creatures of our species, if they are to maintain themselves in existence), and . . . endowed simultaneously with a faculty for conceiving this seeing *as* a seeing from a perspective . . . as capable . . . both of believing in 'reality' [as it appears to our senses] . . . and also of judging this belief a perspective-limitation with respect to a true reality [the transphenomenal 'reality' depicted in the sciences].[55]

What the perspectival theory of knowledge entails is the assumption of a multiplicity of various levels of perspectival 'knowledge' or what amounts to the same thing, perspective-limitations. The often cited formula – 'There are many kinds of eyes. Even the Sphinx has eyes – and consequently there are many kinds of "truths", and consequently, there is no truth'[56] – is largely, but not only, modelled on the scientific disclosure of a plurality of truths which, in turn, nullify the possibility of obtaining holistic truth or the 'truth' of the totality of actuality. In effect, Nietzsche anticipates William James' emphasis upon 'truths in the plural' in opposition to a rationalistic, monistic conception of truth. At the same time he insinuates the inability of science to provide a unified theory of reality or a unitary 'truth'.

Although the conscious relativity of knowledge he had found in the exact sciences provided the basis for his idea of perpectivalism, Nietzsche does not end his analysis of knowledge by holding that all perspectives are of equal value. Rather, he presents his ideal of what knowledge ought to be. Although knowledge is perspectival, 'the *more* affects we allow to speak about one thing, the *more* eyes, different eyes, we can use to observe one thing, the more complete will our "concept" of this thing, *our* "objectivity", be.'[57] That this is a remote ideal is clear when we consider that there are an enormous number of possible perspectives through which we could endeavour to understand phenomena or events. And of course these perspectives are subject to revision, displacement, and what Kuhn later calls 'paradigm shifts'. Lange's *History of Materialism* had already indirectly communicated this in his presentation of the history of scientific theories.

The growth of human knowledge entails the multiplication of new perspectives indefinitely. Given Nietzsche's dynamic conception of actuality and of the self, we can see that the ideal of appealing to all relevant or applicable perspectives in order to understand fully one 'object' or one event ineluctably eludes us. Only an absolute, omniscient being, precisely the kind of being whose existence he denies, could understand the immense synthesis of all relevant perspectives pertaining to one 'object' or one event. It has been said that Nietzsche's perspectivism 'implies that our many points of view cannot be smoothly combined into a unified synoptic picture of their common object'.[58] But, of course, different perspectives yield different 'objects' or different aspects of an object. In notes from the 1880s the 'world' is sometimes considered as the sum of extant perspectives. However, Nietzsche insists upon a process theory of actuality and consequently he must maintain that *at each moment* there are different 'worlds' coming into being. The ultimate complication of the theory of perspectivism, which is often ignored, is that, for Nietzsche, his relations-world is one in which 'the sum' of all points of perspective is 'incongruent'.[59] If we hold him to this position then he could not legitimately claim that all extant perspectives represent *a* world or *the* world. This incongruence corresponds to what he elsewhere calls the 'antithesis character' of actuality.

Despite the extreme to which he pushes his idea of perspectival knowing, he has succeeded in undermining a belief in a single overarching truth, barred the way to absolute truth, and has put in question the exclusive veracity of *any* specific knowledge-perspective of any kind. And it is clear that his entire approach to philosophy, including the projection of his mythopoetic, interpretive possibilities – the 'myth', as he calls it, of the *Übermensch*, the idea of the eternal recurrence of the same, and his anthropomorphic idea of a universal will to power, is modelled on the theoretical projections of the sciences. In place of dogmatic claims to truth, in lieu of 'fundamental truths', he tells us, 'I put fundamental probabilities – provisionally assumed guides by which one lives and thinks'.[60]

Habermas is on target when he emphasizes the effect that the methods and results of the exact sciences had on Nietzsche. In a kind of Sartrean counterfinality the sciences devalue personal knowledge, cultural values, and the aesthetic standpoint. And, as Habermas puts it, scientific theories, for all the technical power their knowledge produces, give no support 'to normative or action-orienting knowledge'.[61] But Habermas goes too far when he accuses Nietzsche of misunderstanding the relation between knowledge and interest because of his supposed empirical orientation. He seems indifferent to the way in which the perspectival way of seeing (originally modelled on the theories and methods of the independent sciences) is employed by Nietzsche in order to open up a new pathway to experimental truths that would intensify the sense of the value of life and make the enhancement of life the goal of existence. The perspectival orientation towards knowledge is, he informs us, 'as deep as our "understanding" can reach today'.[62] And in a number of places he suggests that it requires spiritual strength in order to appropriate and accept the unsettling implications of a perspectival conception of human knowledge, to renounce certainty, to deny the veracity or finality of any point of view, to create values and meaning in the absence of objective foundations.

The reflective thinkers, the scientists, and the artists of today who have not yielded to various forms of dogmatism already live and think in the cognitive domain of Nietzsche's perspectivism.[63] Gradually but persistently the dogmas and absolutes, the fiercely held convictions, the certainties that have been inherited from the remote and recent past are losing their power. Whole cultures may follow Nietzsche's anti-dogmatic footsteps, albeit unknowingly or resistantly, passing through a post-metaphysical stage of thought, then through a post-epistemological orientation. And, with the approach of the close of the century of nihilism he predicted, a new, post-nihilistic dawn may break. Perhaps.

NOTES

1 Friedrich Nietzsche, *Kritische Studienausgabe*, Berlin and New York, Walter de Gruyter, vol. 10, *Nachgelassene Fragmente*, p. 507. (Hereafter cited as KSA followed by the volume, title, and page number or page numbers.)

2 D. Breazeale, trans. and ed., *Philosophy and Truth: Selections from Nietzsche's Notebooks of the Early 1870s*, Atlantic Highlands, NJ, Humanities Press, 1979, 32. My interpretation of what Nietzsche means in these notes differs from Breazeale's claim that Nietzsche is pointing out the circularity of the *Critique of Pure Reason* itself in the sense that it is a work about science (*Wissenschaft*) and is itself supposed to be scientific. Nietzsche, as I try to show, does offer this criticism in a more extended analysis, but he does so in notes from the 1880s.

3 Immanuel Kant, *Kritik der reinen Vernunft*, Hamburg, Meiner, 1956, 9.

4 Ibid.

5 Paul Carus, ed., *Kant's Prolegomena*, La Salle, Illinois, Open Court, 140–1.

6 KSA 12, *Nachgelassene Fragmente*, 264–6.

7 G. Colli and M. Montinari, eds, *Nietzsche Briefwechsel. Kritische Gesamtausgabe*, Berlin and New York, 1975, 12, 160.

8 KSA 2, *Vorrede, MAM*, II, 370.

9 KSA 7, *Nachgelassene Fragmente*, 491: '*Nun aber gibt es keine, eigentlichen Ausdrücke und kein "eigentliches" Erkennen ohne Metapher*'.

10 Cf. George J. Stack, *Lange and Nietzsche*, Berlin and New York, de Gruyter, 1983, chapter VI, 'Human, All Too Human'.

11 KSA 1, *Über Wahrheit und Lüge im aussermoralischen Sinne*, 880–1.

12 F. A. Lange, *Geschichte des Materialismus*, Frankfurt am Main, Suhrkamp, 1974, II, 455 (this is a reprint of the second edition of this work. Volume I was published in 1873 and volume II in 1875).

13 Immanuel Kant, *Anthropology from a Pragmatic Point of View*, trans. Mary J. Gregor, The Hague, Nijhoff, 1974, 53n.

14 Ibid., 53.

15 Ibid., 183.

16 Ibid., 188.

17 Lange, op. cit., II, 694.

18 KSA 13, *Nachgelassene Fragmente*, 258.

19 Lange, op. cit., II, 614.

20 KSA 3, *Die fröhliche Wissenschaft*, III, 471–2.

21 Ibid., 469–70.
22 Cf. C. Lumsden and E. O. Wilson, *Genes, Mind and Culture*, Cambridge, Harvard, 1981.
23 Lange, op. cit., II, 499. Cp. KSA 3, FW V, 627. 'The world has . . . once again become "infinite" to us: in so far as we cannot dismiss the possibility that it *contains infinite interpretations*.' Nehamas seems to take the former ironic comment about the world becoming 'infinite' literally by saying that Nietzsche 'occasionally thought' this. Cf. Alexander Nehamas, *Nietzsche: Life as Literature*, Cambridge, Harvard, 1985, 64. The nature and meaning of perspectivalism is analysed by Nehamas in an effective way, but the various levels of perspective that Nietzsche described are intermixed and the microperspective of 'centres of force' (which complicates an already complicated theory) is not considered. Cf. chapter 2.
24 Nietzsche, *Werke* (*Grossoktav Ausgabe*, henceforth abbreviated to GA), Leipzig, Naumann, 1901–13, XIII, 81.
25 Lange, op. cit., II, 482.
26 KSA 5, *Jenseits von Gut und Böse*, 34.
27 KSA 3, *Die fröhliche Wissenschaft*, III, 472.
28 W. V. O. Quine, 'Natural Kinds', in *Ontological Relativity*, New York, Columbia, 1969, 126.
29 W. V. O. Quine, 'On What There Is', in *From a Logical Point of View*, New York, Harper, 1961, 18.
30 Nicholas Rescher, *Empirical Inquiry*, London, Athlone, 1982, 258–9.
31 James Gleich, *Chaos: Making a New Science*, New York, Penguin, 1987, 5.
32 KSA 3, *Die fröhliche Wissenschaft*, III, 472.
33 Nietzsche, *Werke* (GA), XIII, 21.
34 Ibid., 28. If we hold Nietzsche to the denial of identities in the natural world, this undermines his apparent assumption of sequences of identical histories in his conception of the eternal recurrence of identical individuals and identical event-sequences. It is an understatment to say that the idea of 'eternal recurrence contrasts sharply with the tendency of his other cosmological views' (George A. Morgan, *What Nietzsche Means*, New York, Harper, 1965, 289–90). Elsewhere I've expressed agreement with Bernd Magnus' earlier view that eternal recurrence is a 'countermyth'. (Bernd Magnus, *Nietzsche's Existential Imperative*, Bloomington and London, Indiana, 1978.) Cf. George J. Stack, op. cit., and 'Eternal Recurrence, Again', *Philosophy Today*, Fall 1984, 242–64.
35 Nietzsche, *Werke* (GA), XIII, 21.
36 Nietzsche, *The Will to Power*, trans. W. Kaufmann and R. J. Hollingdale, New York, Random House, 1967, 274–5.
37 KSA 9, *Nachgelassene Fragmente*, 519.
38 Nietzsche, *Werke* (GA), XVI, 171f.
39 KSA 3, *Die fröhliche Wissenschaft*, III, 271.
40 Nietzsche, *Werke* (GA), XV, 434.
41 KSA 7, *Nachgelassene Fragmente*, 424. 'It is not a "matter" of the destruction of science, but of *mastering* it. It is completely dependent upon philosophical insights for its goals and methods, *though it*

frequently forgets this. But the philosophy which gains mastery also has to consider the problem of the degree to which science should be allowed to develop: it has to determine value!' A note from the 1880s reprises this theme and gives us a clue to Nietzsche's concern to have his positive, experimental, Dionysian ideas at least be compatible with scientific knowledge. 'Science shows us the flux, but not the goal: however, it provides the *presuppositions* with which the new goal *must* agree.' *Werke* (GA), XII, 357.

42 KSA 5, *Zur Genealogie der Moral*, III, 404.
43 Carus, op. cit., 123.
44 Ibid., 151.
45 Kant, *Kritik der reinen Vernunft*, 184.
46 Ibid., 166–7. W. H. Walsh calls attention to this difficulty in Kant's account of our knowledge of the natural world. Even though he tries to reinstate a foundation for objective knowledge of nature, Kant's own statements tend to resist this effort. Cf. W. H. Walsh, *Kant's Criticism of Metaphysics*, Chicago, University of Chicago Press, 1975, 88–96.
47 Carus, op. cit., 79.
48 KSA 1, *Über Wahrheit und Lüge im aussermoralischen Sinne*, 886.
49 Carus, op. cit., 82.
50 Lange, op. cit., II, 852–3. In notes from 1885–6, Nietzsche replicates Lichtenberg's observation: 'In the final analysis, man finds in things nothing except what he himself has imported into them; this finding, this importing, is called science.' KSA 12, *Nachgelassene Fragmente*, 153–4. That most of the epistemological material found in notations from the mid-1880s is derived from Lange's *Geschichte* leads me to suspect that, in preparing a work to be called *The Will to Power*, Nietzsche was returning to the 'treasure-house' he had first discovered some twenty years earlier. For this reason, I would have to take exception to a recent judgement on a previous work of mine (*Lange and Nietzsche*). Claudia Crawford avers that 'after taking stock of Lange's work and the specific areas of influence upon Nietzsche, Stack tends to jump to the mature philosophy, relating the initial reactions of the 22-year-old Nietzsche to Lange's work with those of the Nietzsche of the middle and late 1880s'. Claudia Crawford, *The Beginnings of Nietzsche's Theory of Language*, Berlin and New York, de Gruyter, 1988, 69n.
51 Ibid., 498.
52 For an attempt to show that American pragmatism was indirectly influenced by Nietzsche (via the works of F. C. S. Schiller) see George J. Stack, 'Nietzsche's Influence on Pragmatic Humanism', *Journal of the History of Philosophy*, October 1982, vol. 20, no. 1, 369–406.
53 For an early compressed summary of some of Nietzsche's observations on the principles and conceptions employed in the sciences, Vaihinger's appendix to his major work is useful. See Hans Vaihinger, *The Philosophy of As-If*, trans. C. K. Ogden, New York, Barnes & Noble, 1968, 341–62.
54 Kant, *Kritik der reinen Vernunft*, 703.
55 Nietzsche, *Werke* (GA), XIII, 48.
56 Nietzsche, *The Will to Power*, 291.
57 KSA 5, *Zur Genealogie der Moral*, III, 365.

58 A. Nehamas, *Nietzsche: Life as Literature*, Cambridge, Harvard, 1985, 48.

59 Nietzsche, *The Will to Power*, 306. In the evolution of Nietzsche's thought the concept of perspectivalism gradually metastasizes until it reaches the point of extension (in the notes from the late 1880s) to every hypothesized non-extended 'will-point'. Cf. George J. Stack, *Lange and Nietzsche*, chapter IX, 'A Force-Point World'. All perspective knowing is rooted in a value-interpretation. The primary *telos* of this knowing is preservation: 'the *preservation* of the individual, of a community, a race, a state, a church, a belief, a culture' (*The Will to Power*, sect. 259). Man surpasses all other organic beings because he has the capacity to forget his previous 'perspective valuing' and has therefore acquired a multitude of conflicting values. This is the source of his paradoxical nature and a great deal of his suffering. But, for Nietzsche, it is also a sign of spiritual strength and complexity, of a potentiality for further development, advancement, and transformation of his nature. Although Lange was instrumental in calling Nietzsche's attention to 1) the plurality of 'interpretations' (*Auffassungen*) of the world implied by the diverse sensory systems of different species and individual organisms, and 2) the variety of perspectives from which scientists interpret the natural world, he was not the first to stimulate this way of thinking. For it was Ralph Waldo Emerson who insinuated this conception in his mind over the twenty-six-year period during which he read and re-read his essays.

60 Nietzsche, *Werke* (GA), XIII, 72.

61 J. Habermas, *Knowledge and Human Interests*, Boston, Beacon, 1971, 292.

62 Nietzsche, *Werke* (GA), XIV, 7.

63 Many of the tendencies in contemporary science and philosophy illustrate a perspectival orientation towards knowledge, the breakdown of monopolistic, dominating theoretical standpoints (despite anomalies here and there). A distinct trend in recent thought is towards pluralism in theory, method, and conceptual orientation. In psychiatric practice, for example, it is common for multiple perspectives (psychological, familial, social, biochemical, and behavioural) to be brought to bear in the management and treatment of particular conditions. A recent indication of the naturalness of the adoption of perspectival approaches to complex theoretical issues is found in a psychiatrist's attempt to develop a 'synthesis' of philosophy, psychiatry, and neuroscience in an interpretation of 'the mind'. Cf. E. M. Hundert, *Philosophy, Psychiatry, and Neuroscience: Three Approaches to the Mind*, New York, Oxford University Press, 1989.

3 *Schein* in Nietzsche's philosophy

Robert Rethy

The Birth of Tragedy, as Nietzsche readily admits in his retrospective 'Attempt at a Self-Critique', has an 'artist's metaphysics in the background'[1] in which 'art . . . is set out as the genuine metaphysical activity of man', so that 'it is only as an aesthetic phenomenon that the existence of the world is justified'.[2] The context of justification is central to the Schopenhauerian conception of the origin of the 'metaphysical need' with which Nietzsche is working in *The Birth of Tragedy*. Nietzsche protests that by affirming art as the fundamental metaphysical activity he is silently denying morality's pretensions, but the very presence of the problem of justification shows the dark cloud of Schopenhauerian pessimism.[3] Though, as his later formulation in *The Gay Science* of this thought betrays, Nietzsche rejected the very question of 'justifying the world',[4] the 'affirmation' manifested in the eternal return of the same shows the presence, albeit in a transfigured mode, of this conception of 'metaphysics'.

There is another, more traditional conception of metaphysics at work in the 'artist's metaphysics' of *The Birth of Tragedy*, one which is recognizable in Nietzsche's adherence in it to the distinction between 'thing-in-itself' and 'appearance', the cornerstone of the philosophy of Schopenhauer, for whom 'Kant's greatest service is the differentiation of appearance from the thing-in-itself'.[5] Certainly, Nietzsche rejects this metaphysical onset straight away in the 'Attempt at a Self-Critique', criticizing his attempts to 'express strange, new valuations with Schopenhauerian and Kantian formulas',[6] and Nietzsche's metaphysics of a 'primordial one' and its counterpart 'individuals' arguably has more in common with the 'tragic age of the Greeks' than that of the Germans.[7] Our interest, in any case, is not in the metaphysical differentiation, which vanishes in Nietzsche's later thought, but in the 'difference within the difference', the distinction that is visible in *The Birth of Tragedy* between *Schein* or semblance and *Erscheinung* or appearance and, after the elimination of this distinction, in the new opposition, visible in Nietzsche's later thought, between *Schein* and will to power.

SCHEIN AND *ESRCHEINUNG* IN KANT AND SCHOPEN-HAUER

Erscheinung, uncontroversially translatable as 'appearance', is the usual Kantian term opposed to 'thing-in-itself' (see, e.g. B xxi, n.; B xxvii), and bears the general sense of 'object of a possible experience' (B 298) or 'empirical object' (B 299). Kant in the first *Critique* is also concerned with distinguishing *Erscheinung* from *Schein*: objects are 'actually given' in appearance, so that 'the predicates of the appearance can be attributed to the object itself'. To say that these objects are appearances is not to dismiss them as illusion (*Schein*), but to limit them as dependent upon the mode of intuition of the subject, i.e. to deny that they are viewed 'in themselves'. (B 69f.) In fact, the attribution of such predicates to 'things-in-themselves' is the main species of illusion or *Schein* discussed by Kant in the first *Critique*, transcendental illusion (*transzendentale Schein*), whose 'logic' is the subject of the second part of the transcendental logic, the transcendental dialectic as a *Logik des Scheins* (B 349). The 'transcendental logic' gives us the logic of understanding 'in the field of appearances' (B 7): this 'land of pure understanding' is the 'land of truth', 'surrounding by a broad and strong ocean, it is the real seat of illusion (*Sitz des Scheins*)', source of lies.[8]

Due at least in part to the influence of Schopenhauer, Nietzsche's view of the nature of appearance, and thus of the relation of *Erscheinung* and *Schein*, is fundamentally different. Schopenhauer, who psychologizes and biologizes Kantian transcendentalism, views the a priori as the proof of subjectivity rather than as the condition of objectivity:

> If it [the law of causality] is, as Locke and Hume assumed, *a posteriori* . . . then it has an *objective* origin. . . . If, on the contrary, it is, as Kant has more correctly taught, *a priori* given, then it has a subjective origin, and then it is clear that we always remain trapped within the subjective.[9]

Appearances, in so far as they are determined by a priori forms of intuition and understanding, are ineluctably subjective, and thus clearly are continuous with 'illusions', in opposition to the Kantian position already noted. Schopenhauer can thus assert that,

> despite all of its *empirical* reality, the world bears the stamp of ideality and thus of mere appearance. For this reason it must, at least from one side [form] be recognized as akin to the dream, indeed in the same class as this latter.[10]

That *Schein* and *Erscheinung* form a continuum is the sense of the Schopenhauerian use of the 'veil of Maya' to characterize the world of experience.[11] Nietzsche is developing this reading of Kant in a passage such as the following from *The Birth of Tragedy*: totally trapped in semblance (*Schein*), and indeed consisting *of* semblance, 'we are forced to sense it as the truly non-existent, i.e. as a continuous becoming in time, space, and causality, in other words as empirical reality' (sec. 4).[12] The 'land of empirical truth' is at the same time the 'land of total semblance'.

But despite Nietzsche's undoubted dependency on the Schopenhauerian formulation of Kant's epistemology, it would be unfair to reduce his reflections on this issue totally to the earlier philosopher's conception. Beginning with the 'artist's metaphysics' of *The Birth of Tragedy*,[13] it is the ambiguously 'shining' semblance that is primary, that constitutes the world in its visibility, and it is 'appearance' that is a sub-species, granted stability and 'objectivity' by the form of 'empirical reality'. 'The world, in every moment the *attained* redemption of God as the eternally changing and eternally new vision of the most suffering, most oppositional, most contradictory being who knows how to redeem himself only in semblance.'[14] *Schein* constitutes the vision of the divine and the work of the human creator whose luminousness and deceptiveness are co-ordinate to one another, and constitutive of the 'being' of the world.

SCHEIN IN THE BIRTH OF TRAGEDY

In *The Birth of Tragedy* we are introduced to *Schein* in the second paragraph of the first section, right after we learn of Apollo and Dionysus. *Schein* is co-ordinated with the Apollonian 'dream world' and its '*schöne Schein*'. This phrase recurs at many points in *The Birth of Tragedy*, indeed, it ends the paragraph devoted to Apollo at the beginning of the first section, where Nietzsche apostrophizes 'Apollo', 'from whose gestures and looks the whole pleasure and wisdom of "semblance", along with its beauty, speaks to us'.[15] Nietzsche the philologist is well aware of the etymological connection between the two words: 'the beautiful for the Germans the glittering (*das Glänzende*) for the Romans pul-cer, the strong, for the Greeks the "pure" '.[16] More discursively in 'The Dionysian World-View', a preliminary study for *The Birth of Tragedy*:

> The rose is beautiful [*schön*] means only: the rose has a good semblance [*Schein*], it has something pleasantly luminous. Nothing is supposed to have been said about its essence in this. It pleases, it arouses pleasure, as semblance. The will is satisfied through its seeming or shining [*Scheinen*].[17]

In co-ordinating beauty and semblance, Nietzsche is silently revising the Schopenhauerian conception according to which the beautiful is the 'Platonic' idea or the will's adequate objecthood (*Objektität*) as captured by the 'pure subject of knowledge'. Beauty, for Schopenhauer, is thus connected to 'objecthood', or the highest stage of truth an object can attain. 'One thing is more beautiful than another because it eases that pure objective consideration, solicits it, even compels it, in which case we then call it very beautiful.' Hence Schopenhauer can say, 'without truth there can be no beauty in art'.[18] For Nietzsche in his discussion of Apollo in *The Birth of Tragedy*, the 'beautiful semblance of the dream-world', prototype of the Apollonian experience of beauty, is inseparable from a 'feeling that shimmers through of its semblance'. We affirm it in full knowledge of its semblance – love it precisely because it is a dream and not 'the truth'.[19]

The aesthetically pleasurable aspect of *Schein* that is indicated by its connection with *das Schöne* is only one aspect of *Schein* in *The Birth of Tragedy*. In the other, a *schemum etymologicum* is at work as well, only here it is interlingual, from German to Greek. As '*schöne Schein*' inaugurated the previous paragraph, so the next one begins with a reference to the etymology of Apollo's name. 'Apollo, as the god of all plastic forces, is at the same time the prophetic god. He, who according to his root is the "shining" one [*seiner Wurzel nach der "Scheinende"*], the divinity of light, also rules the beautiful semblance of the inner fantasy world.' The Apollonian name referred to is, of course, Phoebus, from φῶς, light, φάω, to shine. As such, Apollo is the god who rules over appearances, φαινόμενα, which shine forth, φαίνονται, or appear with much the same ambiguity as *Schein*, particularly in the φαντάσματα of the fantasy world (κόσμος φαντασμάτων).[20] *Schein* is the power of the visibility of the world in its luminous and pleasing unreality which has a special home in human 'fantasy'. Its honest deceptiveness is its truthfulness, like 'the true non-being – the artwork', and without its moderate self-limitation 'semblance would deceive us as crude actuality' (sec. 1).[21] Semblance, then, functions in *The Birth of Tragedy* as that 'reality' that contains within itself its own negation, its own unreality, hovering on the edge of the abyss of non-being without falling in, maintained by its own self-limitation. This entrancingly self-negating 'show' that points beyond itself not to a stable paradigm but to its own vacancy, is thus the true enemy of a rational philosophy: 'Plato's hostility to art is something very significant. His doctrine's tendency, the path to the true through knowledge, has no greater enemy than beautiful semblance.'[22] Beautiful semblance holds us in thrall with no chance, indeed no desire, for escape.

In the world of *The Birth of Tragedy*, the world as the dream of a suffering creator god, *Schein* is the power constitutive of visibility, and *Erscheinung* is nothing but its flattening-out into *'plumpe Wirklichkeit'* which is deceptive precisely because it lacks the moment of unreality.[23] Far from being 'mere appearance',[24] *Schein* is a *more*, a shining-forth that is also a non-manifesting. Two passages, which stand at the beginning of the fourth and fifth sections of *The Birth of Tragedy*, can help us better to understand the nature of *Schein* and the mechanism of its production.

In the first passage Nietzsche gives his fullest exposition of his 'metaphysics of the primordial one' and of the production of the world from this one. Inverting the traditional relation and valuation of waking and dreaming life, Nietzsche conceives of our world, and ourselves, as the dream, the *Schein* of his artist god, needed for release from his sufferings and contradictions,[25] as Homer needs his gods and Raphael his visions. We ourselves are this *Schein*, which we experience as 'empirical reality'. Yet we are 'in the image of our creator', 'image-makers', 'creators', dreamers, ourselves lovers of semblance. The dream and the dream-like plastic artwork are then the *Schein des Scheins*, a raising of semblance to a higher power that has two opposed meanings: both a 'higher satisfaction' and a 'dis-empowering', or 'demotion'.[26] *Affectively*, the 'shine of shine' raises the joy to a higher power, the joyful release into semblance, 'a still higher satisfaction of the primordial desire for semblance'. To the joy of the dreamer or artist in semblance is added the joy of the creator, of the 'innermost core of nature' which rejoices in this fictive 'show'. Allied to this affective heightening is an ontological diminution. Whereas the positive joy, when raised to a higher power, is augmented, the negative or at least 'fractional' being, when so 'raised', is diminished. Thus, Nietzsche refers to Raphael's *Transfiguration*, in which he presents 'that disempowerment of semblance to semblance' (*Depotenzierung des Scheins zum Schein*). This last difficult phrase[27] – what, precisely, is the 'disempowerment' or 'diminution' of something to itself? – can only be interpreted as meaning that semblance comes to be seen *as such*, in its contrast to the suffering that forms the 'ground of the world'. In the display of this 'ground' we see a level of *Schein* as the *Schein des Seins* or, in another important phrase, the '*Widerschein des ewigen Widerspruchs*' – the 'shining back' or reflection of the eternal contradiction. This *Widerschein*, as can be seen from its two other occurrences,[28] is a 'primary *Schein*' or one that somehow reproduces more faithfully the 'reality' of the ground. The delights of art lie precisely in the 'transfiguration' of this *Widerschein* into a *Scheinwelt* of bliss and painless intuiting. Such is the self-transfiguration of the primordial one and the world-transfiguration of the artist.

The second passage is concerned less with world-creation than with the creation of the lyric poem, and thus also speaks centrally of music.[29] The problem of the lyric poet for 'aesthetic science' is the problem of 'subjectivity' and its individual 'wills and lusts'.[30] Nietzsche here works within a Schopenhauerian framework and since, for Schopenhauer, art depends upon 'release from the will' and hence individual desire, the lyric poet with his passionate concerns is only ambiguously an artist. Nietzsche's resolution is to deny that the 'I' of the lyric poet is the same as 'that of the awake, empirically real man'.[31] The process of creation, as described in this section, is complex and not always clear. The lyric poet, as 'Dionysian', is united with, rather than separated from the primordial one, and this union generates music, an 'image' (*Abbild*) which is itself a 'repetition' of the ground of being. In a process that he will later discuss in more detail,[32] music generates a 'symbolic dream image'. Here again we read of *Widerschein* in the image– and concept-less reflection of the primordial pain in music. Along with this *Widerschein* is a 'redemption in *Schein*' – i.e. the dream image generated by the music. We then discover a *second* reflection, this time not the shining-back of the primordial one, but a shining forth, a *Spiegelung*, in which there is an individual likeness or exemplar, which is the lyric poet's 'I'. The process is thus a four-tiered one: unification, repetition (in music), redemption in semblance (in a symbolic dream image), and mirroring (in individual likeness).

Music stands to the One as the individual image to the semblance. It is the sense of the latter term here that is most puzzling, and a note that is doubtless the preliminary stage of the above text[33] helps us to see that, in contrast to the 'individual' image of the lyric poet, this semblance must be the mythological image. The *Widerschein* of music generates *Schein*, the myth which is then 'mirrored' in the individual: beneath Archilochus and the daughters of Lycambes we see Dionysus and the maenads. The lyric poet's 'I' masks Dionysus, who is himself a mask of the unity of all 'I's', 'the sole truly existing and eternal I-hood, that rests in the ground of things'.[34] Thus 'the I of the lyric poet resounds out of the abyss of being'.[35]

The lyric poet and his combination of Dionysian unity and Apollonian image is a preliminary stage on the way to tragedy, as Nietzsche notes at the end of this passage, in which we encounter the third use of '*Widerschein*'. That it is the 'I' who is the 'subject' of the lyric poem is inessential. He functions 'as a shining-back of eternal being [*als Widerschein des ewigen Seins*]. Tragedy proves how great a distance there can be between the visionary world of the lyric poet and the phenomenon that is, to be sure, closest to him.'[36]

In *The Birth of Tragedy*, then, *Schein* signifies not a 'mere appearance' but a 'beautiful shining' that holds within itself both positive and negative moments of entrancing visibility and dazzling deception. It is the primary aspect of the world in its finite, individuated measure which the plastic artist reproduces in his own *imitatio Dei*.[37] Despite the ontological primacy of the primordial one, there is no path from its dark unity to the 'shining show' of the world. Refusing to affirm Kant's apothegm that 'appearance must be the appearance of something' in the case of semblance, Nietzsche asserts the underivability and independence of *Schein* from *Sein*. In an unpublished note on the Schopenhauerian 'will' as 'thing-in-itself', he notes that, given the unitary nature of the latter, 'the eternal motion, all striving of being is only semblance [*alles Streben des Seins nur Schein*]. Then a totally different, passive power must stand beside eternal being, that of *semblance-mysterion*!'[38]

SCHEIN IN THE GAY SCIENCE

It is well known that the overcoming of such metaphysical mysteries was one of the great concerns of Nietzsche's later work and one of the central tasks of the books from *Human, All Too Human* to *The*

Gay Science. Indeed, the first aphorism of *Human, All Too Human* is devoted precisely to a denial of such metaphysically fixed oppositions in favour of a 'chemistry of concepts and sensations' and of a 'historical philosophy' that denies the 'thing-in-itself', indeed denies 'that there are any opposites outside of the usual exaggeration of popular or metaphysical conception'.[39] This elimination of the duality of appearance and thing-in-itself[40] is in fact the elimination of *both* terms, and the triumph of *Schein*. Appearance, *Erscheinung*, inevitably refers to an opposite outside itself, as the Kantian saying shows, while *Schein* contains the opposite within itself.

We first see this 'triumph of *Schein*' explicitly in *The Gay Science*, the book that marks, in many senses, both a return to the concerns of *The Birth of Tragedy* and a look forward to *Thus Spoke Zarathustra*. At points we can see these two characteristics merging, as in the final aphorism of the original (1882) edition, which 'announces' Zarathustra, and whose title, '*Incipit tragoedia*', hearkens back to the title of Nietzsche's first book. Two aphorisms prior, the aphorism title 'The Dying Socrates' (290), recalls the phrase twice used to such effect in *The Birth of Tragedy*,[41] although the Socrates of *The Gay Science* is a pessimist, not an optimist, and the references to the 'moment', and 'revenge' show the proximity of *Thus Spoke Zarathustra*. More relevant for our purposes, however, are the preface and several aphorisms from the first and second books, the whole of which is centrally concerned with art.[42]

The last section of the retrospective preface, important enough in Nietzsche's eyes to have been revised and republished as the end of *The Wagner Case*, speaks of the rebirth from suffering and the new taste, the new enjoyment in art – implicitly, given the place of this passage in *The Wagner Case*, a non-Wagnerian art, a 'mocking, light, fleeting . . . divinely artistic art'. As an art of forgetfulness, it is a cure of our knowledge. Indeed, what we 'know' is precisely that 'truth is no longer truth when we draw the veil from it', a phrase that certainly recalls the Schopenhauerian 'veil of Maya' that figured so prominently in *The Birth of Tragedy*. The passage ends with an apostrophe of the Greeks, who knew how to stay bravely on the surface, 'to worship semblance [*Schein*], to believe in forms, sounds, words, the whole Olympus of semblance [*Olymp des Scheins*]. These Greeks were superficial – out of depth.'[43] The reference to the Greeks, and more clearly to the '*Olymp des Scheins*', brings the passage into the neighbourhood of *The Birth of Tragedy*, whose 'Attempt at a Self-Critique' was in fact written at the same time. Art is a counterweight to the suffering of life – the subject of the second and third sections of the preface. Art is the recovery of the surface, while philosophy is the response to pain and suffering, a 'going to the ground(s)', going to the depths.[44]

It is only the great pain . . . that forces us philosophers to climb down into our ultimate depths and to reject all trust, all good-nature, all that veils, eases, moderates, to reject whatever it was in which we had previously placed our humanity. I doubt that such a pain 'improves' – but I know that it *deepens* us.[45]

We see that philosophy and art are here related as depth to surface, pain to serenity (*Heiterkeit*).[46]

It is tempting to connect the artistic pathos, the love of *Schein*, to Apollo, and the philosophical descent with the Dionysian descent in *The Birth of Tragedy*. Certainly, art in *The Gay Science* wears a particularly Apollonian guise. Thus, according to an aphorism (81) whose title echoes *The Birth of Tragedy* – 'The Origin of Poetry'[47] – poetry originates in the belief in the magical power of rhythm to force a response, from both human beings and gods. Although the aphorism contains a reference to 'orgiastic cults', Dionysus is not named. Rather, the god who determines the future, Apollo the prophesying god, is mentioned twice. The god of limit and measure can limit or bind the future, and as 'god of rhythm can also bind the goddesses of destiny'. Finally, the power of semblance is not the semblance, but the reality of power – 'semblance at the beginning almost always becomes essence and *acts* as essence', according to an earlier aphorism (58)[48] – so that Nietzsche has no hesitation about admitting, with Homer, that 'the bards lie very often', since the power of semblance, and with it the lie, is the very power of poetry.[49] Indeed, all art is subsumed under the 'cult of the untrue' in the final aphorism of the second book (107) entitled 'Our Ultimate Gratitude to Art'.[50] Here art is characterized as 'the *good* will to semblance' and we again have a covert reference to *The Birth of Tragedy*, in the reformulation of the assertion that 'as aesthetic phenomenon is existence and the world eternally justified'[51] so that it reads 'as aesthetic phenomenon is existence still *bearable* for us'.

But semblance is present in more than art. Art teaches us to love semblance but philosophy teaches us of its universality. This is the burden of aphorism 54 of the first book of *The Gay Science*, 'The Consciousness of *Semblance*' (*Das Bewusstsein vom Schein*).[52]

Nietzsche again uses the image of the dream from which I awaken to realize that I must 'dream on'.

> What is 'semblance' for me now? Truly not the opposite of any essence – what can I assert of any essence except the predicates of its semblance! Truly not a dead mask which one can put on to an unknown X and take off of it! Semblance is for me what acts and lives, that goes so far in its self-mockery so as to let me feel that all there is here is semblance and will o' the wisp and spirit dance and nothing more.

This is the first direct articulation of the primacy of *Schein*, not only as art, but as reality, essence. As the end of the aphorism indicates, it is not only art that finds itself in the element of semblance, but knowledge as well. It is a 'semblance' that the realm of art is 'only' semblance, 'nothing more'. As 'essence' is assimilated to semblance, so knowledge to art: 'among all these dreamers I, too, the "knower", dance my dance. . . . The knower is a means to draw out the earthly dance.'

In *The Gay Science* semblance recovers, after the 'positivism' of Nietzsche's free-spiritedness, its place in Nietzsche's conception of the world as the 'being' of the world as work of art. Indeed, it is for the first time thematized as such. In implicit contrast to *The Birth of Tragedy*, semblance is not the surface accident to the inner Dionysian essence, nor even the 'mask' of Dionysus himself.[53] Semblance holds all in its thrall, not only will o' the wisp (*Irrlicht*) and dreamer, but spirit dance and knower. This dance, as the previous one on poetry, indicates the primacy of the Apollonian realm of beautiful seeming. The later preface, though, introduces a different note. There are depths to this world of surfaces, depths that are perhaps not characterized as 'essence' or primordial one, but yet are depths of suffering and pain, depths that force us to dispense with the veils we so cheerfully affirm at the surface. The preface recognizes that our science is gay out of suffering, as the Greeks were superficial out of depth. The problem of the place of suffering and depth, the place of knowledge in a world of semblance, is one that is touched upon but not answered in *The Gay Science* itself, at least in its first edition: it is the madness of the madman who proclaims the death of God, and the self-induced, mad suffering that animates the 'tragic Prometheia of all knowers'.[54] In a world of surfaces, of semblance, what is 'going to the depths' but madness, an illness from which we may hope to recover or a 'prelude' that announces true science?

SCHEIN BEYOND GOOD AND EVIL

Nietzsche, in a pair of notes written at the time of *Beyond Good and Evil*, articulates the distinction between *Schein* and *Erscheinung*, and the problem of the relation of *Schein* and its underlying depths, in a way that demands their full quotation

> There are fateful words which seem to express knowledge and in fact *hinder* knowledge; one of these is the word 'appearances' [*Erscheinungen*]. The confusion that the 'appearances' create is betrayed by these sentences which I borrow from diverse modern philosophers.

> against the word *'appearances'* [*gegen das Wort 'Erscheinungen'*]. N.B. *Semblance* [*Schein*] as I understand it, is the actual and sole reality of things – that to which all present predicates belong and which can best be characterized by all predicates, even the opposite ones. With the word, however, nothing more is expressed than its inaccessibility to logical procedure and distinctions: thus 'semblance', 'illusion' ['*Schein*'] in relation to 'logical truth' – which however, itself is only possible in an imaginary world. I thus place '*Schein*' not in opposition to 'reality' but rather on the contrary accept semblance as the reality which resists transformation into an imaginative 'truth world'. A more determinate name for this reality would be 'the will to power', that is, characterized from the inside and not from its incomprehensible, fluid Protean nature.[55]

These notes indicate several things quite clearly. First, they show the definitive separation of *Erscheinung*, as a technical term with an opposite separate from itself, from *Schein*. Henceforth, Nietzsche characterizes the world in its visibility as *Schein*, and without further explanation. Second, the latter note helps us better to understand what is *'scheinbar'* in *Schein* – its ability to take on opposite properties or 'predicates', its elusiveness and thus 'inaccessibility to logical procedures and distinctions'. Capable of differing and 'opposed' predicates, it is 'Protean', fluid: becoming. The new opposition is thus not between *Erscheinung* and *Ding an sich*, but between *Schein* and *Verstand* and the *Verstandsbestimmungen* or Laws of Thought. Third, there is the characterization of *Schein* as the 'actual and sole reality of things' (*wirkliche und einzige Realität der Dinge*). This surface may be the 'reality' of the *res*, but such a playful self-display does not allow the philosopher's 'going to the depths'; there are no depths, no 'grounds'. Although *Schein* is the

Realität of things, it need not exhaustively characterize them. If Nietzsche's thought wants to preserve the 'dimensionality' of things, to permit depth as well as surface, inner as well as outer, it needs another, active principle co-ordinate with the passive, negative *Schein* that 'is' characterized by opposed predicates, to which predicates 'belong', and which expresses 'inaccessibility' and 'resistance' to logical operations and transformation.[56] The 'dark interior' of this 'reality' is the 'will to power', which Nietzsche, perhaps with embarrassment, characterizes as merely 'another name' since the relation of cause or ground is a logical relation that is undermined by the world as *Schein*. With this 'other name' we reach the ultimate transposition of the 'fundamental opposition': from essence-appearance or true world-apparent world, to thing in itself-appearance, to will to power-semblance, now not co-ordinated with two gods, but one, seen from 'two sides' or two directions.[57] Might we not follow aphorism 30 of *Beyond Good and Evil* and characterize the 'reality of the world' ex-oterically as semblance, es-oterically as will to power?[58] This question, and its consequences, will form the guiding thread of our investigation of *Schein* in *Beyond Good and Evil*.

Schein, in fact, plays a central role in *Beyond Good and Evil*, if subordinate to its 'inside', the will to power, which forms the leitmotif that unifies the book, itself a 'name' of the god who only appears at its very end, the god who, now, 'understands how to *scheinen*'. Semblance is critical as counterpart, in the very first chapter of *Beyond Good and Evil*, to the 'basic belief of all metaphysicians, belief in the oppositions of value' (section 2). A close reading of this second aphorism, particularly its second part, reveals two questions, only the second of which is really confronted. First, 'whether there genuinely are opposites', and second, 'whether these popular valuations and value-opposites, upon which metaphysicians have pressed their seal are not, perhaps, mere foreground valuations'. The first question concerns the oppositions as such, while the second confronts the value placed upon the opposites. Thus,

> for all the value that may be attached to the true, the truthful, the selfless, it would be possible that a value that is higher and more fundamental for all life must be ascribed to semblance, the will to deception, selfishness, and desire.

Such an assertion, far from denying the opposition of 'truth' and 'semblance', depends upon it in two crucial ways, both with respect to the object of valuation and with respect to the valuation itself. Here the objects valued *are* different – e.g. truthfulness and deceptiveness – as are the valuations themselves, e.g. furtherance and hindrance of life.

The point is more strongly made when we quote similar phrases from the following two aphorisms. According to aphorism 3, philosophy originates in an instinctive sense about what encourages the 'preservation of a particular type of life', and although the relative value of semblance over truth may itself be a mere matter of perspective, the valuation itself and the 'life' it encourages is fixed and determinate. More forcefully still, aphorism 4 begins by objecting that 'the falsity of a judgement is, for us, not an objection to a judgement'. It is a question of 'how far it is life encouraging, life preserving, species preserving, perhaps even species breeding' (*Art-züchtend*). Yet this question, and its possible answer, seems capable of a differential response, indeed must be if Nietzsche's critique of the 'life' that has been preserved by previous philosophers and their religious counterparts is not to be dissolved in the acid of metaphysical *Schein*.[59] Even more so if Nietzsche's conception of the philosopher of the future, according to which 'the genuine philosophers are commanders and lawgivers' who 'say "so shall it be!" ' (211)[60] is not to reduce itself to mere playacting, *Schauspielerei*. '*So soll es sein!*', not '*So soll es scheinen!*'.

The philosopher's vision, or instinct, of 'what is noble' and 'what is base', his understanding of the 'value for life' of semblance and truth, is not itself semblance. In questions of 'life' – of hierarchy, of value, of sex, of man and woman – we return to a fatal determinacy, a 'so *am* I' (my emphasis), and thus to the realm of (my) being and, as aphorism 231 concludes, '*my* truths'.[61] Indeed, in the following aphorism the 'woman-in-itself' is characterized, in direct opposition to the man, as the being to which 'nothing is more foreign, more distasteful, more hostile than truth – her great art is the lie, her highest concern is semblance and beauty' (*der Schein und die Schönheit*). This is placed in direct opposition to 'us men', characterized by 'our seriousness, our heaviness, and our depth', and in implicit contrast to 'our virtue, probity' (*Redlichkeit*), which had been identified and exhaustively anatomized in four previous aphorisms (227–30). Once again we see a central tension in Nietzsche's conception of the world as *Schein*, here put in sexual terms: the harsh, weighty, deep, cruelly legislating (male) philosopher of probity and the tender, flighty, superficial, lovingly playful (female) artist of *Schein*.[62]

A linguistic compound of *Schein*, used in the first chapter of *Beyond Good and Evil*, can help us further to acquaint ourselves with the philosophical unease in a world of semblance. After the discussion of Stoicism in aphorism 9, in which the Stoic is first criticized for his *naïveté* in believing that he can live 'according to nature' and is then affirmed as living 'according to nature' in so far as he 'tyrannizes himself', and which ends with the peroration, 'philosophy is this tyrannical drive itself, the most spiritual will to power, to "creation of the world", to *causa prima*',[63] Nietzsche begins a series of five aphorisms, in four of which (aphorisms 10, 11, 12, 14) the term *Augenschein* appears.[64] Indeed, in aphorism 10 it appears in connection with what Nietzsche designates as 'the problem of the actual and apparent [*scheinbaren*] world', directly after speaking of 'the stronger more vital thinkers who take sides *against* semblance (*Schein*) and speak contemptuously of the "perspectival" '. It is these thinkers, hostile to 'modern ideas' of the 'actuality-philosophasters', who denigrate the credibility of their own bodies as ultimate 'actuality' as they denigrate 'the credibility of the evidence [*Augenschein*] that says "the earth stands still" '. It is striking that here, as elsewhere in this sequence, Nietzsche speaks harshly of '*Schein*' and '*Augenschein*'. In this 'critique of modernity',[65] with its subtitle echoing a previous set of *Principles of the Philosophy of the Future*, modern materialism, along with modern free spirits and 'modern ideas' are all critically evaluated. The enemy of what 'shines before the eye' is the one who does life's work, by striving to transcend the limits and measures of perceptual finitude.[66] The philosopher of the future, unlike Kant, will realize that although 'synthetic judgements a priori' are believed as a 'foreground perspective and evidence' (*Augenschein*), they are 'purely false judgements' (11). Truth is not exhausted by *Augenschein*, nor is philosophy correctly understood as its systematization and justification. Thus, as Nietzsche states in a contemporary note, 'Reason is the philosophy of *Augenschein*.'[67]

The discussion in the twelfth aphorism is the most important one, in so far as it shows us Nietzsche's own contribution to the 'overcoming of *Augenschein*'. This is done, characteristically, in an indirect way, perhaps so that 'the "conviction" of the philosopher does [not quite] step upon the stage' as *his* conviction.[68] Nietzsche speaks of the two Poles who, 'until now', have been 'the greatest and most victorious opponents of evidence' (*Augenschein*), namely Copernicus, who set the earth in motion, and Boscovich,[69] who denied the fixity of the atom in favour of immaterial forces. The third great fusillade against *Augenschein* is the denial of an 'atomistic soul'. This 'attack on the ancient soul concept' has been prepared by modern philosophy from Descartes to Kant (54), but it is only realized by that third great 'Pole', Nietzsche: 'I am a Polish nobleman *pur sang*, in whom there is not the slightest admixture of bad blood, least of all German.'[70] Nietzsche has dis-integrated the soul, destroying this piece of 'superstition' and 'evidence' without, however, eliminating it as a useful 'concept' and 'hypothesis'. Indeed soul, in its original sense 'the principle of life', *anima* and *psyche*, is the central subject of Nietzsche's philosophy. 'Life itself is will to power', we learn in a parenthesis to the next aphorism (13), and psychology, the science of the soul in this sense, is the 'morphology and doctrine of the development of the will to power', once again 'queen of the sciences' which 'is now, again, the path to the fundamental problems' (23). This 'hypothesis of the philosopher' is the animating principle, the 'inside' of the *Schein* which the 'true world' has become and which, as we have seen, is merely a negative designation. The new conception of soul, to return to aphorism 12, is given 'positive content' by Nietzsche: 'mortal souls', 'soul as subject-manyness', 'soul as social structure of drives and affects'. The first conception is obviously a counterpart to the Christian 'immortal soul', the second to the 'absolute unity of the individual soul', the third to the 'equality of souls before God'. Separated from its polemical content, we may characterize soul, whose principle (at least) is will to power, as discontinuous change or 'self-overcoming', manyness or essential relatedness and conflict, and hierarchy or 'commanding and obeying' respectively, all themes easily recognizable from the exposition of will to power in Nietzsche's previous work, *Thus Spoke Zarathustra*. The will to power, then, is not the principle of evidence but rather that which explodes the *Augenschein* of unity from the 'inside', as the very soul of *Schein* and *Augenschein*.

The discussion of aphorism 12 ends with a warning. The new philosopher has been expelled from the 'tropical lushness' of the growths that surrounded the ancient concept into a 'new wasteland and a new mistrust'. Or rather, he has expelled himself, as enemy of semblance and the evidence that shines before the eyes. In the seventh chapter, 'Our Virtues', we learn more about why this has occurred in another sequence of five aphorisms (226–30) leading up to the aphorism on 'man and woman' already discussed.

It should not surprise us that the first in this sequence – entitled 'We Immoralists' – returns to *Augenschein*. According to this aphorism, 'dolts and *Augenschein*' speak against immoralists as 'men without duty', indeed contest that 'we immoralists' can't speak of 'our virtues'. If they had been less doltish, presumably, they would remember aphorism 32, which describes the transition from the moral to the extra-moral age in which we immoralists live as the 'self-overcoming of morality', in which 'morality of purpose' is rejected due to its basis in hidden and self-serving purposes. Thus the evidence or *Augenschein* of immorality hides the final consequences of that very morality.[72] Nietzsche ends the aphorism with a phrase that forms a leitmotif of the five aphorisms, concerned as they are with the related problems of ignorance and semblance: 'we always have the dolts and the evidence against us!'[73]

The dolts are informed, and the evidence of immorality is overthrown, with the first words of the following aphorism: 'Probity, assuming that this is our virtue . . .'. What is probity, intellectual honesty, but the 'purity of mind and soul', 'purity of intention' that is the highest Christian virtue? 'We' are special, have gone 'beyond' Christianity, because we do not let our virtue relax. 'We', 'we immoralists' are enjoined by Nietzsche: 'Let us remain hard, we last Stoics!' – and we recall the characterization of Stoicism, and philosophy, of aphorism 9. The following aphorism, aphorism 228, and its discussion of the English Utilitarians, tell us something about what it means to 'stay hard'. The English moralists are criticized in two different ways: first as advocating a morality of 'usefulness', 'happiness', 'comfort', and 'fashion' (Nietzsche writes the last two in English) – a 'herd morality', in other words, that entails the degeneration of the species through the 'elimination of suffering'.[74] Second, the English moralists are involved in 'cant and moral Tartuffery' – i.e. a lack of probity – in offering as morality what is really English self-justification.[75]

The following two aphorisms (229–30) give Nietzsche's alternative 'morality of probity'. The sign of the refusal to relax in one's virtue is precisely the immoralist's probity about his probity – his own 'virtue' is piteously exposed as cruelty, cruelty towards himself, and this cruelty, the joy in the suffering of others *and* oneself, the joy in the spectacle of suffering, is shown to be the 'harsh foundation' of all 'higher culture'. This process, fascinating in itself but not unfamiliar from the more extended treatment in *On the Genealogy of Morals*, does not concern us as much as the relation discussed at the very end of aphorism 229, which leads to the subject matter of aphorism 230. The process of scientific investigation itself involves cruelty, a cruelty toward 'the basic will of the spirit, which ceaselessly wills and desires semblance and surfaces [*zum Schein und zu den Oberflächen*]. There is, even in every will to know, a drop of cruelty.'

Aphorism 230 falls into two parts.[76] The first gives an exposition of the 'basic will of the spirit', after the appropriately Nietzschean definition of 'spirit' as the 'commanding something that wills to be master and feels that it is master, in itself and around itself', reminiscent of the saying in *Thus Spoke Zarathustra* that 'spirit is the life that itself cuts into life'.[77] The second part speaks of 'the sublime inclination of the knower'. Four apparently disparate elements are united in the exposition of the spirit's 'will to semblance, simplification, mask, cloak, in short will to surface'. First, the will to simplify as a will to incorporate, assimilate, i.e. the logical and categorial 'mastering' of the foreign and the new, familiar in Nietzsche's discussions and critiques of knowledge. Second, the will to simplify as a will to exclude, to ignore, to ignorance itself, in which rather than expand the spirit to include the 'other' as same, the spirit contracts and encloses its horizons, denying the existence of the other to preserve the same, the closing-in of horizons Nietzsche had already seen as 'necessary for life' in the second *Untimely Consideration on History* (*Historie*).[78] Third, 'the occasional will of the spirit to allow itself to be deceived', simplification as a rejoicing in the arbitrariness and constraint of one's 'spiritual household', allied to the enjoyment of art, 'art as the good will to semblance'. Finally, the will to deceive others, a self-simplification through a mask which is also a guarantee of power. Through this 'basic will' spirit may be said to *construct* a world of knowledge, *create* a world of stability, *believe* the presentation of the other and *display* the presentation of itself. Such simplifications and semblances constitute its world. The 'basic will of the spirit' is the will to such a world of *Schein*.

'The sublime inclination of the knower', as the second part of the aphorism tells us, is opposed to this 'basic will'. It 'takes things deeply, from all sides, thoroughly' (*gründlich*). Whether we call it 'cruelty of intellectual conscience' or 'probity, love of truth, love of wisdom, sacrifice for knowledge, heroism of knowledge', it opposes itself to the will to semblance and the semblance it wills to the 'objective world' constituted by the unitary functions of the spirit as intellect and to the provincial limitedness of the 'unfree spirit', to the joy in being deceived of the herd and the studied deceptiveness of the shepherd.

The characterization of it as an inclination (*Hang*) indicates not only its source but its direction – the 'nature' in the 'fearsome basic text [*Grundtext*] *homo natura*' – and the task before such an 'inclination' – 'to retranslate man back into nature'. As natural inclination it is notably free of the taint of Christianity, although Christianity has known how to rename it: in this sense, the self-destruction of the virtue of probity is nothing but its final unveiling as cruelty, a cruelty of spirit in whose final elimination we have less than no reason to believe. Unlike the Christians, 'we' have no wish to rename our 'inclination' a 'virtue', our 'cruelty' 'truthfulness'. But unlike the mere 'free spirits' with their 'modern ideas', we 'free, *very* free spirits' know that we can only eliminate cruelty and suffering by eliminating life itself.[79]

If the 'inclination' points us toward nature, the 'sublimity' of the inclination points us toward tragedy. We are not surprised, then, to discover Oedipus, along with Odysseus, near the aphorism's end. The 'retranslation' of man back into nature demands that man stand before himself and his own nature as he has, 'become hard in the discipline of science' (like Copernicus and Boscovich?), learned to stand, undeceived by *Schein* and *Augenschein*, before the '*other* Nature'. Then, like Oedipus,[80] he can look unblinkingly at the contradictoriness of his own nature, and like Odysseus he will 'deafen' himself to the siren-song of the metaphysical while still, insatiably curious, exposing his vision to its delusory charms. The conflict of the will to semblance and the sublime inclination of the knower, then, rehearses in a non-mythic mode the tragic conflict as exposed in *The Birth of Tragedy*. The only answer to 'why knowledge at all?' is the tragic one – *Moira*, 'a granite of spiritual *fatum*' (231). In affirming its conflict with semblance which is ultimately a conflict with itself, and its fatal advancement to a knowledge that is unilluminated as to its source or end, 'every philosophy' is, indeed, 'a long tragedy' (25).

Thus Nietzsche's late philosophy, at least in one sense, returns to tragedy, the tragedy of the knower at war with the semblance that is the very air he breathes and the earth he treads, and at war with himself and his own ignorance. The appeal to nature is of no more help to the tragic 'Pole' than it is to the sceptical Scotsman in his *Treatise* written a century and a half before. The sphinx at which Oedipus intrepidly looks is the very contradictoriness of nature itself, nature dissolved into a semblance which overtakes him and his own wisdom.[81] Not nature and wisdom, as aphorism 231 makes clear, but 'a granite of spiritual fate', a 'grand stupidity' (*eine Granit vom geistigen Fatum, grosse(n) Dummheit*), are the elements of the thinker's reflection. Previously, in aphorism 55, Nietzsche had discussed cruelty, 'religious cruelty', whose final stage was the sacrifice of God Himself, and the consequent worship of 'the stone, stupidity, gravity, destiny, nothingness' (*den Stein, die Dummheit, die Schwere, das Schicksal, das Nichts anbeten*). The terms of this sacrificial cruelty and the cruelty of the self-sacrificing 'virtue' of probity are strikingly similar. The affirmation of this 'tragedy', this 'ultimate cruelty' is the affirmation of life, the eternal return of the same, in which according to the following aphorism (56) 'we cry, insatiably, *da capo*, and not only for oneself, but for the whole piece and drama, and not only to a drama, but at base for Him, who finds just this drama necessary'. Thus Nietzsche's philosophy under the sign of semblance would be complete, a self-enclosed whole, divinely sanctioned and eternally returning, a drama immune from questions of truth, wrapped in the protective veil of art and semblance.

Yet the tragedy within the tragedy, the real tragedy as viewed 'from the inside', is that the philosopher is not simply animated by the sublime inclination of the *knower*. The true philosopher, the philosopher of the future, according to aphorism 211, is not a scholar, not a 'philosophical labourer' like Kant or Hegel, whose task is the fixing of a great store of valuations into formulas 'whether in the realm of the logical or of the political (moral) or of the artistic'. 'Genuine philosophers, however, are commanders and law-givers: they say "so *shall* it be!", they, first, determine the "whither" and the "why" of man.' They create not a dream but a world: 'Philosophy always creates the world in its image, it cannot do otherwise. Philosophy is this tyrannical drive itself, the most spiritual will to power, to the "creation of the world", to *causa prima*.' The sense of this phrase from aphorism 9, already noted above, is repeated toward the end of aphorism 211. For genuine philosophers, 'their "knowing" is creating, their creating is a legislation, their will to truth is – *will to power*.' The cruelty of the genuine philosopher is not the cruelty of the self-tormenting knower but of the legislator who must exercise his creativity on his fellow men, affirm their suffering, who, as in a note entitled 'The XX Century' is unafraid 'to summon the causes of war'.[82] Indeed, in aphorisms 208 and 209 Nietzsche had discussed the advent of such wars. In the first he speaks quite explicitly about what such philosophical legislation is founded upon, not scepticism, but will, not conciliation but the sharpening of differences: 'the time for petty politics is past; as soon as the next century comes the battle for the mastery of the earth – the compulsion to grand politics'. The second begins by characterizing 'the new warlike age in which we Europeans have obviously entered'.

We needn't multiply our references to Nietzsche's praise of 'war and warriors' nor to his conception of the philosopher's legislative task, nor to the hierarchical principle that animates his social vision, itself the principle of his critique of Christianity and contemporary nihilism. We wish, rather, to raise the question of the relation of these genuine philosophers, bloody wars, and determinate hierarchies to the world of semblance: the relation of artistic tragedy and real suffering.

We can return to the note quoted above 'against the word "appearances" ', or, perhaps more appropriately, end our investigation of *Schein* in *Beyond Good and Evil* with a discussion of its aphorisms 34 and 36. We recall that the unpublished note speaks of semblance as the 'sole reality of things', a reality, however, that does not exhaustively characterize the world – it has an 'inside', the will to power.[83] The thematic discussions of semblance and will to power, in *Beyond Good and Evil*, itself published shortly after this note, are separated, but only by one aphorism, the shortest one in the chapter. Thus, their relation is hinted at but not made explicit. As Nietzsche says in a roughly contemporary note, 'in aphorism books like mine many lengthy, forbidden things and chains of thought stand between and behind short aphorisms'.[84] The theme of hiddenness, unintelligibility, esotericism and masks is a central one of the second chapter, in which these aphorisms occur, and is closely linked with the hiddenness of the will to power itself.

Aphorism 34 begins with the assertion that philosophers have every reason to claim the '*erroneousness* of the world', in fact to conjecture about a 'deceptive principle in the "essence of things" '. After dismissing the 'critical' attribution of this deceptiveness to 'our thinking', Nietzsche raises the deeper question: why not be deceived? 'It is no more than a moral prejudice that truth is worth more than semblance' (*Schein*). Life depends on 'perspectival evaluations and semblances' (*Scheinbarkeiten*), and with the destruction of the 'world of semblance' (*scheinbare Welt*) nothing would remain of the truth. Nietzsche then, in concert with the programme of chapter one, raises the question of the opposition between true and false itself. He asks, apparently rhetorically, 'Isn't it enought to accept shades of semblance [*Scheinbarkeit*] and as it were brighter and darker shades and whole tones of semblance [*Schein*] – different *valeurs*, to use the language of painters?' A world of semblance with internal distinctions, but without the ontological or metaphysical opposition of 'true' and 'apparent', a 'pluralistic universe'. As a world of *Schein*, it is an 'artistic' world, a painter's world, a *Fiktion*. And as to the question of the fiction's author, we have another rhetorical question: why not be as sceptical of the subject's 'truth' as of the object's?

As aphorism 34 poses the self-sufficiency of the 'world of semblance' as a rhetorical question, so does aphorism 36 assert the 'will to power' as the 'intelligible character' of the world only conditionally and subjunctively, in contrast to the, again roughly contemporary, definitive assertion in the note that has become well known as the concluding aphorism of *The Will to Power*.[85] Reading aphorisms 34 and 36 together, we are struck first by their conflict. Here we read, hypothetically, that 'nothing other is "given" to us as real than our world of desires and passions'. 'Reality' is used without hesitation or quotation marks, here and subsequently. Thus, Nietzsche speaks of the 'reality of our drives'; he proposes that the world itself, 'not as a "deception", a "semblance" [*ein Schein*], a "representation" (in the Berkeleyan or Schopenhauerian sense)', 'possesses the same rank of reality as our affect'. The life of our drives is, according to Nietzsche's 'principle' (*wie es mein Satz ist*), 'will to power', so that 'the world seen from within, the world determined and characterized with regard to its "intelligible character" – it would be "will to power" and nothing else'.

Of the many questions these two aphorisms raise, only one need be broached here. What is the relation of the seemingness of the world and its reality? The world of semblance is, here as always, artistic, surface, ironic, fictive. The world as will to power is real – no *Schein* – an inner world, a world of depths, affectively laden with pathos. The outside and the inside, the semblance and the 'intelligible character', the aesthetic and the ethical, a world of artistic *valeurs* that dissolve in an instant into one another and a world of philosophical *Werthe* that are fixed legislatively for centuries, a world of continuous stages and a hierarchical world 'in which we want precisely the opposite of an assimilation, an equalization: we teach estrangement in every sense, we rip open gulfs such as never before existed'. A world in which we can, without embarrassment, speak of the 'actual hierarchy and value difference between men'.[86] What sort of oppositions are these? Does the hypothesis of aphorism 36 answer the rhetorical questions of aphorism 34, beginning from and ending in a reality that is, if not higher, then at least deeper than all *Schein*? The real tragedy, then, would be that the tragedy is real, the wars are fought with real bullets, the slaves are real human beings, and the victims' ashes float into the sky to block out the sun, enfolding us all in the unmistakeably real and impenetrable veil of darkness and death.

The downfall of the 'true world', whose tale is told in *The Twilight of the Idols*, leads also to the destruction of the *scheinbare*, the seeming world.[87] Although 'the opposition of the seeming world and the true world reduces itself to the opposition "world" and "nothing" ' or, otherwise put, 'the "true world", however it has been previously conceived, has always been the seeming world once again',[88] *Schein* has lost its *Scheinbarkeit* with the destruction of the 'true world'. 'The seeming world, i.e. a world viewed, ordered, selected according to values, i.e. in the case according to the viewpoint of usefulness with respect to the preservation and power-augmentation of a determinate species of animal.' Once we recognize not only the illusoriness of the 'true world' but also the rootedness of all *Schein* in an evaluating will to power 'there remains', as this same note of Spring 1888 continues, 'no shadow of justification to speak of semblance [*Schein*] here', since 'reality consists exactly in this particular action and reaction of every individual against the whole'.[89]

Thus, in *The Twilight of the Idols*, after having denounced the 'true world' as the 'seeming world', the invention of ' "Reason" in Philosophy', and having told the tale of its downfall in 'How the "True World" Finally Became a Fable', Nietzsche, in the next chapter, 'Morality as Anti-Nature', answers the question of 'what remains': the principle of the critique of the 'anti-natural' morality as 'hostile to life': 'life itself'. 'When we speak of values, we speak under the inspiration, under the optic of life: life itself forces us to attach values, life itself values through us when we attach values.'[90] As in *Beyond Good and Evil*, we move from an affirmation of *Schein* to its 'inner principle' in three steps.

We see a final indication of the duality and the primacy of the harsh, legislating, valuing will to power at the end of *The Twilight of the Idols*. After the discussion of Dionysus, *The Birth of Tragedy*, and the eternal return of the same, a complex pointing to the artistic resolution we have already adumbrated, the book ends with section 29 from *Thus Spoke Zarathrustra*, III, 'Of the Old and New Tablets', here given the title 'The Hammer Speaks'. Given the subtitle of *The Twilight of the Idols*, 'How One Philosophizes With a Hammer', this 'speech' would seem particularly important. It is a speech that uses the diamond, pressed inside the earth for centuries until it has reached the apotheosis of lustre and hardness, as an image of the will, supremely tensed by its centuries of ascetic discipline.[91] The hardness and harshness of the diamond entails a rejection of weak-hearted pity, an affirmation of implacable destiny, a willingness to cut, to rend to pieces, and thus to create. Creation here is not within the realm of seeming, and we speak of creators, not artists, who can 'write upon the will of millennia as upon bronze'. The legislator's will is the 'hard will' for which bronze and what is 'harder than bronze' is as soft as wax to the touch, as all is soft to the diamond's edge. Inscribing upon the flux of millennia, remaining hard despite the disintegration of the outside into semblance, the Nietzschean philosopher of the future affirms life by affirming its inside, the harsh, brilliant hard inside of the diamantine will to power, whose cutting edge cuts the soft flesh to ribbons, announcing a suffering that is beyond all words, beyond all thought, beyond all *Schein*.

The overcoming of the distinction between *Schein* and *Erscheinung*, or *scheinbare* and *wahre Welt*, does not lead to a world of semblance or its primacy. However strong the attraction of the Greek 'aesthetic vision of the world' for Nietzsche, his world is deep, and deeper than the bright *Schein* of day could ever dream. This generative, destructive, and evaluative inside is the world positively characterized, the world as will to power 'and nothing else'. This is the future philosopher's world, the world of fixed and hard legislation that neither passes away nor passes over into its opposite, but lasts for millennia, inscribed in the hearts and wills of the human race. It is to this legislative task that Nietzsche devoted himself in the last years of his philosophical productivity. Yet once we have seen this, we are forced to wonder whether the legislation can sustain itself 'on the outside' any better than *Schein* can penetrate 'to the inside'. 'The world is will to power – and nothing outside' (*ausserdem*). Once 'outside', what 'is' the will to power?

Many questions arise – old questions, often raised by Nietzsche himself, of whether the 'reality' of our desires is not as *scheinbare* as that of the world, or whether our insights into life or nature possess any special validity. Other questions as well: is the relation of inside and outside safe against the Hegelian dialectic of force and its expression, inner and outer? Is the pathos of the hidden philosophical lawgiver not the mournfulness of the unhappy consciousness whose reality is ever unfulfilled once externalized? Is the progress of *Schein* that we have noted different from, truer than the progress of *Schein* in the *Logic of Reflection*, from *Schein*, through the determinations of reflection, to ground? And since the world does not dissolve into semblance, it matters greatly if the life under whose auspices the diamantine will cuts into humanity is only seemingly higher, that of a seeming master, that the higher man not also be a lower. If so, the 'paradoxical *mysterium* of the ultimate cruelty' would, indeed, 'be left for the generation that just now approaches'. We all, already, know something of that.

NOTES

1 F. Nietzsche, in G. Colli and M. Montinari, eds, *Kritische Gesamtausgabe: Werke*, Walter de Gruyter, Berlin-New York, 1967ff., III, 1, 7, (KGW); *The Birth of Tragedy*, 'Attempt at Self-Critique', sec. 2. All references to Nietzsche's works will be to this edition, and all translation of these and other works is my own. To make it easier to cross-reference, section or aphorism numbers have been supplied in the body of the text wherever practicable.

2 This formulation is taken from the 'Attempt at a Self-Critique', sec. 2 (III, 1, 11) and should be compared with the one in the text (45, sec. 5) which speaks of 'existence and the world' and more importantly has 'eternally' before 'justified'; and with the less confident one toward the end of the book (148, sec. 24) in which 'eternally' has dropped out, and 'appears' replaces the penultimate 'is'.

3 See, for the Schopenhauerian conception of metaphysics, chapter 16 of volume II of *The World as Will and Representation*, A. Schopenhauer, *Sämtlich Werke*, ed. W. Frhr. von Löhneysen, Darmstadt, Wissenschaftliche Buchgesellschaft, 1976, II, 220–3, according to which the deepest problems of metaphysics arise not out of wonder at the existence, but horror at the evil of the world, generating the need for a metaphysical explanation and justification.

4 Nietzsche's rejection of the 'question of the value of existence' is an important theme of *The Twilight of the Idols*. See, especially, the passages at the end of section 5 of 'Morality as Anti-Nature' and section 8 of 'The Four Great Errors' (VI, 3, 80f., 90f.).

5 Schopenhauer, op. cit., I, 564; *The World as Will and Representation*, I, Appendix: 'Critique of Kantian Philosophy'. In *The Birth of Tragedy* we see Kant and Schopenhauer joined together as the philosophers of a new German 'tragic age' (III, 1, 114, sec. 18; 124, sec. 19). In the first passage this kinship is seen precisely in their discovery of the impossibility of elevating 'mere appearance' to the status of 'the innermost essence of things', an epistemological pessimism rooted in the distinction between 'appearance' and 'thing-in-itself' that overcomes the 'logical optimism' inaugurated by Socrates. Contrast Paul de Man, *Allegories of Reading*, New Haven and London: Yale University Press, 1979, 86.

6 KGW III, 1, 13 ('Attempt at a Self-Critique', sec. 6).

7 See KGW III, 1, 148f. (sec. 24) and its allusion to Heraclitus, fragment 52.

8 Kant is quoted following R. Schmidt's edition of *Die Kritik der reinen*

Vernunft, Hamburg, Felix Meiner, 1976. Kant emphasizes the distinction between *Schein* and *Erscheinung* at the beginning of the introduction to 'The Transcendental Dialectic', B 349f.: dialectic, as a logic of illusion, is not to be identified as the doctrine of *probability* as opposed to *certainty*. Still less may *appearance (Erscheinung)* and *Illusion (Schein)* be held to be the same.

9 Schopenhauer, op. cit., II, 21 (*World as Will and Representation*, II, ch. 1).

10 Ibid., II, 12.

11 See ibid., I, 379 (*World as Will and Representation*, sec. 53) for the identification of 'what Kant calls the appearance in opposition to the thing-in-itself and Plato the coming-to-be but never existent in opposition to the existent, never coming-to-be' with 'what the Indians call the veil of Maya'.

12 KGW III, 1, 34f. In passages from Nietzsche, '*Schein*' will be consistently translated as 'semblance' to be distinguished from '*Erscheinung*' which will be translated as 'appearance'. The verbal '*scheinen*' will be translated as 'seem', '*erscheinen*' as 'appear' (unless otherwise noted).

13 KGW III, 1, 7, 11 ('Attempt at a Self-Critique', sec. 2, 5).

14 Ibid., 11.

15 Ibid., 24.

16 KGW III, 3, 5 [123] (Sept. 1870–Jan. 1871).

17 KGW III, 2, 65.

18 Schopenhauer, op. cit., I, 298 (*World as Will and Representation*, I, sec. 41) and II, 679 (vol. II, ch. 44) respectively.

19 KGW III, 1, 22, 23. The following notebook entry may be taken as Nietzsche's comment on the Schopenhauerian 'ideas', although it could easily refer to the Platonic: 'The ideas [*Ideen*] not divine essentialities but illusions' (III, 3, 5 [61] (Sept. 1870–Jan. 1871)).

20 On *Sein* and *Schein*, and their relation to the Greek φαίνεσθαι, see Martin Heidegger, *Einführung in die Metaphysik*, Tübingen, Max Niemeyer, 1966, 75ff. See also *Nietzsche*, Pfullingen, Neske, 1961, I, 195 and *Sein und Zeit*, Tübingen, Max Niemeyer, 1976, sec. 7A (27–31).

21 KGW III, 3, 7 [157] (end 1870–1); III, 1, 24.

22 III, 3, 3 [47] (Winter 1869–70).

23 III, 1, 24.

24 One of Kaufmann's translations. See *The Birth of Tragedy and the Case of Wagner*, New York, Random House, 1967, 34 n. 4. See also Paul de Man, op. cit., p. 91 who seems to neglect the distinction between '*Schein*' and '*Erscheinung*' in the passage in question.

25 It is instructive to compare this passage, III, 1, 34f., with the beginning of 'Of the Backworlders' in *Thus Spoke Zarathustra*, I (VI, 1, 31). See also the note from Autumn 1881: V, 2, 12 [29].

26 KGW III, 1, 35.

27 Kaufmann is forced to translate the two occurrences of '*Schein*' differently: 'demotion of appearance to the level of mere appearance'. (op. cit., 45).

28 The three uses of the term are III, 1, 35: 20 (sec. 4), 40: 6 (sec. 5) and

41: 31 (sec. 5). It is presumably a misprint that generated the variant spelling *'Wiederschein'*.

29 de Man erroneously identifies the earlier passage from section 4 as being from a 'section on the epic', which is actually the concern of section 3 of *The Birth of Tragedy* (de Man, op. cit., 91).

30 KGW III, 1, 39.

31 Ibid., 41.

32 See ibid., 1, 45f. (sec. 6), 69f. (sec. 10), and 103f. (sec. 16). See also III, 3, 8 [29]: (Winter 1870–1–Autumn 1872).

33 Ibid., 3, 8 [7]: 'The lyric poet speaks of himself, but means none but Dionysus. The subjectivity of the lyric poet is a deception. The creative foundation is the Dionysian, primordial pain, which expresses itself in an analogous image, so that we are drawn on to the foundation and not the image.' (Winter 1870–1–Autumn 1872).

34 Ibid., 1, 41.

35 Ibid., 40.

36 Ibid., 41.

37 See ibid., 36 (sec. 4) and 24 (sec. 1).

38 Ibid., 3, 5 [80] (Sept. 1870–Jan. 1871), 118.

39 KGW IV, 2, 19 (*Human, All Too Human*, I, aphorism 1).

40 See ibid., 32–4 (*Human, All Too Human*, I, aphorism 16).

41 KGW III, 1, 87 (sec. 13), 95 (sec. 15).

42 The preface was written for the second edition (1887) and is thus close, both chronologically and spiritually, to *Beyond Good and Evil*, as is the fifth book which was added for this edition.

43 KGW V, 2, 20 (*The Gay Science*, preface, sec. 4).

44 Compare the note of Nov. 1887–March 1888: 'One goes to the ground and perishes when one pursues grounds' (*Man geht zu Grunde, wenn man immer zu den Gründen geht*). KGW VIII, 2, 11 [6].

45 KGW V, 2, 18 (*The Gay Science*, preface, sec. 3).

46 Ibid., 19 (preface, sec. 4). Compare the discussion of Greek 'serenity' (*Heiterkeit*) in *The Birth of Tragedy* (III, 1, 6, 61, 74, 97; 'Attempt at a Self-Critique' sec. 1; sec. 9, 11, 15 of the text).

47 KGW V, 2, 115–18.

48 Ibid., 98.

49 The next aphorism but one speaks 'Of the Theatre', criticizing 'music and art which want to intoxicate their audience'. It speaks in further denigrating tones of 'intoxicants', 'enthusiasts', 'wine', and summarizes by contrasting 'thought' and 'passion' with the 'intoxication' that was so favourably set forth in *The Birth of Tragedy*, still said to dominate the theatre but identified as 'hashish smoking and betel-nut chewing of the Europeans'. There is an obvious contrast between the Apollo of aphorism 84 and the 'Dionysus' of aphorism 86.

50 KGW V, 2, 90f.

51 KGW III, 1, 43 (*The Birth of Tragedy*, sec. 5).

52 KGW V, 2, 90f. *'Schein'* is printed in spaced type in the title.

53 Cf. KGW III, 1, 22, 23 (*The Birth of Tragedy*, sec. 1).

54 *The Gay Science*, aphorism 125: 'The Madman', aphorism 300: 'Preludes of Science'.

55 KGW VII, 3, 40 [52], [53].
56 Compare two contemporaneous notes on the need for an 'inside' of forces, KGW VII, 3, 35 [68] and 36 [31] (May–July and June–July 1885 respectively).
57 In the last aphorism but one of *Beyond Good and Evil* (295), Dionysus is characterized as a god who knows how to 'seem' – '*dass er zu scheinen versteht*'. In *Human, All Too Human*, I, aphorism 15 ('No inside and outside in the world'), Nietzsche rejected the philosophical use of this distinction, and the question of its metaphysical weight in these later discussions remains. The classic exposition and critique of this distinction is in the third chapter of Hegel's *Phenomenology of Spirit* (trans. A. V. Miller, Oxford, Oxford University Press, 1977).
58 On 'esoteric-exoteric', see KGW VIII, 1, 5 [9] (Summer 1886–Autumn 1887).
59 See, for example, aphorism 62 and those of chapter 5 of *Beyond Good and Evil*. Of course, this is a central theme of the whole of *On the Genealogy of Morals*.
60 KGW VI, 2, 148. The characterization of 'the genuine philosophers' is in spaced type.
61 Ibid., 176. 'In every cardinal problem speaks an unchangeable "so am I" [*das bin ich*]: about man and woman, for example.' At the end of this aphorism Nietzsche asserts that 'I have been permitted to get off my chest [*herauszusagen*] some truths about "Woman in itself" . . . my truths.' See also Leo Strauss, 'Note on the Plan of Nietzsche's *Beyond Good and Evil*', *Studies in Platonic Political Philosophy*, Chicago and London, University of Chicago Press, 1983, 190.
62 The characterization of man and woman in *Beyond Good and Evil* 232 has many similarities to that in the preface to *The Gay Science* discussed above, and with which it is roughly contemporaneous, although the latter, in keeping with the artistic focus of the book, is less truculent about the limitations of the 'artistic woman'. Indeed, in *The Gay Science* the aphorisms concerned with art and those concerned with woman are grouped together in book II. See also *Beyond Good and Evil* 127 and 145.
63 It is notable that it is with respect to philosophy that we have the first occurrence in *Beyond Good and Evil* of the 'will to power'.
64 '*Augenschein*' means 'evidence', and has a similar, though not identical formation as its Latin counterpart which forms the basis of the English word. The term is used for legal 'eyewitness' evidence, and is unusual in a philosophical context, where '*Evidenz*' is almost exclusively found.
65 KGW VI, 3, 348 (*Ecce Homo*, 'Beyond Good and Evil').
66 For materialism, see aphorisms 10, 12: for modern 'free spirits' see aphorisms 44, 202, 203; for 'modern ideas' see, in addition to aphorism 10, aphorisms 58, 202, 239, 251, 253, 263.
67 The discussion of Kant is in aphorism 11; the note is found in KGW VII, 1, 2 [141]: Autumn 1885–Autumn 1886. Cf. *Beyond Good and Evil* 134 and 192.
68 See *Beyond Good and Evil* 8.
69 The *Kommentar* to the *Kritische Studienausgabe* (ed. G. Colli and M. Montinari, Munich, Deutscher Taschenbuch Verlag, 1980) notes that

'Ruggiero Giuseppe Boscovich was not a Pole but a Dalmatian' (14: 340).

70 KGW VI, 3, 266 (*Ecce Homo*, 'Why I am So Wise', sec. 3). This passage which continues with undiluted rage against his 'German' relations, mother and sister, was for many years suppressed. See the *Kritische Studienausgabe, Kommentar*, 14: 459–62 on this 'rediscovered' section of *Ecce Homo*. The passage substituted for it and which it was meant to replace, mentions that 'my forefathers were Polish nobility' and notes 'how often I am addressed as a Pole when I travel, and this by Poles themselves, how rarely I am taken for a German'. Compare the roughly contemporaneous letter to Georg Brandes of 10 April 1888 and the letter of 4 January 1889 'To the illustrious Poles'. For further discussion, see C. P. Janz, *Friedrich Nietzsche: Biographie*, Munich–Vienna, Hanser, 1978, I, 26–9.

71 See the preface (KGW VI, 2, 3) and aphorism 54.

72 This process, as is known, is more extensively explored in *On the Genealogy of Morals*, III. See also *The Gay Science* 344 and *Dawn*, preface, sec. 3.

73 Here, *'Augenschein'* retains some of its legal connotations.

74 See, e.g., the discussion of *Beyond Good and Evil* 44 and the distinction between the 'free spirits' and 'free thinkers' to be found in 'all the countries of Europe and equally in America' and the 'free, *very* free spirits' – a locution that recurs at the end of the sequence under discussion in aphorism 230. The distinction is clarified by the note that seems to form the basis of aphorism 44 (VII, 3, 36 [17]: June–July 1885, especially 282f.).

75 For the connection of moral and ethical Tartuffery and lack of probity, see *Beyond Good and Evil* 5.

76 Compare Eckhard Heftrich's lengthy analysis of this aphorism, in his *Nietzsches Philosphie: Identität von Welt und Nichts*, Frankfurt am Main, Vittorio Klostermann, 1962, 111–54.

77 KGW VI, 1, 130 (*Thus Spoke Zarathustra*, II, 'Of the Famous Wise Men').

78 KGW III, 1, 247–50 ('On the Use and Disadvantage of Historical Study for Life', sec. 1).

79 Compare KGW VIII, 2, 11 [133], Nov. 1887–March 1888: 'One recognizes the *superiority* of the Greek man and the Renaissance man, but one would like to have him without his cause and conditions. Until now a more profound insight into the Greeks was lacking.' The final sentence was left off this passage in *Der Wille zur Macht* 882 permitting Alexander Nehamas to use this note in precisely its *opposite* sense. (*Nietzsche, Life as Literature*, Cambridge, Mass., Harvard University Press, 216f.) It is, of course, Nietzsche's own understanding of the Greeks that offers us the possibility of this 'more profound' understanding. See *The Twilight of the Idols*, 'What I Owe to the Ancients', sec. 4–5 (VI, 3, 152–4).

80 For Oedipus as tragic figure, see *The Birth of Tragedy*, sec. 9 (III, 1, 61ff.).

81 For more illumination about the meaning of 'sphinx' in *Beyond Good and Evil*, 1, see the note from the time of its writing (April–June 1885:

VII, 3, 34 [226], headed 'NB. Sphinx', in which the problem of the 'value of truth and falsity' is raised, and which ends with the statement, 'therefore one must deceive and allow oneself to be deceived'.

82 KGW VII, 3, 34 [18].

83 It is notable that Schopenhauer, in the second book of *The World as Will and Representation*, asserts the validity of his insight into the will as 'thing-in-itself' by maintaining that the will is the only possible concept that 'does *not* have its origin in appearance, that does *not* have its origin in mere intuitive representation, but comes from the inside' (op. cit., I, 172; sec. 22).

84 KGW VII, 3, 37 [5], June–July 1885.

85 Aphorism 1067. This note may be found in KGW VII, 3, 38 [10], June–July 1885. See Heftrich's discussion of their relation, op. cit., 68–94.

86 KGW VII, 3, 36 [17], June–July 1885.

87 KGW VI, 3, 75 (*The Twilight of the Idols*, 'How the "True World" Finally Became a Fable').

88 KGW VII, 3, 14 [184], Spring 1888 and 11 [50], Nov. 1887–May 1888 respectively. *The Twilight of the Idols* was finished in September 1888.

89 KGW VII, 3, 14 [184].

90 KGW VI, 3, 80 (*Twilight of the Idols*, 'Morality as Anti-Nature', sec. 5).

91 Cf. *Beyond Good and Evil*, preface, aphorism 188, and especially the discussion of the 'bad conscience' in *On the Genealogy of Morals*, sec. 16–19.

4 Hermeneutics and Nietzsche's early thought

Nicholas Davey

What is tradition? A higher authority which one obeys not because it commands what is useful to us, but because it commands.

(D 9)

INTRODUCTION

The debate concerning Nietzsche's place in Europe's history of ideas has intensified as post-modernist thought challenges the foundations upon which the grand philosophical tradition is built. An advocate of the Derridean assimilation of Nietzsche recently set about the arguments of a defender of Nietzsche's conservative status in the following terms:

> His understanding of Nietzsche (and philosophy) comes across as extraordinarily static, locked in a time warp: little of philosophical importance seems to have happened since Nietzsche's 'collapse' in 1889. . . . Nietzsche the thinker of a revolution that has only begun, the man who suggested as the epitaph of university philosophy, 'it disturbed nobody', has been exceedingly cloistered.[1]

Not that Nietzsche has always had a good time of it in the hands of those who guard the grand tradition. For every Erich Heller, there is a Wilhelm Dilthey intent on cleansing 'the temple of immortals' of Nietzsche's defiling presence. Perhaps it is inevitable that the status of the 'old philologist' should continue to provoke such controversy. The calculated ambiguity of his aphoristic assertions invites pillaging by opposing philosophical causes and the dialectical propensity towards statement and counter-statement guarantees that disputes over his place in tradition will be undecidable so long as critics attend only to the word of his assertions rather than their interplay or context. The historical location of Nietzsche's philosophy remains equally contentious. Despite the bombast with which Nietzsche is claimed for this or that contemporary movement he remains a profoundly transitional figure rooted in the intellectual dispositions of the first half of the nineteenth century. Without doubt he stands on the threshold of the present European philosophical epoch, influencing what lies within it but formed by what now lies outside it. Perhaps no other modern philosopher can simultaneously appear so familiar and yet so remote. Little wonder that he should appeal to post-Heideggerian philosophers and defenders of the grand tradition alike.

This essay will not stand aside from the present debate as it seeks to offer some sanguine historical and philosophical reflections about the formative influences upon Nietzsche's early thought. The aim is to substantiate the case for reading Nietzsche's early philosophy as a hermeneutic project. The early works make it abundantly clear that there *is* a substantial hermeneutic foundation to his thinking which has, astoundingly, been neglected. Attention to this foundation reveals a hermeneutic of considerable complexity and which, when understood, carries considerable implications for the interpretation of Nietzsche's philosophical corpus.

When Foucault comments that 'the only valid tribute to thought such as Nietzsche's is precisely to use it',[2] he echoes the latter's conviction that the value of a philosophy lies in the bricks which can be subsequently used by others 'for better building'.[3] Within post-Heideggerian thought, components of Nietzsche's philosophy have been used to extend and deconstruct hermeneutics whilst within the so-called humanist school, Heidegger's analyses of *Dasein* and temporality are openly in debt to Nietzsche's examination of the human predicament in a 'perpetual becoming in time' (BT 4). Gadamer identifies Nietzsche (with Husserl) as being the philosopher who contributes the concept of 'horizon' to the vocabulary of hermeneutics. Figl suggests that Nietzsche's concept of a life-horizon influences Dilthey's formation of a hermeneutical *Lebens-philosophie*.[4] Conceptual evidence also suggests Gadamer's conception of 'effective history' (*Wirkungsgeschichte*) to be beholden to Nietzsche's analysis of 'moral effects'.[5] More important, however, is Gadamer's recognition that the possibility of philosophical her-meneutics rests upon overcoming the Nietzschean thesis that meaning is not discovered or disclosed in the world but projected into it.[6] In the development of his critical hermeneutics, Habermas extends Nietzsche's analysis of the subjective foundations of knowledge-claims into a theory concerning the inter-subjectively recognizable 'interests' of knowledge. A variant of the stratagem appears in his *The Philosophical Discourse of Modernity* where Nietzsche's critique of the perspectival interests behind knowledge-claims is used to attack the 'self-inflicted systematic constraints' of 'Old Europe's . . . traditional values'.[7] Ricoeur joins Nietzsche, Freud and Marx within a 'hermeneutics of suspicion' and presents Nietzsche as seminal to the development of the 'depth hermeneutics'.[8]

Nietzsche's influence upon the deconstruction of hermeneutics is just as forceful. By combining and extending Nietzsche's critique of individualism and theory of power Foucault constructs a notion of discourse as the oscillation of power relations functioning as autonomously competing communicative systems.[9] Nietzschean perspectivism is the linchpin of Derrida's thesis concerning interpretive undecidability, whilst Vattimo extends Nietzsche's theory of affirmative nihilism into a secular philosophy in which all forms of foundation are cast aside.[10]

Nietzsche's accreditation within post-Heideggerian hermeneutics is without question but it has curious features. Although each of the aforementioned thinkers deploys aspects of Nietzsche's thought, none attend to the hermeneutic foundation of that thought. It is, in this context, extraordinary that Nietzsche who is, as Gadamer once commented, *the* thinker who made a career out of the concept of interpretation, has neither been recognized as a hermeneutic thinker in his own right nor seen his works subject to a sustained examination from such a perspective.[11] It is also invariably true that those who draw upon Nietzsche's thought within post-Heideggerian hermeneutics have come to Nietzsche via the intercession of Heidegger's study. If, however, Nietzsche is approached via an examination of the lines of thought which affect him, the hermeneutic dimension of his philosophy emerges more clearly, revealing a greater radicality of import than the thought of his peer Dilthey. The modern history of hermeneutics merits rewriting for, as this essay will show, Nietzsche's place within hermeneutic thought stands not so much upon his posthumous influence as upon the strength, rigour and independence of his own theoretical articulations.[12]

Part one of this essay will explore certain misconceptions concerning philology which have hindered perception of the hermeneutic elements in Nietzsche's thought. His usage of hermeneutic procedures will then be discussed and it will be suggested that his understanding of Greek tragedy rests upon an appeal to a hermeneutic analogy of an existential nature. The latter, it will be contended, informs Nietzsche's concept of *Lebenshorizonten* which serves two functions. First, it anticipates a notion of fore-understanding which must be identified if the artworks which emerge from such an understanding are to be comprehended. Second, presaging Husserl's and Heidegger's critique of logico-scientific reasoning, the concept of *Lebenshorizonten* is used to attack objectivist tendencies in *Sach-Philologie* and to argue that no learning should be separated from the existential contexts which support it. Part two argues that Nietzsche's appeal to a common existential predicament as the basis of his understanding of Greek culture is not an idiosyncrasy but a universal hermeneutic claim concerning the experience of an epistemological fracturing which severs the individual from reality. Part three looks at the charges of cultural bias and overt subjectivism laid against Nietzsche's reading of the Greeks, and will suggest that from the perspective of contemporary hermeneutics some of the alleged faults of Nietzsche's reading constitute its hermeneutic strength.

1 HERMENEUTICS AND PHILOLOGY

One reason for the overlooking of the hermeneutic dimensions in Nietzsche's thought is that we have become victim to narrow historical categories which prevent philology being thought of as something other than a sequestered linguistic specialism. The efforts of such historians as Schnädelbach reveal that such conceptions are far from the truth, for during Nietzsche's lifetime philology was comparable to a composite multi-disciplinary *Geisteswissenschaft*.[13] A glance at Nietzsche's early lecture programmes reveals such a synthesis of linguistics, history, aesthetics, religion, literature and moral thought. Unlike today, Nietzsche would not have thought of hermeneutics as a distinct branch of philosophical and literary criticism but as an integral part of his classical interests. There is no doubt that he was acquainted with the principal debates within the hermeneutic practice of his day. His library contained approximately 240 volumes devoted exclusively to antiquity. These include the prestigious journals *Philologus* and *Hermes* and volume one of

Wolf's *Vorlesungen über die Geschichte der griechischen Literatur* (1831). The latter argues that the understanding of a text must be prior to its interpretation and that understanding is grasping the thoughts of another by means of outward signs.[14] Paul Forster's *De Hermeneutices Archaeologicae Principiis* (1873?) approaches art interpretation and the nature of human understanding utilizing arguments derived from Kant and Schopenhauer. Volkman's *Geschichte und Kritik der Wolfschen Prolegomena zu Homer* discusses hermeneutical method with particular reference to Wolf and Boeckh. Nutzhorn's *Die Entstehungsweise der Homerischen Gedichte* (1869) analyses Homer's work in terms of the hermeneutic axiom of wholeness, indeed, very much in the manner of Gadamer's recent treatment of *Also Sprach Zarathustra*.[15]

Evidence that Nietzsche was conscious of and deployed hermeneutic procedures can be derived from two sources, the essays on *Diogenes Laertius* and the piece on '*Die Vorbereitung zur Hermeneutik und Kritik*'. In his excellent essays '*Hermeneutische Voraussetzungen der Philologischen Kritik*'[16] Figl detects in the '*Arbeiten zu Diogenes Laertius*' at least four established hermeneutic stratagems: 1) *Konjekturalkritik*, the use of speculative conjecture to determine the original nature of a text below the sediment of historically accrued and transmitted error; 2) *Komparatistik*, the typological identification of forms and structure in works contemporaneous with the one under scrutiny; 3) *Nomothetik*, the aesthetic consideration of transmitted works irrespective of any linguistic analysis and 4) *Kombinatorik*, the linguistic study of phonetic and grammatical structures in classical languages. An indication of Nietzsche's more radical hermeneutic orientation compared to the historicist assumptions supporting the methods of the academic philology of his day can be found in the essay on *Diogenes Laertius*. Even before Dilthey had fully articulated the philosophical and psychological framework he believed necessary for an understanding of an individual's creative intentionality within a prevailing *Weltanschauung*, Nietzsche was striving to delve behind the superficialities of conscious intention. The following extract openly presages his later genealogical method of questioning:

> We want to see more than the finished text, we want to see before our eyes the genesis of a book, the history of its production and birth. . . . We wish that the process of its becoming be slowly uncovered to our view.[17]

What Nietzsche focuses upon as early as 1867 is the cultural *mentalité* which is the enabling condition of an artwork's emergence. The inaugural lecture at the University of Basel reveals his concern not with Homer *per se* but with the collective Greek imagination which achieves embodiment in and through Homer's writing.[18] The procedure is extended in *The Birth of Tragedy* so as to become its central proposition: the Greek tragic dramas exhibit an Olympian mythology which emerges from and gives expression to a collective need to surmount the 'horror of existence'.

> Now it is as if the Olympian magic mountain has opened before us and revealed its roots. The Greek knew and felt the terror and horror of existence. That he might endure this terror at all, he had to interpose between life and himself the radiant dream birth of the Olympian. . . . It was in order to be able to live that the Greeks had to create those Gods from a most profound need.
>
> (BT 3)

As well as anticipating the genealogical approach to meaning this early position hints at Nietzsche's palimpsestic orientation within hermeneutics: to see the surface text as a commentary upon another hidden text.[19]

Another significant manifestation of Nietzsche's early hermeneutic disposition appears in the section of *Einleitung in das Studium der klassichen Philologie*, entitled '*Die Vorbereitung zur Hermeneutik und Kritik*'. Here Nietzsche argues like Wolf that the general concern of hermeneutics is to establish a method of understanding and judging a transmitted work (MA II, 348). Customarily, the transmitted work is a text and in essays such as '*Arbeiten zu Diogenes Laertius*', procedures are elucidated to distinguish a 'pure' text from the inherited versions (BAW V, 157). Yet it would be a gross error to think of Nietzsche as primarily concerned with the restitution of the pure texts for their own sake. His concern is to look beyond the determinate text in order to perceive the indeterminate historical processes which are the source of its being. Reaching beyond the predominance of the printed word to glimpse the existential horizon which conditions any expression entails one of hermeneutic's most difficult problems: how to surmount the difficulties of historical and cultural difference? Nietzsche is alert to it. Because of the enormous distance and difference of nationality, the task of understanding the works of the past represents 'something extraordinarily difficult' (MA III, 348). As 'we have not grown up in the same element', 'the literary and philosophical *personae* of antiquity are to us extremely remote' (ibid.). Grasping the total spirit of an alien culture is thereby impossible but, Nietzsche insists, understanding some of its aspects can be gradually achieved.

> The concern to understand an author or transmitted fact appears very straightforward but with the immense distance and difference of nationality it is something extremely difficult. . . . We must attempt to make our approach by means of analogies. To this extent our understanding of antiquity is a continuous perhaps unconscious parallelization.
>
> (MA II, 348)

The reference to analogy is extremely telling.

Analogical argumentation was carefully analysed by Kant but it is Humboldt who brings it into modern hermeneutics.[20] In the essay 'On the Historian's Taste' (1822) Humboldt readily grasps that 'where two beings (are) separated by a total gap, no bridge of understanding extends from one to the other' (KMV 112). Nevertheless, he is no sceptic and posits a degree of commonness between human beings which facilitates the possibility of understanding.

> Every act of comprehension of a single subject-matter presupposes, as a condition of its possibility, the existence of an analogue in the person who comprehends of that which is subsequently actually comprehended – a preceding original correspondence between subject and object. Comprehension is by no means merely a developing out of the subject, nor a drawing from the object, but rather both at once, for it always consists of the application of a previously present general idea to a new particular instance.
>
> (KMV 112)

Comprehension involves recognizing that both the interpretive field of the subject and the object are in certain respects different manifestations of the same 'form'. The form is not imposed upon the two sides of a hermeneutic interchange but is drawn from the events themselves' (KMV 112). Understanding is thus a grasping of unity in difference, a realization that the concerns of the interpreting subject and the nature and circumstances of the interpreted object are different embodiments of the same form or organizing principle. In the case of Nietzsche, the analogue or shared organizing principle between the modern interpreter and the ancient Greek proves to be a common existential predicament. The point is, however, that in view of the above the '*Arbeiten zu Diogenes Laertius*' and '*Die Vorbereitung zur Hermeneutik und Kritik*' show that hermeneutic procedures and issues *are* both a component of Nietzsche's concerns and fundamental to the evolution of his philosophy.

In their different ways Dilthey, Heidegger, and Gadamer have stressed that to gain an insight into the problems a work addresses its context has to be in part retrieved. That *The Birth of Tragedy* is not just a free-standing essay on Greek literature but a dual response to a crisis within both philology and European culture is frequently overlooked. As its context is a major factor in our appraisal of the hermeneutic dimension of Nietzsche's thought, the concluding part of this section will approach the wider parameters which condition the focus of Nietzsche's first book.

It would be a mistake to see Nietzsche's *The Birth of Tragedy* as the expression of an orthodox romantic longing to return philology to the sophisticated study of antiquity exemplified in the *Altthumswissenschaft* of Winckelmann. Nietzsche's critique of *Sach-Philologie* is grounded upon three charges. *Sach-Philologie* is seriously flawed by 1) overlooking the *Lebenshorizonten* which serve as the productive ground of the cultural achievements of antiquity. 2) encouraging a 'take-it-as-you-find-it' view of antiquity, and 3) failing to provide a coherent extra-theoretical framework capable of both unifying its varied concerns and relating them to the immediate cultural problematics of the day.

With regard to the first charge, the older Wolfian mode of philology looked towards the ideal of reconstructing the factual details of antiquity in all their complexity.[21] Here Nietzsche reacts against the dual assumption that the relics of the ancient world are to be randomly picked out from a hotchpotch of a treasure-chest and interpreted apart from their original context. Though he was not an unthinking reactionary blindly supporting the romantic view of the Greeks as lithe in body and gentle in spirit, he recognizes that the old *Altthumswissenschaft* had its methodological advantages.[22] It interpreted Greek culture holistically, as something circumscribed by a predominant concern with visual beauty. To that horizon was ascribed a teleology of aesthetic perfection. Aside of whether Winckelmann identified as acceptable *Lebenshorizont* for the interpretation of Greek culture, he appealed to Nietzsche for approaching the products of the ancient world not as a myriad of isolated facts apart from a unifying horizon. What Nietzsche attacks in *Sach-Philologie* are the consequences of philological studies evolving from a purely privileged form of cultural learning to a broader academic science. The earlier romantic studies of Greece were boldly defined by the moral and aesthetic enthusiasms of such as Winckelmann which, although questionable, made the subject cohesive by tying it to the artistic and political commitments of its practitioners. Nietzsche was aware that the later Wolfian concern with factual detail fractured the earlier unified conception of Greek study. Not only is the preoccupation with accurate factual reconstruction in principle infinitely extendable but it lacks any internal criterion for what is relevant to its study. The academic study of antiquity's 'facts' stands condemned by Nietzsche of a twofold perversity. It asks the cultural facts of the Greek world to exist *per se* without any reference to their grounding *Lebenshorizont* and assumes that the meaning and value of historical works can be grasped in isolation from the cultural perspective to which they owe their original homogeneity. When in 1867 Nietzsche complained that

> Most philologists lack that elevating total view of antiquity because they stand too close to the picture and investigate a patch of paint, instead of gazing at the big, bold brushstrokes of the whole painting . . . our whole mode of working is quite horrible[23]

he is in part criticizing the overt positivistic foundations of *Sach-Philologie*. Without an identification of the *Lebenshorizonten* that informed both the achievements of antiquity and the study of the ancient world, Nietzsche fears that the cultural and indeed existential significance of the Greek world will be lost.

His anxiety stems from his perception of a link between the lack of methodological homogeneity in the study of the Greek world and the encouragement of a 'take-it-or-leave-it' view of antiquity (UM II, 8). Thus with regard to the second charge, without setting the works of the ancient world within their appropriate *Lebenshorizonten*, they will simply fail to speak of their world and, worse still, be relegated to the status of cultural curios of dubious momentary worth. The study of historical works as 'timeless' decontextualized phenomena silences and condemns them to be nothing more than dumb factual relics incapable of addressing the present. Unlike *Altthumswissenschaft*, *Sach-Philologie* cannot of itself establish any cultural reason as to why the ancient world should be studied. That *Sach-Philologie* might disintegrate without establishing a clear *raison d'être* for itself is not Nietzsche's principal concern. He fears above all that the fragmentation of *Sach-Philologie* would bring in its wake a terrible neglect of the achievements of antiquity. It would inadvertently devalue that cultural achievement – Greek tragedy – most capable of instructively addressing the rise of nihilistic consciousness in modern Europe. It is indeed the problem of existential nihility which structures Nietzsche's reading of Greek tragedy and motivates his passionate defence of ancient studies.

Concerning his third charge against *Sach-Philologie*, Nietzsche suggests in his inaugural lecture at Basel that the motto of the sciences is that 'Life is worth knowing'.[24] *The Birth of Tragedy* argues that this Socratic belief is based on the conviction that Being is worth knowing and that reason can penetrate and correct it (BT 1/3). Of importance here are the consequences of promoting knowledge *per se* and the proclamation that truth is worth knowing in-and-for-itself. Once its localized pragmatic function is repressed and knowledge is promoted as an end-in-itself, vibrant, fertile *Lebenshorizonten* such as that of the tragic age of the Greeks are pushed aside as irrational by an outlook which Nietzsche judges to be both destructive and unproductive. He shares Schopenhauer's concern (which will later be Wittgenstein's too) that a purely scientific outlook cannot of itself generate goals for existence. As was the case with the rise of Socratism in ancient Greece, he senses that the formidable rise of the sciences in nineteenth-century Europe creates the illusion that the pursuit of truth in-and-for-its-own-sake is equivalent to the possession of a *Lebenshorizont* capable of delimiting the value and meaning of human activity. This illusion entails a fateful confusion of truth and value. If truth is the ultimate value everything knowable is of value. Not only does he doubt whether all truth is worth knowing but he also rounds on the proposition that everything true is of equal value. The drive for knowledge in itself is identified as a 'screw without end' (*eine Schraube ohne Ende*, UdW I, sec. 59). If unlimited by cultural aims and values concerning what is and is not worth knowing, there is no end to the discovery of truth. But this disrupts the equation of truth with value. Whereas value implies judgement and selection, infinite truth expectancies imply the opposite. The scientific pursuit of knowledge for its own sake only serves to generate an increasingly confusing mass of facts which, being unrelated to any specific *Lebenshorizont*, will lack any comprehensive significance. Nor does the proliferation of such knowledge encourage practical activity which requires belief in distinct goals and purposes. If science reveals ever more dimensions and possibilities for existence (all judged to be of equal value), nothing can in fact emanate.

> Knowledge is a screw without end: in each instant it becomes operative, an infinity commences which will never give rise to action.

(UdW I, 59)

Nothing can come of scientific reasoning since it cannot limit where analysis might end and action commence. The greater the set of possibilities, the less likely action of consequence will arise. 'Perfect knowledge merely serves to destroy action' (*die vollkommene Erkenntniss tottet das Handeln*, UdW I, 59). The inner logic of such sciences as *Sach-Philologie* drives them towards cultural inconsequentiality if not sterility. Yet greater danger arises when logico-deductive reasoning usurps the role of myth, masquerades as a *Lebenshorizont* and turns its critical weapons against the creative but rationally unjustifiable intuitions at the heart of myth. Here reason demands rational justification where none can be given. As it assumes that only that which is rational can be justified, reason will, in demanding justification, destroy the deep beds of fantasy and imagination from which the intuitions of myth spring. Nietzsche concludes that the (culturally inadvertent) purpose of science is world destruction (*der Zweck der Wissenschaft ist Weltvernichtung*, UdW I, sec. 60) and, regarding the questions of rational justification, accuses scientific reason of deep hypocrisy. Though it demands reasons where none can be given, neither can it justify its own normative premises. Scientific reasoning too contains an element of fantasy, seminal assumptions and intuitions obtained by the 'wing beat of fantasy', a 'springing from possibility to possibility' (KSA 7, 19.77). If both scientific rationalism and myth share elements of fantasy and intuition, the question becomes which of the two is more efficacious in promoting a cultural *Lebenshorizont* capable of contending with mankind's existential predicament. There is no doubt where Nietzsche's commitment lies.

In his critique of scientific rationalism, Nietzsche is not only taking sides in the philological dispute between learning and knowledge but giving voice to precisely the worries that Husserl was to articulate in his *Crisis of the European Sciences* concerning the severing of scientific-technological concerns from the *Lebensinteressen* that nurture them.[25] Furthermore, his critique of *Sach-Philologie* is interwoven with a broadly historical appraisal of the crisis confronting European culture. The *Kulturkritik* is based upon the ontological *Leitmotif* which permeates all of Nietzsche's philosophy: the principle of Becoming which asserts everything to be in flux, to be finite and to lack intrinsic meaning. The principle undoubtedly underwrites the central existential motif of *The Birth of Tragedy*; that life is a horrible absurdity. The real measure of the Greek cultural achievement is accordingly that the tragedies embody a remarkable pre-theistic response to the existential *malaise*.[26] Whereas on the one hand Socratic rationalism and the intellectual faiths it spawns seek redemption from the existential predicament by believing in and pursuing a true world of Being and whilst, on the other, Christian religion searches for release from actuality by believing in an after-world, the pre-Socratic Greek had no option but to confront and overcome actuality in this-worldly terms. There was no fleeing into the comforting fictions of other more real, more just worlds. The pivotal cultural importance of Greek tragedy for Nietzsche is its status as an insurpassable exemplar as to how art might confront and overcome life within actuality and in so doing so beautify it as to present existence as deeply desirable. Nietzsche's book could have been entitled 'The Death of Tragedy' as one of its key arguments is that the tragic-aesthetic solution to the existential predicament is both subverted and supplanted by the easier doctrines of Socratic rationalism and theistic religion. They posit redemption in a true world of Being as already available to the faithful rather than as having to be achieved by an individual's transformation of his predicament through his own artistic powers. What fuels the *Kulturkritik* of *The Birth of Tragedy* is the historical premonition that the Socratic and theistic faiths in fictional worlds of Being and truth, which have been the mainstay of post-pagan European culture, are collapsing. Due to the metaphysical critiques of Kant and Schopenhauer, Nietzsche believes the optimism of theoretical culture (the belief that 'all the riddles of the universe could be known and fathomed', BT 18) is crumbling, soliciting the emergence of nihilism. The burning cause of Nietzsche's anxiety (which ingeniously links the *Kulturkritik* to the attack on *Sach-Philologie*) is the fearful anticipation that in the nihilistic wrath of disillusionment to be unleashed against all forms of truth seeking, philology – the very subject which houses an insight into the only art form capable of providing an exemplar for the overcoming of nihilism – will itself be destroyed and with it the last hope of averting the dawn of Europe's darkest age. By keeping before its mind the 'immeasurable value' of the 'Hellenic prototype' (BT 19), Nietzsche's endeavour to reform *Sach-Philologie* is no mere attempt at a palace revolution but a sustained effort at making the subject and its transmission of ancient wisdom culturally relevant to a Europe withering at the collapse of its traditional intellectual and religious faiths.

The hermeneutic components within Nietzsche's thought and the academic and cultural context in which they are deployed show how questionable it is to regard his thinking as either revolutionary in the sense of breaking with tradition or eccentric in the sense of standing outside it. It is a reform of *Sach-Philologie* that Nietzsche was looking for and not its destruction, for the latter would entail the loss of the only cultural exemplar capable of overturning nihilism. The problems which Nietzsche addresses in his discipline and cultural epoch are not placed on the agenda by him. It is he who responds to their emergence.

2 *THE BIRTH OF TRAGEDY* AND ITS HERMENEUTIC FOUNDATIONS

In his *Science of Logic*, Hegel attacks those philosophers who 'begin, like a shot from a pistol, from their inner revelation, from faith, intellectual intuition, etc. and who would be exempt from method and logic'.[27] Nietzsche's early analysis of Greek tragedy rests upon the intuition that Greek mythology stems from a nauseous insight into the horrific nature of existence. Hegel's remark forces the question whether there is anything philosophically substantive to Nietzsche's account of tragedy, and if there is a hermeneutic basis to the existential analysis of Greek tragedy how can it parry the charge that it amounts to nothing more than an unwarranted projection of nineteenth-century ennui upon antiquity? To answer these questions the existential analogy which underpins the argument of *The Birth of Tragedy* must be considered.

The Birth of Tragedy enunciates, through the voice of Silenus, Nietzsche's convictions concerning the ontological primacy of Becoming and the nihility of Being upon which he never ceases reflecting.

> Oh wretched ephemeral race, children of chance and misery, why do you compel me to tell you what it would be most expedient for you not to know? What is best for you is utterly beyond your reach: not to be born, not to *be*, to be nothing. But the second best for you is – to die soon.
>
> (BT 3)

These sentiments are, however, not entirely personal as *The Birth of*

Tragedy sets them within a Schopenhauerian framework whereby they acquire the form of a universal existential claim which grounds a hermeneutic theory of understanding. Schopenhauer's philosophy is no mere surrogate for Nietzsche's renunciation of Christianity but a coping stone of his hermeneutic.[28]

To set the conceptual parameters of Nietzsche's assimilation of Schopenhauer, the following should be remembered about the principle that 'all is in flux'. Like Heraclitus and classical Buddhist thinkers, Nietzsche accepts it as a verbal assertion of an empirically self-evident truth. It carries a nauseous connotation only when it is perceived to contradict antithetical beliefs in permanent substance, the continuity of the self and intrinsic meaning. Schopenhauer's conception of a 'Becoming without Being' implies that actuality lacks that which redeems its finitude. Existential nausea is tied to the capacity of the principle of Becoming to render empty previously held assumptions about Being and intrinsic meaning. Existential nihility denotes that moment of awareness in which pivotal beliefs about self-identity and Being are exposed as vacuous. Let us now turn to Schopenhauer. The argument to be pressed is that within Schopenhauer's philosophy is a substantial epistemological structure which when seen in the context of Nietzsche's hermeneutic concerns provides the latter with a rigorous framework for a theory of cross-cultural and existential understanding.

The Kantian thesis which Schopenhauer adapts is the argument that our mode of cognition 'is peculiar to us and though not necessarily shared by every being, is certainly shared by every human being' (CPR A, 42). It is not so much the existence of a common cognitive structure which draws Schopenhauer but the asymmetric relation within that framework between how the world may be thought of a priori and how it is experienced a posteriori. What he focuses upon and what subsequently becomes of central importance for Nietzsche is that moment in an individual's consciousness when he experiences that 'fearful dread' symptomatic of a fundamental shift in how the nature of existence is perceived. The shift is from that frame of mind in which the individual assumes that how he thinks of the world actually is the world to that in which he becomes aware of the radical disjuncture between the intelligible world as it is constructed in thought and the unintelligible world of actual experience. In *The Birth of Tragedy* Nietzsche pinpoints the argument when he comments that

Schopenhauer has depicted for us the tremendous *terror* which

seizes man when he is suddenly dumbfounded by the cognitive
form of phenomena because the principle of sufficient reason . . .
suffers an exception.

(BT I)

The terror which embodies this shift exhibits a circular movement
involving an explicit return to what was already implicitly the case.

For Schopenhauer the implicit but initially unrecognized truth of
existence is that all beings are individuated phenomenal forms of a
blind striving, of a universal will which seeks nothing other than
self-perpetuation. The world as phenomenally objectified will is an
eternal becoming without intrinsic purpose. The 'real existence' of
an individual is thus no more than an unimpeded flight from the
present into the past, an 'ever-deferred death'. This existential truth
simpliciter (though certainly not Schopenhauer's evaluation of it) is
adopted wholesale by Nietzsche and is dubbed 'Dionysian wisdom'.

We are to recognize that all that comes into being must be ready
for a sorrowful end; we are forced to look into the terrors of
individual experience.

(BT 17)

How is that that this existential truth remains initially unrecognized
within an individual's consciousness, and when it is recognized why
is it recognized with such shock?

As will in objectified form, the individual operates from within
the framework of ordinary consciousness pursuing his aims oblivious
to the futility of his real existence. By drawing a veil across the real
nature of an individual's existence, illusion is one of the devices
whereby the universal will perpetuates itself. The dominant
illusions of ordinary consciousness are epistemological in character.
They are 1) the belief that a knowing subject is a priori a free,
changeless being and that 2) what the subject experiences as an
intelligible world – the phenomenally perceived world ordered and
judged according to the categories of the intellect – is indicative of
the nature of the real world. The illusion that what is represented as
the world within cognitive consciousness *is* the actual world is the
product of that synthesis of sensuous intuition and judgemental
categories of reason which is the core of Kantian epistemology.
Schopenhauer deviates slightly from Kant by adding causality to the
forms of sensuous intuition, a deviation which Nietzsche follows
(BT 4). Kant never considers, however, the possibility of a

mismatch between the realms of sensuous intuition and the categories of reason giving rise to an utterly unintelligible experience. It is on this possibility that Schopenhauer dwells. The occurrence of such incongruities enables the individual to slip between the illusions of pre-reflective consciousness and perceive the true nature of existence.

One of the incongruities Schopenhauer has in mind relates to the problem of causality. The belief that the world is 'an orderly arrangement of occurrences in which one change necessarily conditions and brings about other predictable changes' (WWR I, 23) results from a successful fusion of the categories of intuition with those of the understanding. Yet this belief and the synthesis that produces it can be ruptured by the realization that causal explanation, so often heralded as the criterion of the intelligibility of events, merely gives rise to a *reductio ad absurdum*. What is more, causal explanations fail to explain why phenomena behave in the way that they do. As Nietzsche will also argue, they only describe the order in which events take place, explaining nothing of their why and wherefore. According to Schopenhauer, therefore, causality cannot render the phenomenal world intelligible. In conclusion, the naïve belief of ordinary consciousness that perceived reality is an intelligible reality is vulnerable to a twofold disruption. Either those occurrences which break expected patterns of temporal and spatial location or the realization that the principle of sufficient reason cannot causally explain the origin and purpose of worldly events can bring on the realization that the world is not as pre-reflective consciousness would have us believe, a world which is a priori intelligible.

The primary consequence of such epistemological fractures is the undermining of the grounding assumption of pre-reflective consciousness – the a priori conviction that the knowing subject is a free effective agent. Schopenhauer argues that the knowing subject can sustain a belief in its own efficacy as long as it can manipulate phenomena and this it can do only when the latter conform to the forms of its sensuous intuition and reason. When the synthesis of reason and sense falls apart the world given to the subject no longer appears as a given intelligible field, supplicant to its imperious designs, but as a senseless Becoming quite unintelligible when viewed from the perspective of sufficient reason. This is the epiphany of reflective consciousness.

Reflective consciousness embodies the fragmentation of Kant's synthesis of sense and reason. Once the fracture has occurred, the knowing subject feels itself to be on the one hand a priori a free effective subject capable of conceving a world which is intelligible but which cannot be concretely perceived and on the other hand it knows itself a posteriori to belong physically to an unintelligible finite world of Becoming. The tension between what a subject conceives of as an intelligible existence and what he perceives as his actual unintelligible existence constitutes the existential horror which is at the root of reflective consciousness. It is that sense, as Nietzsche might later have put it, of an individual feeling that he ought to belong to a world that does not in fact exist whilst actually belonging to a world that he feels ought not exist. So long as the principle of sufficient reason is esteemed as the sole criterion of intelligibility, existence will appear without meaning, to be nothing more than an 'ever deferred death'. Within this framework of assumptions, the pessimistic conclusion that we are at bottom something that ought not to be (WWR II, 41), that 'this very real phenomenal world of ours with all its suns and galaxies, is . . . nothing' (WWR I, 71) is perhaps inevitable. Here Schopenhauer's argument closes its circle. The individual subject realizes that his true being is and always has been will. The ahistorical aspect of the position is not an epistemological thesis concerning the universality of a cognitive framework but the view that, given the principle of sufficient reason can be incompatible with the nature of phenomenal reality, the epistemological fracture between sense and reason and the accompanying existential dread it provokes is an *imminent possibility for all individuals regardless of culture and historical location*. This is of crucial importance for Nietzsche. The epistemological fracture which Schopenhauer describes encapsulates one of what Nietzsche describes as 'the eternal problems of life'. It is the various responses, specifically the Greek response, to this timeless existential condition that concerns him. This ahistorical insight into the existential predicament is utilized by Nietzsche as the basis of his hermeneutic approach to Greek tragedy.

Though it unquestionably derives from Schopenhauer, Nietzsche's formulation of the existential problem is simpler. It is concerned both with the experiential primacy of finitude and the incommensurability of fixed concepts with the flow of actuality. If individual being is no more than a meaningless arising and passing away, the question is how can such a scepsis be overcome? Is life possible once its futility has been exposed? Nietzsche believes like Schopenhauer that not all human beings attain a true consciousness of the nature of existence. He recognizes that pre-reflective cognitive knowledge makes the nature of existence apparently intelligible with its illusion that reason's categories are indicative of what is actual. Thus emerges that 'unshakeable faith' that thought 'can penetrate the deepest abysses of being and that thought is capable not only of knowing being but even of correcting it' (BT 15). Nietzsche clearly follows Schopenhauer in the suggestion that the root of existential anxiety lies in the implicit tension between the nature of actual existence and that ideal intelligible existence constructed in thought and misconstrued as reality itself. The illusion that the actual world is intelligible stems from confusing the concept of a thing with the actual nature of that thing. However, as the world represented in thought will be represented according to the categories of intelligible being, the form of the represented world will inevitably display the intelligibleness of the categories that constitute it. But, as Nietzsche states, in the case of the actual world 'all knowing is a reflection within determinate forms which do not themselves exist . . . Nature knows no forms' (KSA 7, 19[133]). As knowledge reduces perceived actuality to its forms the illusion arises that the world is intelligible: 'the concept pencil is confused with the thing which is the pencil' (KSA 7, 19[242]). This obversation leads to what becomes the epistemological *Leitmotif* of his philosophy, namely, that in the actual world of Becoming, static concepts based upon the fixed categories of reason can never remain congruent with the world they represent. Thus, somewhat inevitably, the illusion of pre-reflective consciousness concerning the intelligibility of the perceived world is within the actuality of Becoming always prone to imminent collapse.

Nietzsche also intimates that in a world where the principle of sufficient reason is not adequate to reality, any belief that it is will eventually founder as the very thing that it promotes – the belief in the attainability of rational truth – will prove self-defeating. As he comments in *The Birth of Tragedy*, 'science spurned by its powerful illusions speeds irresistibly towards its limits where its optimism, concealed in the essence of logic, suffers shipwreck' (BT 15). It is the occasion of such calamities which explode the illusions of pre-reflective consciousness and give rise to the experience of mankind's existential predicament: that sense of being cast out of an intelligible world into a meaningless realm of flux. Nietzsche's history of the demise of rationalistic thought from Socrates to contemporary nihilism is no more than a historical making explicit of the implicit ahistorical truth of human existence, namely, that for beings who operate solely within identity-based frameworks of reason, existence in actuality will always appear terrifyingly meaningless.

It can be concluded that the existential insight which serves as the foundation of Nietzsche's early hermeneutic does not rest exclusively upon a personal intuition but also upon a philosophical ground which draws heavily upon an aspect of Schopenhauer's argument which few commentators have touched upon let alone have seen relevant to an understanding of Nietzsche's approach to hermeneutic understanding. Once again it is clear that he is not standing outside tradition but drawing upon and extending arguments from the context within which he is working.

The foregoing discussion was prefaced by the question of how Nietzsche can construct and justify a hermeneutic relation between the contemporary and antique worlds? It is his account of the existential predicament which serves as the basis of his hermeneutic. His articulation of that predicament proclaims an ahistorical conception of the human situation which traverses the difficulties of cultural differentiation. It can be argued that an aspect of Nietzsche's position is more attractive than the ahistorical elements in the arguments of either Schopenhauer or Dilthey. Whereas the latter appeals to the universality of either cognitive frameworks or relatively stable experiential categories, Nietzsche never states that he believes in a common cognitive or experiential framework. He is committed to the historical transience of epistemological and interpretive categories. Admittedly, the predicament of which he speaks appears constant even if in some instances it remains merely latent in those philosophical or religious perspectives which have not suffered an epistemological fracture. Yet he never supposes the experiential nausea experienced by the Greek to be qualitatively the same as that felt in a post-monotheistic culture. They are nevertheless different forms of a common or shared existential predicament which permit analogies to be constructed between them. Moreover, Nietzsche's argument implies a more radical thesis. By virtue of the reduction of the complexities of perception to the relative simplicities of conceptual thought, *any cognitive framework will be incommensurable with the actuality of Becoming*. Though two cultures may operate within different cognitive schema with mutually exclusive presuppositions, both may share approximate forms of that existential anxiety which results from the realization that reality as conceived within either schema is not congruent with the actual. In other words, an insight into the fundamental nothingness of human existence provides Nietzsche with a device for overcoming the problem of historical distance in interpretation. At the same time he acquires the basis of an inter-subjective mode of aesthetic interpretation.

The claim that *The Birth of Tragedy* rests upon a philosophical foundation which grounds an inter-subjective approach to under-standing will no doubt seem curious. Nietzsche's idiosyncratic style, his devoted appeals to Wagner and Schopenhauer and his concerns with the existential seem too obvious an expression of personal concerns. The subjective dispositions of Nietzsche's work are indeed visible. They reveal his instrumentalist concerns with such questions as 'How is existence possible in a world where there is no truth?', 'What can be learned from the Greeks?', and 'How can the circumstances surrounding the death of Greek tragedy' assist in the birth of a new German culture? The personal and (then) highly contemporary focus of such questions was extremely remote from the dominant historicist and objectivist tendencies of the academic philology practised during Nietzsche's lifetime. Yet despite the acknowledged personal perspective, Nietzsche's interests are not merely idiosyncratic. They embody the contemporary and localized cutting edge of a universal predicament, which in the form of an ontology of flux and an associated doctrine of nihility provides the foundation of his hermeneutic practice.

The question of what might be learned from the Greeks is not for Nietzsche an academic one. The spirit of his hermeneutics belongs to the Aristotelian tradition which enshrines the conviction that interpretive understanding should not give rise solely to abstract appreciation but praxis. The existential problematic which domin-ates Nietzsche's reading of Greek tragedy is that of nihility. His exposition of the problematic is two-tiered. On one level the issue is treated abstractly. The experience of epistemological fracture and the sense of nihility it gives rise to is regarded as a forever imminent possibility. The concrete form which the experience of nihility takes on, however, depends upon the cultural and historical location of the individual. Nietzsche clearly recognizes that the Greek sense of existential nausea cannot be straightforwardly the same as that experienced by a post-Christian European. Yet the fact that these two forms are different historical embodiments of a common existential predicament evidently relates them. Without doubt the cultural conviction that underwrites *The Birth of Tragedy* is that modern European culture is being forced by the hand of its own scientific rationalism to confront the spectre of nihilism. The purpose of Nietzsche's approach to Greek culture is not arcane but a matter of crucial relevance in contemporary cultural analysis. The value of understanding the aesthetics of Greek tragedy is that it serves as an exemplar of how existential nihility can be confronted. Here, once again, Nietzsche steps away from the dominant historicist strand within the philology of his epoch.

The past if reconstructed in its own terms cannot say anything to the present as it will simply have ceased to be relevant to contemporary concerns. It can only address the present when the present has pressed its questions upon it, questions which for Nietzsche cluster around the problem of the existential.[29] The artistic achievements of the past come to life only when we place 'our questions' to them.

> These works can only survive through our giving them our soul and our blood. This alone enables them to talk to us. . . . We honour the great artists less by that barren timidity that leaves everything, every word, every note as it is, than by energetic endeavours to aid them continually to new life.
>
> (HAH II, 126)

Yet, as has been argued, the questions with which Nietzsche interrogates Greek tragedy are not solely *his* or *our* questions. They are questions which reflect the contemporary form of a shared existential predicament. Thus Greek tragedy can speak to the contemporary mind because the question which informs it is a form of the same question which informs our interest in the Greek artworks. Nietzsche's account of aesthetic experience is therefore unequivocally instrumentalist. As Silk and Stern have so aptly perceived, when Nietzsche asks the question 'What is Greek tragedy?', he means, 'What is Greek tragedy for?'.[30] As can now be seen, the answer which declares tragedy to be both formed by and a transformation of existential awareness is not a bolt from the blue but fits consistently within the epistemological and ontological positions which frame his thinking. In formal terms, Nietzsche's position promotes a consistent yet critical extension of Schopenhauer's aesthetic instrumentalism.

As aesthetic representation offered, according to Schopenhauer, an insight not into particular objects but into their universal form he believed that aesthetic experience offered an escape from the appetites of the will which focused not on abstractions but on possessable particulars. The instrumental value of aesthetics was its ability to negate life's conatic force and open the possibility of release from the sufferings of desire. Nietzsche clearly recognizes the different order of experience which aesthetic perception represents but it does not thereby cease to serve life's interests. Rather than inducing its abnegation of life, an insight into life's inevitable finitude can – when transformed by aesthetic experience – promote an insatiable desire for living life to the full.

The fusion of an aesthetic instrumentalism with a theory concerning the imminent possibility of epistemological fracture and its attendant existential nausea bring the principal components of Nietzsche's hermeneutic into place. That hermeneutic enables him to ask of any form of aesthetic production whether it attempts to surmount the existential predicament or to escape it.[31] Once the framework of Nietzsche's hermeneutic becomes apparent his interpretation of antiquity need no longer be viewed as an unwarranted projection of nineteenth-century ennui upon the past but as an attempt to engage with and understand Greek art within the parameters of a common existential predicament. This approach does not imperiously subject Greek aesthetics to Nietzsche's idiosyncratic concerns. It allows two cultures to engage with one another within a common existential framework. Nietzsche is careful never to diminish the enormous differences between his world and that of the Greeks. In the second *Untimely Meditation* he comments, 'I do not know what meaning classical studies could have for our time if they were not untimely, that is to say, acting counter to our time' (UM II, Foreword). Within the boundaries of a common existential predicament it is the very otherness of the Greek world that enables the contemporary world to view antiquity as an exemplar. The concept of existential nihility provides Nietzsche with not only a device for overcoming the problem of temporal and cultural distance within hermeneutic interpretation but also a hermeneutic framework which philosophically entails a great deal more than the unwarranted projection of cultural pessimism upon the historical past.

3 *THE BIRTH OF TRAGEDY* FROM THE PERSPECTIVE OF HERMENEUTIC ANALYSIS

The question of subjectivity

In the critical storm that broke over the publication of *The Birth of Tragedy* the alleged subjectivism of Nietzsche's approach to Greek culture drew intense criticism. Wilamowitz's pamphlet *Philology of the Future* focused on Nietzsche's abandonment of the historicist stratagem of interpreting historical events solely in terms of the categories contemporaneous with their epoch.[32] Nietzsche's extra-scholarly concerns – his tendency to conceive of the intellectual crisis of his time as the inevitable culmination of a sequence of metaphysical fictions emanating from Socratic rationalism – were judged by Dilthey to exhibit a complete lack of understanding concerning the 'real sciences'[33] and an amateurish approach to historical facts. Yet historical hindsight permits another view. Paradoxically, the very philosophical and cultural dimensions of Nietzsche's book which so many of his contemporaries belittled as extraneous pieces of subjectivity are judged within post-Heideggerian hermeneutics to be the necessary 'givens' of any historical interpretation. It fell to Heidegger to explode the myth of pre-suppositionless interpretation so dear to Wilamowitz and Dilthey. Heidegger also developed the view that 'understanding is tradition engaged in an endless conversation with itself and its own recapitulation'.[34] In so far as Nietzsche approaches Greek tragedy within the common framework of a universally shared existential predicament his argument not only presages Heidegger's but looks forward to Gadamer's historical hermeneutic of question and answer. Furthermore, the sense of a cultural crisis that his own age must face, a crisis which emerges from the unmasking of Socratic rationality as myth, embodies an attempt to employ an understanding of the past in order to mediate the nature of an envisaged historical future. Such an 'extra-scholarly' concern may have been anathema to Wilamowitz and Dilthey but it fell once more to Heidegger to insist that the historically projective nature of all interpretation means that an approach to any historical work entailed *ipso facto* a projection of that history's envisaged unfolding.[35] Considered within the perspective of philosophical hermeneutics, the supposed 'subjectivity' of Nietzsche's approach to Greek aesthetics begins to emerge as its enabling condition of that approach, as the horizon within which he receives and amends his understanding of Greek culture. The critical analysis of German philology, the taking of sides in the debate between *Sach-Philologie* and *Altthumswissenschaft*, the concern with cultural nihilism and the desire to preserve the existential insights of Greek tragedy are all interests which are undeniably 'subjective' in the language of the nineteenth-century philology but for philosophical hermeneutics these interests determine the possibility of such an analysis.

Philosophical hermeneutics also offers an insight which reveals Nietzsche's reading of Greek tragedy to be something other than a projection of nineteenth-century ennui upon antiquity. Heidegger

argues that though the presuppositions of an individual's interpretation of a work are subjective in the trite sense of belonging to
him and not to the work, in another profounder sense they do not
just belong to the individual as appendages to his subjectivity but
are constitutive of his existence as a member of a cultural
community. What will appear as subjective within one perspective,
emerges as an ontological characteristic in another. The central
argument of *The Birth of Tragedy* anticipates this ontological
overcoming of subjectivity. What announces itself as 'subjective' –
the seeming wilfulness of Nietzsche's existential insight – appears
within the perspective of philosophical hermeneutics as an appeal to
a universal predicament. In the moment of epistemological fracture
there is an experimental sameness indicative of a universal
existential situation. Though the structures of meaning man attaches
to existence change, the experience of estrangement from actuality
remains eternally the same. It is a revelation of that which eternally
remains the same: the irresolvable tension between an individual's
finite existence and his ability to conceive of timeless realms of
meaning which can neither be realized nor made commensurate
with actuality. Thus the hermeneutical structure of Nietzsche's
thinking depends upon a common existential condition. It enables
'us' in Nietzsche's terms, to put 'our questions' to the Greek world
and, at the same time, to use the Greek tragic perspective to focus
upon our world. In so far as Nietzsche's hermeneutic rests upon a
universal existential predicament, it anticipates Heidegger's existential hermeneutic. Furthermore, in so far as it seeks not a repetition
of the Greek experience but a means to finding our answer to a
universal existential dilemma, Nietzsche's hermeneutic foreshadows
Gadamer's hermeneutic of question and answer. Finally, the insight
into mankind's existential predicament seems to hint at an early
formulation of the doctrine of the eternal recurrence. That which
will return eternally as the same and that which is eternally the same
is the moment in which the existential predicament is inwardly
realized.

Historical distanciation: Nietzsche's reversal of the classic her-
meneutic problem

The problem of historical distance is central to the development of
modern hermeneutics. Thinkers such as Dilthey assume that
whereas the past with its foreign categories is not easily accessible
the present is well formed and intelligible. Nietzsche makes no such

assumptions about the present. He seeks to utilize the past for shaping the contemporary epoch, deriving from it a creative model to solve the problem of cultural nihilism.

The argument is premissed by a metaphysically derived construct concerning the absurdity of human existence in a world of perpetual flux. This construct provides *the* question with which he can analyse if not diagnose the typology of works of the past. Given the absurdity of existence, how is life possible? This is a question for us as well as for the Greeks. Once put to the ancient Greeks, 'our' question produces the reasoned answer that they responded to and overcame the absurdities of existence with their tragic dramas. This art form redeemed their nauseous insight into the nihility of being. Art, Nietzsche concludes, therefore makes the overcoming of nihility and the affirmation of life possible. The point is not to achieve an ingenious insight into the art of antiquity but to use the latter's response to the existential predicament in order to illuminate how modernity might also face it. The hermeneutic significance of his stance is that it strives not to allow us to see the Greek world through Greek eyes, i.e. to reconstruct it in its own terms, but to look at *our* world through the tragic perspective of ancient Greece. That the radicality of Nietzsche's hermeneutic procedure has not been recognized or given its proper place within the history of modern hermeneutics is astonishing. That his position anticipates well-articulated stances in twentieth-century hermeneutical aesthetics can be seen if we briefly compare the central thrust of Nietzsche's attempt to use Greek tragedy as an aesthetic-existential exemplar with an argument within Gadamer's *Truth and Method*.

Nietzsche's presentation of Greek tragedy as an ideal exemplar of an aesthetic response to the existential situation presupposes an effective relationship between the immediacy of human experience and the remoter abstractness if not unreality of an artwork. Gadamer approaches this relationship in terms of a contrast between the indeterminate openness of ordinary experience and the closed determinacy of the artwork.[36] Ordinary experience is presented as being 'open' in the sense that as human beings we are from our birth 'thrown' into a cultural situation in which a great number of questions are at play. Within the temporal flow of experience these are never definitively resolved. Some are set aside, some forgotten and others retrieved. In this respect Gadamer comes close to Nietzsche's conception of human experience as being a realm of conflict and contradiction, as containing no end which would give sense to the whole flow of perceptions. In contrast to the openness of experience, the nature of an artwork is thoroughly determinate and closed. If an artwork is aesthetically successful, it is so because it achieves its end. An aesthetic whole is thereby realized. The artwork is thus truly fictional in so far as its closed aesthetic qualities make it quite unlike the indeterminacy of anything in the experiential world. Nietzsche and Gadamer are in accord that art is not of this world. However, the ontological distinctions between art and the world do not sever it from the world. To the contrary, it is precisely what might be called art's other-worldliness, its aesthetic completeness, that gives it this-worldly value. By offering what ordinary experience never can – a determinate structure of meaning – art can complete what in experience can only remain as an open possibility. Art takes up what exists in actuality as unrealized possibility and by turning it into the stuff of fiction realizes the latent ends within those possibilities. By imaginatively completing the indeterminacies of actual experience art is existentially instructive in so far as it reflects what might have been or might be. The significance of art is that it can frame and conclude experience in such a way as to allow us to map the indeterminacies of actuality. The same pattern of argumentation can be detected in Nietzsche's work.[37] Greek tragedy is appealed to as a means to clarifying the latent potentiality for nihilism in the modern world. For Nietzsche, the collapse of Christianity, a growing awareness of the implications of Kant's destruction of rationalist metaphysics, and the increasing fragmenta-tion of European culture point toward the real possibility that the intellectual and cultural beliefs which have served since the time of Socrates to blind human beings from the actual nature of their being, will no longer be able to do so. Nietzsche does not claim that a cultural catastrophe is in consequence logically inevitable but he is terrified of its likelihood. His invocation of Greek tragedy can be seen to have a dual purpose. First, it is to precipitate precisely the (latent) cultural situation it must overcome. The dramatic represen-tation of life as meaningless expedites latent anxieties about existence without sense. In Gadamerian terms, the artwork concretizes the indeterminate fear that life lacks meaning. The second side to Nietzsche's invocation of Greek tragedy is to present it as a cure for precisely the existential condition it exacerbates. Its portrayal of the flux of existence by means of powerful aesthetic images does not terrify but fascinates with its motion and beauty. Greek tragedy achieves an aesthetic disposition which can accom-modate itself to and celebrate actuality as the only world. The function of tragic art is thus joyous world affirmation. Nietzsche evidently hopes that an acquaintance with Greek tragedy will galvanize the contemporary experience of nihilism and show how art can transform it into an affirmation of actuality. Whereas for Gadamer art's function is to illuminate the indeterminacies of experience by realizing certain of its latent possibilities, for Nietzsche the function of Greek tragedy is to precipitate the experience of nihilism and offer an aesthetic analogy to demonstrate that it can be transformed into an ecstatic affirmation of existence. What this brief comparison between Gadamer's hermeneutical aesthetics and Nietzsche's demonstrates is that Nietzsche's concern with Greek aesthetics is never a concern with an aesthetic form in and for its own sake. His approach to aesthetics is functionalist and genealogical from the start. The hermeneutical thrust of Nietzsche's position and indeed its historical novelty is that a knowledge of the classical past is deployed to serve as a catalyst and prophylactic for an anticipated contemporary cultural crisis. The classic hermeneutic problem of historical distanciation is reversed. The task for Nietzsche is not to retune the contemporary mind to perceive the past according to its own canons of interpretation, but to utilize an understanding of an historical art form in order to galvanize and transform the cultural problems of the contemporary world.

4 CONCLUSIONS

We have seen that the proper perception of the hermeneutic element in Nietzsche's early thought has been hindered by the dominance of limited concepts of philology. Scrutiny of his early lectures and writings reveals that not only was Nietzsche aware of hermeneutic procedures but that he also deployed them. Prominent amongst these is the concept of understanding by analogy which via a mediation of Schopenhauer's epistemology with Nietzsche's own ontological convictions develops into a hermeneutic theory of the existential predicament. That theory informs his account of Greek tragedy and serves as the foundation of his concept of *Lebenshorizonten*. Accordingly, he argues, an understanding of cultural productions can only be achieved by a comprehension of the *Lebenshorizonten* which enable such works to emerge. Anticipating Husserl's and Heidegger's critique of logico-scientific reasoning, the notion is used to criticize the objectivist pretensions of philology and to float the argument that all learning must be shaped and directed by an awareness of the existential parameters which surround it.

Most important is Nietzsche's attempt to use an analysis of the existential predicament as a means to hermeneutic understanding across different *Lebenshorizonten*. Finally, in view of the insights won by twentieth-century philosophical hermeneutics, Nietzsche's reading of Greek tragedy can no longer be dismissed as purely subjective. The existential and cultural preoccupations of Nietzsche's reading achieve a novel solution to the problem of historical difference by suggesting that a determinate understanding of the past must be deployed to the end of shaping the indeterminacies of the present. It can be contended then that Nietzsche's place within hermeneutic thought does indeed stand upon the strength and ingenuity of his individual analyses.

REFERENCES

The title abbreviations employed in this paper are as follows. For the works of Nietzsche these initials are used.

BT *The Birth of Tragedy*, trans. W. Kaufmann, Vintage, 1967.

UM *Untimely Meditations*, trans. R. J. Hollingdale, Cambridge University Press, 1983.

HAH *Human, All Too Human*, trans. R. J. Hollingdale, Cambridge University Press, 1986.

D *Daybreak*, trans. R. J. Hollingdale, Cambridge University Press, 1982.

GS *The Gay Science*, trans. W. Kaufmann, Random House, 1974.

Z *Thus Spoke Zarathustra*, trans. R. J. Hollingdale, Penguin, 1969.

BGE *Beyond Good and Evil*, trans. W. Kaufmann, Random House, 1966.

TI *The Twilight of the Idols*, trans. R. J. Hollingdale, Penguin, 1986.

WP *The Will to Power*, trans. W. Kaufmann and R. J. Hollingdale, Weidenfeld and Nicolson, 1969.

MA The Musarionausgabe edition of Nietzsche's *Collected Works*, Munich 1920–.

KSA *Friedrich Nietzsche Sämtliche Werke, Kritische Studienausgabe*, Deutscher Taschenbuch Verlag, de Gruyter, 1980.

UdW *Die Unschuld des Werdens, Nietzsche's Nachlass, Sämtliche Werke*, ed. A. Bäumler, Kröner, 1978.

BAW *Nietzsche Werke*, ed. A. Bäumler, Munich, 1940.

References for other frequently cited works are:

CPR Immanuel Kant, *The Critique of Pure Reason*, trans. N. K. Smith, Macmillan, 1970.

WWR Arthur Schopenhauer, *The World as Will and Representation*, trans. R. F. J. Payne, Dover, 1966, 2 vols.

PG Georg F. W. Hegel, *Phänomenologie des Geistes*, Suhrkamp, 1974.

KMV Kurt Mueller Vollmer, *The Hermeneutics Reader*, Oxford University Press, 1986.

Other works will be cited in the appropriate notes. When quoting Nietzsche's individual texts, I have followed the convention of citing the section number, not the page. When quoting from editions of his work, the last number refers to page numbers.

NOTES

This essay is a reduction of the first part of a much larger study of Nietzsche and hermeneutic thought, currently under completion. The foundations of the present essay were laid in my article 'Nietzsche's Aesthetic and the Question of Hermeneutic Interpretation', *British Journal of Aesthetics*, vol. 26, no. 4, Autumn 1986.

1 See David Wood's letter to the Editor (*Times Literary Supplement*, 1–8 June 1989), replying to Michael Tanner's 'Dim Perceptions Of Clear Ones', a composite review of recent studies of Nietzsche (*Times Literary Supplement*, 12–18 May 1989).
2 'I prefer to utilize the writers I like. The only valid tribute to thought such as Nietzsche's is precisely to use it, to deform it, to make it groan and protest.' Michel Foucault, ed. Colin Gordon, *Power-Knowledge*, Sussex, Harvester, 1977, 54.
3 '*Error of Philosophers* – The philosopher believes that the value of his philosophy lies in the whole, in the building: posterity discovers it in the bricks with which he built and which are then often used for better building: in the fact, that is to say, that that building can be destroyed and nonetheless possess value as material.' (HAH Assorted Maxims, 201).
4 See Johann Figl's article, 'Nietzsche und die philosophische Hermeneutik des 20. Jahrhunderts. Mit besonderer Berücksichtigung Diltheys, Heideggers und Gadamers', in *Nietzsche-Studien*, 1981/2, vol. 10/11, 408–41.
5 This resides in Nietzsche's frequently asserted argument that alleged 'truths' or substantive values have no effect within history but only the *interpretation* of the supposed 'truths'. See HAH 126, D 105 and D 307.
6 See H. G. Gadamer's 'Text and Interpretation' in *Hermeneutics and Modern Philosophy*, ed. Wachterhauser, State University of New York Press, 1986, 388.
7 J. Habermas, *The Philosophical Discourse of Modernity*, Oxford, Polity Press, 1987, 366–7.
8 Ricoeur's phrase 'the hermeneutics of suspicion' probably derives from Nietzsche who in his 1886 preface to *Human, All Too Human* states that his writings have been called a 'schooling in suspicion' for they look upon the world with a 'profound suspiciousness'.
9 Michel Foucault, *The History of Sexuality*, New York, Vintage, Random House, 1980, vol. 1, 82 and 98.
10 See Gianni Vattimo, *The End of Modernity*, Oxford, Polity Press, 1988, ch. 10.

11 This was a conversational remark made by Gadamer at a Heidegger Conference at St Edmund's Hall, Oxford, April 1986.
12 I must here acknowledge J. P. Stern's and M. Silk's study *Nietzsche on Tragedy*, the suggestive inadequacies of which developed lines of thought upon which this essay has been built. For my judgement of this text see my review of it in *Journal of the British Society for Phenomenology*, 1985, vol. 16, no. 1, 88–91.
13 See H. Schnädelbach, *Philosophy in Germany, 1831–1933*, Cambridge, Cambridge University Press, 1984, 111–26.
14 F. A. Wolf, *Vorlesungen über die Geschichte der griechischen Literatur*, ed. Gurtler, Leipzig, 1831, 271–302.
15 H. G. Gadamer, 'Das Drama Zarathustras' in D. Goicoechea, ed., *The Great Year of Zarathustra*, New York and London, University Press of America, 1983, 339–69.
16 J. Figl, 'Hermeneutische Voraussetzungen der Philologischen Kritik', in *Nietzsche-Studien*, 1984, vol. 15.
17 BAW V, 126.
18 C. P. Janz, *Nietzsche Biographie*, Munich, Carl Hanser Verlag, 1978, vol. I, 270.
19 'Every philosophy is a foreground philosophy – that is a hermit's judgement: "There is something arbitrary in his stopping here to look back and around; there is also something suspicious about it." Every philosophy also *conceals* a philosophy; every opinion is also a hide-out, every word a mask' (BGE 289).
20 Examples of Kant's analogical arguments are to be found in Kant's *Critique of Teleological Judgement*, trans. Meredith, Oxford University Press, 1978, 136–7.
21 See J. P. Stern and M. Silk, *Nietzsche on Tragedy*, Cambridge University Press, 1981, 12.
22 The term *Altthumswissenschaft*, literally the science of antiquity, refers to the old classical humanist tradition of learning represented by such as Winkelmann whilst *Sach-Philologie* refers to the later academic study of antiquity which was dominated not by a culturally homogeneous idea of learning (what Nietzsche occasionally refers to as wisdom) but by the quest for knowledge for knowledge's sake. This point is further discussed by Stern and Silk, op. cit., 12.
23 See Nietzsche's letters to Gersdorff, 6 April 1867 and to Rohde, 20 November 1868, cited by Stern and Silk, op. cit., 23.
24 C. P. Janz, op. cit., 270.
25 For an elaboration of this point see Jorg Schreiter, *Hermeneutik, Wahrheit und Verstehen*, Akademie Verlag, Berlin, 1989, 153–5. This is a notable text as it is the first full-length study of contemporary hermeneutics to appear within the German Democratic Republic. I am indebted to Gabriele Stammberger for drawing my attention to it.
26 Recent studies of pre-Islamic Arabic poetry point to a similar use of poetic structures in which 'the celebration of life is entwined with a tragic sense of the inevitability of death and the infinite nature of life itself'. See Kamal Abu-Deeb's article 'Towards a Structural Analysis of Pre-Islamic Poetry', *International Journal for Middle Eastern Studies*, 1975, vol. 6, 148–84.

27 G. F. W. Hegel, *Science of Logic*, trans. Miller, London, Allen & Unwin, 1969, 67.

28 Hollingdale for example comments, '*The World as Will and Idea* had (for Nietzsche) replaced the Bible. It was not an intellectual decision: it was a conversion, a way out of a crisis.' R. J. Hollingdale, *Nietzsche*, London, Routledge & Kegan Paul, 1973, 51.

29 This theme is succinctly expressed in the essay 'On the Uses and Abuses of History': 'If you are to venture to interpret the past you can do so only out of the fullest exertion of the vigour of the present' (UM 11, 94).

30 J. P. Stern and M. Silk, op. cit, 296.

31 The point is developed further by Nietzsche in *The Gay Science* where he suggests that 'every art, every philosophy may be viewed as a remedy and an aid in the service of growing and struggling life: they always presuppose suffering and sufferers. But there are two kinds of sufferers: first, those who suffer from an over-fullness of life – they want a Dionysian art and likewise a tragic view of life, a tragic insight – and then those who suffer from the impoverishment of life and seek rest, stillness, calmness, still seas, redemption from themselves through art and knowledge' (GS 370).

32 See J. P. Stern and M. Silk, op. cit., 98.

33 Dilthey refers to the *Geisteswissenschaften* as 'real' sciences. See *Selected Writings*, Cambridge, Cambridge University Press, 1976, 116–18.

34 Z. Baumann, *Hermeneutics and Social Science*, London, Hutchinson, 1978, 170.

35 See W. Pannenberg, *Theology and The Philosophy of Science*, Darton, Longman & Todd, 1976, 197, 198 and 201.

36 See H. G. Gadamer, *Truth and Method*, Sheed & Ward, 1979, 99–108.

37 Nietzsche's epistemologial instrumentalism pursues this line exactly. Concepts and categories do not reflect the nature of reality *per se* but offer a framework of schematizations whereby the complexities of experience can be ordered. See WP, 515: 'Not to "know" but to schematize – to impose upon chaos as much regularity and form as our practical needs require . . . to subsume, to schematize, for the purpose of intelligibility and calculation . . . only when we see things, coarsely and made equal, do they become calculable and useful for us.'

5 Nietzsche, the self, and Schopenhauer

Christopher Janaway

Nietzsche vehemently attacks the traditional conception of the unitary self. This essay tries to show that some of the undermining of that conception had already been done in Schopenhauer's work. We should not ignore the obvious fact that while Nietzsche is a philosopher of cultures, classes and epochs, Schopenhauer's view of knowledge and ethics remains firmly ahistorical.[1] Nevertheless, if we first try to inhabit Schopenhauer's point of view, we can look forward to Nietzsche and illuminate him from one (partial) perspective.[2] For Nietzsche's opposition to Schopenhauer's conceptions of the subject and of the will is interwoven with more positive debts to his predecessor's philosophy, and he by no means fully overcomes its problems and tensions.

I

Schopenhauer's account of the self unfolds dramatically throughout the course of *The World as Will and Representation*.[3] The drama is consciously and artistically executed, constructed of tensions, reversals, and resolutions. We begin with an account of the subject of knowledge. The subject is 'that which knows everything and is known by none', it is 'the bearer of the world, the condition of all appearance, of all object'.[4] Subject and object are 'necessary correlates' in that, first, there can be no subject without object, and no object without subject, as Schopenhauer frequently asserts; and second, *subject* and *object* are mutually exclusive categories: 'Since the representing I, the subject of knowing, as the necessary correlate of all representations, is their condition, it can never itself become representation or object.'[5] 'Our knowledge', Schopenhauer says in another passage, 'like our eye, only sees outwards and not inwards, so that, when the knower tries to turn itself inwards, in order to know itself, it looks into a total darkness, falls into a complete void.'[6] Visual metaphors predominate in Schopenhauer's account of the subject of knowledge. Another which he uses is that of the focal point – the extensionless point at which rays converge when focused by a concave mirror. Such, for him, is the subject of representations: the mere point at which they all converge. He embraces the corollary that the subject is not spatial or temporal, or capable of causal interaction with anything in the empirical world. The subject if purely that point from which whatever is known or experienced is known or experienced. It is necessary to the world, but never a part of it.

As may already be apparent, Schopenhauer's account of the subject of knowledge, despite its novel style of presentation, is thoroughly Kantian. This subject is that of the transcendental unity of apperception.[7] It is the 'I' of the 'I think', which Kant says 'must be able to accompany all my representations', the self that must exist as the unitary subject of a collectivity of *Vorstellungen* or representations. Its existence is constituted by its self-consciousness – that is, by its being able to ascribe each of many *Vorstellungen* to itself as a single subject. Beyond that we have no licence to claim any knowledge of the subject itself – because there is no experience of it as such, only of its states passing in 'inner sense'. I shall refer to this conception as that of the transcendental subject, meaning by that the subject considered non-empirically, as a mere condition of the possibility of experience. The Kantian transcendental subject is not 'the soul as substance' which Nietzsche so often criticizes as a fiction.[8] It is no substantial entity at all, no *thing* of any kind within the world. Schopenhauer is fully aware of this: 'the subject', he says, 'though simple (being an extensionless point) is not for that reason a substance (soul), but a mere state'.[9]

The transcendental subject serves as the origin of conceptual classification under the a priori categories. Though Schopenhauer prunes the Kantian system drastically here, his view is closely continuous with Kant's. He contends that space, time and causality are modes of organization among a subject's representations, rather than of the world 'in itself', and that without these modes of organization there could be no experience of objects and, indeed, no objects. Further, space and time together form what Schopenhauer calls the '*principium individuationis*'. Only what occurs as an object in space and time is capable of individuation. There are thus no individuals at the level of the 'in itself'. Nor is the subject (which is never an object for itself) an individual either. (Hence the inadvisability of considering Schopenhauer a solipsist.)

This initial facet of the subject is striking, and may incline us to think that everything to follow will be a version of something Kantian. According to his own official programme, Schopenhauer holds this transcendental subject of knowing fixed and supplements it with other elements in a single coherent picture. But another way of reading his work is to see him as undermining the transcendental subject in a series of moves, each of which in some manner turns away from epistemology as the axis of orientation. We are left with something much more nakedly problematic, and not properly containable within the Kantian terminology of subject and object, appearance and thing-in-itself.

The first step away from Kant comes with Schopenhauer's insistence that an objective view of the knowing intellect is equally as tenable as the Kantian subjective view. Though scornful of a materialist world-view which aspires to reduce everything including the subject to states of matter – what he calls the philosophy of 'the subject that forgets itself in its own reckoning' – he is prepared to concede that: 'materialism too has its justification. For it is just as true that the knower is a product of matter as that matter is the mere representation of the knower'.[10] The materialist world-view on its own is one-sided. But so is Kantian philosophy. Kant leaves an unbridgeable gap between philosophy and physiology, because he does not countenance the 'objective view of the intellect'. Such a view

> takes as its object not our own consciousness, but beings given in outer experience . . . and it investigates what relation their intellect has to their other properties, how it has become possible, how it has become necessary, and what it achieves for them. The standpoint of this method of consideration is empirical: it takes the world and the animal beings present in it simply as given, using them as its starting point.[11]

The investigations Schopenhauer has in mind will be 'zoological, anatomical, physiological', will reveal the human subject as an animal, the intellect as 'springing from the organism', and – most tellingly – Kant's synthetic unity of apperception as 'the focal point of the activity of the whole brain'.[12] Materialist explanations of consciousness cannot be total because they must ignore the essential viewpoint of the subject. But that viewpoint alone is also incapable of giving a complete account. We are objects as well as pure subjects. Empirical science must supplement transcendental epistemology.

The next dramatic reversal similarly relies on relinquishing the supremacy of epistemology and the account of the subject which epistemology requires. Superficially it is simply a move back towards a metaphysics of the kind Kant had sought to stamp out – a metaphysics of the 'in-itself'. Schopenhauer now argues that, contrary to the initially premissed Kantian position, we can know what we are in ourselves. In ourselves, 'seen from within', we are *will*. And this gives us the key to a metaphysical account of the world as a whole, at the level of the thing-in-itself. I shall not discuss the global aspect of Schopenhauer's *Willensmetaphysik*, only the core of it which concerns the self. The starting point is our awareness of our own actions, which necessitates our being rooted in the world of objects in a way in which the pure transcendental subject of knowledge can never be. All objects are known to the transcendental subject as something other than itself. It hovers outside the whole of the world, like 'a winged angel's head without a body'.[13] But within my subjective experience, one particular object is privileged – my body. Schopenhauer argues in effect that what makes this body mine is its being the manifestation of will. His argument depends on the claim that willing is bodily acting: that there is no separable 'purely mental' state of willing, which is merely the cause of action. To will is to act, and to act is to move the body. Hence in being the subject of willing I must be embodied. Action shows that the account of the transcendental subject cannot be an exhaustive account of the self.

Indeed, Schopenhauer goes on to suggest that will is our essence. Supposedly, the awareness of willing in acting takes us beyond representation to the thing-in-itself, which for Kant remained an unresolved mystery. This, at any rate, is what Schopenhauer would sometimes like to say. The dichotomy of subject and object, in terms of which representation is defined, is to be left behind. In willing and acting I am not a subject aware of a distinct object. I, the subject, grasp what I, the subject, really am. But Schopenhauer cannot easily say this because he has stipulated that any form of awareness has the subject/object structure of representation. He has to have recourse to the notion that in awareness of action the subject of knowing knows, as object, a distinct subject of willing, and nevertheless is identical with it, since the word 'I' embraces both. This is a poor account of self-consciousness. But holding out for unmediated knowledge of the thing-in-itself would have been no improvement. The thing-in-itself must be strictly unknowable, and anything known must fall within 'our representations'. At the key point of dislocation from Kant, Schopenhauer cannot state a coherent theory because of his wholesale retention of Kantian terminology. Yet the move away is decisive. The subject is a subject of will as much as of knowledge and as such must be empirically embodied.

Having reached the conception of the self as essentially willing via the questionable metaphysics of the will as thing-in-itself, Schopenhauer hangs on to this thread a number of important insights, whose theme is that from both the objective and the subjective points of view the will has primacy in us. The will functions here more as a central hypothesis that can explain a variety of observed phenomena. But to understand these insights we have to be aware of the unusual and wide sense which accrues to the concept of will. To begin with, Schopenhauer suggests that will should be applied to a wide range of mental states: 'all affections and passions' are 'only more or less strong . . . movements of one's own will, which is either checked or let free, satisfied or unsatisfied' – hence 'all desiring, striving, wishing, longing, yearning, hoping, loving, and enjoying' and their 'opposite', negative affections come under the heading of 'will'.[14] But the concept of will is widened in another way, so that it does not apply solely to what we would call mental states. The will becomes for Schopenhauer a very generalized principle of striving or end-directedness that manifests itself in the human body and its behaviour, both at a conscious and at an unconscious level. There are conscious acts of will, caused by rational motives, and identical with actions. But then there are all the bodily processes that do not presuppose consciousness, such as digestion, growth, reflex reaction – these are also empirical manifestations of the end-directedness that is our true essence. Or, as Schopenhauer puts it, they are objectifications of the will. (This does not mean that any being has consciously entertained the 'ends' involved, nor that there is some overall end to which the world is directed. Phenomena have piecemeal teleological explanations for Schopenhauer, but the world in itself is emphatically purposeless.)

Ultimately such processes are subservient to a single end for the human organism, that of survival within its environment. That our behaviour, and our very formation as organisms, are governed by this end is what Schopenhauer means by his famous claim of the primacy of the will to life (*der Wille zum Leben*). Not only the will to survive, but the will to produce life, to reproduce, are embraced in this concept. Hence Schopenhauer writes, 'The genitals are the real *focus* of the will, and are therefore the opposite pole to the brain, the representative of knowledge.'[15] This last comment, however, is a little misleading. For the brain too is a manifestation of the will in an organism striving consciously and unconsciously for survival. Schopenhauer is prepared to say that 'teeth, gullet and intestinal canal are objectified hunger; the genitals are objectified sexual impulse',[16] but also that the brain and the nervous system are the objectified 'will-to-know'.[17] The brain, and hence the capacity for knowledge, are explicable in terms of their function of preserving and enhancing the life of the organism in which they appear. Hence the 'ultimate substratum' of willing and knowing is the same – it is the will manifesting itself in an organism. Rationality, and even consciousness, do not belong to the will essentially, which is why Schopenhauer often refers to it as 'blind'. Rationality and consciousness are secondary phenomena, in that they are explicable in terms of the ultimate ends they serve for an organism, ends which do not themselves presuppose rationality or consciousness.

Schopenhauer's doctrine of the primacy of the will has many aspects, of which I shall note three that are of greatest importance. First, Schopenhauer suggests that from the subjective point of view our mental life is shot through with the influence of the underlying will. Phenomena confront us as imbued with a complex positive or negative significance corresponding to the ends, interests, and drives which are basic to our psychology. Many of these drives are pre-rational and for the most part elude our conscious control. Hatreds, fears, and sexual drives exist in us unconsciously and can be seen to influence our actions.[18] Second, the classifications which we impose on the world of our representation are all those of an organism bent on manipulating its environment. Our capacity for knowledge, and the forms that knowledge takes (including scientific knowledge) are to be explained in terms of our being possessors of will. Third, the self is not unitary. We find ourselves to be compounded out of two elements: will, which is in itself blind and pre-rational, and intellect, which springs out of the will to fulfil certain of its ends, but which, in human beings, can arrive at a self-consciousness of itself as a subject of knowledge and rational thought. We tend to consider ourselves simply to be such an intellect, but in truth, for Schopenhauer, our psychology is a perpetual struggle between the two elements, with the will remaining primary.

There is a final twist to this drama.[19] Exceptionally, the subject of knowledge can free itself from the will. This occurs in aesthetic experience, 'by . . . *losing* oneself completely in the object, i.e. forgetting precisely one's individual, one's own will, and remaining only as pure subject, as clear mirror of the object'.[20] By ceasing to exercise one's individual will towards an object, one comes to shed the modes of connectedness governing our ordinary will-bound experience, experiencing the object out of space, out of time, and out of its causal bonds with other things. Correspondingly, one's consciousness of oneself changes – one is, for oneself, in these brief moments, no longer an individual, but a clear mirror of the object, 'pure, will-less, painless, timeless *subject of knowledge*'. One becomes, as Schopenhauer also puts it, 'the one world-eye that looks out from all knowing beings'.[21] The aesthetic state brings us to a truer contemplation of reality than that given by the will-bound classifications we impose as individual members of a particular species of organisms. Schopenhauer suggests that it is Platonic Ideas (somewhat adapted to the context) that we are enabled to grasp when in this state. A prolongation of this 'timeless, will-less' condition is at the heart of Schopenhauer's view of ethics too. In abstaining from imposing one's individual will on the world one comes to 'see the world aright', as not containing a fundamental division between 'I' and 'not-I'.

As final salvation Schopenhauer envisages the prospect of turning against the will in its individual manifestation within oneself – of the total denial of the will. A proper account of these aspects of Schopenhauer is well beyond the scope of this paper. But we should note in passing Schopenhauer's view of responsibility. He argues persuasively for determinism, but recognizes that this leaves untouched the sense of being 'the doer of the deed', or the feeling of responsibility. The problem is: how to account for it? Schopenhauer is critical of Kant's well-known solution involving the notion of noumenal causality – for there can be (even by Kantian principles) no causal connection between the noumenal and the empirical. Schopenhauer's 'solution' is like Kant's but without the prospect of the noumenal self's having any effect on the empirical chain of events. It is simply that we must conceive ourselves as having an intelligible (non-empirical) character, an immutable being (*esse*) outside of the deterministic empirical world, and that it is for this being that we hold ourselves responsible.[22]

We have seen a trend in Schopenhauer to undermine the privileged status of the Kantian transcendental subject of knowledge which he uses as his own epistemological starting point. His introduction of the concerns of the theory of action, physiology, biological teleology, and the psychology of irrational and unconscious motivation are all couched in metaphysical terms as a doctrine about the will as thing-in-itself. Yet the reversion to pre-Kantian metaphysics is at the same time his way of progressing beyond Kantian epistemology. Never again, one is tempted to say, will it be possible to conceive the self as a wholly rational, self-conscious subject of knowledge confronting a world of objects from some point outside that world. On the other hand, by retaining a basic Kantian framework, Schopenhauer contrives to hold that very conception in a tension – both unstable and creative – with his new insights. The supposedly necessary conceptions of the transcendental subject of knowledge is left in an extremely vulnerable position, wholly external to the spatio-temporal and incapable of any kind of causal interaction with it. Equally, that of the moral intelligible character, with its different Kantian origin, has become so stranded as to threaten extinction.

The aspiration towards a pure, will-less subject should not be mistaken for a return to the Kantian transcendental subject. That subject knows mere empirical things according to the classifications of time, space and causality and is ultimately explicable as end-seeking and manipulative – an outgrowth of will. The pure subject of knowing is an older, Platonic notion, expressly designed to penetrate beyond Kantian appearance, and to contemplate what is in a timeless, painless, and will-less condition. While producing a theory that the self is fundamentally a blindly striving, limited, pain-ridden product of organic functions, Schopenhauer never loses a sense that it ought to be a pure Platonic soul. This conflict is close to the root of his pessimism. But he is also conservative enough to think that, despite what we are, the state of purity is one which we might at least, with difficulty, attain.[23]

II

Nietzsche's early infatuation with Schopenhauer and his later repudiations are well enough known. I shall examine a few salient passages of particular interest from the Schopenhauerian perspective. First, we find Nietzsche attacking the conception of a pure, will-less subject. Thus in *The Genealogy of Morals* he writes:

From now on, my dear philosophers, let us guard ourselves

better against the dangerous old conceptual fabrication which set up a 'pure, will-less, painless, timeless subject of knowledge'. Let us guard ourselves from the clutches of such contradictory concepts as 'pure reason', 'absolute spirituality', 'knowledge in itself'; here the demand is always for us to think of an eye that cannot be thought of at all, an eye that is supposed to have no direction, one in which the active and interpreting powers that are a condition of seeing's being a seeing *of something*, are supposed to be suppressed, or absent. Thus what is demanded is always a nonsense and an inconceivability of an eye. There is *only* perspectival seeing, *only* perspectival 'knowing'; and *the more* affects we allow to have their say over something, *the more* eyes, different eyes, we are able to engage on the same thing, the more complete will be our 'concept' of this thing, the more complete our 'objectivity'. But eliminating the will altogether, removing the affects one and all, just supposing we could to this: would that not mean *castrating* the intellect?[24]

This is not simply a commentary on Schopenhauer, since Nietzsche's aims are wider than that. But the model for the inconceivable eye is Schopenhauer's world-eye, as the direct reference to the 'pure, will-less, painless, timeless subject of knowledge' shows. Schopenhauer's last (Platonic) refuge from the will is here explicitly blocked. The only 'objectivity' that survives Nietzsche's attack is radically different from that to which Schopenhauer aspires, and is to be understood

not as 'disinterested contemplation' [*Anschauung*] . . . but as the capacity to have one's For and Against *in one's control*, and to cast them off and on: so that one precisely knows how to make the *variety* of one's perspectives and affect-interpretations useful for knowledge.[25]

Occupying the greatest possible sum of partial 'interested', or will-bound, perspectives is Nietzsche's new prescription for 'objectivity'.

Why must the 'pure, will-less subject of knowledge' be abandoned? To be a subject is to experience something. To experience something presupposes active interpretation. Thus far, Schopenhauer ought to agree. But then a subject that imposes no interpretation on whatever confronts it, and merely mirrors the world, should be impossible. The conception of the Platonic self is incompatible with that of the actively interpreting subject which knows only its own objects according to its own imposed rules, and never the thing-in-itself (or the Ideas), Nietzsche forces us to resolve this tension in Schopenhauer by giving up the Platonic notion. But he does not stop there. Knowledge always involves interpretation – but what explains how we interpret and classify? As we saw, Schopenhauer's answer was in terms of the will. And – though this needs some careful qualification later – Nietzsche gives a similar answer. It is the will which cannot be extirpated without castrating the intellect. It is our 'affects' which interpret[26] 'our needs . . . our drives and their For and Against'.[27] And 'every drive is a kind of lust to rule; each one has its perspective that it would like to compel all the other drives to accept as a norm'.[28] Any subject's experience emanates from a partial perspective because it is at the service of, and limited by, the subject's own drives and affects – which would, in Schopenhauer's terms, be manifestations of will *par excellence*. Nietzsche's terms 'drive' (*Trieb*) and 'affect' (*Affekt*) are elusive. Provisionally, we might understand a drive to be a disposition to behave in certain ways, whose existence and operation are not wholly within the conscious control of the subject who manifests it. We might understand an affect to be a state of feeling with a positive or negative value for the subject who feels it. But Nietzsche uses the terms very widely and often seems to draw little distinction between a drive and an affect. Dispositions to behave and feelings of the value of their activation in behaviour are not clearly separable for him.

What further unifies drives and affects for him is their rootedness in the will to power. At least on the surface of it, there is a strong parallel with Schopenhauer in Nietzsche's claim that 'In the case of an animal, it is possible to trace all its drives to the will to power; likewise all the functions of organic life to this one source'.[29] Nietzsche seeks to impugn the notion that any conception of the way things are is ever adopted or retained because of its correspondence with an independent reality. For example, he says that 'The usefulness of preservation . . . stands as the motive behind the development of the organs of knowledge . . . they develop in such a way that their observations suffice for our preservation . . . a species grasps a certain amount of reality in order to become master of it, in order to press it into service'.[30] 'Logic and the categories of reason' are for Nietzsche merely 'means towards the adjustment of the world for utilitarian ends (thus, "in principle", toward an expedient *falsification*)'. Their ultimate 'criterion of truth' is 'merely the *biological utility of . . . a system of systematic falsification*: and since a species of animals knows of nothing more important than preserving itself, one might indeed be permitted to speak here of "truth".[31] If 'fabrication' and 'falsification' are colourful terms for something like 'merely subject-dependent modes of classification, to which no "external" reality corresponds', then Schopenhauer must agree: knowledge is not a matter of contact with a world beyond our own *Vorstellungen*. And how do we explain what we do nevertheless call 'knowledge'? We must regard humanity from a biological point of view, as a species concerned with its own preservation, and explain its modes of classification as best serving a need, or drive, or attempt, to become master, to press the world into service. 'Truth is the kind of error without which a particular species of life could not life. The value for *life* is ultimately decisive.'[32]

Thus we can discern, within Nietzsche's opposition to Schopenhauer, the outline of an argument which itself has Schopenhauerian roots. The will underlies and explains those classifications of the subject that pass for knowledge, and they correspond to nothing independent of the subject. If this is so, there can only be perspectival knowing, only affect-interpretation. Hence the yearning for the condition of a 'pure will-less subject' must be abandoned as a nonsense. In effect, it is variants of Schopenhauerian premisses – 1) that knowledge concerns relations between representations existing only for a subject, and 2) that the capacity for knowledge is explanatorily less basic than the will – which combine to rule out his conservative retention of what I have called the ideal of the pure Platonic soul.

However, in arguing for a Schopenhauerian basis to Nietzsche's claims here, we run the risk of drastic over-simplification, chiefly because of aspects of Nietzsche's doctrine of the will to power carefully skirted so far. I offer no definitive view on this crucial and vexed issue. But we must face up to a number of differences between the will to power and the Schopenhauer doctrine of the will. First, Nietzsche decisively rejects the notion of an all-pervading will to *life* – 'for life is merely a special case of the will to power; it is quite arbitrary to assert that everything strives to enter into *this* form of the will to power.'[33] Instead 'every living thing does everything it can not to preserve itself but to become *more*':[34] increase, self-enhancement, maximum effect on the rest of the world are more fundamental than merely continuing to live. Yet, important though this difference is, it is not of itself a fatal objection to my claims so far. Provided we remind ourselves that the manifestations of the will to life are subsumable under the wider heading of will to power, which has many other manifestations, then what Schopenhauer said about the will to life might still contain some truth. After all, Nietzsche himself characterizes interpretation in terms of 'biological utility', 'value for life', and 'preservation'.

There is, however, a difference of greater importance for us. This is the fact that, while Schopenhauer strives for an explicitly metaphysical doctrine of the will, identifying it with the thing-in-itself, Nietzsche repudiates any such notion. Not that he is averse to Schopenhauerian rhetoric at times. For example, he exclaims '*This world is the will to power – and nothing besides!* And you yourselves are also this will to power – and nothing besides!'[35] He contemplates explaining 'our life of drives in its entirety' (*unser gesammtes Triebleben*) as the expression of '*one* fundamental form of the will', speaks of reducing 'all organic functions' to the will to power, and designating '*all* effective force univocally as: *will to power*'. 'The world seen from within', he continues, 'the world determined and designated according to its "intelligible character" – it would be "will to power" and nothing else.'[36] Unless Nietzsche is inconsistent on a global scale, this must be rhetoric, rather than a variant of Schopenhauer's metaphysics of the 'in itself', for Nietzsche certainly considers 'the "thing-in-itself" nonsensical' and writes: 'That things possess a constitution in themselves quite apart from interpretation and subjectivity, is a quite idle hypothesis: it presupposes that interpretation and subjectivity are not essential, that a thing freed from all relationships would still be a thing.'[37]

It is coherent to view Nietzsche's doctrine of will to power as itself an interpretation, a hypothesis which allows one to 'master' as much of phenomenal reality as possible, rather than as an attempt to characterize the world as it is in itself.[38] But it must be noted that for Nietzsche this is a singularly privileged hypothesis, which is to be allowed precedence over all others, and which is global in its explanatory ambition. There may be no such *thing* as the will to power – only a flux of processes inconceivable except in relation to one another – but 'will to power' is the overall description which for Nietzsche best captures a quality present throughout the world. In this respect the use made of the doctrine is, after all, not so radically different from that to which Schopenhauer puts his doctrine of the will. Kaufmann has written that 'Nietzsche based his theory on empirical data and not on any dialectical ratiocination about Schopenhauer's metaphysics, as is so often supposed erroneously.'[39] But, as we saw, Schopenhauer himself uses his metaphysical claim as a peg on which to hang generalizing explanations (rather of the kind Kaufmann has in mind) concerning a wide range of psychological, biological, and other phenomena. The ease with which Nietzsche adopts Schopenhauerian modes of expression reflects this fact, rather than his predecessor's distinctly metaphysical aspirations, which Nietzsche consistently rejects. We might say that Schopenhauer remains caught in a metaphysical conception of the 'in itself' which does not best serve all his explanatory aims, while Nietzsche adopts the rhetoric of that conception.[40]

Without going back on the points of difference between the doctrine of will to power and Schopenhauer's doctrine of will, we can still make a case for regarding Nietzsche's position as analogous to Schopenhauer's, in the following way: both posit as a basic explanatory feature of human beings a non-conscious, non-rational principle which is apparent in multiple drives and affects that permeate cognition, and to which the unitary self-conscious subject is secondary. We may also note the primacy Nietzsche assigns to the body. Belief in the body has certainly, he asserts, been more fundamental at all times than belief in 'soul' or 'ego' or 'subject'; the phenomenon of the body is 'the richer, clearer, more tangible phenomenon: to be discussed first, methodologically'.[41] In a notable section of *Thus spoke Zarathustra* he goes further. Body is primary because 'the creating body created the spirit [*den Geist*] for itself as a hand of its will' – almost as Schopenhauer said. But the body remains also the true self (*das Selbst*):

> 'I' say you and are proud of this word. But the greater thing is what you will not believe in – your body and its great wisdom: it does not say I, but does I.

> Behind your thinking and feeling, my brother, stands a mighty commander, an unknown wise one – it is called self. It dwells in your body, it is your body.

> Your self laughs at your I and its proud leaps. 'What are these leaps and flights of thought to me?' it says to itself. A roundabout way to my ends. I am the leading string of the I, and the prompter of its concepts.[42]

In some passages in *The Will to Power* Nietzsche thinks of the body as a collectivity, a multiplicity of cells and organic functions, bound together by a fluctuating set of quasi-social power-relations. But the body, and physiology, are still 'the starting point', and enable us to 'gain the correct idea of the nature of our subject-unity, namely as regents at the head of a communality' – at the head, but a) dependent upon, and b) of the same kind as, the forces beneath.[43] For Schopenhauer, the self-conscious intellect is an 'outgrowth of will'. For Nietzsche, our being a 'subject-unity' depends on our being primarily an organic plurality, with all organic functions to be interpreted finally as modes of will to power.

III

The analogies I have argued for, if they are genuine, are only one side of the story. In this final section I shall pursue some more fundamental divergences. As we saw, Schopenhauer deliberately holds his theory of the 'blind' will in tension with his conceptions of the subject. Nietzsche's declared position is deeply at odds with this, for two reasons. One is that for him there is no 'I' – that the unitary subject, whether of thought, knowledge or action, is an outright illusion. The other is that 'will' has to be interpreted in a new way.

In attacking the 'I' Nietzsche is in part taking as his target the conception of the soul as *substance*, a view well undermined already by Kant, with powerful assistance from Schopenhauer.[44] But these two philosophers persist in holding that I must conceive myself, not indeed as a substance, but as a single, united subject, claiming a collection of representations and – in Schopenhauer's case – bodily actions, as *mine*. This view too Nietzsche aims to discredit. He is suspicious of the reasoning 'There is thinking: therefore there is something that thinks'.[45] It is not that he attacks only the conclusion here, or only the inference made. He also attacks the premiss – 'thinking' is just as much a fiction as the subject of thinking. 'Thinking is merely a relation of . . . drives to each other,'[46] it is 'a quite arbitrary fiction, arrived at by selecting one element from the process and eliminating all the rest', and the conception of *something that thinks* is 'a second derivative of that false introspection that believes in "thinking" . . . that is to say, both the deed and the doer are fictions.'[47] (Similarly, as the last clause hints, neither 'willing' nor such a *thing* as 'the will' – as the subject of action – really exists.[48]) Nietzsche would rather view the mental life as a complex, ever-changing interweaving of forces, without discrete episodes of re-identifiable types classifiable as 'thinking' or 'willing'. But there must be some story as to what *is* the case (what 'the process' is): we glimpse it here:

> The assumption of one single subject is perhaps unnecessary;
> perhaps it is just as permissible to assume a multiplicity of

subjects, whose interaction and struggle is the basis of our thought and our consciousness in general? A kind of aristocracy of 'cells' in which dominion resides? To be sure, an aristocracy of equals, used to ruling jointly and understanding how to command?

My hypotheses: The subject as multiplicity.[49]

Similarly again, 'there is no will', but rather 'the multitude and disgregation of impulses and the lack of any systematic order among them result in a "weak will"; their coordination under a single predominant impulse results in a "strong will"'.[50]

As to why we believe in an 'I' – in part this is simply a special case of what Nietzsche thinks generally true with regard to interpretation. 'However habitual and indispensable this fiction may have become by now – that in itself proves nothing against its imaginary origin: a belief can be a condition of life and nonetheless be false.'[51] There is a line of argument here[52] which is powerful against idealists such as Kant and Schopenhauer: space, time and causality are admitted to be the subject's impositions on the data of experience – but what about the subject itself? Interpretations must (presumably) have some origin – but why must that origin be the kind of unitary subject we interpret ourselves to be? It might be suggested that the difference between Nietzsche and Schopenhauer here is not as great as it appears. After all, Schopenhauer expresses his view of the subject's status by calling it not just a 'mere focal point' – something with only virtual existence – but also an 'illusion', since, for him, the will alone is 'what there is'. With Schopenhauer the career of the 'I' reaches terminal crisis. It must serve as the notional point of origin for our indispensable interpretations of the world, whilst at the same time a more fundamental explanation is wheeled into place – that of the organism whose 'will-to-know' engenders a brain, and thereby the illusion of a single subject of representations. Thus, it might be said, Nietzsche's use of the concept of will to power to destabilize the subject is not wholly new. He says that the belief in the 'I' is indispensable to us – in the sense that 'to let it go means: being no longer able to think' – but that this is compatible with its 'corresponding to no reality'. What is new is the shift Nietzsche makes in the sense of 'indispensable'. If Schopenhauer's subject was a 'necessary illusion', it was because it was supposedly an a priori presupposition of all experience. For Nietzsche, belief in the subject can be indispensable only to the extent that it enhances life or subserves the will to power.

But the picture is still incomplete until we have taken account of Nietzsche's un-Schopenhauerian conviction that belief in a unitary self or subject, and indeed the will to power manifested in that belief, have a history. The will to power is that of a particular class of people, who had a need to separate out in the human being an enduring *locus* of responsibility, a core or substratum which brought about thought and action, but which itself remained the same, and could have brought things about otherwise. The weak, the powerless, the oppressed 'have a *need* for the belief in the indifferent, freely-choosing "subject", arising from the instinct of self-preservation, self-affirmation'.[53] By this means the strong can be held responsible for their exertion of strength, and the weak can gain power over them. 'People were thought "free" in order to be judged and punished – so that they could become guilty: and as a consequence every action *had* to be thought of as willed, and the origin of every action as lying in consciousness.'[54] But, claims Nietzsche, there is no such neutral substratum: 'there is no "being" behind doing, operating, becoming; "the doer" is merely added to the deed.'[55]

Once again, however, Schopenhauer can be seen as inadvertently pointing the way, by stretching an (in Nietzsche's view) erroneous conception to its limit – as witness his role in 'the fable of intelligible freedom' told in *Human, All Too Human*.[56] Here Nietzsche portrays a search back through the effects of action, to action itself, to antecedent motives, to the essence (*Wesen*) from which they spring: a search for something for which a person may be made responsible. Schopenhauer is a thoroughgoing determinist, but nevertheless notes the common feeling of displeasure we attach to our actions (he calls it the consciousness of guilt) and concludes from this that our intelligible Being, outside of empirical reality, is free. Nietzsche labels this a 'fantastic conclusion', which overlooks the fact that the feeling we call guilt may not be justified. By pushing the responsible self fully out into the non-empirical realm, with no possibility of causal influence on it, Schopenhauer prepares the ground for the final realization that there is no such responsible self at all. There is no more a willing 'I', for Nietzsche, than there is an 'I' that thinks or knows.

These, then, are some of the reasons supporting Nietzsche's claim that 'The "subject" is not something given, it is something added and invented and projected behind what there is.'[57] 'What there is', according to Nietzsche's privileged hypothesis, is a process consisting of a multiplicity of impulses or drives occurring within a single organism. These drives are better or worse co-ordinated, more or less subservient to a single dominating impulse. Drives and their associated affects are the origin of interpretations, which often purport to be knowledge, but always subserve some manifestations of will to power. And one among these interpretations is the belief in a unitary 'I'. A familiar difficulty arises here: Nietzsche forbids us to ask 'Who interprets?'[58] but it is far from clear whether we should obey him. It may be that interpretation requires no single, unchanging subject.[59] But does not Nietzsche's preferred talk of a multiplicity of community of subjects ('soul as subject-plurality' (*Subjekts-Vielheit*), 'soul as social construction of drives and affects'[60]) rely on a kind of personification of the sub-personal – in that we must still use the concept *subject* even if not of any single entity? Or are we ultimately to jettison these descriptions and acquiesce in an entirely subjectless view of the sub-personal processes out of which the need to believe in an 'I' is to emerge? In that case it begins to look as if a distant descendant of the Schopenhauer 'blind' organic will – shorn of metaphysical pretensions, pluralized, historicized – nevertheless wins out.

Nietzsche has a way of fending off this consequence, but it lands him, I believe, in some difficulty. So far I have kept alive the impression that the will to power is akin to Schopenhauer's will in being solely a 'blind' manifestation of forces within an organism. But that is a wrong impression. As I said earlier, Nietzsche offers a new sense of 'will':

> Schopenhauer's basic misunderstanding of the *will* (as if craving, instinct, drive were the *essence* of will) is typical: lowering the value of the will to the point of making a real mistake. Also hatred against willing; an attempt to see something higher, indeed that which is higher and valuable, in willing no more, in 'being a subject *without* aim and purpose' (in the 'pure subject free of will'). Great symptom of the *exhaustion* or the *weakness* of the *will*: for the will is precisely that which treats cravings as their master and appoints to them their way and measure.[61]

It is a commonplace that Nietzsche combats pessimism and nihilism by substituting the will's affirmation for its Schopenhauerian denial. But notice how Schopenhauer is here accused of devaluing the will by *misconceiving* it. Having split up the self into intellect and will, and whilst insisting that the will is primary, Schopenhauer clearly regards will as something *at whose mercy* the individual subject is – something from which we suffer, that it would have been better to be without altogether. (How poignant that one's very essence should be thought in a sense external to oneself, and a danger to oneself!) Against this, Nietzsche urges the notion of that which masters and gives direction to cravings and instincts. The choice is not between suffering at their mercy on the one hand and suppressing or escaping them entirely on the other. Though each drive is itself a striving for power,[62] will is exercised chiefly in directing these forces within oneself. And it is in this positive self-assertion with respect to the 'blind' strivings in oneself that Nietzsche finds his new taste of value: 'The highest man would have the greatest multiplicity of drives, in the relatively greatest strength that can be endured';[63] but *Blind compliance* with an affect . . . is the cause of the *greatest evils*. Greatness of character does not consist in not possessing these affects – on the contrary, one possesses them to the highest degree – but in having them under control.'[64] So, if we continue to think in terms of a 'blind' quasi-Schopenhauerian will that manifests itself unbidden in the body and in a multiplicity of drives (this is part of Nietzsche's picture), then we must not neglect the all-important controlling or harnessing aspect of the will to power, which enables sublimation of drives and the ultimate control of 'self-overcoming'.

As Alexander Nehamas has eloquently argued,[65] one of Nietzsche's prime concerns is with the notion of creating the self. Here the self one creates ideally has the kind of unity associated with a work of art or a fictional character. It is a stylistic unity constructed out of a diversity of elements: 'the creation, or imposition, of a higher-order accord among our lower-level thoughts, desires and action'.[66] The significance of Nietzsche's injunction to 'become who you are' is that one creates oneself, progressively over one's life, rather than finding a pre-existing unity that one timelessly is. Nehamas gives an example:

> In counselling himself to become who he is, Zarathustra becomes able to want to become what in fact he does become and not to want anything about it, about himself, to be different. To become what one is . . . is to identify oneself with all of one's actions, to see that everything one does (what one becomes) is what one is. In the ideal case it is also to fit all this into a coherent whole and to want to be everything one is: it is to give style to one's character; to be, we might say, becoming.[67]

If we sought to pursue the analogy with a work of art, we would have to ask: what is the raw material from which the self is formed, and what is the end-product? But that would be misleading. For

Nietzsche there is no end-product: one never statically remains the self that one becomes, since one is constantly becoming it. And there is no real distinction between 'raw material' and 'product'. I am the flux of weak and strong drives and affects, the multiplicity, over time and at any one time, contained within the body's greater organic unity; the self that I create is in a sense nothing over and above this multiplicity, but is constituted only by the taking of an attitude towards it. Surely, though, it is here that the genuine philosophical difficulty lies for Nietzsche. He may escape the terminology of 'material' and 'product', but, keen though he has been to do so, he cannot relinquish that of *agency*. For there must be something that gives style, imposes accord, identifies with all of its actions, harnesses or controls the many drives and affects.[68] I must own these actions and states, or acknowledge them as mine. I must be that which takes an attitude to them.[69]

Without the notion of this imposing agency – the harnessing or controlling will identified earlier – the supposed achievement of 'becoming oneself' is a nonsense. Let us recap. Nietzsche encourages us to conceive acting, thinking and feeling as subjectless processes occurring within an organism, leaving no residue that acts, thinks, and feels, and that could have acted, thought, or felt otherwise. And I am supposed to be the inter-relation or community of these processes, nothing more. How do I then 'become' myself, or 'create' myself? Perhaps it is simply the case that among the flux of states that (subjectlessly) occur, some are second-order states that affirm a positive attitude towards other states? But this is surely not enough: one is to affirm of one's states and actions 'I accept this as mine', or 'I accept this is myself' – and such affirmation of something *as one's own* cannot occur unless one is already a self that is more than a conglomeration of the states or actions it takes an attitude to. So the question arises: how has one become that *affirming* self? If by one's own imposition of order, then the supposed achievement of becoming oneself depends always on its own prior completion: I must be an order-imposing self before I can become one. On the other hand, if one has grown to be a self capable of affirming its own states through no exercise of agency, and merely as part of the course of nature, then it is not, after all, the above-described process of affirmation or order-imposition which constitutes one's becoming a self.

It may be that Nietzsche would have us happily embrace these paradoxes. Whether we should do so is a further question. I urge merely that we recognize the insuperable tension in his position.

Either the self dissolves without remainder into a multiplicity of subjectless (unowned) processes – the descendant of Schopenhauer's 'blind' organic will – or it is possible to exert one's will, in Nietzsche's new sense, to organize and harness this flux, and create a unified self. The former alternative Nietzsche must ultimately abhor as *'un monstre et un chaos'*.[70] But to embrace the latter alternative is to accept that one is not exhausted by the multiplicity of subjectless processes, and somewhere along the line has become an agency capable of recognizing its states as its own, and fashioning them into a character with style. Thus, while rejecting as an illusion the notion of a subject distinct from its states Nietzsche has nevertheless to conceive the self as something more than a flux of many processes, and has to reckon with the question: how does this harnessing, affirming self arise out of the subjectless flow? Even here he remains closer than he might like to think to the ambit of *The World as Will and Representation*. He inherits few of that work's doctrines, but is haunted by echoes of its deepest dilemmas.

REFERENCES

Works by Nietzsche

BGE   *Beyond Good and Evil. Prelude to the Philosophy of the Future*, trans. W. Kaufmann, New York, Random House, 1966.
TI   *Twilight of the Idols*, trans. R. J. Hollingdale (with *The Antichrist*), Harmondsworth, Penguin, 1969.
OGM   *On the Genealogy of Morals*, trans. W. Kaufmann and R. J. Hollingdale (with *Ecce Homo*), New York, Random House, 1969.
HH   *Human, All Too Human*, trans. R. J. Hollingdale, Cambridge, Cambridge University Press, 1986.
WP   *The Will to Power*, ed. W. Kaufmann, trans. W. Kaufmann and R. J. Hollingdale, New York, Random House, 1968.
Z   *Thus Spoke Zarathustra*, trans. R. J. Hollingdale, Harmondsworth, Penguin, 1960.

Departures from the translations listed are indicated in the notes, and have been made on the basis of the relevant texts in the *Kritische Gesamtausgabe*, ed. Giorgio Colli and Mazzino Montinari, Berlin, Walter de Gruyter, 1967–78.

Works by Schopenhauer

W   *The World as Will and Representation*, 2 vols, trans. E. F. J.
(W1, W2)   Payne, New York, Dover, 1969.

On the Freedom of the Will, trans. Konstantin Kolenda, 2nd edn, Oxford,
Blackwell, 1985.
Parerga and Paralipomena, 2 vols, trans. E. F. J. Payne, Oxford,
Clarendon Press, 1974.
On the Fourfold Root of the Principles of Sufficient Reason, trans. E. F. J.
Payne, La Salle, Illinois, Open Court, 1974.
Schopenhauers sämtliche Werke, ed. Arthur Hubscher, 7 vols, 3rd edn,
Wiesbaden, Brockhaus, 1960.
Der handschriftliche Nachlass, ed. Arthur Hubscher, 5 vols, Frankfurt am
Main, Kramer, 1970.

Translations from Schopenhauer are my own, though I have
consulted and cited the published translations listed above.

Other works

Clark, Maudemarie, 'Nietzsche's Doctrines of the Will to Power'.
Nietzsche-Studien, 1983, vol. 12, 458–68.
Davey, Nicholas, 'Nietzsche, The Self and Hermeneutic Theory', *Journal of
the British Society for Phenomenology*, 1987, vol. 18, 272–84.
Deleuze, Gilles, *Nietzsche and Philosophy*, trans. Hugh Tomlinson,
London, Athlone Press, 1983.
Janaway, Christopher, *Self and World in Schopenhauer's Philosophy*,
Oxford, Clarendon Press, 1989.
Kant, Immanuel, *Critique of Pure Reason*, trans. Norman Kemp Smith,
London, Macmillan, 1929.
Kaufmann, Walter, *Nietzsche: Philosopher, Psychologist, Antichrist*, Prin-
ceton, Princeton University Press, 1st edn, 1950; 4th edn, 1974.
Müller-Lauter, W., 'Nietzsches Lehre vom Willen zur Macht', *Nietzsche-
Studien*, 1974, vol. 3, 1–60.
Nehamas, Alexander, *Nietzsche: Life as Literature*, Cambridge, Mass.,
Harvard University Press, 1985.

NOTES

1 Cf. Nietzsche's strong comment at WP 366: 'That the history of all
phenomena of morality could be simplified in the way Schopenhauer
believed . . . only a thinker denuded of all historical instinct, and one
who had eluded in the strangest way even that strong schooling in
history undergone by the Germans from Herder to Hegel, could have
attained to this degree of absurdity and *naïveté*.'
2 In 1950 Walter Kaufmann wrote (specifically concerning the doctrine of
will to power) that 'Nietzsche's position is best elucidated by comparing
it not with Schopenhauer's, as has generally been done, but with Hegel's

(*Nietzsche: Philosopher, Psychologist, Antichrist*, Princeton, Princeton University Press, 1st edn, 1950, 236). Forty years later, there seems little danger of neglecting Hegel – and, if anything, a tendency to play down the systematic influence of Schopenhauer. One interesting exception is Deleuze, who sees the significance of both, and one of whose comments is apposite here: 'If we do not discover its target the whole of Nietzsche's philosophy remains abstract and barely comprehensible. The question "against whom" itself calls for several replies' (*Nietzsche and Philosophy*, trans. Hugh Tomlinson, London, Athlone Press, 1983, 8).

3 I explore Schopenhauer's account of the self in more detail in my *Self and World in Schopenhauer's Philosophy*, Oxford, Clarendon Press, 1989.

4 *The World as Will and Representation*, trans. E. F. J. Payne, New York, Dover, 1969, vol. 1, 5. Hereafter, this work as a whole is referred to as W, vol. I as W 1, and vol. II as W 2.

5 *On the Fourfold Root of the Principle of Sufficient Reason*, trans. E. F. J. Payne, La Salle, Illinois, Open Court, 1974, 208.

6 *Parerga and Paralipomena*, trans. E. F. J. Payne, Oxford, Clarendon Press, 1974, vol. ii, 46.

7 Cf. *Critique of Pure Reason*, B131–5, B157–9, Schopenhauer is aware of his affinity with Kant: 'If we summarize Kant's utterances, we will find that what he understands by the synthetic unity of apperception is, as it were, the extensionless centre of the sphere of all our representations, whose radii converge towards it. It is what I call the subject of all knowledge, the correlate of all representations' (W 1, 451–2).

8 Cf., e.g., WP 485, 487, 488.

9 W 2, 278. It would have been more accurate to say that the subject is a mere presupposition of experience, but I take the metaphors to make essentially this point.

10 W 2, 13.

11 W 2, 272.

12 W 2, 277.

13 W 1, 99.

14 *On the Freedom of the Will*, trans. Konstantin Kolenda, 2nd edn, Oxford, Blackwell, 1985, 11.

15 W 1, 330.

16 W 1, 108.

17 W 2, 258.

18 See, e.g., W 2, 209–10, 512–14.

19 Final in terms of the exposition in W. But Schopenhauer's notebooks reveal this as one of the earliest parts of his philosophy to fall into place. On this, see my *Self and World in Schopenhauer's Philosophy*, 27–31.

20 W 1, 178.

21 W 1, 198.

22 See *On the Freedom of the Will*, 93–9.

23 On this combination of progression and regression in Schopenhauer, cf. Nietzsche's comment: 'Against the theory that an "in-itself of things" must necessarily be good, blessed, true, and one, Schopenhauer's interpretation of the "in-itself" as will was an essential step; but he remained entangled in the moral-Christian ideal . . . . As soon as the

thing-in-itself was no longer "God" for him, he had to see it as bad, stupid, and absolutely reprehensible' (WP 1005). In Schopenhauer's self-understanding, it was, as I have said, a Platonic, rather than a Christian ideal that motivated him. For Nietzsche, on the other hand, 'Christianity is Platonism for "the people" ' (BGE preface).

24 OGM iii, 12 (my translation).
25 OGM iii, 12.
26 Ibid.
27 WP 481.
28 Ibid.
29 WP 619.
30 WP 480.
31 WP 584 (translation slightly altered from that of Kaufmann and Hollingdale).
32 WP 493.
33 WP 692. Cf. Z ii, 12 ('Of Self-Overcoming') 'Where there is life, there too is will: but not will to life, rather . . . will to power. Much is valued higher by the living than life itself; yet out of the valuing speaks – the will to power' (my translation).
34 WP 688.
35 WP 1067.
36 BGE 36 (my translation).
37 WP 558, 560.
38 This is brought out clearly by Alexander Nehamas: 'What there is is always determined from a specific point of view that embodies its particular interests, needs, values, its own will to power'; but 'the will to power is not a general metaphysical or cosmological theory. On the contrary, it provides a reason why no general theory of the character of the world and the things that constitute it can ever be given' (*Nietzsche: Life as Literature*, Cambridge, Mass., Harvard University Press, 1985, 81, 80).
39 Kaufmann, *Nietzsche: Philosopher, Psychologist, Antichrist*, 207.
40 An alternative view is that 'will to power' is used by Nietzsche as a 'self-conscious myth which gives us a picture or image of reality which is not intended to provide knowledge, but *is* supposed to play a role in the interpretation of experience and the furtherance of life' (Maudemarie Clark, 'Nietzsche's Doctrines of the Will to Power', *Nietzsche-Studien*, 1983, vol. 12, 461). This seems to capture the attitude that should be taken to the 'will to power' doctrine by someone holding Nietzsche's views about knowledge and truth. He can only claim, in circular fashion, that his doctrine is better because it increases one's power, or enhances life: cf. W. Müller-Lauter, 'Nietzsches Lehre vom Willen zur Macht', *Nietzsche-Studien*, 1974, vol. 3, 45–9. Nietzsche seems happy with this circularity: 'Supposing that this also is only an interpretation – and you will be eager enough to make this objection? – well, so much the better' (BGE 22). The 'myth' status of the doctrine of will to power is a consequence of Nietzsche's theory about philosophical theories. Yet he does treat the doctrine as a general hypothesis that is responsive to the phenomena and supplants other 'false' doctrines.
41 WP 489, (cf. also 659, 491).

42 Z i, 4 ('Of the Despisers of the Body') – my translation (and somewhat violent selection of extracts from a continuous passage).

43 WP 492, cf. 488, 490.

44 In BGE 54 Nietzsche contrasts the *former* belief in the soul (naïvely misled by the subject–predicate structure of 'I think') with the attack on this belief in '*die ganze neuere Philosophie*' since Descartes, and including Kant. However, in the preface to the same work, he treats the subject- and I-superstition as a version of the soul-superstition.

45 Cf. WP 484.

46 BGE 36.

47 Cf. WP 477.

48 WP 668, 692, 46.

49 WP 490.

50 WP 46.

51 WP 483.

52 Cf. 487.

53 OGM i, 13 (my translation).

54 TI vi ('The Four Great Errors'), 7 (my translation).

55 '*zum Tun bloß hinzugedichtet*' – merely a fictional addition to the deed, OGM i, 13.

56 HH i, 39.

57 WP 481.

58 WP 556.

59 As is argued by Nicholas Davey, 'Nietzsche, the Self and Hermeneutic Theory', *Journal of the British Society for Phenomenology*, 1987, vol. 18, esp. 281.

60 BGE 12 (my translation), and see WP 490, quoted above.

61 WP 84.

62 Cf. WP 481, 'a kind of lust to rule' (*Herrschsucht*).

63 WP 966.

64 WP 928. Kaufmann and Hollingdale translate '*blinde Nachgiebigkeit*' as 'blind indulgence'.

65 Nehamas, *Nietzsche: Life as Literature*, ch. 6.

66 Ibid., 188.

67 Ibid., 191.

68 'Mere variations of power could not feel themselves to be such: there must be present something that wants to grow and interprets the value of whatever else wants to grow' (WP 643).

69 Equally passive compliance with one's states is impossible if one is but the conglomerate of those states, and nothing besides. Compliance implies the possibility of choice, and hence a chooser. Schopenhauer's 'denial of the will' has likewise always seemed an act of will.

70 WP 83.

6 Marx and Nietzsche: the individual in history

Ian Forbes

> The unfinished problems I pose anew. . . . Man becomes more profound, mistrustful, 'immoral', stronger, more confident of himself – and to this extent 'more natural': this is 'progress'.
>
> (Nietzsche, 1968a, 123)

A radicalized individuality is the least well-explained product of nineteenth-century thought. This is partly the result of the temper of the century, which divided itself with respect to materialist versus idealist, holist versus atomist, and collectivist versus individualist approaches to philosophical method, scientific inquiry, normative issues and political prescription. In practice, a very particular conception of the individual emerged and came to underpin the dominant individualist explanations of western society. Effectively, the concept of the individual was annexed by liberal thought, and it is a jealously guarded piece of ideological property. Not only was the individual claimed for a methodological approach, but the individual was also said to exist in a certain way.

Alternative accounts of the individual have suffered the double burden of having to deny the existence of the individual seen as a norm while attempting to establish the existence of a differently conceived and understood individual. A new or distinctive language to describe the individual has not been forthcoming. No other term has quite the cachet of 'the individual' – since it denotes not just a single person, but also a unique and self-conscious being, distinguishable from all others. Liberal and radical interpretations actually have in mind much the same human creature – someone distinct, with capacities and powers – such that the struggle is over establishing the content of the individual, the origin, nature and extent of social and historical influence, and the implications for social and political organization. The problem for radically alternative conceptions of the individual is that the vocabulary and political and economic order of the west implicitly confirm individualist assumptions and conclusions alike. As Fred Dallmayr has observed:

> In modern Western society, little effort is required to show that ego-references have become so strongly sedimented in ordinary experience as to function as taken-for-granted parameters. It seems to me that it would be pointless to deny the importance and effectiveness of individualism in given historical contexts – although one may very well question its ability, as a philosophical doctrine, to account for itself.
>
> (Dallmayr, 1981, 138)

Nevertheless, the tradition of radical thought by definition tilts at all available windmills, so the concept of the individual must be open to continual challenge, especially in the face of its plausibility. In the past, the major arguments have focused on the existence or not of the individual, and have taken many forms and turns. Mainstream Marxism, or the 'master' narrative, maintains that the individual does not exist except as an ideological category, that, scientifically speaking, we are all social beings, determined by our economic and social circumstances. The psychoanalytic turn suggests that more naturalistic forces, drives deep within our unconscious, are at the heart of our being and actions. Most recently, post-structuralist approaches deny the elements of being an individual – there is no self in existence, no subjectivity to locate, no basis for an account of individualness apart from the context of life and language.

Karl Marx and Friedrich Nietzsche are by now heavily implicated in these old and new traditions. However, it is argued here that interpretations of Marx and Nietzsche have consistently underplayed the consequences of their contributions to an alternative understanding of the individual in history. Marxist thought, focusing on the economic roots of social and political discord and the mechanisms for a productively effective future, has neglected to develop an account of the new freedoms and responsibilities of post-capitalist existence. Nietzschean interpretation, on the other hand, has swung between a fear of nihilism and aristocratic radicalism and the glorification of the kind of relativism given such a spur by Nietzsche's aesthetic and moral critiques.

Recent explorations of Nietzsche and Marx tend to emphasize the incompatibility of their rival systems of thought. Nancy Love, for example, argues that: 'By pursuing the origins of modern society, Marx discovers the dominant economic interests and Nietzsche reveals its dominant psychological ones' (1986, 8). While Marx and Nietzsche cannot be compressed into the same theoretical mould, it can certainly be demonstrated that their critiques have been formative influences in the subsequent development of western perceptions of self and change in society. Equally, both thinkers place themselves within a historicizing tradition of understanding and discovery. They presume the existence of change and discontinuity, crucial aspects of which have already occurred, are unfolding in their present, and will exercise a major influence on the immediate future. Marx and Nietzsche accept the necessity for change, but neither is didactic about its ultimate outcome. Marx is prescriptive, given the possibility for an organizationally different and socially just society, while Nietzsche is encouraging about the prospects for a creative mode of being despite the realities of organization.

THE REAL MARXIAN INDIVIDUAL

Marx is a severe critic of individualism, seeing it as the basis of liberal idealism and a key element in the ideology of capitalism. The underlying principle for him is the concept of the abstract individual. His principal objections are to atomistic views of the person and ahistorical approaches to society. In this respect his attacks on those who perpetrate these philosophical errors has an undiminished potency, notwithstanding subsequent attempts to modify the claims and theory of individualism (O'Neill, 1973). Individualism, for Marx, was equated with the distinction between the self and others that is implicit in an exchange economy, where interactions reflect the transmission of the result of human activity. It is no surprise then to find that Marx described the egoist as 'an individual separated from the community, withdrawn into himself, wholly preoccupied with his private interest and acting in accordance with his private caprice' (1975, 26). The direct result of the exchange society and the division of labour on which it is based, however, is a process that is contradictory. 'Instead of the individual function being the function of society, the individual function is made into a society for itself' (ibid., 148). Despite the increasing sophistication of society and the advancement of humanity, there was nevertheless 'a diminution of the *capacity of each man* taken *individually*' (ibid., 373). Such passages indicate that Marx did employ the historical materialist method to analyse non-economistic matters. His view of historical development presupposes that change brought about at the level of social organization will ultimately produce change in our basic human nature, and so change the possibilities and create the conditions for new social forms (Forbes, 1990). In general terms, Marx's view of a history made up of epochs and his theory of change point to an evolving individuality connected in materialist terms to the increasing sophistication of social and technological existence.

The strongest element in Marx's story of the development of the human individual emerges in the transition from feudalism to capitalism. Feudal individuality was a restricted and parochial experience, with strong reliance on pre-scientific and traditional patterns of thought and behaviour. The move to capitalism meant that the person effectively had opportunities for a greater under-standing of the world, and that understanding made greater control over action possible. In other words, developing rationality and emotionality meant that agency could take new and more potent forms. Under capitalism, the development of humanity undergoes significant advance. The powers and potentialities of individuals begin to be freed from the restraints of mystical explanation or sheer ignorance. The antagonism with nature within feudal existence, arising from the alienation from nature, and the subjugation of the forces of production to that nature, begins to be resolved with capitalism. Humans realize that they can control, however imperfectly, themselves and their environment. Marx believed that social change could produce altogether new social forms which dispensed forever with society based on exploitation of human by human, and even of nature by humans.

The account of the individual is closely connected to the progression of capitalism, through which individuals become more aware of themselves and their abilities, powers and needs. This kind of development is the direct outcome of Marx's view of the developing relations of production.

> When we consider bourgeois society in the long view and as a whole, then the final result of the process of social production always appears as the society itself, i.e. the human being itself in its social relations. . . . The conditions and objectifications of the process are themselves equally moments of it, and its only subjects are the individuals, but individuals in mutual relation-ships, which they equally produce and reproduce anew.
>
> (Marx, [1857–8] 1973a, 712)

The success of new kinds of human activity in conjunction with the developing forces of production is to be understood in a number of ways. First, there was the delimiting or cathartic effect on society. Humans are invested with the ability to break down or through the conditions of their existence, and establish a new comprehension of themselves in a world of their making. Second, Marx was making another claim about the nature of capitalist society – that it was producing very favourable conditions under which individuals were freed from mystifications about themselves which served to maintain a system of exploitation.

Marx suggests that some powers of humanity were indeed nascent and remained dormant until the development of capitalism made their expression a concrete reality. History, then, is not just made by living human individuals but also confronts them in the present. History is the context that confines and shapes living human individuals but it does not, cannot, define what it is to be human.

> In the present epoch the domination of material conditions over individuals, and the suppression of individuality by chance, has assumed its sharpest and most universal form, thereby setting individuals a very definite task. It has set them the task of replacing the domination of circumstances and of chance over individuals by the domination of individuals over chance and circumstances.
>
> (Marx, 1973b, 117)

Put another way, Marx is referring to the development of a most extensive autonomy as a principal feature in the historical progress of humankind. This is not the autonomy of Kant, who posits an agent in contrast to the material and social world. Rather, this is an autonomy of being in a more complete and individuated sense. In *Capital*, for instance, Marx sets out in some detail the way that capitalist private property brings about a general pattern of human development. First of all, the change from the fusion of 'the isolated, independent working individual with the conditions of his labour' to 'formally free labour', is a 'metamorphosis' which 'decomposed the old society throughout its depth and breadth' (1976, 928). Certainly this is destruction, for Marx, but it is also a great clearing away of tradition, involving a refreshing disregard for the ostensible limits to the possible, and demonstrating the potential of human social organization. This is in the context, moreover, of 'the development of social production and of the free individuality of the worker himself' (ibid., 929). The framework of individuality and production provides the basis of Marx's developmental approach. As Wood puts it, 'the development or "self-genesis" of man in history is for Marx fundamentally an expansion of man's productive powers' (1981, 33).

> The act of reproduction itself changes not only the objective conditions – e.g. transforming village into town, the wilderness into agricultural clearings, etc. – but the producers change with it, by the emergence of new qualities, by transforming and developing themselves in production, forming new powers and new conceptions, new modes of intercourse, new needs, new speech.
>
> (Marx, 1964, 93)

These two processes – the changes in objective and human conditions – are inseparable, or are elements of the same historical interplay of one upon the other. On this basis Marx is able to extrapolate beyond the relative efficiency and potential material abundance of capitalist society. In the juxtaposition of individual and social production, he was critical of a mode of production which made individuals subservient. Both individuals and social production, equally, are historical products, yet Marx claimed that it was the position of individuals *vis-à-vis* the production process which is the major concern in the organization of society (1976, 493).

> Capitalist production, when considered in isolation from the process of circulation and the excesses of competition, is very economical with the materialized labour incorporated in commodities. Yet, more than any other mode of production, it squanders human lives, or living labour, and not only blood and flesh, but also nerve and brain. Indeed, it is only by dint of the most extravagant waste of individual development that the development of the human race is at all safeguarded and maintained in the epoch of history immediately preceding the conscious reorganization of society.
>
> (Marx, 1959, 88)

Thus Marx distinguished clearly between humankind as a whole and the life of the individual. The development brought about at the level of humankind Marx most definitely wanted to be realized for all individuals. Indeed Marx argued that this was the drift of historical development.

The bedrock of Marx's explanation is the abstraction of the living individual as a subject in history. The existence of humankind as a subject is crucial, because it requires that the subject has content, a content which may not be immediately identifiable, or converted into a list of properties and characteristics. Nevertheless, that content is assumed to exist. That is, the subject, humankind, is not a historical constant but is capable of changing and developing by being culturally expanded and becoming more universal, whereas the object, nature, has remained, at the most general level, the same. Certainly nature has been modified, checked or extended, but it cannot regenerate the changes imposed upon it as a matter of course in the way that human subjects can. This is not a simple change.

> For the first time, nature becomes purely an object for humankind, purely a matter of utility; ceases to be recognized as a power in itself; and the theoretical discovery of its autonomous laws appears merely as a ruse so as to subjugate it to human needs.
>
> (Marx, 1973b, 410)

In particular, the development of humankind is the outcome of this interaction between humanity and nature, identifiable as a propensity and a quality of human nature, one which can therefore have a role in the making of history by the forces of its existence and the drive of its potentiality and capacity:

> the direct production process . . . is then both discipline, as regards the human being in the process of becoming; and, at the same time, practice, experimental science, materially creative and objectifying science, as regards the human being who has become, in whose hand exists, the accumulated knowledge of society.
>
> (Ibid., 712)

Production takes place in the context of the basic *power* of humans to modify nature and their social existence. In so doing they modify themselves, becoming not what they essentially are but what is possible given the development of the forces of production achieved in previous epochs, and under more primitive modes. Humankind, both becoming and stretching the limits of what it is possible to become, makes clear advances over nature, and alters the interaction between nature and society. The fruit of this form of change can be referred to as the progress of individuality, wherein living human beings become individual in so far as their social existence – their practical, sensuous life activity – is more and more under their control, and where their decisions and reactions approximate successively to reality: 'the universal appropriation of nature as well as of the social bond itself by the members of society' (ibid., 409). This move toward control over the material and social world represents a stage in the development of society, 'in comparison to which all earlier ones appear as mere *local developments* of humanity' (ibid., 409–10). This development of humanity leads directly to

> the discovery, creation and satisfaction of new needs arising from society itself; the cultivation of all the qualities of the social human being, production of the same in a form as rich as possible in needs, because rich in qualities and relations – production of this being as the most total and universal social product, for, in order to take gratification in a many-sided way, he must be capable of many pleasures, hence cultured to a high degree – is likewise a condition of production founded on capital.
>
> (Ibid., 410)

Notwithstanding its capitalist character and form (and therefore the brutality of its exploitation), Marx clearly saw the general development of humanity creating the possibility for a specifiable and identifiable role for human agents who are universally rich in needs and culture. Individuality (that propensity to understand and control as a conscious choice) increases dramatically. And with that change, whose midwife was the forces of production, the new relations of production reveal more of the capacities of human nature. If individuality develops in history, then it must mean that control over nature and human history develops, at least as a potentiality.

> Man is equated with self. But the self is only *abstractly* conceived man, man produced by abstraction. Man *is* self. . . . The self abstracted and fixed for itself is man as *abstract egoist*, egoism raised to its pure abstraction in thought.
>
> (Marx, 1975, 387)

For Marx it is not just the objective world of economic relations that counts. Individuality also relates to the degree of autonomy that is to be found in any social organization. This autonomy refers to the 'limitations of general self-consciousness', such that Marx wished to deny that all individuals were allied by the level of their consciousness with the rest of society. But in this rejection of the Hegelian Absolute Idea also lies the correct way to perceive individuals and their self-consciousness. At the level of theory, individuality is to be seen as a result of long history, the outcome of the progressive development of the forces of production. As such individuality is a materialist conception since it has developed entirely in the context of the labour of humans under successive modes of production, and incorporates the progressive shift to more complex relations of production, which implies the extension and articulation of the faculties of humans (Forbes, 1989a).

The real achievement of capitalism is the development of human wealth. The wealth of humankind means to be faced by a combination of daunting challenges and exhilarating freedoms. Control over nature is not enough; Marx also dares humankind to take control over its own (human) nature. That is, humankind is the responsibility of every individual in the course of their own life. Individualistic decisions with an exclusive focus on the self become a poor form of the choices of the free individual, who will always choose with full awareness as a member of humankind. It becomes impossible to live for oneself in the liberal-bourgeois expectation of a greater social good arising magically or mysteriously. Marx enjoins human individuals to express their full potential, without limitation, taking into account only that such potential has been brought into existence by historical progression. The manifestation of the creative potential of each individual serves as its own teleological justification, and explains his preference for communism over capitalism or barbarism. Communism would mean 'the liberation of each single individual', 'the control and conscious mastery of these powers which, born of the action of men on one another, have till now overawed and governed men as powers completely alien to them', and 'the development of a totality of capacities in the individuals themselves' (Marx, 1970, 55, 92). Only then will 'self-activity coincide with material life, which corresponds to the development of individuals into complete individuals and the casting-off of all natural limitations' (ibid., 93).

Marx regarded the existing development of the individual as an achievement in its own right. The historical process produces conscious, determining individuals who live beyond the constraints and definitions of economically and politically defined class structures. They are to live, co-operatively and realistically, in respect of the realms of necessity and freedom. Agency and autonomy are key features of these individuals, representing a naturalism at a high level of cognitive, social, and historical development.

NIETZSCHE'S EXTRA-MORAL INDIVIDUALITY

Nietzsche's approach to the individual in history offers a different perspective on the possibility of naturalism. He establishes a dialectic not of materialism but of change. That is, he is concerned with the way in which reality and appearance are intertwined such that we confuse the two, so preventing ourselves from seeing where change has already occurred, and is about to take place. The individual is a principal site of historical change, and the first task for Nietzsche is to destabilize the convention that the subject exists.

To achieve this, Nietzsche must assemble the necessary elements for understanding society, history, and human existence. In his rejection of the dichotomy between willing and doing, for example, he attacks two popular fictions concerning the notion of the self: first, that there is an inner being that is somehow frustrated and prevented from acting authentically in society; and second that such a self must will itself into being and doing:

> popular morality . . . separates strength from expressions of strength, as if there were a substratum behind the strong man which was free to express strength or not to do so. But there is no such substratum; there is no 'being' behind doing, affecting, becoming; 'the doer' is merely a fiction added to the deed – the deed is everything.
>
> (Nietzsche, 1966b, I, 13)

Instead of looking for a being behind an action Nietzsche sees action as a manifestation of will to power in that action. There is no self-conscious subject expressing an inner self by a deliberate choice of actions. Rather, it is the sum of actions that constitutes being, revealing the orientation of the whole being toward life. Nietzsche also denies that society can ever progress and improve itself under the impetus of socially conscious political activity. For him, such a reification of the social being places a limitation on a fully human existence. 'If we wished to postulate a goal adequate to life, it could not coincide with any category of conscious life; it would rather have to explain all of them as a means to itself' (Nietzsche, 1968a, 707).

This does not imply a circular or merely mentalistic 'consciousness of consciousness'. The will to power operates to bring a person into a position of power over something, in the process of which that person changes. However, one does not exercise will to power with strict teleological intent, in Nietzsche's view, as if the will were a guiding consciousness 'behind' action.

> The fundamental mistake is simply that, instead of understanding consciousness as a tool and particular aspect of the total life, we posit it as the standard and the condition of life that is of supreme value: it is the erroneous perspective of *a parte ad totem* – which is why all philosophies are instinctively trying to imagine a total consciousness, a consciousness involved in all life and will, in all that occurs, a 'spirit', 'God'.
>
> (Nietzsche, 1968a, 707)

Consciousness is relegated from a position of power over individual and collective action and progress to a secondary utility of the primary force of will to power. The devaluation of consciousness as a precursor to positive action highlights the subjective, value-laden cloudiness of rational thought processes as they strive for metaphysical comprehension of *telos* and essences. For him, the act of becoming conscious is but a midpoint in the process of action being perfected, and becoming automatic: 'in such a way that we are conscious of a condition only when the supposed causal chain associated with it has entered consciousness' (Nietzsche, 1968, 479). Consciousness-related action, therefore, will be contrived and imperfect in the sense that such action is not autonomous and independent from value-orientations currently held at the conscious level. It is only when consciousness recedes and action becomes unconscious that one achieves 'a perfect automatism' (Nietzsche, 1968a, 523).

> All perfect acts are unconscious and no longer subject to will; consciousness is the expression of an imperfect and often morbid state in a person. Personal reflection as conditioned by will, as consciousness, as reasoning with dialectics, is a caricature, a kind of self-contradiction – A degree of consciousness makes perfection impossible – Form of *play-acting*.
>
> (Nietzsche, 1968a, 289)

Nietzsche's deprecation of the introspective and self-aware individual illustrates how radical a departure is his explanation of consciousness when compared to the image and function of consciousness implicit in liberal individualist thought. The rational and virtuous individual, constructing selfhood by carefully expanding consciousness and moral probity is no ideal for Nietzsche (1966a, 30).

The hierarchy of sub-conscious, conscious, and automatic states that Nietzsche develops suggests that there must be a redefinition of the ontological development of humanity. It is a decisive move away from the conception of the individual as a unified subject progressing toward perfectibility. This is an attack upon the popular view, that humanity can only advance through society, and will continually improve as a result of meaningful social relations: 'All communities make men – somehow, somewhere, sometime "common" ' (1966a, 284). In so doing Nietzsche rejects the notion of the single subject, or the abstract individual.

> The assumption of one single subject is perhaps unnecessary; perhaps it is just as permissible to assume a multiplicity of subjects whose interaction and struggle is the basis of our thought and our consciousness in general? A kind of aristocracy in 'cells' in which dominion resides? To be sure, an aristocracy of equals, used to ruling jointly and understanding how to command?
> *My hypothesis*: the subject as multiplicity.
>
> (Nietzsche, 1968a, 490)

This hypothesis undermines any faith in the realm of conscious reasoning and, by implication, truth itself. If the subject is a multiplicity that defines our consciousness, and not vice-versa, then the demand of the hitherto 'rational' mind for certainty is frustrated, or, more accurately diagnosed as a chimera, a fantasy. In Nietzsche's opinion, this problem has been avoided in several ways, notably in the belief in either a 'saving grace' of immortality after death, world historical processes, the perfectibility of humankind, or the importance of a separate individualness which calls for a limited state and a society of negative freedoms:

> 'nothing has any meaning' – this melancholy sentence means 'All meaning lies in intention, and if intention is altogether lacking, then meaning is altogether lacking, too.' In accordance with this valuation, one was constrained to transfer the value of life to a 'life after death', or to the progressive development of ideas or of mankind or of the people or beyond mankind; but with that man had arrived at a *progressus in infinitum* of purposes: one was at

last constrained to make a place for oneself in the 'world process'.

(Nietzsche, 1968a, 666)

Nietzsche's characterization of wo/man as will to power in a world of energy in continual flux creates a demanding and uncompromising position from which to view human development (1968a, 1067). He is suspicious of any attempt to structure human progress through rationalistic or moralistic prescriptive theories, and regards the need to belong within or create an ordered system as a moral (or philosophical) capitulation and a compete lack of integrity. In this context the emerging nihilism of the nineteenth century, with its suggestion that there exists a certainty that all is uncertain and false, may have been treated charitably by Nietzsche as an understandably pessimistic reaction to Enlightenment attitudes toward existence. On the other hand, he rejects the pessimistic reaction in principle, on the grounds that 'modern pessimism is an expression of the *modern* world – not of the world of existence' (Nietzsche, 1968a, 34). Nietzsche's partial acceptance of nihilism is thus largely on the basis that it can bring about the necessary destruction of the valuations of the modern world, and the cleansing of modernity of the false and facile prescriptions of Christianity and contemporary social theory – both democratic and socialistic (1968a, 784). Nietzsche can condone nihilism's cathartic negativism, therefore, in order to demonstrate more clearly a contrary and more sophisticated understanding of wo/man. It is Zarathustra who informs us of a vital and positive aspect inherent in overcoming the modern world.

And life confided this secret to me: 'Behold', it said, 'I am *that which must always overcome itself*. Indeed, you call it a will to procreate or a drive to an end, to something higher, farther, more manifold; but all this is one, and one secret.'

(Nietzsche, 1968b, 227)

Thus Nietzsche conjoins will to power and the eternal recurrence by emphasizing that wo/man is life, implying that wo/man is in a continual struggle against life and therefore him or herself. Of even greater significance, however, is Nietzsche's perception that in such a struggle against these inseparables of life and self wo/man will be transfigured by the process of constantly overcoming at least some of the conditions of self and life confronted at each moment. 'What is great in man is that he is a bridge and not an end: what can be loved in man is that he is an *overture* and a *going under*' (ibid.,

127). By expanding the notion of overcoming to incorporate the *development* of wo/man, rather than seeing it simply as an aspect of behaviour, Nietzsche conceptualizes humans not merely as a species, but human within a cultural-biological typology of civilization. It is Nietzsche's suggestion, therefore, that wo/man with knowledge of self will disappear at each overcoming, to be replaced by a new being. The act of overcoming will continue, since it is fundamental that each new being will strive to overcome itself, even though it can have no conscious or unconscious perception of a future state.

> Put briefly: perhaps the entire evolution of the spirit is a question of the body: it is the history of the development of a higher body that emerges into our higher sensibility. The organic is rising to yet higher levels. Our lust for knowledge of nature is a means through which the body desires to perfect itself. . . . In the long run, it is not a question of man at all: he is to be overcome.
>
> (Nietzsche, 1968a, 676)

While Nietzsche's articulation of this new wo/man, and the vocabulary he uses to evoke the process of transformation, are obscure and fundamentally different from the idioms of Enlightenment perfectibilitarianism or Marxist materialism, it is worth noting that Nietzsche is engaging in quite the same theoretical optimism, namely, *that wo/man in history shall preside over a personal re-creation*. Nietzsche agrees that the false individuals of contemporary society must be transcended, but he stresses the transcendence, the becoming, rather than the new or emerging form of being:

> whatever exists, having somehow come into being, is again and again reinterpreted to new ends, taken over, transformed and redirected by some power superior to it; all events in the organic world are a subduing, a *becoming master*, and all subduing and becoming master involves a fresh interpretation, an adaptation through which any previous 'meaning' and 'purpose' are necessarily obscured or obliterated.
>
> (Nietzsche, 1966b, II, 12)

The emphasis on becoming serves as a criticism of any approach which uses an analysis of a particular society to formulate prescriptions for a new society and to project the behaviour and beliefs of its constituents. Nietzsche denies that there can be such knowledge beyond any one transformation of wo/man, because each change demands an entirely fresh evaluation of what wo/man is – in effect, a new 'genealogy of morals'. Such an evaluation, since it is in the context of a new being, is unrelated to any prior set of valuations that went to form the basis of the initial social criticism, and the valuations that go to make up a social criticism have no automatic relation to future states of wo/man (Forbes, 1989b). Rather, all valuations concern wo/man becoming a new being, applying to the transfigurative process as it unfolds, and not to the new being when that occurs.

1 Becoming does not aim at a *final state*, does not flow into 'being'.
2 Becoming is not a merely *apparent state*; perhaps the whole world of beings is mere appearance.
3 Becoming is of equivalent value every moment; the sum of its values always remains the same; in other words, it has no value at all, for anything against which to measure it, and in relation to which the word 'value' would have meaning, is lacking. *The total value of the world cannot be evaluated*; consequently philosophical pessimism belongs among comical things.

(Nietzsche, 1968a, 708)

Thus Nietzsche rejects all ideality and teleology. In doing so he appears to be offering, with no apology to those interested in certitude or scientific method, a vision of recurring differences of becoming, and so redefining our world as a 'fable and approximation on the basis of a meagre sum of observations' (Nietzsche, 1968a, 616). The false world, the one seen and lived in, is one to which wo/man's will to power is opposed, and which it seeks to overcome. Failing to oppose this world, and every definition it offers of itself, is to collaborate with that fable. 'To impose upon becoming the world of being – that is the supreme will to power' (Nietzsche, 1968a, 617). Nietzsche's antipathy to the fable of the modern world provides an illuminating juxtaposition of core ideas in his thought. His concept of transfiguration is based upon both the notion of wo/man as will to power, and the idea of eternal recurrence.

The theory of eternal recurrence is, on his own admission, a restatement of the Heraclitean concept that the whole world is involved in constant change, and that change alone is changeless (EH, 'Birth of Tragedy', 3). For Nietzsche, the concept demands of wo/man that s/he learn not only to accept things as they are, but be able to cope with a future that will consist of things occurring as they have. Thus wo/man must know that s/he is never an end toward which s/he must strive. Rather, s/he must continue to struggle toward each new becoming. Struggle, therefore, features as an underlying principle both in Nietzsche's presentation of will to power and in his theory of eternal recurrence. The will to power, as we have seen, is an affect of becoming, imposing 'automatism' on being. This becoming is not then an end, but a new beginning and a new becoming of recurring will to power.

Rebelling against the studied negativism of nihilism, Nietzsche attempts to incorporate, theoretically and practically, the positive aspects of nihilism into his revitalizing celebration of existence itself. In this way, Nietzsche was careful to differentiate himself from nihilism, and indeed all popular social and philosophical move-ments, while still being able to validate some basic nihilistic propositions. For example, the negativism of nihilism was at least functionally progressive since it led to the destruction of current moralities, a process Nietzsche regarded as a necessary cleansing therapy for wo/man. Nihilism was not an end point or a mere disintegration of existing things, but a preparation for the future.

> I perceived that the state of disintegration, in which individual natures can perfect themselves as never before – is an image and isolated example of existence in general. To the paralysing sense of general disintegration and incompleteness I opposed the *eternal recurrence*.
>
> (Nietzsche, 1968a, 417)

In effect, Nietzsche shows the nihilistic critique of Christian morality to be a necessary, but not sufficient, condition for the understanding and acceptance of human existence. Still on this methodological plane, the theory of eternal recurrence serves as yet a further, necessary, therapeutic process, which must remain – in the long term – equally insufficient for the development of the sovereign individual. The archetypal Zarathustra, Nietzsche rejoices in the task he set himself of destroying the hold of conventional morality over humanity. Nietzsche did not wish to supplant contemporary valuations with communitarian ideals based upon individualism and the possibility of a just and well-ordered sovereign state. Although Nietzsche gives some indications that his ideas have specific ramifications for the future structure of society, our attention is focused repeatedly on the individual as one important first principle. Nietzsche criticizes all views of human nature offering specific and well-defined sets of characteristics that, allowed their free play, would constitute pretended descriptions of human beings. His concept of continual becoming insists upon the impossibility of any original notion of what man will, much less should, eventually be.

Nietzsche views wo/man in the context of personal orientation, not to nature (morality), but to *existence* (the *affect* of will to power). This goes beyond valuations of wo/man's behaviour as real or unreal, natural or unnatural, social or unsocial, moral or immoral. Instead of seeing individuals in a universalistic sense, Nietzsche differentiates between types of wo/man as well as types within a single individual. Just as he noted that slave and master moral value-orientations will exist side by side within the one psyche, he makes his appeal to higher beings as a category, and the higher being within the individual, to overcome false interpretations of self and the modern world. Thus Nietzsche avoids the need for a class analysis. If various representations of humanity are present within a single individual, then that individual is responsible for personal existence, and it is not just the social milieu which dictates the resulting level of humanity. Moreover, Nietzsche's thought constitutes an attack on the objectification of individuals and social forces, as if they can be separated and then analysed.

> That things possess a constitution in themselves quite apart from interpretation and subjectivity, is a quite idle hypothesis: it presupposes that interpretation and subjectivity are not essential, that the thing freed from all relationships would still be a thing.
> (Nietzsche, 1968a, 560)

His rejection of the notion of a 'thing-in-itself' can be applied with some success to the existence of an abstract individual, and Nietzsche's criticism is indeed highly reminiscent of Marx's critique on this issue (Lukes, 1973, 75–7). Nietzsche implicitly, and Marx explicitly, perceive the idea of the individual abstracted from the social environment to be a fundamental impossibility. Any agreement is short-lived, however, since Nietzsche also rejects the 'objectivity' inherent in Marx's materialistic assumptions concerning the development of the individual.

> Conversely, the apparent *objective* character of things: could it not be merely a difference of degree within the subjective? – that perhaps that which changes slowly presents itself to us as 'objectively' enduring, being, 'in-itself' – that the objective is only a false concept of a genus and an antithesis *within* the subjective?
> (Nietzsche, 1968a, 560)

This calls for a restructuring of our personal orientation to the world, however difficult that may be.

> Means of *enduring it*: the revaluation of all values. No longer joy in certainty but in uncertainty; no longer 'cause and effect' but the continually creative; no longer will to preservation but to power; no longer the humble expression, 'everything is *merely* subjective', but 'it is also *our* work! – Let us be proud of it!'
>
> (Ibid., 1059)

Only at this stage in the development of wo/man is it possible to assess the types of changes that Nietzsche regards as conducive to progress for humankind. On the basis of his genealogy of morals, the will to power is seen as creative of the disposition of wo/man to conquer the conditions of life, while the theory of eternal recurrence encourages a consciousness of strength, thus permitting the old valuations of morality to be questioned and displaced.

This amounts to a reinstatement of the psychological 'instinct' as the basic ordering principle for individual life. This is wholly superior to a merely socially determined existence and is for Nietzsche a potent and meaningful naturalism that is alone capable of producing progress for humankind. This naturalism is a harsh and demanding one, presupposing that the social nature of humankind is not a moral value at all. It is at last possible, Nietzsche argues, to see that the idea of the social being has served its specific purpose for nature and humankind. 'To breed an animal *with the right to make promises* – is not this the paradoxical task that nature has set herself in the case of man? Is it not the real problem concerning man?' (Nietzsche, 1966b, II, 1).

The importance that Nietzsche places on the right to make promises signals a demanding reappraisal of the prerequisites for real and enduring change in the world, with singular reference to the individual. The individual here is a representative of humankind rather than a collection of abstract entities. For this reason, individuality cannot be assessed in terms of autonomy and freedom with respect to the requirements that society imposes. Instead, individuality is an achievement of the species. In this respect Nietzsche is both distant from and close to the approach of Marx, since both demand great things of individuals, in terms of their ability to deal with the world at a high level of abstraction and understanding:

> man must first have learned to distinguish necessary events from

chance ones, to think causally, to see and anticipate distant eventualities as if they belonged to the present, to decide with certainty what is the goal and what the means to it, and in general be able to calculate and compute. Man must first of all become *calculable, regular, necessary*, even in his own image of himself, if he is to be able to stand security for *his own future*, which is what one who promises does!

(Ibid.)

The individual, then, is not given autonomy and freedom within a social structure, but develops the capacity for action that is autonomous and independent from what are seen as physical and social realities. Nietzsche definitely breaks new ground here, surpassing the flights of fancy in the *German Ideology* (Marx and Engels, 1973) over the ideal communist existence with a much more credible vision of post-revolutionary, transfigured existence. Most challenging of all is the notion that an individual could, in an age of positivist social theorizing, *know* the intended goal, promise to achieve it, and be aware that all succeeding events *must* produce that goal. Nietzsche does not succinctly justify this proposition, nor does he hedge his bets by relying on faith or fate: he insists that the individual is the source and provider of absolute certainty regarding goal and action. The right to make promises is no more than the logical conclusion to his entire philosophical labour on humans, morals and society. It leads him to argue that the sovereign individual has been made possible by the very social and moral processes that he catalogued and condemned in his genealogy of morals and critique of philosophy.

If we place ourselves at the end of this tremendous process, where the tree at last brings forth fruit, where society and custom at last reveal *what they have simply been the means to: then we discover that the ripest fruit is the sovereign individual*, like only to himself, liberated again from the morality of custom, autonomous and supramoral (for 'autonomous' and 'moral' are mutually exclusive), in short, the man who has his own independent, protracted will and the *right to make promises*.

(Nietzsche, 1966b, II, 2)

The sovereign individual, then, represents the achievement of the overcoming of the necessary foundations of social morality. Such an individual becomes strong in accordance with the degree of independence from external social and moral constraints, and it is at this point in his thought that Nietzsche may reintroduce the concept of willing. It is the will of the sovereign individual which enables him or her to take control of the conditions of existence. Instead of merely *possessing* free will, the sovereign individual *commands* will, and makes it a servant to the totally human activity of valuing and creating values. It is this which transforms individuality into a new kind of power, and establishes a new potential for social existence.

> The 'free' man, this possessor of a protracted and unbreakable will, also possesses his *measure of value*. . . . The proud awareness of the extraordinary privilege of *responsibility*, the consciousness of this rare freedom, this power over oneself and fate, has in his case penetrated to the profoundest depths and become instinct, the dominating instinct.
>
> (Ibid.)

With this image of freedom and responsibility, this combination of power and autonomy, Nietzsche completes a complex historical picture of the emergence and development of individuality in history. It culminates in a confidence in the most demanding of moral, and therefore political and social, revolutions.

CONCLUSION

Marx and Nietzsche foresee, expect and desire the most radical social change, and argue that its inevitability arises out of an explicitly historical approach to social understanding. Both share responsibility for creating the perspectival prism for the twentieth century. They are united in their rejection of the abstract individual in all philosophy. Each provides a foundation for the exploration of individuality, and presages either a Nietzschean kind of radical individual autonomy or its Marxian counterpoint of a realized social individuality. Marx argued for an historical materialist analysis of the individual in history, while Nietzsche concentrates on a genealogical account of the development of individuality.

The second major commonality concerns agency. Both need an account of agency which will permit judgements about the quality of human action in society, and both see agency as something to be achieved as a higher form of naturalism. The reiteration of instinct and the powerful reconceptualization of agency implicit in Nietzsche's thought demonstrates a naturalism which finds its complement in Marx's focus on a historicized human nature and vision of free individuality. As Richard Schacht observes:

> Rather like Marx . . . Nietzsche thus advocates and exemplifies what might be called an *anthropological shift* in philosophy. By this I mean a general reorientation of philosophical thinking, involving the attainment of what might be called an *anthropological optic* whereby to carry out the program of a de-deification and reinterpretation of ourselves and our world.
>
> (Schacht, 1988, 71)

Nietzsche's desire was to reinterpret conceptions of history and their usefulness to existence in general and the future in particular, in order to develop and precipitate necessary and progressive change in the world. He describes a different and delimiting view of the human condition notable for its rejection of an essentially static description of the human individual and the concept of the unified self. By definition, wo/man is constantly undergoing change, such that transfiguration is the notion that best conveys the sense of wo/man continually becoming something s/he is not already. That this process should remain non-teleological, infinite and even dangerous presents no difficulty to Nietzsche, but it does challenge any political thought, any political morality which seeks certainty in society.

The contrast with Marx's attempt to encourage a rational, controlled transition to a new social order suggests that the Enlightenment modernism and twentieth-century post-modernism is played out in the differing approaches to the individual discussed here. This had led to the suggestion that Marx's logical heir is Habermas, who inevitably finds himself in conflict with Foucault and Derrida taking the Nietzschean turn. However, the different histories of the individual demonstrate that Nietzsche and Marx share a concern with progress, whether it is of a moral or material kind. As such, it is more accurate to describe their contributions by seeing Nietzsche as the Dionysus to Marx's Apollo. They, and their accounts of the individual in history, presuppose each other. Both thinkers locate reality and social assertiveness about life outside morality but in a valuational system which is human and individual. Change, like individuality, is available. The tasks for the political philosopher, in other words, derive not from method and approach, but from an exploration of ourselves in history. Nietzsche 'follows' the achievements of Marx by adding yet another vast dimension to the potential for human understanding.

BIBLIOGRAPHY

Dallmayr, F. (1981), *Twilight of Subjectivity*, Amherst, Massachusetts University Press.

Forbes, I. (1989a), 'Marxian Individualism', in M. Cowling and L. Wilde (eds), *Approaches to Marx*, Milton Keynes, Open University Press, 135–48.

—— (1989b), 'Nietzsche, Modernity and Politics', in J. R. Gibbins (ed.), *Contemporary Political Culture*, London, Sage, 218–36.

—— (1990), *Marx and the New Individual*, London, Unwin Hyman.

Love, N. S. (1986), *Marx, Nietzsche, and Modernity*, New York, Columbia University Press.

Lukes, S. (1973), *Individualism*, Oxford, Blackwell.

Marx, K. (1959), *Capital*, vol. III, F. Engels (ed.), London, Lawrence & Wishart.

—— (1964), *Pre-Capitalist Economic Formations*, E. Hobsbawm (ed.), London, Lawrence & Wishart.

—— (1973a), *Grundrisse*, Harmondsworth, Penguin.

—— (1973b), *The German Ideology*, C. J. Arthur (ed.), London, Lawrence & Wishart.

—— (1975), 'Economic and Philosophical Manuscripts', in K. Marx, *Early Writings*, trans. R. Livingstone, Harmondsworth, Penguin, 1975, 279–401.

—— (1976), *Capital*, vol. I, Harmondsworth, Penguin.

Nietzsche, F. [1886] (1966a), *Beyond Good and Evil*, in *Basic Writings of Nietzsche*, W. Kaufmann (ed.), New York, Modern Library.

—— [1887] (1966b), *Genealogy of Morals*, in *Basic Writings of Nietzsche*, W. Kaufmann (ed.), New York, Modern Library.

—— (1968a), *The Will to Power*, W. Kaufmann (ed.), New York, Random House.

—— [1883–5] (1968b), *Thus Spoke Zarathustra*, in *The Portable Nietzsche*, W. Kaufmann (ed.), New York, Viking.

O'Neill, J. (ed.) (1973), *Modes of Individualism and Collectivism*, London, Heinemann.

Schacht, R. (1988), 'Nietzsche's *Gay Science*, Or, How to Naturalize Cheerfully', in *Reading Nietzsche*, R. C. Solomon and K. M. Higgins (eds), New York and Oxford, Oxford University Press, 68–86.

Warren, M. (1988), *Nietzsche and Political Thought*, Cambridge, Mass., and London, MIT Press.

Wood, A. (1981), *Karl Marx*, London, Routledge & Kegan Paul.

7 Nietzsche and the problem of the will in modernity

Keith Ansell-Pearson

No other concept in Nietzsche's corpus is more controversial and has met with such a wide variety of interpretations than that of will to power. Heidegger demands that we interpret the notion in terms of Nietzsche's consummation of the modern philosophical project which begins with the Cartesian positing of the human *ego* as the source of all meaning and value in the world. On this reading, the will to power signals the 'triumph' of man's technological will to domination and mastery which characterizes the *Machtpolitik* of the modern age. A more common reading is one which understands will to power in terms of a psychological metaphysics where the 'power' (over persons and things) posited in the notion replaces 'life' or 'happiness' as the object of the 'will'. In this manner Nietzsche's central philosophical notion is understood as little more than an inversion of Schopenhauer's positing of a will to life: where Schopenhauer demands that we negate the blind and destructive will, Nietzsche teaches that we should affirm its nihilistic striving. There is also a well-established tradition which argues that the notion of will to power is best understood as a contribution to an understanding of the nature of human autonomy and self-realization. A recent examination of the relationship between Nietzsche and political thought by Mark Warren argues that when construed in terms of a philosophy of praxis the doctrine of will to power can provide the basis for the articulation of a 'postmodern' conception of human agency in which the autonomous will is conceived not as an abstract metaphysical essence, but as the historical realization of certain social and cultural practices.[1] Warren argues for a marriage of Kant and Nietzsche in which a philosophy of power (where power denotes the self-reflective desire of the human subject to become a self-determining centre of action) is combined with an ethic of equal respect derived from Kant's notion of a kingdom of ends. It is with this Kantian supplementation of Nietzsche that Warren believes some of the worst excesses of the exploitative will to power can be overcome.

In this essay I propose to examine the notion of will to power (*der Wille zur Macht*) in terms of its status as a metaphor for self-legislation within the context of Hegel's recognition of the notion of the will as a defining moment of modernity. My argument is structured as follows. First, I shall discuss the importance of Rousseau's account of the will for understanding the problematic of modernity and then examine Hegel's critical appraisal of the attempts by Rousseau and Kant to establish the will as the foundation of 'right'. Second, I shall examine the meaning of 'will' and 'power' in the formulation 'will to power', and then move on to locate the nature of Nietzsche's challenge to Rousseau and Kant. Nietzsche's challenge, I shall argue, lies in posing the relationship between autonomy and morality as one of mutual exclusivity. Thus, a marriage of Kant and Nietzsche is not as easy as one might wish. The key question which arises in this context is the one raised by Alasdair MacIntyre: to what extent does Nietzsche's conception of the autonomous will of the supra-ethical sovereign individual represent not an alternative to the conceptual scheme of liberal individualist modernity, but rather one more representative moment of its internal unfolding?[2] This essay is an attempt to outline a context in which this question can be fruitfully posed.

I

The notion of the 'will' is without doubt one of the most unclear notions in philosophy. Replete with ambiguities and contradictions it is used to explain and account for a wide range of experiences. On the one hand, it is conceived as an appetite or desire (Hobbes's 'last appetite in deliberation').[3] On the other hand, it is elevated to the status of a moral causality; that is, the fact that actions can be attributed to a source in free agency is what gives them their distinctly *moral* character. The key notion implied here is that actions are 'intentional'. We can only experience a sense of injury if we believe that someone acted with the *intention* of harming us. As Rousseau noted, it is the intention to hurt, not the harm done, that constitutes the sense of moral injury or wrongdoing we experience.[4]

One commentator has clarified this double reading of the will by drawing a distinction between the 'will' viewed in terms of a physiological psychology, where it is conceived simply as the efficient cause of action; not as a faculty that can legitimize what is elected, and the 'will' conceived as an elective faculty (a free causality) which binds us to something once we have freely chosen it.[5] Considered as an elective faculty the notion of the will has its origins in Christianity.[6] Modern thought politicizes the notion and, beginning with Rousseau, voluntarism becomes a foundational moment of the conception of the relationship between the individual and society characteristic of modernity. Expressed at its weakest the modern self declares to itself: I shall obey only those powers to which I have freely granted my consent. It is the 'will' which is located as the source and ground of this consent.

Rousseau, for whom thinking about the problem of the will constituted a confrontation with the very abyss of philosophy, both clarifies and confuses key facets of the nature of the mysterious entity we call the 'will'. For Rousseau the 'will' is what defines human freedom. Rousseau esteems human freedom so much that he believes that for a person to renounce their freedom is tantamount to them renouncing their status as a human being ('the rights and duties of humanity'). It is through the 'will' that freedom, whether natural, moral, or civil, exists. But we can only 'know' the will through the 'sentiment' of our own individual will. For Rousseau willing is a purely spiritual act which transcends all laws of determinism. The 'will' is a faculty of the soul which inaugurates spontaneous motion, that is, motion which is self-determining and not externally caused (autonomous, as opposed to heteronomous, in Kant's vocabulary). For Rousseau any 'free' action is made up of two factors, the moral and the physical, that is, the 'will' which determines it and the 'power' which executes it.[7] Willing discloses its nature through doing. It is the experience of a free will, in particular the resistance of instinct, which gives a person a sense of their distinctive human nature. Why? Because, says Rousseau, it is through the recognition that one has the capacity not to obey but to resist that we gain a consciousness of our freedom.[8] However, such resistance is only possible through the faculty of judgement – 'the power of comparing and judging'. (It is on the relationship between will and judgement that Rousseau's confusion begins in that he construes the will as both the *ground* of judgement and as *guided* by it.)

Rousseau shows quite brilliantly that having a sense of *power* over one's self and one's environment is dependent on the experience of a free will. It is a perspective shared by Nietzsche when he argues that the will is not only a complex of sensation and thinking but, above all, an 'affect of command' (BGE 19). Considered in such terms the 'will', Nietzsche says, is 'the distinguishing feature of sovereignty and of strength' (GS 347). Rousseau's understanding of the will, however, is faced with a number of problems when the attempt is made to establish the principle of free will as the principle of morality (that is, determining whether actions are 'good' or 'bad'). It is here that Nietzsche's understanding of willing takes a radical turn away from the original insights of Rousseau.

In Rousseau the notion of free will is closely allied to his belief in the natural goodness of humanity. On the one hand he believes that the origin of 'evil' lies in man: 'Providence has made him free that he may choose the good and refuse the evil'.[9] But on the other hand, he maintains that the free will wills only the good. All wrongdoing is the result of external causes whether that be a weak will or social degeneration. Here we touch upon a crucial difference in the thought of Rousseau and Nietzsche. Rousseau believes in a natural order of the self which corresponds to a natural moral world-order of good and evil. 'Wickedness' is caused by the self-interest or vanity (excessive *amour-propre*) that is the product of degenerate social conventions and is a purely artificial sentiment. Against the rule of self-interest Rousseau claims that 'the eternal laws of nature and of order do exist'.[10] Moreover, 'if there is no God, the wicked are right and the good man is nothing but a fool'.[11] Nietzsche seeks to undermine the basis of Rousseau's faith – a faith in morality – by teaching that life has to be understood as being *beyond* good and evil. Nietzsche argues that what we call 'evil' may be no more than the result of a slave revolt of morality by which certain actions are declared to be the result of vanity and pride (hence 'bad' in Rousseau's schema) and other actions the result of 'good' sentiments of pity and humility. In this way Nietzsche attempts to separate the 'will' from notions of moral judgement, and to posit human action as being beyond the opposition of 'good' and 'evil'. Good and evil actions have to be understood in terms of a necessary creative entwinement.

In Rousseau we see that the status of the will is ambiguous in that although it is posited as the ground of 'right', of political legitimacy and sovereignty, it must also be recognized as the source of the kind of excessive *amour-propre* which has led to a degenerate civilization and the rule of an illegitimate social contract in political life based on a purely artificial moral inequality. In Kant, as in Hegel later, a distinction is made between *der Wille* and *die Willkür* as a way of distinguishing between the will as source of command and sovereignty (the legislating will) and the will as a faculty of choice and arbitrary preference, the latter being no more than the reflection of the personal desires of the individual subject and not something inherently rational and universal. Hegel overcomes the ambiguity of the will with the paradoxical idea that the will must learn to *will* its own will. Interestingly, the same idea is to be found in Nietzsche in the form of Zarathustra's teaching that willing liberates because it creates (Z, 'Of the Spirit of Gravity').[12] As we will see, a similar contrast to that made between the capricious will and the reflective will can also be seen to inform Nietzsche's thinking on will to power in that the notion defines both the basic human instinct for growth and development (for 'freedom'), which could take the form of relationships of exploitation and domination, and the noble ideal of self-mastery in which the emphasis is placed on attaining power over oneself and where the exercise of power over others is seen as a mark, not of strength, but of weakness.

Hegel follows Rousseau in constructing a philosophy on the principles of political right on the basis of a notion of will.[13] In paragraph 258 of *The Philosophy of Right*, for example, he commends Rousseau for adducing the will as the principle of the modern state. For Hegel the modernity of Rousseau consists in his attempt to establish the principle of the autonomous will as the principle of *freedom*. As Rousseau put it in his famous definition: 'The mere impulse of our appetites is slavery, while obedience to a law we prescribe to ourselves is liberty'.[14] For Hegel it is the 'right of subjectivity', that is, the right of the individual to be free as an individual, as opposed to free as a bourgeois, a Jew, a Catholic, or a Protestant, etc., which constitutes the difference between antiquity and modernity, and which is captured in Rousseau's definition of freedom.[15] It is Kant who takes Rousseau's definition of liberty one step further by conceiving the free will as one which is entirely free of all empirical determination. The will is now defined as the capacity to act in accordance with maxims of action which are objective and universalizable. The key question which emerges for modern thought is whether it is possible to arrive at a notion of the political – the realm of the public and the universal – from something which is particular and contingent, namely the 'will'. It is a problem which is clearly evident in Rousseau's beguiling and provocative formulation of the general will. Rousseau's definition of liberty as self-legislation has to be seen in the wider context of his radical attempt to overcome the antinomies of modern political life (consent and coercion, autonomy and authority, etc.) by showing that there is no necessary opposition between the autonomous individual will and the social law. The paradoxes of Rousseau's thought result from his attempt to discover a vocabulary which will demonstrate this overcoming. However, the key question which arises for modern political thought is whether a social ethic of community is possible on the basis of the primacy of the individual will. One of Rousseau's most pertinent critics on this point is Hegel.

Hegel criticizes Rousseau for conceiving the general will as no more than the common element among particular wills and not as the absolutely rational element in the will. Hegel links Rousseau's teaching on the general will with the tyrannical turn taken by the French Revolution. Tyranny comes about when the attempt is made to create an immediate identity between the particular and the universal. What is missing from Rousseau's conception of the general will, of his conception of the relationship between individual and society, is a notion of mediation. Rousseau defines the fundamental problem of political theory as that of creating 'a form of association which will defend and protect with the whole common force the person and goods of each associate, and in which each, while uniting himself with all, may still obey himself alone and remain as free as before'.[16] Quite rightly Hegel accuses Rousseau of being disingenuous here, for in becoming a moral being (a citizen), the individual will not remain 'as free as before', but will in fact *become* free. The transition from nature to society (from a condition of natural liberty to civil liberty) brings about a transformation in human nature, and implies that freedom must be either restricted or transformed. Rousseau himself recognized this: 'The passage from the state of nature to the civil state produces a very remarkable change in the nature of man, by substituting justice for instinct in his conduct, and by giving his actions the morality they formerly lacked.'[17]

In detecting duplicity in Rousseau's formulation of the antinomies of modern political life Hegel in fact misreads the context of that formulation. It should be said in Rousseau's defence that his central insight into modernity is that given the reality of civil society, a society of atomized sovereign individuals,[18] there is no sufficient reason why any mediation should occur. It is precisely tyranny that Rousseau fears and locates as the main danger of modern society.[19] Thus, the most striking feature of Rousseau's political thought is not that it posits a mere aggregation of particular wills or that it advocates the subjection of the particular to the universal – both common criticisms – but rather that it appeals directly to the self-interest of the possessive individual of civil society as a way of constituting an ethical and juridical community of free and equal human beings.[20] Hegel fails to appreciate that Rousseau attempts to rationalize the will by generalizing it, by educating the will away from particularity and capriciousness.[21]

What Hegel neglects in his critical reading is the ironic use of enlightened self-interest in Rousseau. This use is nowhere more apparent than in the piece known as 'The General Society of the Human Race' which formed chapter two of the original version of the *Social Contract*. Rousseau poses a challenge to Hegel when he argues that it is not a question of showing the individual what justice is, but of showing it what interest it has in being just. Rousseau conceives the task of political education (a task for the legislator) as one of putting the process of sociability in the direction of a complete and profound transformation of human nature, 'of transforming each individual, which is by itself a complete and solitary whole, into part of a greater whole from which it receives its life and being'.[22] Given the lack of any general association, Rousseau says, we are compelled to create new ones. As a result of this *moral* transformation of human nature the isolated individual of civil society will become 'good, virtuous, and compassionate. In short, the man who wanted to be a fierce brigand will become the most firm support of a well-ordered society.'[23] Rousseau is important because he so clearly recognizes that the fundamental problematic of modernity is that of our predicament as bourgeois individuals.

The influence of Rousseau on Kant's ethics is well known.[24] Kant's attempt to establish the ground for a metaphysic of morals bears testimony to the schizophrenic experiences of the modern ethical consciousness, full of rancour towards itself for failing to live up to the strictures of its severe morality and full of resentment towards forms of otherness which deviate from established rational norms and do not match the lofty moral standards it has established for itself. Morality becomes based on a permanent war between nature and reason, inclination and duty, between self-love and the cruel, awkward strictures of the categorical imperative: 'Act only on that maxim through which you can at the same time will that it should become a universal law.'[25] We are entrusted the task of creating maxims of moral behaviour as if they were universal laws of nature, that is, as if there was nothing more natural in the world than in the individual creating universal maxims of action.

For Kant human free will lies not in the capacity to choose for or against the moral law, but rather in the emancipation of subjectivity from any empirical determination. But, as Charles Taylor has noted, Kant only succeeds in purchasing moral autonomy at the price of vacuity since he deprives the morally autonomous individual of any social and historical world within which to act.[26] Kant is quite explicit on the cruel nature of the categorical imperative and on the task of the human being emancipating itself from its animality. He speaks of reason as having to continually 'reject', 'strike down', and 'humiliate' the natural inclinations.[27] The individual does not achieve wholeness and universality by, in Nietzsche's words, 'giving style to its character' (that is, creating a coherent and unified self), but by splitting itself in two and existing in self-division and self-laceration.

Hegel's originality as a political philosopher attempting to sublate the antinomies of modern social life consists in grounding a notion of the political not in universal characteristics of human nature or in the idea of human rights, but in the notion of ethical life (*Sittlichkeit*).[28] It is with this notion that Hegel attempts to educate the abstract will of modernity about its realization in a concrete ethical order (a community of wills). The duties we assume are not the abstract or general ones of Kant's categorical imperative, but contextual and particularized ones which are inseparable from the social domain and the sphere of activity in which we are active.[29] Hegel's main critique of Kant is that he has restricted ethics to *Moralität*, that is, to a set of abstract universal principles of conduct which have no grounding in the ethical life of a people or a community. Because of this restriction Kant's political theory cannot advance beyond the problematic of liberalism which is that of harmonizing individual wills. The problem of politics remains that of limiting the negative freedom – the *Willkür* – of each so that it can peacefully co-exist with that of all others under a universal law. But so construed politics (right) has not been established on the basis of the autonomous will but on irrational and immoral nature. Nietzsche's observation is appropriate here: 'Kant believed in morality, not because it is demonstrated in nature and history, but in spite of the fact that nature and history continually contradict it' (D, preface 3).

For Hegel, as for Nietzsche, the phenomenon of willing is above all something complex.[30] In any simple act of willing we can distinguish three moments. First, there is the 'negative' moment of pure indeterminacy, the ability of the will to negate every content which would restrict it. It is this conception of the will which Nietzsche regards as dangerous and derived from a philosophical mythology surrounding the human subject or ego. Second, there is the 'positive' moment of the particularization of the ego in which the ego gives itself differentiation and determination. Third, there is the unity of both these moments in which the will posits itself as its own negative and yet retains its identity and universality. Hegel's argument, contra Kant, is that Kant's conception of the autonomous will cannot get beyond the first negative moment because as soon as it posits a determination it has become heteronomous and limited. The novelty of Hegel's own formulation of the will is that it does not conceive of the will simply in terms of a faculty. The will that is free is a will which rests on a unity of willing and thinking.[31] Of course, abstracted from the context of a phenomenological presentation of the will, these remarks have the character of assertions and not a demonstration. What Hegel seeks to demonstrate in the account of the will which is developed in the *Philosophy of Right* is that the ability or capacity of the subject to choose from a range of options is not freedom but mere wilfulness or arbitrariness. Wilfulness – the belief that freedom means doing whatever one likes by giving free reign to one's impulses – is defective because the wilful person is unable to shape its impulses and desires into a coherent, ordered whole, within which it achieves a unity of willing and thinking. As a result it cannot attain a universality of willing but remains governed by the purely accidental and contingent. When Hegel speaks of the will learning to will its will as its own will, he means that the self has succeeded in achieving this unity and coherence of action. In Nietzsche's terms, which Hegel anticipates, there is no separation between the doer of the deed and the deed itself (one has *become* what one *is*).[32] The self is able to recognize itself in its actions – to the extent, Nietzsche says, that it can declare to itself 'I willed it!' (Z, 'Of Redemption'). When the will is able to declare this to itself it has achieved self-affirmation, as opposed to the limited and negative form of self-determination found in Kant which is really a state of indetermination (freedom in negativity). The crucial insight of Hegel's here is that the will is not something apart from its expression in action (which explains why he refuses to speak of it in terms of a mysterious faculty). The choices and commitments a person makes define 'who' they are. Here the will wills itself not out of a lack – out of a desire to negate any specific content which would define it – but from the confidence of its own self-affirmation. As freedom under law, willing is necessarily self-reflective and can only exist in the context of a community of wills.

In spite of his immense achievement in defining the specific moment of modernity Hegel, as Patrick Riley has noted, does not make clear how a new self-conscious *Sittlichkeit* is possible after the historical unfolding of a new ruinous subjectivism and individualism.[33] Could it be precisely recognition of this problem which informs Nietzsche's deepest insights into the ethical and political dilemmas of modernity?

> To say it briefly – for a long time people will still keep silent about it! – What will not be built any more henceforth, and cannot be built any more is a society [*Gesellschaft*] in the old sense of that word; to build that, everything is lacking, above all the material. *All of us are no longer material for a society*; this is a truth for which the time has come!
>
> (GS 356)

II

Is the doctrine of will to power, as many hold, a doctrine which posits à la Hobbes a universal and natural desire for domination and mastery over others? Or is it, as some have argued, a doctrine of self-mastery in which 'power' denotes not domination over another but self-overcoming? Essential to understanding the notion is our ability to grasp what Nietzsche intends by the terms 'will' and 'power' in the compound formulation of 'will to power'.

Nietzsche's remarks on the will do not constitute a unified and coherent teaching. Instead, he views the phenomenon of willing in a number of contexts and from a number of perspectives. First, he argues that the will considered as a faculty of the soul is part of a philosophical mythology surrounding the human ego (TI, pp. 37–8, pp. 48–9). Second, he argues that the notion of the subject in possession of a free will is the historical product of the slave revolt in morality (GM I, 13).[34] Third, he argues that it is quite arbitrary to assert that willing can be identified with Schopenhauer's will to life – this is merely one form of the will to power (KSA 8, p. 301; WP 692). Fourth, he argues that if we wish to adhere to a belief in the causality of the will then that efficient causality has to be understood as will 'to power' (BGE 36). Fifth and finally, he argues that the will to power cannot be equated with a mere striving for power, where the desire for 'power' is akin to the utilitarian conception of the desire for 'happiness', but that above all the will to power denotes a *commanding* will (a will which wills itself) (KSA 13, p. 54; WP 668).

Present in Nietzsche's scattered and inconsistent remarks we find the ambiguous understanding of the will as an efficient causality and as a moral causality (the legislating or commanding will) which is common to the philosophical tradition. We are not necessarily dealing with an incompatibility here, but with the difference between a psychological will and a self-reflective will. Certainly, it cannot be denied that Nietzsche is highly suspicious of the notion of a free will. In the *Genealogy of Morals* he puts forward the argument that the notion of a subject which is free to act is an invention of a slave revolt in morality by which the weak and the oppressed attribute responsibility for their weakness and oppression to the intentional actions of the strong and powerful who allegedly act with a view to inflict pain and suffering on them. The weak type of human being, Nietzsche argues,

> *needs* to believe in a neutral independent 'subject', prompted by an instinct for self-preservation and self-affirmation in which every lie is sanctified. The subject (or, to use a more popular expression, the *soul*) has perhaps been believed in hitherto more firmly than anything else on earth because it makes possible to the majority of mortals, the weak and oppressed of every kind, the sublime self-deception which interprets weakness as freedom, and their being thus-and-thus as a *merit*.
>
> (GM I, 13)

Here Nietzsche is exposing the *illusion* of sovereign individuality which consists in believing oneself to be free when one in fact is enslaved. In *On the Genealogy of Morals* Nietzsche employs the will to power as a principle of 'historical method' in order to disclose the misrecognized will to power of the weak and the oppressed. Under certain historical circumstances the will to power assumes the form of a will to dominate, not on account of the largely instinctual and pre-reflective actions of the 'masters', but via the slave revolt in morality which internalizes the will to power. It is at this point in the social evolution of the human animal that intentions are ascribed to action and man develops a 'soul'. In what is ultimately an inversion of Rousseau's teaching on the natural goodness of humanity and the problem of civilization, Nietzsche argues that it is only on the soil of this dangerous priestly form of existence that the human being becomes an interesting animal, because only here does the soul acquire depth as it learns how to become *evil* (OGM I, 6). Thus, Nietzsche ends up with a justification of the spirit of *ressentiment* and revenge which the weak and oppressed have injected into history (OGM I, 11). Nietzsche does not disagree with Rousseau that civilization has corrupted humanity but laments the fact that it has not been corrupted sufficiently (D 163).

At its most elemental the will to power denotes an instinct for freedom, where freedom means growth, development, expansion, etc. George Stack is surely right when, following Walter Kaufmann, he argues that with this notion Nietzsche shows a deep understanding of the nihilistic and destructive expressions of the will to power but does not advocate them.[35] On the contrary, Nietzsche's teaching is that man must overcome this primitive energy of will to power and learn how to transform it into higher, creative forms. The need to direct power over others is, in fact, a reflection of the weak person's feeling of impotence. The person who has overcome their will to power by co-ordinating their instincts into a unified and coherent whole is someone who does not depend on the praise or blame, or on the suffering, of others for their sense of power. The sublimated will to power is not to be identified with the Hobbesian desire for glory, or with what Rousseau never stops criticizing as the deformation of the human being in the form of an inflated sense of self-worth as in vanity (*amour-propre*). As Nietzsche writes:

> Benefiting and hurting others are ways of exercising one's power over others. . . . Certainly the state in which we hurt others is rarely as agreeable in an unadultered way, as that in which we benefit others; it is a sign that we are still lacking in power, or it shows a sense of frustration in the face of this poverty; it is accompanied by new dangers and uncertainties for what power we do possess, and clouds our horizon with the prospect of revenge, scorn, punishment, and failure. . . . What is decisive is how one is accustomed to *spice* one's life: it is a matter of taste whether one prefers the slow or the sudden, the assured or the dangerous and audacious increase of power. One seeks this or that spice depending on one's temperament.

(GS 13)

Nietzsche's model of the sublimated will to power is that of Goethe whose life and art he celebrates on account of its achievement of a unanimity of thought, feeling, and willing: 'Goethe disciplined himself into a whole, he *created* himself' (TI, pp. 102–3). He defines a noble culture in terms of an education in which one learns three things – to see, to think, and to speak and write. Regarding the first, he writes:

> Learning to *see* – habituating the eye to repose, to patience, to letting things come to it; learning to defer judgement, to investigate and comprehend the individual in all its aspects. This is the first schooling in spirituality: *not* to react immediately to a stimulus, but to have the restraining, stock-taking instincts in one's control. Learning to *see*, as I understand it, is almost what is called in unphilosophical language strong will-power [*starken Willen*]: the essence of it is precisely *not* to 'will', the *ability* to defer decision. All unspirituality, all vulgarity, is due to the incapacity to resist a stimulus – one *has* to react, one obeys a stimulus. In many instances, such a compulsion is already morbidity, decline, a symptom of exhaustion. . . . To stand with all doors open, to prostrate oneself submissively before every petty fact, to be ever itching to mingle with, *plunge into* other people and other things, in short our celebrated modern 'objectivity', is bad taste, is ignoble *par excellence*.
>
> (TI, pp. 64–5)

Nietzsche's predilection for aesthetic notions to describe the sovereign will to power is consonant with his rejection of morality and with his articulation of a philosophy of the future which seeks to be beyond good and evil (that is, beyond moral judgement). As we shall see, Nietzsche departs not from the definition of the will as self-mastery, but from the attempt of Rousseau and Kant to universalize the maxims of a legislating will, to arrive at a notion of 'morality' from a notion of 'autonomy'.

Nietzsche's attempt to conceive of a model of will to power which is beyond the spirit of *ressentiment* finds its best expression in section 290 of *The Gay Science* where he identifies the noble self as a person who is able to give style to their character. In contrast to Kant's divided moral self which is forever trying to achieve the moral purity demanded of it by the categorical imperative, Nietzsche envisages a form of aesthetic selfhood in which the self is able to fit its strengths *and* weaknesses into an artistic plan 'until every one of them appears as art and even weaknesses delight the eye'. It is notable that Nietzsche explicitly refuses to employ any notion of moral judgement in describing this aesthetic model of subjectivity. The only criterion he will allow is an aesthetic one: 'In the end, when the work is finished, it becomes evident how the constraint of a single taste governed and formed everything large and small. Whether this taste was good or bad is less important than that it expressed a single taste!' Style in this context denotes the ability of the self to subject itself to some kind of discipline. 'It will be the strong and domineering natures', Nietzsche informs us, 'that enjoy their finest gaiety in such constraint and perfection under a law of their own; the passion of their tremendous will relents in the face of all stylized nature, of all conquered and serving nature.' Conversely, Nietzsche says, it is weak natures 'without power over themselves who *hate* the constraint of style. . . . Such spirits – and they may be of the first rank – are always out to shape and interpret their environment as *free* nature: wild, arbitrary, fantastic, disorderly, and surprising.' Here it is not a question of Nietzsche positing some dubious neo-conservative aestheticism, as Habermas would have us believe, but of identifying a form of subjectivity in which the destructive morality of good and evil has been overcome. As in Hegel the emphasis is on the self achieving a unity and coherence of action. Habermas's claim that Nietzche's genealogy of morals is a conservative, aestheticist enterprise since it equates the question of validity and value with that of ancestry and origin, so that what is 'earlier' (the 'good and bad' of the nobles) is 'better', is misdirected. It is Rousseau's construal of the problem of civilization which for Nietzsche merits being labelled as 'conservative' in that Rousseau's critique rests on a privileging of what is natural/original over what is artificial/historical (the pre-reflective sentiment of pity over the artificial sentiment of vanity).[36]

In *Thus Spoke Zarathustra* will to power is presented as a new virtue (a bestowing virtue) which constitutes 'a new good and evil'. As a doctrine on the nature of sovereignty (of 'commanding' and 'obeying') the will to power conceives of the unity of doer and deed, of self-legislation and self-execution, of *will* and *power*. The person who commands has the power to become judge, avenger, and victim of their own law (Z, 'Of the Way of the Creator'). Heidegger illuminates Nietzsche's teaching on the commanding will when he writes that the person who commands has at their conscious disposal the means for effective action. In other words, the commanding will is a self-reflective will and can be nothing other.[37] The commanding will is a will which has the power to actualize itself. This leads Heidegger to argue that what the will *wills* in will to power is not something it merely strives after because it is simply lacking in this something (namely, power), but rather what the will wills it has already for the will wills *itself*.

By positing the unity of 'will' and 'power' in the formulation 'will-to-power' Nietzsche attempts to overcome the notion of the will found in the philosophical tradition in which the will is conceived metaphysically as a noumenal substratum lying behind all action, and which posits a metaphysical doer behind every deed. This conception is faulty for Nietzsche in that it attributes divine powers of action to the human will, in which the will itself is conceived as some kind of lordly instigator and manipulator of events in the world. This conception is nothing but a vain anthropomorphic conceit by which the human ego attempts to dominate the world in the illusion that it can become master of it. In fact, we already find present in Nietzsche's understanding of the will the critique of anthropomorphism which Heidegger will later deploy against Nietzsche's own formulation of the will to power, when he argues that the notion represents the apotheosis and fulfilment of the modern metaphysics of subjectivity.

In the formulation 'will to power' the notion of 'power' serves to designate the manner in which living things express themselves. To appreciate the self-reflective nature of the notion of will to power it is necessary to recognize that an important part of Nietzsche's argument is that one should not construe the relation between will and power simply in terms of a 'will' freely expressing its 'power'. Thus, for example, he claims that the will as perceived by psychology hitherto is a generalization and does not exist.

The terms 'will' and 'power' are ambiguous ones. To 'have' power means to have the ability to do or effect something, to act upon a person or a thing. 'Power' denotes a physical or mental strength which is a kind of energy or force. In book two, part seven of his *Essay on Human Understanding*, for example, Locke defines power as a simple idea received from sensation and reflection. In observing ourselves we derive pleasure from seeing that we can exercise control over our body (moving limbs at will for example), and the effects this control has over other bodies. In its legal sense 'power' means command over others (dominion, rule, supremacy, domination, etc.). In the sixteenth century the French writer Jean Bodin defined law in terms of the commands of the sovereign power. Following Bodin, Hobbes conceived law as 'the words of him that by right hath command over others'. Law is command in the sense that it lies in the power of the one who commands to compel obedience. Similarly Nietzsche conceives of the will to power in tems of a doctrine on the nature of 'commanding' and 'obeying'. In section 19 of *Beyond Good and Evil* he conceives of 'morals' in terms of 'relations of supremacy' (relations of commanding and obeying) under which the phenomenon of 'life' arises: law, force, will, and power – all these notions are closely allied in the thought of will to power. If law is thought of in terms of will to power, then it is possible to appreciate that all law is posited from its ground in 'life', that law can be either active force or reactive force. For what is law if not force given recognition, limits, boundaries, and so on?

If power is a kind of will – as is evident from Locke's construal of power – then equally power can be construed as a kind of will. The 'will' denotes a desire, a longing, inclination, and a striving for something. But it also means command in the sense that one has the determination that something shall be done either by oneself or another. Will is also conceived as consent or permission, a faculty of choice (a *free* will) by which we can pledge ourselves to something and be held accountable to others for our actions. It is also, finally, the power of directing our actions without constraint, the power of being autonomous. The notion of 'will to power' represents Nietzsche's attempt to show the unity of will and power and, in doing so, to overcome the opposition which governs metaphysical thinking between freedom and necessity. In becoming what we are we become will to power. The will to power thus obligates us because it defines what we are: the question is to what extent do we *recognize* ourselves as such a will and to what extent we *will* our will as a 'will to power'.

In his writings Nietzsche carries out an important 'epistemological' critique of the notion of will, in which he criticizes the idea of 'I will' in the same terms that one might criticize the *naïveté* of Descartes's positing of the 'I think' (it simply takes the existence of the 'I' for granted). Rousseau and Kant follow the philosophical tradition by construing the will in metaphysical terms as an underlying reality. Here the will is conceived as that which brings about spontaneous effects, as a kind of causality by which we are able to act upon the world. The basis of Nietzsche's argument against this construal of the will is to argue that because it relies on metaphysical properties of human agency (such as the ego and consciousness), it is led to posit the will in terms of a unified essence (the 'subject') which lies behind all action and thus ends up positing the relationship between man and the world in dualistic terms. It is our belief in causality which lies at the basis of this erroneous conception of human action. With this belief we separate the deed from the doer, the process of doing (acting) from a substance (the ego), and then decide whether or not this 'subject' is free to act.

With this critique of the subject Nietzsche is directing our attention to the reification embedded in language. Our psychological categories all derive from the illusion of substantial identity which goes back to an ancient belief in the truth of grammatical categories. In section 22 of *Beyond Good and Evil*, for example, Nietzsche argues that instead of viewing the notions of cause and effect as conventional fictions which we use for the purposes of designation and communication (and 'not explanation'), we naturalize ('reify') them by understanding them as concepts which explain the real nature of things. But in reality there are no causal connections or necessities and no 'rule of law'. Through the reification of language we simplify the complex reality of our existence as a plurality of subjects, drives, affects, and wills. Thus, what language designates with the term will is, as Michel Haar has pointed out, a complex and belated sentiment which accompanies the victory of one impulse over others, and the translation into conscious terms of a temporary state of equilibrium intervening in the interplay of affects, drives, and impulses. Like consciousness, the will for Nietzsche is not a beginning but an end. What we call 'will' is in reality a plurality of instincts and impulses, a symptom and not a cause.

Nietzsche's awareness of the reification of concepts explains why he explicitly and gaily defines his own theory of the world as will to power in terms of 'only an interpretation'. When we will what actually takes place, Nietzsche says, is that we feel a force come into operation and achieve a triumph without our knowing anything about it; the illusion arises when we take this feeling as a sign of a free causality. In reality it is simply a matter of strong and weak wills; the former being a 'will' which is able to harmonize its multifarious forces and drives and which accepts the chaos it is because it is strong enough to affirm it as something to be cultivated and overcome; the latter cannot bear the thought that it is a chaos and a mere overcoming, and so strives to eliminate and repress certain forces and drives in an effort to achieve an illusory mastery over itself (to be being and not becoming).

For me the crucial idea contained in the thought of will to power is that of attaining freedom through necessity, which revolves around the task of *becoming* what one *is*, namely, 'will to power'. By positing the unity of 'will' and 'power' Nietzsche seeks to overcome the reifying language of metaphysics *and* the conception of the abstract will found in the tradition of moral theory. But in order to overcome the ethical tradition of western metaphysics it becomes necessary for Nietzsche to show that the task of becoming those that we are – new, unique, and incomparable – denotes not a moral enterprise or task but a labour which is essentially and fundamentally paradoxical and aporetic (one example of this given by Nietzsche is that in order for one 'to become what one is' one must not have the faintest idea what one *is*). Recognition of the unique and incomparable nature of self-creation means that Nietzsche is compelled to abandon the task of moral philosophy and its claims to providing a set of universal prescriptions or rules of conduct. I shall now turn to examining what this abandonment of a philosophy of morals means for understanding Nietzsche's relation to Kant.

III

Nietzsche subscribes to Rousseau's conception of autonomy in which the only valid law is the one which the self has legislated for itself. But in what way does Nietzsche's understanding of the will conceived as a principle of autonomy – that is, as the command of a self-legislating will which has overcome 'the mere impulse of appetite' – differ in key respects from that found in both Rousseau and Kant?

An important part of Nietzsche's revolution in ethics must surely reside in his overturning of what we understood by morality. In section 335 of *The Gay Science* Nietzsche dismisses one by one the main candidates for supremacy in our moral vocabulary. The notion of the categorical imperative is dismissed as little more than a selfish deceit on the part of the weak soul which is simply not strong enough to affirm itself in its own uniqueness and independence. Nietzsche argues that it is utterly selfish to experience one's own judgement as a universal law. The positing of conscience as providing the firmness needed for our moral judgements simply reflects the stubbornness and stupidity of a slothful self which refuses to engage in the creative labour of self-overcoming by which it continually creates itself anew. The firmness of our moral judgements might only be a reflection of personal abjectness. Instead, Nietzsche invites us to 'become those who we are', that is, those who are new, unique, and incomparable, who create themselves and who give themselves laws. But here Nietzsche is giving expression to an aporia, not setting up a new moral philosophy. The attempt to become those who we are is strangely and necessarily paradoxical for the unique and incomparable individual is precisely that which cannot be either identified or compared *qua* individual. Nietzsche insists that the law of mechanism of our actions is indemonstrable since the attempt to establish the 'right' maxim of action presupposes a judgement of 'right'. 'Every action that has ever been done', Nietzsche writes, 'was done in an altogether unique and irretrievable way' (GS 335).

Although a notion of autonomy is crucial to Nietzsche's understanding of the unique sovereign individual, he is aware that the definition of the individual in terms of a self-legislating will is peculiar to modernity. Thus, for example, he notes that today all teachers of law start from a sense of self and pleasure in the individual as if this had always been the foundation of law. But, he argues, during the longest period of the human past, to stand alone and experience things as an individual, neither to obey nor to rule, was considered to be not a pleasure but a punishment: 'one was sentenced to individuality' (GS 117).[38] Nietzsche conceives of a historical process in which society and what he calls the morality of custom (*die Sittlichkeit der Sitte*) produce the fruit of the sovereign individual, an individual which is autonomous and 'supra-ethical' (*übersittlich*): autonomous and ethical are mutually exclusive in the sense that to be autonomous is to be beyond the standpoint of customs within which there is no scope for individuality (OGM II, 2).[39] Thus, Nietzsche speaks of the emancipated individual who is master of a free will and who has earned the '*right to make promises*'. The story which Nietzsche narrates of how responsibility originated involves a pre-voluntaristic process of political obligation that leads to a cultivation of a *memory* of the will so that between the original declaration of intent and the actual discharge of the will an entire world of circumstances can be interpreted without breaking the chain of the will. Nietzsche is insistent that the appearance of this 'astonishing manifestation' of the sovereign individual has a long history and a variety of forms behind it. The 'right to affirm oneself' is a ripe fruit but also a *late* fruit (OGM II, 3). In section 262 of *Beyond Good and Evil* Nietzsche speaks of the uncanny and dangerous point in history having been arrived at when 'the "individual" appears, obliged to give himself laws and to develop his own arts and wiles for self-preservation, self-enhancement, and self-redemption'. He wishes to alert our attention to the potential dangers of this phenomenon of the 'individual':

> Again danger is there, the mother of morals, great danger, this time transposed into the individual, into neighbour and friend, into the alley, into one's own child, into one's own heart, into the

most personal and secret recesses of wish and will: what may the moral philosophers emerging in this age have to preach now?

(BGE 262)

Nietzsche looks forward to a possible future lawgiving founded on the idea that 'I submit only to the law I myself have given in great and small things' (D 187). However, he sharply criticizes any attempt – such as we find in Rousseau's general will or in Kant's categorical imperative – to define autonomy in terms of objective and universalizable laws or rules. For Nietzsche this is to deceive us into thinking that the individual can attain the standpoint of the universal merely by generalizing its own particularity and to spare us the task of self-creation (the labour of self-overcoming). The selfishness which is concealed by the seemingly outward altruistic appearance of the categorical imperative is described by Nietzsche as 'blind, petty, and frugal' since it betrays the fact that we have not yet discovered or created ourselves and our own laws (GS 335). It is necessary, Nietzsche argues, that each one of us should create our own virtues and our own categorical imperative (AC 11).

For Nietzsche the great problem with Kant's formulation of morality in terms of a kingdom of ends of self-legislating rational beings is that it naïvely assumes that everyone knows what kind of actions will benefit the whole of humanity. Kant's ethical theory 'is like that of free trade, presupposing that universal harmony *must* result of itself in accordance with innate laws of progress'. From this critique of Kant Nietzsche evinces a Machiavellian understanding of creative political life: 'Perhaps some future survey of the requirements of mankind will show that it is not at all desirable that all men should act in the same way, but rather that in the interest of ecumenical goals whole tracts of mankind ought to have special, perhaps under certain circumstances even evil, tasks imposed upon them' (HH 25). For Nietzsche this is a task of 'culture', but one which he recognizes is very difficult to achieve in the absence of any pre-established ethical universality.[40] 'Only if mankind possessed a universally recognized *goal*', he tells us, 'would it be possible to propose "thus and thus is the *right* course of action"; for the present there exists no such goal. It is thus trivial and irrational to impose the demands of morality upon mankind' (D 108).

It needs to be asked, however, whether Nietzsche is not guilty of misunderstanding Rousseau and Kant's attempt to unite autonomy and morality in that the aim is not simply to universalize particularity but precisely to *overcome* it. In Rousseau, for example, self-legislation is not merely a political metaphor for strong will to power but a notion which denotes the creative and legislative act of a new political ethic of solidarity and community (the greatest paradox of Rousseau's thought concerns the nature of this moral transformation – to achieve it we would have to be *before* 'the law' what we should *become* by means of 'the law'). Of course, hovering around the Rousseauian vision of a general will is the spectre of the doctrine of forcing someone to be free in which self-choosing gives way to right-acting. For Nietzsche, however, human action has to be understood as 'beyond good and evil', that is, as beyond the moral judgement which Rousseau wishes to impose on it. What Nietzsche seeks to question most in Rousseau's political vision is the value-basis on which sovereign individuals emancipated from the morality of custom enter into social relationships with one another. This for Nietzsche is the decisive question to be asked of moral and political philosophy in a condition of modernity. In Rousseau he locates the 'moral' origins of the social contract in the sentiment of pity. His own political vision is one which envisages sovereign individuals creating a form of association not out of fear, weakness, or pity, but out of strength, independence, and bravery. Such individuals want not the pity of a social contract but the courage of the overman. 'The man of "modern ideas" ', Nietzsche writes contra Rousseau, 'is immeasurably dissatisfied with himself: that is certain. He suffers – and his vanity wants him only to suffer with others, to feel pity' (BGE 221).

Perhaps the key question to be asked of Nietzsche's politics is whether the attainment of power over oneself (as in autonomy) necessarily entails exercising power over others (as in domination). The attraction of Kant's notion of a kingdom of ends is that it rests on an ethics in which each and every individual is treated as an end-in-itself and not as a mere means to an end, that is, it recognizes the dignity of every human being. Whether accepting Nietzsche's attack on the universalistic claims of morality involves endorsing a culture in which some are treated as 'instruments' for the end of aristocratic cultivation remains a contentious and crucial question.[41] It seems clear that Nietzsche develops a very idiosyncratic reading of Kant's ethics when he suggests that it is a question of each individual creating their own categorical imperative. Although Nietzsche proposes this conception of self-legislation in terms of a position 'contra Kant', it could be argued that he has in fact misread Kant. For surely the point of the categorical imperative is that it is a maxim of action which, through the criterion of universalizability, supplies human action with a moral aspect. Kant's argument is that human autonomy, if it is not to result in solipsism, necessarily entails universality. To be a singular and unique human being, which clearly is what each individual is, and to create and construct rules or maxims of behaviour through the exercise of one's own individual will, does not preclude that one's actions can be universal in a moral sense.[42] It is precisely the creative basis of individual willing (as self-legislation) which Kant wishes to emphasize in the notion of the categorical imperative.

There are, however, a number of problems with any attempt to impose a Kantian conception of morality on Nietzsche's philosophy of power. For Nietzsche the notion of a kingdom of ends creates little more than a formal equality between sovereign individuals and comes dangerously close to positing a slave morality in which the self defines its identity not through self-affirmation but by negating the independence and difference of the other. In a Kantian kingdom of ends the self declares that it would like to treat the other as an end in itself and not as means to an end, and to be treated as an end in itself in return, as it is too weak to affirm itself in its own uniqueness and independence (Nietzsche's Calliclean argument that the basis of altruistic behaviour can always be found in egoism). Moreover, Nietzsche wishes to abandon the notion of the human subject conceived as a fixed, moral point of reference. The achievement of genuine autonomy is not to be understood as 'moral' since there are no fixed or pre-established moral rules and conventions by which free, spontaneous, and creative human action can be judged. The essential nature of 'free' agency is that of self-creation, and for this one needs to be beyond good and evil. Ultimately, however, in the absence of any ethical universality Nietzsche presents an informative but disabling choice between the overman and the herd – a choice which always threatens to degenerate into either solipsism or barbarism.

Self-conscious modernity is based on the recognition that once the will has become detached from social and cultural practices there then arises the problem of the authenticity and identity of the self. It is at the moment of its emancipation from tradition, custom, God, etc., that the self experiences contingency and fragility. It is necessary however, to be sceptical about recent claims that Nietzsche's philosophy of will to power is able to provide the foundation for a postmodern conception of human agency – a conception which eschews a metaphysics of the ego or subject in favour of a radical historicization of subjectivity – since the positing of a notion of power as subjectivity or autonomy represents an insufficient motive for the constitution of an ethico-political community in that each individual's desire for autonomy (will to 'power') could easily result in a war of all against all. Without some conception of a substantive, not merely formal, ethics subjectivity remains either trapped within itself as in the case of the beautiful soul or faced with the constant threat of a Hobbesian warlike condition breaking out. But in problematizing the link between autonomy and morality Nietzsche's thought depicts the tense and difficult relationship between the particular and the universal which characterizes modernity in a highly instructive manner.

REFERENCES

For the original German I have used the *Kritische Studienausgabe* (KSA) edited by G. Colli and M. Montinari, Berlin, Walter de Gruyter, and Munich, Deutscher Taschenbuch Verlag, 1967–77 and 1988, in fifteen volumes. References in the text and in the notes are to sections, not page numbers, unless stated otherwise. Readers should note that I have adopted the practice of modifying translations for the sake of uniformity and accuracy without explicitly stating so.

BT   *The Birth of Tragedy*, trans. W. Kaufmann, New York, Random House, 1967.
HH   *Human, All Too Human*, trans. R. J. Hollingdale, Cambridge University Press, 1986.
D   *Daybreak*, trans. R. J. Hollingdale, Cambridge University Press, 1982.
GS   *The Gay Science*, trans. W. Kaufmann, Random House, 1974.
Z   *Thus Spoke Zarathustra*, trans. R. J. Hollingdale, Penguin, 1969.
BGE *Beyond Good and Evil*, trans. W. Kaufmann, Random House, 1966.
OGM *On the Genealogy of Morals*, trans. W. Kaufmann and R. J. Hollingdale, Random House, 1969.
TI   *Twilight of the Idols*, trans. R. J. Hollingdale, Penguin, 1968.
AC   *The Anti-Christ*, trans. R. J. Hollingdale, Penguin, 1968.
WP   *The Will to Power*, trans. W. Kaufmann and R. J. Hollingdale, Random House, 1967.

NOTES

1 Mark Warren, *Nietzsche and Political Thought*, Cambridge, Mass., MIT Press, 1988. On the role of Nietzsche in the postmodern turn in western thought see also Ian Forbes, 'Nietzsche, Modernity, and Politics', in John Gibbins (ed.), *Contemporary Political Culture. Politics in A Postmodern Age*, Sage, London, 1989, 218–36; Robert B. Pippin, 'Nietzsche's

Farewell: Modernity, Pre-Modernity, and Post-Modernity', in Bernd
Magnus (ed.), *Nietzsche*, Cambridge University Press (forthcoming);
Henning Ottmann, '*Nietzsches Politische Philosophie. Versuche in
Postmoderner Politik*', in Walter Gebhard (ed.), *Friedrich Nietzsche.
Willen zur Macht und Mythen des Narziss*, Frankfurt am Main, Peter
Lang, 1989, 107–29.

2 Alasdair MacIntyre, *After Virtue. A Study in Moral Theory*, London,
Duckworth Press, 1981, 240–1.

3 Thomas Hobbes, *Leviathan*, ed. C. B. MacPherson, Middlesex,
Penguin, 1968, ch. 6.

4 Jean-Jacques Rousseau, *Discourse on the Origins of Inequality*, trans.
G. D. H. Cole, London, Dent, 1972, 66. Nietzsche also locates the
historical birth of morality at the moment when the origin of an action is
understood to reside in intention. But the intention is merely 'a sign and
symptom which is in need of interpretation' BGE 32.

5 P. Riley, *Will and Political Legitimacy*, Cambridge, Mass., Harvard
University Press, 1982, 1–22.

6 See for example, Albrecht Dihle, *The Theory of Will in Classical
Antiquity*, Berkeley, University of California Press, 1982, 80–6; Hannah
Arendt, *The Life of the Mind: Willing*, New York, Harcourt Brace
Jovanovich, 1978, 3–7, 84–110; see also G. W. F. Hegel, *Philosophy of
Right*, trans. T. M. Knox, Oxford University Press, 1967, para. 124.

7 Jean-Jacques Rousseau, *The Social Contract*, trans. G. D. H. Cole,
London, Dent, 1972, bk. III, ch. I.

8 Rousseau, *Discourse on the Origins of Inequality*, 53–5.

9 Jean-Jacques Rousseau, *Émile*, trans. Barbara Foxley, London, Dent,
1974, 243–4.

10 Ibid., 437.

11 Ibid., 255.

12 Hegel, *Philosophy of Right*, paras 15–26. Compare Nietzsche, Z, 'Of the
Virtuous': 'That *your* Self be in the action, as the mother is in the child:
let that be the maxim of *your* virtue!'.

13 The term *Recht* means either 'right' or 'law'; in Hegel it refers to 'the
entire normative structure of a people's way of life, not just their civil
rights and liberties but the whole system of ethical norms and values . . .
informing a culture'. Steven B. Smith, 'What is "Right" in Hegel's
Philosophy of Right?', *American Political Science Review*, March 1989,
vol. 83, no. 1, 3–18, 5.

14 Rousseau, *Social Contract*, I, VIII.

15 Hegel, *Philosophy of Right*, para. 124. See also para. 260.

16 Rousseau, *Social Contract*, I, VI.

17 Ibid., I, VIII.

18 As used by Hegel and Marx 'civil society' is a concept which defines the
historical separation of state and society characteristic of the modern
'bourgeois' epoch. It refers to the economic domain in which individuals
interact in terms of the free exchange of goods and commodities
(including labour), and where society becomes conceived along the lines
of a 'market'. According to Manfred Riedel, civil society for Hegel is a
depoliticized society in which the 'political' and 'civil' have become
separated. See his important study, *Between Tradition and Revolution*.

The Hegelian Transformation of Political Philosophy, Cambridge University Press, 1984, 129–56.

19 On this point see Asher Horowitz, *Rousseau, Nature, and History*, University of Toronto Press, 1987, 198–200.

20 In his now classic study, *The Political Theory of Possessive Individualism*, Oxford University Press, 1962, C. B. Macpherson argues that the 'possessive' quality of liberal individualism lies in its conception of the individual as the proprietor of its own person and capacities owing nothing to society for them. Political society itself is conceived as a calculated device for the protection of property and maintenance of orderly relations of exchange.

21 On this point see Riley, op. cit., 163.

22 Rousseau, *Social Contract*, II, VII.

23 Ibid., 161–2.

24 See E. Cassirer, *Rousseau, Kant, and Goethe*, Connecticut, Archon Books, 1961; George A. Kelly, *Politics, Idealism, and History, Sources of Hegelian Thought*, Cambridge University Press, 1969; Stephen Ellenburg, 'Rousseau and Kant: principles of political right', in R. A. Leigh (ed.), *Rousseau After Two Hundred Years*, Cambridge University Press, 1982, 3–35. Nietzsche was well aware of Rousseau's influence (the influence of 'a moral tarantula' – D, preface 3) not only on Kant, but on modern German culture as a whole. See section 216 on 'German Virtue' of *The Wanderer and His Shadow*, trans. R. J. Hollingdale, Cambridge University Press, 1986.

25 I. Kant, *Groundwork of the Metaphysics of Morals*, trans. H. J. Paton, New York, Harper & Row, 1964, 88.

26 C. Taylor, *Hegel and Modern Society*, Cambridge University Press, 1979, 76–8.

27 Kant, *Critique of Practical Reason*, trans. Lewis White Beck, Bobbs-Merrill, Indianapolis, 1956, 75–6.

28 See Z. A. Pelczynski's introduction to his *The State and Civil Society. Studies in Hegel's Political Philosophy*, Cambridge University Press, 1984, 8–9. In para. 33 of *Philosophy of Right* Hegel argues that Kant's principles of action explicitly 'nullify' and 'spurn' the standpoint of ethical life.

29 See Z. A. Pelczynski, 'Political community and individual freedom in Hegel's philosophy of the state', in Pelczynski, op. cit., 66.

30 Hegel, *Philosophy of Right*, paras 5–7. Compare Nietzsche, BGE 19: 'Philosophers are accustomed to speaking of the will as if it were the best-known thing in the world. . . . Willing seems to me to be above all something *complicated*, something that is a unit only as a word.'

31 See Donald J. Maletz, 'The Meaning of "Will" in Hegel's *Philosophy of Right*', *Interpretation*, 1985, vol. 13, no. 2, 195–212. See also his essay, 'Hegel on Right as Actualized Will', *Political Theory*, February 1989, vol. 17, no. 1, 33–51.

32 See Hegel, *Philosophy of Right*, para. 118: 'The self-consciousness of heroes (like that of Oedipus and others in Greek tragedy) had not advanced out of its primitive simplicity either to reflection on the distinction between act and action . . . or to the subdivision of consequences. On the contrary, they accepted responsibility for the

whole compass of the deed.' Compare Nietzsche OGM I, 13: 'there is no
"being" behind doing . . . "the doer" is merely a fiction added to the
deed – the deed is everything.'
33 Riley, op. cit., 165.
34 But see *The Wanderer and His Shadow*, 9, where Nietzsche says that
'The theory of the freedom of the will is an invention of *ruling* classes.'
See also BGE 260 where Nietzsche argues that we need a *Typenlehre* of
master morality and slave morality.
35 G. J. Stack, *Lange and Nietzsche*, Berlin and New York, Walter de
Gruyter, 1982, 286–7.
36 See the lectures on Nietzsche in J. Habermas, *The Philosophical
Discourse of Modernity. Twelve Lectures*, Cambridge, Mass., MIT
Press, 1987. For an important contribution to the debate on the relation
between aesthetics and politics in Nietzsche see Tracy Strong,
'Nietzsche's Political Aesthetics', in M. A. Gillespie and T. B. Strong,
Nietzsche's New Seas, Chicago University Press, 1988, 153–75.
37 M. Heidegger, 'The Word of Nietzsche: "God is Dead" ', in *The
Question Concerning Technology and Other Essays*, trans. William
Lovitt, New York, Harper & Row, 1977, 77. In addition to Heidegger's
reading, I have learned most on the meaning of will to power from
Michel Haar, 'Nietzsche and Metaphysical Language', in D. B. Allison
(ed.) *The New Nietzsche*, Cambridge, Mass., MIT Press, 1985, 5–37.
38 See also GS 21 and 143. In *Assorted Opinions and Maxims*, 366,
Nietzsche speaks of active and successful natures in terms of agents who
act, not in accordance with the dictum 'know thyself', but in accordance
with the commandment '*will* a self and thou shalt *become* a self'.
39 Nietzsche's notion of the *die Sittlichkeit der Sitte* should not be confused
with Hegel's notion of *Sittlichkeit*. 'Mores' (an important notion in
Montesquieu and Rousseau) indicate a pre-reflective mode of ethical
existence, where ethical life for Hegel is both rational and individuated.
David S. Thatcher has recently argued that Nietzsche's use of the phrase
'morality of custom' may not be as original to him as he would have us
suppose. He suggests that Nietzsche's immediate source may have been
Walter Bagehot's *Physics and Politics* of 1872, which Nietzsche was
certainly familiar with. See Thatcher, '*Zur Genealogie der Moral*: Some
Textual Annotations', *Nietzsche-Studien*, 1989, vol. 18, 587–99, 591. In
addition, I would suggest that Nietzsche was influenced by John Stuart
Mill who, in the introduction to his essay of 1859 *On Liberty*, draws a
contrast between 'custom' and the 'sovereign individual'. Nietzsche's
library contained a German edition of Mill's complete works. See Karl
Brose, '*Nietzsches Verhältnis zu J. S. Mill*', *Nietzsche-Studien*, 1974, vol.
3, 152–74.
40 It should be noted that Kant's thinking itself anticipates this move to
'culture' in the third critique, the *Critique of Judgement*, trans. J. C.
Meredith, Oxford University Press, 1972, appendix, sec. 83.
41 For a detailed examination of this point see James H. Read, 'Nietzsche:
Power as Oppression,' *Praxis International*, April–July 1989, vol. 9,
72–87. See also John Andrew Bernstein's hostile but instructive study,
Nietzsche's Moral Philosophy, London and Toronto, Associated University Presses, 1987. In BGE 273 Nietzsche illuminates his position on

'means' and 'ends' in the context of a discussion on what is noble: 'A human being who strives for something great considers everyone he meets on his way either as a means or as a delay and obstacle – or as a temporary resting-place. His characteristic *graciousness* toward his fellow men becomes possible only once he has attained his height and rules . . . every means conceals the end.'

42 For a recent defence of the categorical imperative see Agnes Heller, *A Philosophy of Morals*, Oxford, Basil Blackwell, 1990. Heller illuminates the link between autonomy and morality when she argues that becoming what one is (a 'good' person) is necessarily bound up with the authenticity of our actions.

I would like to thank Hayo Krombach and David Owen for their helpful comments on an earlier draft of this essay.

8 Autonomy and solitude

J. M. Bernstein

1 Autonomy, self-legislating and self-determining individuality, is the foremost achievement of modernity and its despair. What looks like the essential structure of autonomy designates a movement of the will whereby if it is governed by anything other than itself alone it loses itself, it becomes heteronomous. Heteronomy refers to any determination of the will that governs it from without, where what is without, outside, other is simply what is not the will either metaphysically (essentially) or through the work of incorporation. Which is why attaining autonomy has meant either isolating the will, through doubt or conceptual refinement, from everything that could be considered, logically or actually, external to it in order that it might then be in a position to will only itself, its freedom; or, especially in political contexts, reclaiming for the will what originally belonged to or was produced by it but has become alienated or reified in opposition to it – what has become separated from it and come to rule it from without. Despite appearances to the contrary, this latter move equally requires the *isolation* of the will from its products, even if they are truly morally or metaphysically its, since unless there is a means of identifying the will as intrinsically my or our will, unless the will has a specifiable character and integrity apart from what it wills, then there will be nothing for its products to stand over and against, overwhelm, dominate, and control. Autonomy depends upon locating, above all through the self-reflective self-purification of sceptical doubt, some essential characterization of the will in order that its true, legitimate and rightful, scope and provenance with respect to what lies outside it can be established.

Alternatively, when autonomy is specified through the isolation of the moral will from its products there comes to be specified at the same time a series of items that are the will's others: the body, desire, need, feeling, history, tradition, community, other persons and their wills. But these others, as the alienation/reappropriation (incorporation) pattern of movement for overcoming heteronomy indicates, may appear, from a more or less acute angle, as what is intrinsic to the self, subject or will, not without at all but more inside than what is otherwise claimed as inner and essential. The purification of the will equally strips the will of any empirical identity, its being *this* will because immersed in this body, with these fundamental desires formed through this unique history in this community. Unless the will can have a passive determination, an empirical, physio-historical characterization, it will lack any worldly being, any concrete actuality, and hence become a will opposed to all content – its autonomy a purity against all possible worlds. From this angle, austere and pure autonomy is alienated, and the overcoming of heteronomy is a work of (re-)incorporation, reclaiming for the will its reified content and determinations. A substantial autonomous will can will itself only by willing the heterogeneous manifold that makes it the will it is.

The difficulty here is that when we reclaim for the will and self its physical body and its socio-historical 'body' we lose a grip on what can be thought of as *opposing* autonomy, on what is or might be considered to be a heteronomous determination of the will. If the will lacks an intrinsic inner nature, then nothing can be truly outside it; and without an inner/outer distinction there is no emphatic autonomy/heteronomy distinction to be drawn. Yet, it is this distinction that has structured both the modern critique of traditional societies and the reiterated political critique of authoritarian regimes. Critical autonomy necessarily requires some normative criterion for identifying what 'belongs' to the will in its essential nature.

In the aporia of autonomy modernity attains its limit and refutation. Metaphysically, this aporia concerns the rigid *dualism* of passivity and activity, subject and object (only the purely active belongs to the subjectivity of the subject); formally, this aporia concerns the question of what the *content* of the will is, whether the will can have a content and remain a free will; materially, this aporia concerns the changing, shifting and indeterminate, *boundaries* of the self or subject, where such a being can be said to begin or end. If there can be no essential determination of the self or subject, and if the shifting boundaries of identity – from the extreme of the pure activity of thinking and willing to the extreme of sheer external givenness – are co-extensive with the will, then the hope of instituting a substantial conception of autonomy must collapse. Nietzsche, I will argue, continues the project of modernity as autonomy while interrogating its limits and intriguing its dissolution.

2 Nietzsche is a social philosopher; the force of his critique of Platonism, Christianity ('Platonism for the people'), representation and truth is misplaced if it is considered only a theoretical, contemplative critique detachable from the way in which the values designated by those terms have informed life, the practices of peoples. Philosophy for Nietzsche is always and everywhere a worldly praxis, a work of valuation, and hence a work of critique and transformation. Philosophy self-consciously appropriates its praxial and valuing fate when, in the experience of nihilism, in the experience of the highest values devaluing themselves and losing their capacity to inform practice, it perceives that history as one of heteronomy, as one in which the will has posited a series of significations above itself as its determining ground.

Nietzsche places this claim in the context of a hypothetical narrative stretching from the pre-morality of pre-history, where actions were judged by their consequences, to the present. In the second stage of this narrative, as an 'after-effect' of the rule of aristocratic values, the will incorporated God and good into itself; this led to the development of a morality of intentions (rather than consequences), which occurred, could only have occurred, under the aegis of a (moral) will to truth – here the truth of moral action. The self-overcoming of morality, moral self-reflection, interrogates the unreflected presuppositions ('intention', 'will', 'I', etc.) of morality in its traditional sense (BGE 32).[1] Because, on the one hand, Nietzsche relocates and re-identifies metaphysical thinking as moral thinking, as valuing, estimating and judging; and, on the other hand, conceives of the interrogation of the morality of intentions as an application of its own standards of truth and truthfulness to itself (an enlightening of Enlightenment about itself) such that morality is realized and completed in its methodological self-reflection, his critique of modern morality becomes the radical continuation of the critique of heteronomy begun by Descartes and Kant which overturns the firm ground of self and will discovered by them. Nonetheless, the shifting ground of valuation created and discovered by Nietzsche, the will to power, must itself be subject to determination – rational, moral or conceptual – if its autonomous and heteronomous instances are to be distinguishable. The 'law' or ideal determination of the will to power, that which specifies those instances when it wills itself and nothing more, Nietzsche terms 'the eternal recurrence of the same'. The will to power is the *ratio essendi* of eternal recurrence, while eternal recurrence is the 'law' of the will to power. Nietzsche's position is the mimetic fulfilment and collapse of Kant's where freedom (*Willkür*) is the *ratio essendi* of the moral law, and the moral law (*Wille*) is the *ratio cognoscendi* of freedom. *Willkür* is to *Wille* as will to power is to eternal return.

3   Kant opens his *Critique of Practical Reason* with an antinomy, the antinomy of heteronomy. Traditional morality was the search for the true determining ground of the will, presupposing through- out that the will was determined by some object external to it. This object could be: the Platonic good, the commands of God, happiness, perfection, virtue, etc. However the moral good was characterized, it could only relate to the will through desire. If the will is related to its object through desire, then only two possibilities are available: either the will contingently desires the good or it necessarily desires the good. If the will only contingently desires the good, then the good does not obligate and the objectivity of morality is lost. We cannot be obligated to pursue a principle based only on subjective susceptibility since the obligation to pursue it could only arise in consequence of the accidental correspondence between desire and the good. Conversely, if we were necessarily compelled to seek the good – the desire for the good always (causally) determining the will – then, again, obligation would be lost: we cannot be obligated to do what we cannot help but doing. Morality is possible only if the will is free and the relation between the will and the good is neither causally necessary nor contingent. All object-oriented theories of morality necessarily fail to satisfy these two criteria; hence, morality is possible only if what is moral is determined by the will. And if what the will determines as its good is to obligate, then it must be co-extensive with the freedom of the will and be applicable to all possible wills (thereby formally bypassing subjective susceptibility). This is Kant's 'Copernican turn' in ethics; from henceforth the will determines the good, giving the law to itself, rather than the good giving the law to the will.

Morality is the self-binding of the will that is simultaneously a self-lawfulness of self-legislation. The principle of autonomy is that man is subject to his own yet universal legislation. Like pre-modern thinkers, Kant figures the ordering of the soul in political terms. In this regard he contrasts autonomy with autocracy, which is the 'power which the soul has over all faculties and over the whole condition, i.e., the power to subject this condition, without compulsion, to its own free choice'.[2] Autocracy, literally 'self-rule', is a relation of power. Kant contends that man must give this autocracy its full scope 'otherwise he becomes a plaything of other forces and impressions which withstand his will and a prey to the caprice of accident and circumstance'. The political analogy is uppermost in Kant's thoughts here: 'Our sensibility is a kind of rabble without law or rule; it requires guidance even if it is not rebellious.' Autocracy is a necessary condition for autonomy, but not the same as it. Autonomy obtains if I am subject not to the power I employ against myself, but to the law that I give myself. 'Autonomy is distinguished from autocracy as Rousseau's republic, the law-governed state, is distinguished from despotism.'[3] One question in the contestation between Kant and Nietzsche is which is the autocrat and which the defender of autonomy; or even: can the distinction between autocracy and autonomy be sustained?

4 What Kant regards as the theoretical errors of traditional, object-oriented morality Nietzsche investigates under the title of 'nihilism'; nihilism is the socio-historical actuality of object-oriented, heteronomous moral thought. In its most emphatic sense, nihilism refers to the fact that peoples have sought the meaning of their lives in objects outside themselves, in objects that they, or their ancestors or betters, have created. What distinguishes Kant and Nietzsche, however, is that the latter asks after the why, wherefore and consequences of heteronomy as well as investigating its formal characteristics. People would not have sought meaning elsewhere, in the beyond, if life was not conceived as riven with suffering, evil, transitoriness, strife, destruction and failure. Nihilism is not only heteronomy but is also a normal condition of life that expresses its tendential untenability; this untenability conditions the practice of estimating life against values extrinsic to it, values that devalue existence in favour of what is not susceptible to life's tendential untenability. 'Morality', in its narrow sense, is Nietzsche's general term for the heteronomous positings employed to measure life. In so far as morality gives life – evil and suffering included – meaning, in so far as it salvages the integrity and dignity of man and allows it to be comprehended and known, morality has prevented man from despising himself, and hence denying life completely: 'Morality was the great antidote against practical and theoretical nihilism' (WP 4).

Morality as an antidote to nihilism as a normal condition, the aspect of nihilism that leads to or generates heteronomy, points to the question of the *value* of morality (OGM, preface, 3). Hetero-nomous morality, which is itself an expression of life and will to power, secures the worth and dignity of individuals by positing ideals that compensate (through interpretation, prohibition, projection, etc.) for forces that tend to undermine individuals' capacity to have values, to engage in valuing *überhaupt*. Kant comes closest to engaging with the value of morality, and hence with nihilism as a normal condition, in the very place where a Nietzschean would look: his moral theology. There Kant does concede that the value and truth of the moral law is psychologically damaged and undermined by the facts of existence. Moral theology is a defence mechanism against life's refutation of morality. When the moral man looks around him what does he see? That 'deceit, violence, and envy will always be rife around him'; that no matter how worthy of happiness a man is nature will subject him to the 'evils of deprivation, disease, and untimely death' as it does all its creatures; and that all men will remain subjected to those evils until 'one vast tomb engulfs them all (honest or not, that makes no difference here) and hurls them . . . back into the abyss of the purposeless chaos of matter from which they were taken.'[4] Kant concedes that if these facts are true and remain uncompensated, if there are no grounds for hope, if moral worth and happiness were to remain radically disconnected and the human condition incapable of amelioration, then while morality would remain a priori true, its claim valid, it would become psychologically implausible and unsupportable. But to say this is just to admit that the validity of a moral ideal is non-detachable from the conditions under which it is possible for us to sustain belief in it. Since values and ideals provide orientation for life practices, then the value of morality is co-extensive with believing in those values. Belief is necessary for life; and incorporating in morality the conditions that make belief possible will be the centre of Nietzschean affirmation. Belief and reverence are what Nietzschean affirmation are about.

Kant's 'postulates of pure practical reason', his philosophy of history and his eschatological politics address, individually and collectively, the worth or value (for life) of autonomous morality; but in so doing they concede morality's non-autonomy, its conditioning by life. In each case, however, Kant's response to the problem of the value of morality displaces the worth of morality from the moral subject (and the moral law) to what would redeem its strivings. But if what would redeem the strivings of the moral subject are external to it, then the worth of those strivings cannot be autonomous.

Nietzsche appears to concede that it was Kantian autonomy that broke 'open the cage'; but in conceding this he wants at the same time to separate the principle of autonomy from the moral law; the former is a principle of self-binding that restricts the will to paths of action that do not abrogate its supreme authority, while the latter commands the autonomous will to actions that could be done by all.[5] Nietzsche sees the moral law undermining autonomy: 'For it is selfish to experience one's own judgement as a universal law; and this selfishness is blind, petty, and frugal because it betrays that you have not yet discovered yourself nor created for yourself an ideal of your own, your very own' (GS 335). If we mediate our will through its possible willing by others, we dispossess ourselves of the worth or value our willings as our own, as autonomous. So it was the categorical imperative that led Kant *'astray'*, leading him back to God and the immortality of the soul (GS 335; Nietzsche's inclusion of freedom with the other two postulates is, to be sure, textually accurate but philosophically problematic).

Reverence and fear for the moral law is a levelling of man, a reduction of him to what is shareable by the rest of the herd; as such it displaces and prohibits the soul from having reverence for itself (BGE 259, 287); reverence for the moral law weakens the will to value by making the shareability of an end a condition for having it, thus displacing the pursuit of autonomy by a good external to it, namely, shareability or universality. Because universality turns against autonomy it undermines what gives values their worth in the first instance: that 'I' desire and will them. The categorical imperative's levelling effect undermines the presumptive worth of those who attempt to act *under* it, and thus its apparent or intended humanism becomes an anti-humanism, a nihilism: 'together with the fear of man we have also lost our love of him, our reverence for him, our hopes for him, even our will to him' (OGM I, 12).

Nihilism as a normal condition leads Kant back to the postulates, but this compensatory mechanism could have been anticipated since the categorical imperative itself is heteronomous, driving a wedge between the self and its willing that undermines the autonomy of the will and alienates man from himself.

and between the Shaman of Tungus, the European prelate who rules church and state, the Voguls, and the Puritans, on the one hand, and the man who listens to his own command of duty, on the other, the difference is not that the former make themselves slaves, while the latter are free, but that the former have their lord outside themselves, while the latter carries his lord in himself, yet at the same time is his own slave. For the particular – impulses, inclination, pathological love, sensuous experience, or whatever else it is called – the universal is necessarily and always something alien and objective.[6]

This, of course, is Hegel not Nietzsche.

5   If moral theology (or eschatological, progressive politics) is a necessary addendum to morality, and Kant concedes that it is, then the psychology of morality, the valuing of morality with respect to life, is internal to moral reflection and not a mere accessory or supplement. So-called Nietzschean vitalism, his turn to psychology and life, is the *logical* extension of the unsurpassable question of moral motivation, the motivation to morality and the motivation of morality. Belief in moral reason becomes irrational when it excludes either self-reflection or the conditions of its employment; but the conditions for the employment of moral reason are not themselves rational in the narrow sense since they must include sustaining belief in reason and morality as life practices; and, tendentially, all object-oriented, heteronomous moral codes and theories undermine belief in valuing since they devalue or suppress the activity of valuing, valuing-giving and creating, itself. Heteronomous moralities turn against valuing for the sake of keeping valuing alive; but this is a limited strategy since tendentially heteronomous moralities also undermine valuing. This is the third sense of nihilism and the centre of Nietzsche's critique and genealogy of (so-called) objective morality and truth: nihilism is the history whereby the self-defeating structure of heteronomous morality terminates in a condition where no value can be willed, where the will would rather will nothing than not will at all (OGM III, 1). Conversely, Nietzsche's own strategy in lodging this genealogical critique is a continuation of transcendental reflection; his questioning of heteronomous morality is equivalent to an interrogation of the necessary conditions that make valuing possible.

6   Nihilism is heteronomy; where heteronomy now includes whatever prohibits the will from willing itself. Morality, in its traditional sense, is best construed as the will's positings of what it believes would secure its worth and belief in itself in conditions that tendentially undermine *both*. If pure practical reason undermines the will's self-relation, then pure practical reason is heteronomous.

Hence, the will's self-relation, its autonomy, now includes acknowledgement of what the will needs in order to continue willing. Indeed, the default of the claims of pure practical reason entails that a true morality must satisfy the conditions of autonomy, internal coherence (there is no outside to autonomous reason), psychological sustainability (both of the worth of the self and belief in that worth), and empirical plausibility. But these, of course, are just a slightly refined set of criteria for truth.

What does not satisfy these criteria, however, are traditional conceptions of truth, truth as correspondence and disinterested objectivity. Such truth is heteronomous precisely because it takes itself to be an unconditional end; but this belief blocks its psychological conditions for existence, namely 'faith in truth': ' "faith", must always be there first of all, so that science can acquire from it a direction, a meaning, a limit, a method, a *right* to exist' (OGM III, 24). To have faith in truth is to believe that truth is worth pursuing; but to believe truth is worth pursuing puts truth as an object of volition in the same position as all the other objects of heteronomous morality. If the pursuit of truth is heteronomous, then its pursuit will equally involve a depreciation of its conditions of sustainability; belief in truth, where that belief is repressed, where truth is not recognized as a value, entails, then, the affirmation of a world other than 'life, nature, and history'. Truth cannot be an unconditional end and hence cannot be good without qualification. But to say this is to make truth a moral good, a valued good, where the question of the value of truth reveals the primacy of valuing, and hence practical reason, over contemplative reason which now necessarily appears as heteronomous when regarded as independent from moral practice.

The moral critique of objective truth immediately generates an argument parallel with a second Kantian autonomy argument, viz., the argument that runs from the fact that the objects of desire or inclination have only a relative value dependent on their being desired or wanted, to the claim that it is only in virtue of the estimate or judgement of value that we confer value on desire and its objects, that without that estimate an object lacks worth, and that we can estimate apparent goods, items desired, as worthless; and thence to the conclusion that we are ends in ourselves or unconditioned ends since things only get their value by being chosen, and hence choosing (judging, estimating, valuing) cannot itself be valued since it is the necessary condition for there being value at all.[7]

Applying this pattern of argumentation to the question of truth: if truth must be valued to be sought, then it and those who seek it unconditionally are means, 'instruments', 'mirrors' but not unconditional ends: they belong in 'the hand of one more powerful' (BGE 207). The modern truth-seeker is the 'most sublime type of slave', but he is 'no goal, no conclusion and sunrise, no complementary man in whom the rest of existence is justified'. However, truth was sought, and in being sought it was valued; its being valued is what conferred on it the power to govern those whose end it became. But since nothing, including pure practical reason, is valuable in itself, then all values are posits, products of acts of valuing. Because those acts cannot be modelled on anything anterior to them, the belief in such again turning valuing into heteronomy, then valuing is the *creation* of values. 'Genuine philosophers', those for whom modern scholars are instruments and mirrors, 'are commanders and legislators: they say, "thus it shall be!" They first determine the Whither and for What of man. . . . Their "knowing" is creating, their creating is a legislation, their will to truth is – will to power' (BGE 211). As it stands, this claim appears peremptory: Why should creating, will to power, rather than the creating will of the individual be the end in itself?

7   Nietzsche's most austere presentation of his autonomy argument appears in *Thus Spoke Zarathustra*, 'Of the Thousand and One Goals' (Z I, 15). The thousand goals are the heteronomous and conditional ends of humanity thus far; the 'one' is autonomy: creation, legislation, self-legislation itself. The thousand goals bespeak a condition of plurality and relativism; in so far as we cannot adequately choose between those values, then relativism becomes nihilism: values become valueless. Following classic anti-relativist lines, then, Nietzsche contends that unless there is one goal, something of unconditional worth, there can be no goals. If one goal for humanity is lacking then 'is there not still lacking – humanity itself?'

Hitherto there have been a thousand goals, each the goal, the end, the truth of the thousand peoples there have been. Each people must have a goal in virtue of which it claims worth for itself as being the people it is. The collective identity of a people and their self-evaluation are both necessary and reciprocally conditioning elements of any group being a people. Which is why a people cannot evaluate itself 'as its neighbour evaluates'. Over every people there hangs a table of values: the valuings that constitute a people's collective identity. Since a people must believe in its values, and believe in them in opposition to competing collective value ascriptions, then a people's table of values are their self-ascriptions of their worth, their idea of who they are and the goodness of that for themselves and in relation to others. These values reflect the conditions (its needs, land, sky, and neighbours) under which and through which a people were able to constitute itself and sustain that collective identity. Hence its table of values is 'the table of its overcomings'. What has been hard to achieve a people calls 'praiseworthy'; what has been hard to achieve and necessary for its existence it calls 'good'; and what relieves the greatest need, the rare, the hardest of all, i.e., what unconditionally appears to furnish the condition for all other goods, 'it glorifies as holy'. In this way tables of values represent both the identity and conditions of existence for peoples: 'Whatever causes it to rule and conquer and glitter, to the dread of its neighbour, that it accounts the sublimest, the paramount, the evaluation and meaning of all things.'

If tables of values, of good and evil, are self-ascriptions, then regarding this fact generally, from the outside, objectively, entails that these tables collectively cannot be understood as taken, found, or given. The generality of the phenomenon requires an account that can provide an explanation for the totality. Nietzsche's reductive account explains the anthropological facts of the case. Further, as we have already seen, to regard a people's table of values as taken, found, or given would entail relativism, nihilism, and the antinomy of heteronomy. We must then say that 'man first implanted values into things to maintain himself – he created the meaning of things, a human meaning'. Therefore, valuing is creation, and valuing 'is the jewel of all valued things', the unconditioned condition of values.

Thus far, however, only collective valuings have been mentioned. Nietzsche concedes this point: peoples were the first creators of value, only later were there individual creators; or rather, *the individual is the latest creation*. Nietzsche provides an account of this creation in the second essay of *On the Genealogy of Morals*. Nietzsche's only point in *Zarathustra* is that in so far as the individual is a creation, then individuals cannot be unconditioned ends either plurally or collectively. Hence man, plurally or collectively, is not an end in itself because it is a conditioned end, created. However, it does follow from the creation of individuals that valuing as the only unconditioned good has devolved from peoples to individuals. Which individual or individuals? If not individuals collectively or plurally, then only those who self-legislate self-legislation and value creation, those who make unconditioned autonomy their end. The one goal of humanity which gives it to itself, redeems it, is the autonomous legislator.

8   How, then, does Nietzsche construe post-Kantian autonomy, the effort of unconditioned legislation/creation? What sort of will is the will to power? Willing, Nietzsche contends, is something complicated whose only unity is in the word itself (BGE 19). To begin with, willing involves a plurality of sensations: towards, away from, and an accompanying muscular sensation which commences even before we put our body in motion. The antecedents of all actions are inclinations, endeavours, drives, and their sensory accompaniments. Second, every act of will is subject to a ruling thought; to will, as opposed to react, be moved, undergo a reflex action, requires a thought of 'where to' and/or 'away from' of the action to be done. The ruling thought, as will become evident directly, is both the thought of what is to be willed and the identification of the doer with that thought. Third, and most significant, willing involves an affect, 'specifically the affect of command'. If all acting occurs under conditions in which plurality of drives are present and may be acted upon – to sit, stand, walk, think, read, eat, look left or right – then all action involves selection and a conquering by one drive over others. The autocracy which philosophers typically regard as a specific achievement of moral volition is for Nietzsche an element, however weak or evanescent, present in all willing. The term 'freedom of the will', Nietzsche declares, is essentially the affect 'of superiority in relation to him who must obey'. In every act of will there is 'the straining of attention, the straight look that fixes itself exclusively on one aim, the unconditional evaluation that "this and nothing else now". . . . A man who wills commands something within himself that renders obedience, or that he believes renders obedience.'

Nietzsche hypothesizes that metaphysical accounts of willing lose sight of its inner duality, the fact that in every willing we are both commanding and obeying, through the fact that typically obedience is so routine, so predictable that it disappears from sight. It is this that leads to the belief that willing suffices for action, and only the rare occasions of conflict, either between desires themselves or between a desire and duty, provide a reminder of the facts of the case. All willing is an autocratic achievement. Thus, 'freedom of the will' must come to mean not merely doing what one wants to do (the occurrence of an action in consequence of a drive, without external impediment is sufficient for that – which is just freedom of action), but having the will one wants to have.[8] To have the will one wants to have occurs when one's ruling thought succeeds in ruling; and this counts as 'my' freedom because to have a ruling thought is a reflexive identification of oneself with that thought. Who I am, *my* will, is a work of self-identification with the striving or desire that dominates in the battle for power. To act out of character or to feel oneself in the grip of a compulsion is just to say that the drive one identifies as one's own has failed, and hence one's actions were not those of a free will – it was not me acting. '*L'effet c'est moi.* What happens here is what happens in every well-constucted common-wealth; namely, the governing class identifies itself with the success of the commonwealth.' Where Kant conceives of our multiple desires and inclinations as a rabble, Nietzsche simply states that our body is a 'social structure composed of many souls'.

9   Now what separates Nietzsche's account of willing from what is otherwise a fairly standard Humean analysis is its third element, the *affect* of command. Each willing brings with it a feeling of achievement and power (or, where the ruling thought fails to rule, its opposite). This feeling, since it is constitutive of willing itself, becomes thereby the overall affective condition of willing. In heteronomous willing this affect is achieved indirectly: by getting myself to do God's will or that of the categorical imperative I nonetheless master myself (in accordance with a reified third). This is why no self is ever fully adequate to a heteronomous end: the achievement of the good is always my achievement. Hence, the self is always and necessarily in competition with an extrinsic goal; if willing is an autocratic achievement, then in a lateral sense all successful willing is a success for one of the body's many souls. To do God's will or to obey the categorical imperative absolutely would entail the extinction of the self utterly. Extrinsic ends, then, are those that have been incorporated into the self but are consistently regarded *as* external. If they were external, in truth, they could not rule. Thus externality and internality are neither spatial relations, nor relations of passivity and activity; rather, they designate a form of self-relation: in heteronomous willing I do not identify the ruling thought as mine, as a creation of my will, and hence as an expression of my autonomy.

In strict terms, the will to power is only the affect of command and its satisfaction. Since it is a necessary element of willing, short of self-extinction, then Nietzsche is entitled to claim that wherever there are found living creatures, there also will be found will to power, even 'in the will of the servant' (Z II, 12). Will to power is just one element of willing, but it is the very element that has been suppressed by the tradition, and the one whose existence explains why nihilism is a more radical condition than relativism. Nihilism engenders the inability to will anything; it signifies a lifeless life without goals of any sort, and without the possibility of believing in goals: life without faith. This state of affairs is the direct consequence of the long history of believing in unconditional heteronomous goods. As unconditional those goods displace the self in the autocratic hierarchy of successful willing. When those goods reflectively undermine themselves, when truth is discovered not to be an unconditioned end, then all the ends are missing and nothing appears to occupy, or to be worthy of occupying, the place of the dominant soul. Nihilism is spiritual exhaustion, the loss of the possibility of reverence for or faith in anything. But faith, the affective relation between self and ruling thought, where the self is already a self-relation between multiple souls within the same body, is the affective condition for having a ruling thought. As such, it is antecedent to the affect of command; but since faith could not exist without command, then it is best to say that faith is the affect of command as seen from the perspective of obedience. Faith and the affect of command are the affects of the will to power as seen, felt, from contrasting perspectives. They are the constitutive self-affections of the will. Faith as affective 'belief in' through self-affection constitutes the being of the self from the perspective of obedience; it is both consequence and condition of all 'freedom of the will'.

The will to power is the structuring of willing that explicates the possibility of Nietzschean faith. This is why Nietzsche can respond to the troubled voice who asks if there is nothing but the will to power does it mean that God is refuted and the devil not: 'On the contrary!' (BGE 37). In place of the mysterious self-affection of the soul that produces 'reverence' for the moral law in Kant, a reverence that 'demolishes my self-love',[9] Nietzsche institutes the reverence the noble soul has for itself, a 'faith', 'some fundamental certainty that a noble soul has about itself, something that cannot be sought, nor found, nor perhaps lost' (BGE 287). Nietzsche locates the self-affection of the soul in precisely the same place as does Kant, and with the same intended effect: reverence, belief, and faith.

10   Although will to power in its austere sense refers to just the affective dimension of willing, Nietzsche's standard usage is a legitimate metonymy: will to power refers to the whole complicated complex of willing under the name of just one of its parts.

The structure of will to power is autocratic. Like Kant, Nietzsche wants (and needs) to distinguish between three instances: anarchy (where there is no ruling thought, no hierarchy, no reflective self-relation); moral anarchy (covering all heteronomous willing: for Kant this typically occurs when the ruling thought is prudential, and for Nietzsche when it is unconditioned); and autonomy. For Kant, unless all desires are subject to the requirement of the moral law, hence universal legislation, some desire rules and there is only a 'semblance of self-mastery'.[10] But if any desire rules, then the will does not rule (*self*-legislate). 'In self-mastery', Kant states, 'there resides an immediate worth, for to be lord of oneself is to be independent of all things.' Self-mastery is complete only when the will is constituted as independent of all desires; but this can occur only if there is a law of the will that itself is free from all sensible determination. Such a law could not have a content, since any content would be empirical and hence engender heteronomy. Therefore, only the form of what determines the will can constitute its autonomy; and that form can only be that of lawfulness itself, that is, determination by universal law. Thus the will (*Willkür*), which is the capacity for choice and action, has as its intelligible condition the moral law, which gives to the will a principle not subject to empirical conditions, and hence provides the guarantee of its autonomy. Heteronomy is possible because *Wille* (the rational will – which does not 'will' anything, but only legislates what ought to be willed) and *Willkür* (the executive faculty, the capacity for choice and choosing) are not identical. We can will for or against the moral law, *Willkür* being lodged between the solicitations of sensibility and the law of reason (which is reason as law); when willing against its rational ground the will becomes heteronomous. Conversely, autocracy becomes autonomy and the will (*Willkür*) attains to its essence when it is governed by *Wille*.

For Nietzsche, because heteronomous willing is still willing, a will to power, and indeed may be, temporarily, life-promoting (involve an increase in power), then he requires not just a descriptive way of separating autonomous from heteronomous willing, but a practical or normative criterion for distinguishing heteronomous from autonomous willing. Nietzsche too needs a way of separating the 'semblance of self-mastery' from the real thing, the will to power of the ascetic priest from that of the complementary man. Contemplatively, the distinction is straightforward: heteronomous willing regards the ruling thought *as* unconditioned, where any item that is regarded as unconditioned is thereby *practically* external or extrinsic to the will. Now since Nietzsche conceptualizes theoretical reason as an always already subtended moment of practical reason, then the practical or moral question of autonomy becomes: how must the will *regard* itself if it is not to fall into heteronomy? What self-relation would constitute an act of will as being autonomous? And this amounts to asking: what relation must there be between a self and its ruling thought if the ruling thought is to be autonomous? But, finally, this question can be reduced to: what thought constitutes a ruling thought as autonomous? The thought that constitutes a ruling thought as an autonomous thought is the direct Nietzschean analogue of the categorical imperative, with this difference: since the will to power specifies an affective self-relation, then the intelligible structure of the will to power will not specify a logical condition (universality) for a ruling thought, but rather an 'attitudinal' relation. How must I relate myself to my ruling thought if it is going to be autonomous? A valid Nietzschean imperative will designate the necessary relation between a self (which is itself a reflective identification) and its will that would constitute a willing as autonomous.

11 Although the thought of eternal return has a ruling thought for its direct object, in fact that self-affecting self-relation as a whole points beyond itself. Recall, nihilism as a normal condition designates the irremovability from the world of evil (formally for Nietzsche: the transgression of given conceptions of moral goodness), suffering, cruelty, domination, and the transitoriness of all things. Recall too the despair of the Kantian moral man at the sight of these items. In *On the Genealogy of Morals* Nietzsche reductively interprets the ascetic ideal as the truth of the history of heteronomous willing; the ascetic ideal is, for Nietzsche, the definitive heteronomous response to nihilism as a normal condition. The ascetic ideal stands to nihilism as a normal condition as eternal return will stand to the radical nihilism of modernity once the ascetic ideal has finally collapsed. In both cases comes the refrain that human endeavours have been in vain, 'that something was lacking, that man was surrounded by a fearful void – he did not know how to justify himself, to account for, to affirm himself: he suffered from the problem of his meaning' (OGM III, 28). And what

man suffered from was not suffering itself but the meaninglessness of suffering. In the ascetic ideal suffering was interpreted and given meaning, and thereby gave sustenance and direction to the will. Thus what affectively conditions heteronomous thought, what drives and motivates heteronomy is the meaninglessness of suffering, where suffering is understood metonymically as nihilism in its form as a normal condition of life. The justification for Nietzsche's metonymy here is that suffering formally involves the negative, passive relation between an organism and its environment and the felt response to that passive, negative relation. Thus suffering can designate, for example, physical suffering or the transitoriness of things. Suffering is the creaturely, as opposed to creative, condition of humanity. 'In man *creature* and *creator* are united' (BGE 225).

12   If all willing is a commanding and obeying, if in all willing man is creator and creature, and heteronomous willing involves giving to suffering a permanent meaning, then autonomous willing is only possible if one *accepts* absolutely the meaninglessness of the equally absolute effort of giving meaning, creating and legislating. The thought of eternal return is the necessary creaturely thought that must qualify every ruling thought as a commanding. But what is the meaning or value of such a radical acceptance? How does the thought of eternal return evade the grasp of nihilistic despair? One must answer this question in two steps: i) What are the analytic characteristics of the thought of eternal return that allow it its position of privilege?; ii) in virtue of those characteristics, how does the thought of eternal return distinguish autonomous from heteronomous willings?

The central answer to i) is that eternal return is a creaturely *thought*, it is the active thinking of what is itself passive (as passive), and thus, in virtue of its terms, the absolute conferring of value and meaning on what is the negation of meaning *because the negation of meaning, non-meaning, is not its opposite but co-constitutive of it*. It is the co-constitutive role of suffering (destruction, need, contingency, time, etc.) that requires its affirmation. Although Kant's epistemology, arguably, makes suffering in the form of sensibility constitutive, the subsumptive relation between the categorical imperative and desire irredeemably makes the unconditionally good a priori independent of passivity. All unconditionality necessarily entails heteronomy. In contrast, the thought of the eternal return of the same marks the passage between creator and creature, meaning and meaninglessness, activity and passivity. In the thought of eternal return one regards creations as creatures and, at the same time, all creatures as creations. To regard all creations as creatures is to regard all meanings as meaningless (as life and nature); to regard all creatures as creations is to regard meaninglessness as constitutive of meaning giving. Thus the thought of eternal return images, simultaneously, *physis* becoming *nomos*, and *nomos* becoming *physis*. Eternal return does not represent any, possible or actual, state of affairs (and hence is not a metaphysical truth of any kind); it expresses the *practical* entanglement of creature and creator, that is, it expresses the reflective self-comprehension that the entanglement of creatureliness and creativity must have for an agent. Any thought that attempted to transcend this entanglement would, *a fortiori*, be denying a condition of willing.

Eternal return is, then, ii) both the law and the *ratio cognoscendi* of the will to power in the precise sense that it stipulates what willing under the will to power requires us to think (what our self-relation must be) if we are not to abrogate our capacities as wills to power, and how, in so relating ourselves to ourselves will to power is comprehended as the auto-transformation of valuing into life and life into valuing. To be willing, to want to have this moment come back eternally is to be willing for it to be forever creature and forever creation; and to will this is to affirm oneself (beyond oneself) since if one accepts the thought of eternal return then nothing, including the lapse of all my willings into meaninglessness, can deprive 'this' act of willing of its validity and worth. Conversely, and it is the converse consideration that gives the thought of eternal return its power, if for any act we can conceive of conditions under which we might desire that the act and its consequence did not occur, then we must be desiring that the past had been other than it is; but since the past is closed, it cannot be other than it is; therefore, to want the past other is to want the past to be future, which is absurd. Worse, to desire that what one has done has not been done is to desire and not desire the same thing. The temporal spacing that typically makes this look plausible – 'I desired it then; I desire now that I not desired it then' – evades the temporal simultaneity that is the condition for making the second desire worth having. All of what have been called regret, remorse, guilt, all backward-looking emotions that seek to undo the past, involve a refusal of creatureliness and suffering. Finally, a will that routinely suffers from remorse or regret can do so only under the condition that not its willing but something else is of supreme value, something whose worth remains untouched by the worthlessness (wrongness, evil, cruelty, destructiveness) of one's acts. In order to regret an act one must measure it not against one's will and thereby what one can will, but against some constant norm that measures the will, against, say, the good or the categorical imperative. Thus to wish the past or present otherwise is necessarily to will heteronomously. Since suffering is a constitutive element of life, then heteronomous morality is always a morality of remorse or regret, always a will against past willings, always a denial of what it is to will, to act, to value (WP 585).

The thought of eternal return is the intelligible form of the affective aspect of the self-affection involved in all willing. Because eternal return is the intelligible double of will to power, the thought of eternal return qualifies the ruling thought of a willing as 'for the sake of' the affective aspect of the self-affection constitutive of all willing. This 'for the sake of' binds willing to itself; in affirming 'this' willing, and by extension all my willings, I free myself to willing, valuing, and legislating without remorse or regret. But to act without the possibility of remorse or regret is to accept absolute responsibility for all my doings and valuings, and thereby have the self-reverence that makes valuing possible. As a virtue or character trait, the self-relation that eternal return legislates qualifies all one's willing as worth doing because done unconditionally (despite being absolutely conditioned).[11]

13 Although there can be little doubt that eternal return is meant as the law and *ratio cognoscendi* of will to power, Nietzsche barely discusses it in his published writings, and his alter ego, Zarathustra, does not himself proclaim it (Z III, 13). There are a number of reasons for this, including the unteachableness of autonomy (and generally any teaching which has a first-person, performative structure), and the fact that given the natural order of rank amongst human beings, as always also natural beings, it is contingent that one be able, have the power, to will eternal return (one may be crushed by the thought of it); finally, Nietzsche is aware that even if eternal return does express our categorical imperative, the imperative designed for the tranformation of passive into active, affirmative nihilism, he cannot, on pain of contradiction, demonstrate why he or anyone else *ought* to make it supremely authoritative for themselves. If eternal return ought to be supremely legislative, then it becomes another unconditional, dogmatic thought, an ideal incompatible with its own logical content. Alternatively, if eternal return lacked that logical content, if it were not able practically to

distinguish autonomous from heteronomous willings, then, it would be critically and practically empty. Its critical and practical *force* is not distinguishable from its logical content (even if that content is exhausted in its practical significance, in its performance). Eternal return is a categorical imperative – 'Always will so that you can, at the same time, will that what you do could be willed once more and innumerable times more' – that, when regarded as a categorical imperative immediately cancels itself out: it becomes something other than and external to the self-relation it legislates. Thus Zarathustra: ' "This – is now *my* way: where is yours?" Thus I answered those who asked me "the way". For *the* way – does not exist.' That eternal return is the way and the way does not exist is what makes *Zarathustra* 'A Book for Everyone and No One'.

Like some contemporary moral philosophers,[12] Nietzsche denies that reasons for action that are not *mine* (a drive of my body) can obligate: we cannot be obligated to do what, given who we are, we have no reason (drive or desire) to do: 'external' reasons cannot be obligatory because 'I' have no reason or motive for obeying them. But unlike modern moral philosophers, this never entails for Nietzsche an easy individualism or a reduction of morality to prudential reasoning: 'The philosopher as *we* understand him, we free spirits – *is the man of the most comprehensive responsibility who has the conscience for the over-all development of man*' (BGE 61; emphasis mine). Responsibility derives from a relation between a context and a self-relation. The self-relation at issue is of nihilism as loss of faith (the interruption of the relation between myself and my affective conditions of willing), and the context is of that experience as conditioned by the objective devaluation of all values. To experience the world like 'this', nihilistically, makes me responsible for 'the over-all development of man', since only by legislating/ creating beyond good and evil, only by becoming one 'who creates a goal for mankind and gives the earth its meaning and its future . . . who creates the quality of good and evil in things' (Z III, 12), only by bearing 'the burden of all who obey' (Z II, 12), only thus can *I* will autonomously. The fate of my willing, my being able to act autonomously, is non-detachable from what historically and socially have constituted the conditions and nature of willing heretofore. *I* can act autonomously only by the actual transformation/transvaluation of all values, by, thus, creating and conferring new values and meanings on the earth and its future, and so legislating for all humanity. So my duty to myself, grounded in my reverence for myself, entails, given the historical collision between my needs and the nihilistic denouement of all previous history that I inhabit, that I can only satisfy my duty to myself by taking up and becoming responsible for humanity as a whole.[13]

Autonomy is not Kantianly universalizable since to treat all others as moral agents would deny the creaturely condition of willing; Kantian respect would make others, those external to my will, unconditioned ends. Nietzschean autonomy and obligation entails responsibility *for* others not *to* them; they are moral patients not moral agents. But this does not remove responsibility, but rather redirects it: 'responsibility for' all others, which again is just my autonomy, my becoming 'judge and avenger and victim' of my own law, is universal in scope (the entire history of humanity resides in me). This is why Nietzsche can say that the complementary man, the philosopher of the future is one 'in whom the rest of existence is justified' (BGE 207). With the man who can will autonomously humanity finally discovers its – one – end.

14 Let us ignore the hyperbolic excess of these claims; the question still remains: what is it to be responsible for the development of humanity? After all, that responsibility is for Nietzsche just the converse side of *my* becoming autonomous. Since my autonomy ultimately is justified by my self-relation, the affective increase in willing to act autonomously (creatively), then autonomy is still primarily a self-affection, something solitary, private and beyond communication. Thus doctrines, works of legislation and creation devolve into moments of my spiritual becoming, 'steps to self-knowledge, sign-posts to the problem we *are* – rather to the great stupidity we are, to our spiritual *fatum*, to what is *unteachable* very "deep down" ' (BGE 231). Autonomy is a work of solitude, since language (BGE 268) and community (BGE 284) both have a reductive tendency to claim the self for what is outside it. Thus the truth of autonomous existence is never to be found in the works or deeds of autonomous beings (BGE 269, 289). Because there is an inevitable incommensurability between autonomous self-affection and its products, because creation materialized is creaturely, and thus a betrayal of autonomy, because autonomy is always a spiralling form of autocracy that requires difference and the 'pathos of distance' (BGE 257), then *what* is legislated by the autonomous self is a matter of indifference; or better, what is important is that there be autonomous legislation. But if nihilism is nothing but heteronomy, the history of the denial that willing is will to power, then this consequence is hardly surprising.

15   With the advent of modern nihilism, the culmination of passive nihilism, heteronomous morality no longer can aid the will. Moreover, it was this

> morality itself [that] damned up such enormous strength and bent the bow in such a threatening manner; now it is 'outlived'. The dangerous and uncanny point has been reached where the greater, more manifold, more comprehensive life transcends and *lives beyond* the old morality; the 'individual' appears, obliged to give himself laws and to develop his own arts and wiles for self-preservation, self-enhancement, self-redemption.
>
> (BGE 262)

The emptiness of autonomy as a social ideal is prescribed by the structure of 'living beyond'.[14] Living beyond is self-overcoming; self-overcoming being the incessant realization that whatever is created turns creaturely and thus must be opposed: 'Whatever I create and however much I love it – soon I have to oppose it and my love: thus will my will have it' (Z II, 12). Autonomy is only the transgression of boundaries, valuing only transvaluation, going beyond, living beyond. Because what willing is categorically for is the affective moments of the self-affection whereby the individual relentlessly comes to be, a second order aporetic incommensurability between creator and creature becomes inevitable. It is this incommensurability, the necessity for sustaining the 'pathos of distance' which, finally, is a perpetual distancing of the self from itself, that enforces solitude, mask, and irony. Autonomous beings are hermits, the living dead, entombed in life because forever living beyond creatureliness, while striving for a creaturely life, a life in community, that only death can provide:

> this whole subterranean, concealed, mute, undiscovered solitude that among us is called life but might just as well be called death – if we did not know what will *become* of us, and that it is only after death that we shall enter *our* life and become alive, oh, very much alive, we posthumous people!
>
> (GS 365)

Eternal return raises to a historico-metaphysical fate the very duality between creator and creature, activity and passivity, self and world that it was designed to overcome. Nietzsche's radicalization of Kantian autonomy terminates in the worldless, death-in-life solitude of the philosopher-legislator. That solitude reveals autonomy as an empty social ideal since it is solitude with its remorseless self-overcomings that is the truth of eternal return rather than any content that the philosopher-hermit might create and legislate. Yet, the path to it was not idle, for Nietzsche's question 'How is morality possible?' discovered the Achilles' heel of Kantian morality: that its 'good reason' for performing an action is permanently detached from motive and desire. But having desires is not the same as having values, valuing requires belief in and reverence for values. But, if reverence for value requires self-reverence (which is both a reverence for the valuer and a reverence for the valuing making the valuer possible), then the trajectory of autonomy makes the conditions necessary for reverence simultaneously ones that prohibit anything worth valuing having a place. Nietzsche's formalism, like Kant's, demonstrates the emptiness of the moral will. The search for an autonomy beyond autocratic rule always transpires in but another autocracy, another power without virtue. This should be unsurprising since the drive for autonomy is always a refusal of community and mediation, a refusal of dependency on the will of another. This is doubly marked in Nietzsche: first, through his reduction and introjection of political rule to 'superiority of soul' (OGM I, 6); and second, through the consequential untransformed Stoicism in his thought of autonomy (BGE 227). Another way of saying this would be to point out that Nietzsche's doctrines, above all will to power and eternal return, undermine the abiding pathos of Nietzschean discourse: his reverence for the noble Greeks, his disgust for modern man because not worthy of reverence (and lacking it), his terrible sense of responsibility for us. Autonomy becomes autocracy when the reverence for man that makes autonomy worth pursuing is absent. Perhaps, then, we had better say that *our* difficulty, the aporia of modernity, its limit and refutation, is just the reflective belonging together and utter historical opposition between autonomy and reverence.

NOTES

1 Works are cited in the text by abbreviations and by section number.
BGE *Beyond Good and Evil*, trans. Walter Kaufmann, New York, Random House, 1966.
OGM *On the Genealogy of Morals*, trans. Walter Kaufmann and R. J. Hollingdale, New York, Random House, 1969.
GS *The Gay Science*, trans. Walter Kaufmann, New York, Random House, 1974.

WP   *The Will to Power*, trans. Walter Kaufmann and R. J. Hollingdale, New York, Random House, 1967.

Z   *Thus Spoke Zarathustra*, trans. R. J. Hollingdale, Baltimore, Maryland, Penguin Books, 1961.

2 For this and the next quote: I. Kant, *Lectures on Ethics*, Louis Infield, New York, Harper & Row, 1963, 140.

3 Rüdigner Bittner, *What Reason Demands*, trans. Theodore Talbot, Cambridge, Cambridge University Press, 1989, 76.

4 I. Kant, *Critique of Judgement*, trans. Werner S. Pluhar, Indianapolis, Hackett Publishing Company, 1987, 87, 452.

5 Bittner, op. cit., 76ff.

6 G. W. F. Hegel, *On Christianity: Early Theological Writings*, trans. T. M. Know, New York, Harper Torchbooks, 1961, 211.

7 For a good account of this argument see Christine Korsgaard, 'Kant's Formula of Humanity', *Kant-Studien*, April 1986, vol. 77, 183–202.

8 Harry Frankfurt, 'Freedom of the Will and the Concept of a Person', *Journal of Philosophy*, Jan. 1971, vol. 67, 5–20.

9 I. Kant, *Groundwork of the Metaphysics of Morals*, trans. H. J. Paton, New York, Harper & Row, 1964, 401n.

10 I. Kant, *Lectures on Ethics*, op. cit., 140.

11 After writing this paper I discovered a deeply analogous analysis by Jean-Luc Nancy, ' "Our Probity!" On Truth in the Moral Sense in Nietzsche', in Lawrence A. Rickels (ed.), *Looking After Nietzsche*, Albany, State University of New York Press, 1990. Roughly, working through GS 335, Nancy interprets the relationship between probity and physics much as I interpret eternal return and will to power, and doing so as a way of revealing how Kantian Nietzsche is. Nancy puts the issue I am working through here in these terms (p. 76): '*Redlichkeit* is a moral conscience consisting in nothing other than conformity to the law of *physics*. The *moral* character vanishes or is sublimated – or is perhaps transvalued – in a knowledge of the law of nature, a knowledge which comes out immediately as evaluation, as a *Gewissen* evaluating this *Wissen* of universal evaluation. Physiology becomes axiology – but in opposition to all axiology. Such is *Redlichkeit*.'

12 E.g. Bittner, op. cit., and, above all, the writings of Bernard Williams, especially the articles collected in *Moral Luck*, Cambridge, Cambridge University Press, 1981.

13 Clearly the present analysis lacks an account of Nietzschean obligation, the key to which is doubtless his views on conscience and probity. See Nancy, op. cit., esp. 76–8.

14 For a perspicuous account of 'living beyond' see Werner Hamacher's ' "Disgregation of the Will": Nietzsche on the Individual and Individuality', in Thomas C. Heller *et al.* (eds), *Restructuring Individualism: Autonomy, Individuality and the Self in Western Thought*, Stanford, Stanford University Press, 1988, 106–39.

9 Affirmation and eternal return in the Free-Spirit Trilogy

Howard Caygill

Shall we do this, friends, again? Amen, and *auf Wiedersehn!*
Epilogue, *Human, All Too Human*

The question of where the thought of eternal return belongs has haunted the reading of Nietzsche's philosophy. There is some doubt whether it belongs to him at all, or if it does, where it stands in respect to his other thoughts of 'will to power' and 'overman'. It is a thought difficult to place, one which disturbs any attempt to gather his thinking under the traditional titles of theoretical and practical philosophy. And while it appears in some respects marginal to his philosophy, eternal return is claimed by Nietzsche in *Ecce Homo* as its centre – the 'highest formula of affirmation' and the 'basic thought' of *Also Sprach Zarathustra* (1883–5).

One response to the difficulty of placing eternal return is to expel it altogether. This option was taken by Alfred Bäumler in *Nietzsche der Philosoph und Politiker* (1931) where the thought is relegated to the realm of biographical idiosyncrasy, so clearing the field for an alignment of will to power and overman. Although few would today admit to following Bäumler's reading, its consequences are evident in many contemporary critiques and defences of 'Nietzscheanism'.[1]

A more subtle form of relegation casts eternal return as an esoteric doctrine whose hidden ubiquity may be established by a scrutiny of what Nietzsche wrote but did not publish in the manuscripts and notebooks from the 1880s. This approach combines the pleasures of close textual scholarship with the virtue of leaving an open verdict on where to place eternal return. But it also threatens to divert the search for eternal return into unravelling the textual difficulties posed by Nietzsche's projects, notebooks, and jottings.[2]

In this essay eternal return will be read as the outcome of the crisis of judgement rehearsed in the 'Free-Spirit Trilogy' of *Human,*

All Too Human (1878–80), *Daybreak* (1881), and *The Gay Science* (1882). This approach, recommended by Nietzsche in *Ecce Homo*,[3] emphasizes the difficult, aporetic character of the doctrine over its systematic relation to 'will to power' and 'overman'. In this reading eternal return becomes, in Kantian terms, a 'statement' of the 'enigma' or 'puzzle' of liberation, and not its 'solution'.[4] The difficulty of placing eternal return marks its resistance to the classic topic of philosophy and its intimation of new philosophical spaces.

I

The translation of Nietzsche's philosopheme into the classic distinction of theoretical and practical philosophy informs many readings of his work. Theoretical philosophy is discovered in the relation of will to power's 'becoming' and the 'being' of eternal return, while practical philosophy is found in the 'legislative' will to power of the 'sovereign' overman. Such a translation informs Heidegger's designation of Nietzsche's philosophy as the 'end of metaphysics' in the text of his Nietzsche lectures from the 1930s.[5] However this text, whose importance for reading Nietzsche cannot be overestimated, becomes extremely apprehensive when thinking about eternal return and its relation to 'will to power' and 'overman'. It constantly exceeds its own interpretative limits in a movement later thematized in the non-metaphysical reading of Nietzsche developed in *What is Called Thinking* (1954).

One of the subtexts of Heidegger's lectures is the restoration of eternal return in the wake of its dismissal by Bäumler and company.[6] He does so by 'including' eternal return within will to power, suggesting that they say and think the same thought:

> We call Nietzsche's thought of the will to power his sole thought. At the same time we are saying that Nietzsche's other thought, that of the eternal return of the same, is of necessity included in the thought of will to power. Both thoughts – will to power and eternal return – say the same and think the same fundamental character of beings as a whole.
>
> (Heidegger, 1961, III, 10)

Nietzsche's 'other thought' is 'included in' the thought of will to power by virtue of the metaphysical dichotomy of being and becoming. The terms of this theoretical inclusion were later described by Heidegger as 'the way of continuance through which will to power wills itself and guarantees its own presencing as the being of becoming' (Heidegger, 1950, 22). So while eternal return is recovered from the oblivion decreed by Bäumler, it is 'included' in a metaphysical dichotomy which it cannot but disrupt.

Another defence of eternal return offered in the lectures is practical, and involves the inclusion of eternal return in a metaphysics of the temporality of *Dasein*. The moment of eternal return is a 'collision' of past and future in the resolute decision:

> Whoever stands in the Moment is turned in two ways: for him past and future *run up against* one another. Whoever stands in the Moment lets what runs counter to itself come to collision, though not to a standstill, by cultivating and sustaining the strife between what is assigned him as a task and what has been given him as his endowment.
>
> (Heidegger, 1961, II, 56–7)

Heidegger correctly and profoundly identifies the key to understanding this moment – a moment of the greatest weight or the greatest liberation – as the manner in which it is affirmed. It is how we say yes to the return of 'every pain and every joy' that determines the meaning of the moment.[7] He distinguishes the affirmation of a spectator (the dwarf in *Zarathustra*) from one who stands resolutely in the moment and decides between past and future. But the choice Heidegger offers between irresolute and resolute affirmation does not exhaust all the options. There is also the affirmation of one who is in the moment but free from the choice which it poses, the free spirit, whose yes neither affirms nor negates the times of past, present, and future.

The way in which Nietzsche came to this yes through the 'historical philosophy' announced in *Human, All Too Human* will be examined below. It involves liberation from judgement rather than grasping the freedom to judge and decide resolutely. In Heidegger's reading, the moment of liberation occurs when eternal return and will to power cross each other in the resolute decision which affirms ecstatic temporality: 'Strange – are we to experience something that lies behind us by thinking forward? Yes, we are' (p. 135). Such affirmation characterizes authentic *Dasein*; we forfeit liberation if we avoid this decision of the moment since:

> we no longer ponder the fact that as temporal beings who are delivered over to ourselves we are also delivered over to the future in our willing; we no longer ponder the fact that the

temporality of human being alone determines the way in which the human being stands in the ring of beings.

(p. 136)

But perhaps there is another form of avoidance,[8] one which is not inauthentic but whose affirmation is beyond the past and future of the moment of *Dasein*; perhaps the strange thought is not exhausted by past and future united in the moment of willing? For eternal return points beyond man and time, beyond *Dasein* and ecstatic temporality, perhaps beyond the ontological difference of being and beings. The complexity of Heidegger's narrative at this point, his admission that 'Nietzsche knew and experienced a great deal more than he sketched out or fully portrayed', points to an uneasiness with the proposed alignment of the moment of eternal return with ecstatic *Dasein*.

The interruptions of the lecture's narrative by apprehensions of the excess of eternal return are transformed into the rhythmic tropes of *What is Called Thinking*. Here Heidegger lets his reading of Nietzsche sway in and out of metaphysical dichotomies. One trope makes eternal return 'the supreme triumph of the metaphysics of the will that eternally wills its own willing' (Heidegger, 1954, 104) while the other makes it rehearse the *difficulties* of such thinking. In the latter, 'Nietzsche's attempt to think the Being of beings makes it almost obtrusively clear to us moderns that all thinking, that is, relatedness to being, is still difficult' (ibid., 110). In the first trope eternal return is included within metaphysical dichotomies as a supplement to a philosophy of the will, while in the second it breaks their bounds and becomes the site for the crisis of thinking. With the second thought Nietzsche is no longer the philosopher of will to power who completes the metaphysics of presence, but the thinker who turns thinking into thanks – not recompense but devotion – one whose difficult thought is a remembrance of 'what is unspoken', of what has not been sent down or destined to be present.

The example of Heidegger's subtle rhythmic movement between immanence and externality in the later reading has until recently had few imitators. His 'inclusive' reading of the 1930s has been more influential, even in a text as unsympathetic to Heidegger's general project as Deleuze's *Nietzsche and Philosophy* (1962). This text locates Nietzsche's philosophy as a 'radical transformation of Kantianism', one in which the Kantian problematic of synthesis in judgement is transformed into the synthesis of forces effected through will to power and eternal return:

He understood the synthesis of forces as the eternal return and thus found the reproduction of diversity at the heart of synthesis. He established the principle of synthesis, the will to power, and determined this as the differential and genetic element of forces which directly confront one another.

(Deleuze, 1962, 52)

The principle of will to power and the principle of eternal return achieve the synthesis of judgement, but at the cost of closure, for 'Return is the being of becoming, the unity of multiplicity, the necessity of chance' (ibid., 189). Eternal return is thus brought under judgement as the supplement necessary to bring the becoming of will to power to presence or to stabilize it in synthesis. This is to 'include' eternal return within will to power, and to subordinate both to the oppositions of metaphysical thinking.

While Deleuze's reading of Nietzsche stabilizes eternal return in a synthetic judgement, Derrida's reading develops Heidegger's later thought that eternal return marks the crisis that destabilizes judgement. In his reading of *Ecce Homo* in *Otobiography* (1982) eternal return is less the metaphysical negotiation of being and becoming than the difficult attempt to think beyond metaphysical dichotomies. Reading Heidegger against Heidegger, Derrida writes:

The point is that the eternal return is not a new metaphysics of time or of the totality of being, et cetera, on whose ground Nietzsche's autobiographical signature would come to stand like an empirical fact on a great ontological structure. (Here, one would have to take up again the Heideggerian interpretations of the eternal return and perhaps problematize them.) The eternal return always involves differences of forces that perhaps cannot be thought in terms of being, of the pair essence–existence, or of any of the great metaphysical structures to which Heidegger would like to relate them.

(Derrida, 1982, 46)

Derrida turns Heidegger's late reading of Nietzsche against the early lectures, preferring the 'difficulty' of eternal return to the 'solution' of the will eternally willing itself. For Derrida, as for Heidegger in *What is Called Thinking*, this enigma poses itself in the uncontainable affirmation of eternal return.

Derrida's return to Heidegger's later reading of Nietzsche underlines the way in which the difficulty of eternal return forces a return to the question of Nietzsche's affirmation. In both cases the 'yes' of eternal return is thought as a 'yes' before 'yes and no', an affirmation before affirmation and negation. It is not a resolute yes, nor a yes spoken in judgement, but a yes that both enables and disturbs judgement. The character of this unspoken yes before yes and no – a yes that is not of the logos – is beautifully described by Rosenzweig in *The Star of Redemption* (1921) as 'the silent attendant of every sentence, the confirmation, the "so be it", the "amen" behind every word'.[9] This affirmation is not willed, it is before the subject and its willing; nor is it a judgement, but is before, and yet confirms and upsets, the giving of judgement.

The readings of eternal return intimated by Heidegger and developed by Derrida are confirmed when the thought is read as the summation of the Free-Spirit Trilogy. The trilogy is concerned with evoking a crisis of judgement, of achieving a liberation from the measures of 'man' while respecting them, of affirming while paying a penance for yes and no. It develops the thought of eternal return as the 'highest formula' of an affirmation which both conserves and disrupts. This affirmation and disruption is contained in Nietzsche's analysis of the 'calling' (*Aufgabe*), an idea central not only to the trilogy, but to the whole of his authorship. Indeed, the notions of return and originality developed in the context of the 'calling' of the 'free spirit' are crucial to understanding Nietzsche's presentation of eternal return as something which 'if it took hold of you would transform you as you are or would lie on your actions as the greatest weight' (GS, 341).

II

In *Ecce Homo* Nietzsche describes how he signed for the receipt of the thought of eternal return, some time in August 1881, with the phrase '6000 feet beyond Man and Time'. His signature states the condition and consequence of receiving the affirmative formula of eternal return to be an elevation beyond 'man and time', one which is both task and achievement. It was the projective and retrospective character of the formula which impelled Nietzsche to return to the Free-Spirit Trilogy in the prefaces he wrote to each volume in 1886[10] and in his 'autobiography' (*Ecce Homo*) of 1888. I shall begin with the autobiographical return.

The presentation of the Free-Spirit Trilogy in *Ecce Homo* challenges the assumption that Nietzsche's authorship was progressive. Far from tracing a development through his writings before and after *Zarathustra*, Nietzsche insists on a qualitative break in his authorship. The writings before and including *Zarathustra* represent the 'yes-saying *part*' (*der jasagende Teil*) and the later writings the 'no-saying, no doing *half* [*neinsagende, neintuende Hälfte*] of my calling [*Aufgabe*]' (EH 310). This division of the 'calling' is crucial to understanding Nietzsche's view of his authorship. For the yes-saying part is not the simple complement of the no-saying half, as if they added up to some integral calling, but belongs to a completely different order of affirmation.

The texts of the no-saying half have become the canonical sources for Nietzsche's philosophy. Yet they were described by their author as mere 'fish hooks' intended to catch those who 'would offer their hands for destroying' and contribute to 'conjuring up a day of decision' (EH 310). The second half of the calling, in other words, engages on the terrain of previous and current values, and attempts to institute a state of crisis and decision. Their manifesto character distinguishes them from the texts of the 'yes-saying' part of his authorship which Nietzsche described as 'monuments', as sites for the return and remembrance of his calling.

Far from being the positive propaedeutic for the later negative texts, the affirmation of the trilogy and *Zarathustra* emerges from a working through of a crisis of yes and no. They do not complement the later texts since they already contain the *whole* of Nietzsche's philosophy. The return of negation in the writings after *Zarathustra* is not defined against the affirmation achieved in eternal return, but is tied to the same crisis of yes and no which the free spirit had overcome. The 'fish hook' texts were addressed to the 'agitated, power-hungry society of present-day Europe and America' (D 148) in a language they would understand and in a manner intended to provoke the return of the liberating destruction already experienced by the free spirit.

Human, All Too Human, the first book of the Free-Spirit Trilogy, is described in *Ecce Homo* as the 'monument of a crisis'. One of its preconditions was its author's 'profound alienation from everything that surrounded' him at the first *Bayreuther Festspiel*, when Wagner descended among the Germans and draped himself in 'German virtues'. The alienation was experienced as a break between memory and actuality, with Nietzsche waking up to feel that he was dreaming. As he 'leafed' through his memories he could find 'no shadow of similarity' between the Wagner before him and the Wagner of Tribschen. There was no discernible relation between the present and the past.

The shock of 'recognizing nothing' led first to a general

impatience with the forgetting of self or 'selflessness' of 'idealism' and then to an 'inexorable decision' against 'yielding, going along, and confounding myself'. Wagner had become for Nietzsche the 'opiate' of the *Reich*, and Bayreuth the place where Germans could 'forget themselves, be rid of themselves for a moment – what am I saying?' For *five or six hours'* (EH 287). Against this Nietzsche determined to 'return to myself', 'to recall and reflect on myself', to liberate his self from what did not 'belong' to him. He presents his negation in terms of recovering possession: the free spirit is one 'that has *become free*, that has again taken possession of itself' or one which has 'recovered' itself.[11]

The recovery of what was his own required 'rigorous self-discipline' on the part of Nietzsche, but here an ironic note enters the triumphant autobiographical narrative. The 'self-discipline' required is passive, that of a patient '*commanded*' by sickness to be still; it is a discipline 'of lying still, of leisure, of waiting and being patient. – But that means, of thinking' (EH 287). Nietzsche introduces a complication into the classic schema of loss, struggle, and recovery through which he seems to describe the genesis of *Human, All Too Human*. The complexity of his autobiographical narrative is underlined by his claim to have avoided 'the little word "I" ' which exemplified the 'monstrous surenes [with which] I got hold of my task and its world historic aspect' (EH 288). The book which seemed to be about the recovery of the 'I' becomes the book in which the 'I' is avoided.

The avoidance and the recovery of the 'I' are not necessarily incompatible, nor does self-discipline rule out lying still and being patient. But these movements are quite different from the classic dialectic of loss, self-disciplined labour and recovery. In *Human, All Too Human* 'Idealism's' trope of recovering its own is arrested and brought to a standstill:

> This is war, but war without powder and smoke, without warlike poses, without pathos and strained limbs: all that would still be 'idealism'. One error after another is coolly placed on ice; the ideal is not refuted – it *freezes* to death.
>
> (EH 284)

This 'dialectic at a standstill' confirms the description of the book as the 'monument' at once to a 'crisis' (EH 283) and to 'rigorous self-discipline' (EH 288). It is monumental in the sense of placing the movement of loss, struggle, and recovery in a different time, one beyond loss and recovery. The attempt to remember the lost 'I' is made into a monument or object of remembrance, and in doing so it changes its significance. What is recovered in remembrance is new and original, even if it had always been present.[12]

The same refusal to move from loss to recovery informs Nietzsche's autobiographical recall of *Daybreak*, the second volume of the trilogy. The 'effect of the book is negative' but 'this in no way contradicts the fact that the book contains no negative word, no attack, no spite' (EH 290). The self-discipline required to execute this 'campaign against morality' imitates the languor of a 'sea animal basking among rocks'. Nietzsche teases his reader with the suggestion that the book might be read as a 'liberation from all moral values, in saying yes to and having confidence in all that has hitherto been forbidden, despised, and damned'. But he ends a beautiful description of how the yes of this negative book expels 'morality' in an outpouring of 'light, love and tenderness', by freezing the yes with the question 'Or?': 'This book closes with an 'or?' – it is the only book that closes with an 'or?'.

Nietzsche remembers that it was with *Daybreak* that he began his 'campaign against a morality that would unself man' (EH 292). But this negative campaign did not imply a positive one which would re-self man, return him to himself. The yes and the no of the campaigns for and against are disturbed by the question 'or?' – or is there something more than saying yes and no? Must the no to the priestly memory which 'conserves what degenerates' imply a yes to a memory which conserves what regenerates? For Nietzsche this implication would confine thought to an 'idealistic' movement of loss and recovery, of negation and affirmation. He affirms against this particular trope the need to avoid solutions and to conclude with questions: the 'no' to morality and the 'yes' to the forbidden, despised, and damned are equally questionable.

What is recovered or affirmed is not necessarily that which was lost, but might be something new and original. This is how Nietzsche recalls *The Gay Science* where the 'highest hope' or the freedom won was not what was sought, but 'something incomparable' (EH 296). From it emerged the beginning of *Zarathustra*, and, in the penultimate paragraph (§341), the first and most perfect expression of the thought of eternal return.

In remembering the Free-Spirit Trilogy in *Ecce Homo* Nietzsche shows how the liberation achieved in these texts was not the recovery of a self that had been lost and forgotten. The autobiographical narrative of *Ecce Homo* transforms the movement of self-discovery characteristic of its genre to a movement of questioning, one which re-invents the meaning of the signature 'Nietzsche'. When Nietzsche does his duty and asks 'Above all do not mistake me for someone else' he is not presenting his real self against the mistaken self, but asking that the question of his signature, of what he meant, of what belonged and did not belong to him, be kept open – *Nietzsche oder?*

A similar insistence on the questionable nature of his work informs Nietzsche's earlier return to the trilogy in the prefaces he wrote for each of the works in 1886. Here the ironic undermining of autobiographical trope of *Ecce Homo* is anticipated in a magisterial contribution to the venerable genre of the self-destructing philosophical preface. The return of the trilogy announced and performed by these texts once again puts the nature of Nietzsche's calling in question.

III

Nietzsche added prefaces to the books of the Free-Spirit Trilogy several years after they were completed. They were retrospective prospects for books which were, he said, already dated when he wrote them.[13] Nevertheless, their re-issue remained timely, and what he said in the preface to *Daybreak* applies to them all: 'This preface is late but not too late – what, after all, do five or six years matter?' (D, p. 5). He does not return to deliver his own or philosophy's funeral oration – Hegel's painting 'grey in grey' in the preface to the *Philosophy of Right* – but to announce the recovery of his calling; he returns to announce his return.

In the preface to Part One of *Human, All Too Human* dated Nice, Spring 1886, he describes his 'recovery' as 'a temporary self-forgetting' (HH, p. 5). The preface to Part Two, written in Sils Maria in September 1886, offers a more startling image of the author's departure and return: while his pessimistic anti-romantic insights 'have often made him jump out of his skin' he has 'always known how to get back into it again' (p. 210). Similarly, in the 'belated' preface to *Daybreak* dated 'Ruta, near Genoa, in the Autumn of 1886', he assures his friends that the 'underground man' will return, and that 'in this late preface which could easily have become a funeral oration' he is pleased to announce 'I have returned and, believe it or not, returned safe and sound' (D, p. 1). The preface to *The Gay Science*, written at the same time and the same place, assures us that Herr Nietzsche has recovered, and returned from profundity to superficiality. In all the prefaces

Nietzsche seems to depart and return – he does not stay still long enought to watch with Hegel as a shape of life grows old.

The prefaces are full of gratitude for the return, and unanimous that what has returned is something new, something unprecedented. The preface to Part One of *Human, All Too Human* presents this return of the new as the 'riddle of liberation', and it will be examined at length below. But what is it that can return as new? In the preface to Part Two of the same book Nietzsche describes it as 'the return of our calling' (*Aufgabe*) and praises this return as 'the *greatest* of life's gifts, perhaps the greatest thing it is able to give of any kind', its reward.

The return of the calling is the discovery of something new and original. But discovery simply renames the calling's property of being both a process of discovery and the object discovered, the way and the goal. Nietzsche's calling is both what he is and the search for what he is, there is no distinction between them. But the calling is also other, strange, a tyrant without a name: 'That concealed and imperious something for which we for long have no name until it proves to be our calling – the tyrant in us takes a terrible retribution for every attempt we make to avoid or elude it' (HH, p. 211). Nietzsche goes on to say that there can be 'no return to health', no recovery unless we 'burden ourselves more heavily than we have ever been burdened before'. The calling has always been there, but in 'alleviated' form;[14] with its return the tyrant is named and while still demanding satisfaction it ceases to exact retribution.

Nietzsche's description of the calling as 'nameless' but effective anticipates the terms of his later description of 'originality' in §261 of *The Gay Science*. Originality is the ability 'to see something that does not bear a name and can still not be named even though it stares us all in the face'. The calling, or the nameless, is both revealed and concealed and can only be named in its return – which is always too late. The return is always questionable, and this burden of the question must be borne to the extent of becoming *the greatest weight*.

Nietzsche ends his preface by claiming that he holds this 'novel and strange' perspective 'as much for myself as, occasionally at least, *against* myself' (p. 214). But even this statement of the calling is questionable and provokes the question, 'do you want me to prove this to you? But what else does this long preface – prove?' What else indeed – the reply is a return of the question.

The return of the calling as something new and questionable also informs the preface to *Daybreak*. The same 'concealed and imperious something' drives the single-minded, unalleviated excavations of the 'subterranean man':

> Does it not seem as though some faith were leading him on, some consolation offering him compensation? As though he perhaps desires this prolonged obscurity, desires to be incomprehensible, concealed, enigmatic, because he knows what he thereby also acquires: his own morning, his own redemption, his own *daybreak*?

> (D, p. 1)

Yet this faithful excavator – worthy pioneer – is engaged in investigating and digging out an ancient faith – faith in morality. If this seems contradictory, then 'you do not understand me?' For this excavation of faith in morality, even faith in reason, is undertaken '*out of morality!*'.

It is the calling of faith and 'men of conscience' *not* to want 'to return to that which we consider outlived and decayed, to anything "unworthy of belief", be it called God, virtue, truth, justice, charity'. There is a return to the tradition of 'German integrity and piety of millennia' but one which makes it new and strange. The questionable descendants of this tradition, 'its heirs and the executioners [*Vollstrecker*] of its innermost will' are those who deny with joy and achieve 'the *self-sublimation of morality*'. The return is an execution of tradition in both senses of the word, as the fulfilment of its testament and as its destruction. This questionable execution, with its destructive fulfilment of tradition, is both the calling of faith and its sublimation into something new and unprecedented.

The questionable calling is renamed 'philosophy' in the preface to *The Gay Science*. Philosophers are perpetually jumping in and out of their skins, for they

> have traversed many kinds of health, and keep transversing them, have passed through an equal number of philosophies; they simply *cannot* keep from transposing their states every time into the most spiritual form and distance: this art of transfiguration *is* philosophy.

> (GS, p. 35)

The philosopher returns from the exercise of the calling as something new, informed with the question, 'a different person, with a few more question marks – above all with the *will* henceforth to question further, more deeply, severely, harshly, evilly, and quietly than they had questioned heretofore' (p. 36). The joy in the question is the privilege of those 'knowing ones' who 'learn to forget well, and to be good at *not* knowing'. They 'return *newborn* having shed their skin . . . with a second dangerous innocence in joy, more childlike and yet a hundred times subtler than they had ever been before' (p. 37). The modality of the calling – the return anew of the question – has now become that of philosophy.

The question of the return of the calling is directly addressed in the preface to Part One of *Human, All Too Human*. The first edition of the book was not prefaced, but carried the subtitle: 'A Book for Free Spirits'. These free spirits, Nietzsche explains in the preface, were his 'invention' – in both senses of fabrication and discovery – for 'free spirits of this kind do not exist, did not exist' (HH, p. 6). Yet he is in no doubt that they could exist, and will exist 'physically present and palpable and not, as in my case, merely phantoms and a hermit's phantasmagoria' (p. 6). Indeed, he will provoke their advent by describing the ways by which they will appear: 'I see them already coming, slowly, slowly; and perhaps I shall do something to speed their coming if I describe in advance under what vicissitudes, upon what paths, I see them coming' (p. 6). Once again it is a question of originality, of naming what can be seen, and in so naming to create new 'things' (GS §58).

The free spirit is called to undergo the experience of the 'great liberation', a vocation which Nietzsche unfolds in four stages. The first stage is a release from the fetters of obligation. Under the tyranny of the calling the free spirit learns contempt for its past – 'the youthful soul is all at once convulsed, torn loose, torn away – it does not know what is happening. A drive and impulse rules and masters it like a command' (p. 7). The contemptuous glance back points to this first stage of the calling as being an 'enigmatic, question-packed, questionable victory' (p. 7). For the cruelty of this immoral wilful stage – the stage which has come to typify vulgar 'Nietzscheanism' – is a destructive sickness, a vengeful inversion of values.

This stage is followed in Nietzsche's genealogy of the free spirit by the two stages of *ataraxia* – the suspension of judgement. The first marks a distance from judgement:

One lives no longer in the fetters of love and hatred, without yes, without no, near or as far as one wishes, preferably slipping away, evading, fluttering off, gone again, again flying aloft; one is spoiled, as everyone is who has at some time seen a tremendous number of things beneath them.

(p. 8)

The second stage of the suspension of judgement is a return to 'what is close at hand'. The free spirit looks back in gratitude, and 'only now does he see himself'. The calling becomes manifest, and is repulsed in favour of the 'happiness that comes in winter, the spots of sunlight on the wall' (p. 9). And yet this suspension of judgement in the convalescent's *dolce fa niente* is not the end of the calling, merely its abeyance. For the calling returns in 'the riddle of the great liberation which had until then waited dark, questionable, almost untouchable in memory' (p. 9) and returns as something new and terrible.

The return of the calling is itself the 'great liberation'; in recognizing it the free spirit is freed of the past, present, and future. Nietzsche describes the temporality of the calling in the following terms:

The secret force and necessity of this calling will rule among and in the individual facets of his destiny like an unconscious pregnancy – long before he has caught sight of this task itself or knows its name. Our calling commands and disposes of us even when we do not yet know it; it is the future that regulates our today.

(p. 10)

However, this is not the ecstatic temporality which Heidegger discerned in the eternal return. For the return of the calling is not in time, nor does it negate or affirm judgement. This is underlined at the point in the preface when Nietzsche has the calling name itself in recalling the free spirit's vocation:

You shall get control over your for and against and learn how to display first one and then the other in accordance with your [calling]. You shall learn to grasp the sense of perspective in every value judgement – the displacement [*Verschiebung*], the warping [*Verzerrung*], and apparent teleology of horizons and whatever else pertains to perspectivism; also the bit of stupidity in every opposition of values and the intellectual penance that must be paid for every for and against.

(p. 9)

The calling of the free spirit is imperious – it makes itself known as the task which is, has been, and is to be followed. And this is no less than judgement's questioning of judgement, which for the free spirit manifests itself as 'the problem of the order of rank' (p. 10).

Before further pursuing the problem of the 'order of rank' it might be well to close this section on Nietzsche's prefaces by returning to Hegel's preface to the *Philosophy of Right*. Both thinkers consider their prefaces to be late additions to a delayed philosophy. For Hegel philosophy is too late to 'give instruction' because its shape of life has grown old: 'By philosophy's grey in grey it cannot be rejuvenated but only understood. The owl of Minerva spreads its wings only with the falling of the dusk.' So too for Nietzsche, the return of philosophy's calling is always too late, and remains in question. But it is this remaining in question which marks the *daybreak* of philosophy, its originality and its beginning. The return of the calling marks a renewal and is what prevents the Nietzschean preface from becoming a funeral oration.[15]

IV

The itinerary of the free spirit transformed the problem of judgement into the problem of rank. The free spirit began its calling with the yes and no of 'human, all-too-human' judgement. These were refused in the first, evil stage of the free spirit's liberation, and their opposites revalued. Then the free spirit refused to judge for or against – it deemed judgement to be below it and even unhealthy for it. But judgement returned in the problem of rank – but this return established a new non-human measure, a new for and against which did not simply invert or ignore the old yes and the old no, but which 'sublated' them. It was beyond human measure, and inhabited a penitential time, remembering and mourning the necessary injustice of its measure. Its affirmation was 'beyond man and time'.

In the preface to *Human, All Too Human* Nietzsche describes the calling's return in the demand to pay penance for the ineluctable displacement and warping of judgement: 'you must learn to understand the necessary injustice in every for and against'. The free spirit must affirm a judgement which warps and displaces, is unjust, one which would normalize originality, measure the immeasurable, compare the incomparable, and identify the different. And it must do so because it recognizes that there can be no originality without norm, no immeasurable without measure, no incomparability without comparison, no difference without identity. There is a necessary violence and injustice in judgement which manifests itself in law. But it is open to the judgers to recognize this violence and to pay penance for it, and this is what is *more* than human.

Nevertheless, Nietzsche's penance calls for more than the recognition of the necessary injustice of judgement. Like the calling it executes the traditional oppositions of judgement, destroying while fulfilling them. The penance of the free spirit is an affirmation of judgement which is beyond and before its yes and no. This is underlined in section 32 of *Human, All Too Human* where Nietzsche suggests 'We are from the beginning illogical and unjust beings and are able to recognize this: this is the greatest and unresolvable discord of Being' (HH, p. 28). The possibility of recognizing that we are illogical and unjust rests on two modalities of discrimination, one within and one beyond judgement. In the case of logical judgement, there is an illogic that says no to logic, but there is also an alogic that is beyond logical affirmation and negation. In the case of justice, there is an injustice that says no to justice, but also an ajustice beyond the affirmations or negations of just judgement. The penance of the free spirit is directed beyond such oppositions as logic/illogic, justice/injustice to their realization and destruction. Nietzsche describes the *via negationis* of penance as a purification, and his model, cited approvingly in *The Gay Science*, is Ekhardt's saying 'I ask God to rid me of God' (GS, 292, p. 235). It is the prayer of a creature to God to rid him of having to think God in terms of the opposition creature/God.

The character of the Nietzschean penance – what Heidegger later called 'devotion' – is developed in the discussions of logic/illogic and justice/injustice in the Free-Spirit Trilogy. The no-saying half of his calling simply inverts the conventional privilege enjoyed by one term over its other, while the yes-saying part affirms and destroys the very opposition of the terms by putting them into question. Remaining with *Human, All Too Human*, Nietzsche writes in §18 on the 'Fundamental Questions of Metaphysics':

> The first stage of the logical is the judgement: and the essence of judgement consists, according to the best logicians, in belief. The ground of all belief is the sensation of the pleasurable or painful in relation to a perceiving subject.
>
> (HH, p. 21)

He approaches this 'fundamental question' by systematically

undermining the notion that judgement can have a ground or a foundation. The basis of the belief that founds logic is the distinction of pleasure and pain; but this itself is not fundamental since it is based on the further distinction of perception and non-perception. This distinction in turn surrenders to the more fundamental belief that everything is one. But the one depends on the distinction between identity and plurality, which depends in its turn on those of existence and non-existence, uniqueness and repetition. But these distinctions themselves are already derived, and foundations appear as displaced oppositions.

The exposure of the displacements of judgement is pursued in section 32 in terms of evaluation. All evaluations are partial, and we have no logical right to a total evaluation (the right to employ logic cannot be derived logically) because

> the standard by which we measure our own being is not an unalterable magnitude . . . and yet we would have to know ourselves as a fixed standard to be able justly to assess the relation between ourself and anything else whatever.
>
> (p. 28)

Logically and justly, 'we ought not to judge at all' – but it would not be human to live without judging, since the name '*Mensch*' for Nietzsche means the measurer and the judger.

Nietzsche goes on to reverse the previous founding of logical evaluation on pleasure/pain, saying that – 'all aversion [*Abneigung*] is dependent on an evaluation, likewise partiality [*Zueignung*]' (p. 28). Nietzsche makes the *Ab* (away) and *Zu* (toward) in *Abneigung* and *Zuneigung* denote the operation of a drive: 'A drive [*Trieb*] toward something or away from something . . . without some kind of knowing evaluation of the worth of its objective does not exist in man.' The disposition of the drive towards and away (a modality which constitutes good and evil in *ressentiment*) is itself based on an evaluation, but this in its turn is founded on the drive. In this passage Nietzsche drives the human notion of measure into distraction, showing that it is necessarily aporetic. And far from seeking a solution to this aporia, as Habermas claims, Nietzsche insists that we recognize and pay penance for it.

In *Daybreak* Nietzsche twists the tangles of judgement by introducing the problem of the 'other' or 'neighbour'. In section 118 on the question 'What then is our Neighbour?' Nietzsche anticipates the discourse on the thousand and one goals in *Zarathustra*. The border which marks the difference between my neighbour and I cannot be thought in terms of the simple opposition of inner and outer:

> What do we understand to be the boundaries of our neighbour, I mean that by which he so to speak engraves [*einzeichnet*] and impresses [*eindruckt*] himself on to [*auf*] and into [*an*] us . . . our knowledge of him is like a hollow but informed space.
>
> (D, p. 118)

The neighbour is both engraved and impressed *on to* us as if we were surfaces, but also impressed and engraved *into* us – the operation anticipates the punitive inscription of the offence in Kafka's story *The Penal Colony*.[16] In place of Kafka's archaic machinery of the law, Nietzsche's inscription of the boundary *is* the boundary; its action cannot be thought since it is the condition of thought. The simultaneously constituting and constituted border can only be known as a 'hollow but informed space', neither inner nor outer, 'World of phantoms in which we live. Inverted [*verkehrte*] upside down, empty world, yet dreamed as *full* and *straight*.'

To fill the informed void by postulating a 'theory of power' to effect the inscription of the boundary is less a solution than an avoidance of the difficulty. The difficulty has to be recognized and then atoned for in an affirmation which is not one of judgement. The previous paragraph of *Daybreak* entitled 'In Prison' describes the boundary as both a prison wall and a web, simultaneously enclosing and extending:

> it is by these horizons, within which each of us encloses his senses as if behind prison walls, that we *measure* the world, we say that this is near and that far, this big and that small, this is hard and that soft. . . . We sit within our net, we spiders, and whatever we may catch in it, we catch nothing at all except that which allows itself to be caught in precisely our net.
>
> (p. 117)

Our various systems of distinction fall within definite limits; the limit or prison wall is reflected back and constitutes a network of differences which determine what can appear. However, it is with the knowledge of the neighbour that this otherwise invisible limit becomes perceptible as an informed void.

The breakdown of our knowledge of the neighbour manifests the injustice of our measure and judgement. The experience of the 'informed void' brings the illogic and injustice of human measure and judgement into recognition. The recognition of the collapse of measure and its network of differences is at the core of Nietzsche's conception of the yes-saying free spirit. Returning to Kafka's *The Penal Colony*, the name of the crime being expiated is written on to and into the flesh of the prisoner. For Nietzsche the return of the injustice of measure is in the recognition of the proper name 'human' inscribed on and in the body. In the section of *Human, All Too Human* on 'Man as the Measurer' Nietzsche writes:

> Perhaps all the morality of mankind has its origin in the tremendous inner excitement which seized on primeval men when they discovered measure and measuring (the word *Mensch* indeed, means the measurer, he desired to *name* himself after his greatest discovery!). With these conceptions they climbed into realms that are quite immeasurable and unweighable but originally did not seem to be.

The recognition of the collapse of measure has two possible consequences. The first remains within measure, and is the all-too-human yes and no of nihilism, while the other exceeds measure and is the unmeasured affirmation of the free spirit.

The relation between the penance for the all-too-human yes and no and the affirmation of the more than human is worked through in the well-known aphorism section 335 of *The Gay Science*, 'Up with Physics'. Here Nietzsche distinguishes between the Kant of synthesis in judgement and the Kant who having 'broken open the cage' of moral judgement was led back into it by the postulates of God, Soul, Freedom and Immortality. Kant's escape from the cage through critique and legislation is the paradigm for Nietzsche's demand for penance and legislation. The critical project of establishing the 'extent and the limits' of understanding through critique presupposes the transcendence of limit, not in terms of the metaphysical postulates, but in terms of legislation. The philosopher 'is not a worker in the field of reason, but the lawgiver of human reason' (*Critique of Pure Reason*, A839/B867) and it is because philosophers give the law that they can establish its limits.

For Nietzsche, the legislative giving of limit avoids becoming simply another founding of judgement if it is accompanied by penance: 'Let us therefore limit ourselves to the purification of our opinions and evaluations and to the creation of new, proper tables of the good' (GS, 335, pp. 255–6). Both purification and legislation, the 'intellectual penance' for yes and no and the giving of new law tables, are themselves already limited: *Beschranken wir uns*. The law of *this* limitation, the giving of the giving of law, is beyond-law.

It is not measured in terms of the yes and no of a normalizing subject, but is the creative and original affirmation of law.

Such an affirmation cannot be made within the 'prison wall' or 'cage' of judgement except in terms of the paradoxes into which the prisoner's language falls when driven beyond its web of distinctions. One such an occasion is the celebrated call for the return of what we are. Here Nietzsche clearly refers to the notion of the calling which informs the Free-Spirit Trilogy: 'We, though, want to become those we are – the new, unique, the incomparable, the self-legislating, the self-creating' (*Wir aber wollen die werden wie wir sind, – die Neuen, die Einmaligen, die Unvergleichbaren, die Sich-selber-Gesetzgebenden, die Sich-selber-Schaffenden*) (GS, p. 266). Walter Kaufmann humanizes this passage in his translation by introducing 'human beings who are new . . . , etc.'; but they are absent in Nietzsche. It is not 'men' (*Mensch*) who are called to give themselves law, create themselves, but those whose calling is to fulfil and destroy human measure. The 'we' want to return, to become what 'we' are called to be; yet the 'we' are not measurers; 'we' affirm and act beyond the distinctions of new/old, unique/repeated, incomparable/comparable, legislating/legislated, creating/created. The giving of the free spirit in each case 'executes' the limit of these oppositions.

The new, the unique, the incomparable cannot be named; 'their' calling is not the affirmation of a given limit but a limitless giving which exceeds the bounds of human measure. With this Nietzsche both fulfils and destroys the tradition of judgement. The classical doctrine of judgement was inseparable from a doctrine of invention, and it was the suppression of this relation in early modernity which led to the warps and displacements of judgement first identified as such by Kant.[17] His transcendental logic and its phenomenological development by Hegel tried to rethink the relation of judgement and invention. For judgement to take place there must be an appropriation or a giving of place which is more than judgement and which cannot be described in its terms. This giving, which does not bear a name but which stares us all in the face, is the yes for judgement which is before and beyond its yes and its no. By returning to the human, all-too-human of judgement, Nietzsche fulfils this tradition in the 'creative legislation' of the free spirit which liberates affirmation from the opposition of judgement's yes and no.

The penultimate aphorism of the first edition of *The Gay Science*, 'The Greatest Weight', speaks of this '*Ja-und Amen*' before yes and no. When the demon whispers that everything in life must return 'all in the same series and sequence' he is stating something which stares us all in the face – that judgements must both return and be made anew. Such a thought becomes overwhelming, able to transform or destroy, when it is made into a question: 'Do you desire this once more again and innumerable times more?' (p. 274) or, in other words, 'do you want to judge?'. The question itself is a judgement on whoever is asked it, since it shows that the yes and no of wanting *this* rests on a yes and amen before every yes and no. To want this yes is to want a singularity which cannot be generalized, cannot be named, and which exceeds the limits of judgement.

The extreme statement of *eternal* return – one beyond time – leads paradoxically to an affirmation of singularity. To affirm the yes before yes and no leads beyond the universal and particular of judgement. A portrayal of this affirmation is the 'Yes saying, Yes laughing' of Zarathustra in *'das Ja- und Amen-Lied'* which closes Part III of *Also Sprach Zarathustra*. The double yes would have everything return in order to release it from time. To affirm the judgement of eternal return, to answer yes to its question (yes, saying), is to make a nonsense of the generalizations and measures of judgement (yes, laughing). The rigorous affirmation of eternal return pays penance for judgement by executing its original sin of generalization. Judgement is the return of measure to the singular, but when this return is made eternal it is driven to its limit in absurdity. And at that wicked moment of parody, the 'greatest burden' changes into the greatest joy.

With the statement of the eternal return at the end of the Free-Spirit Trilogy Nietzsche recovers his calling. he recapitulates '6000 feet beyond Man and Time' what had already been said 'lying back amid the grasses' in the 'epilogue' 'Among Friends' to *Human, All Too Human*. The folly of this 'fools-book' is but 'Reason coming to its senses', and it does so in the repeated refrain:

Shall we do this, friends, again? Amen, and *auf Wiedersehn!*

BIBLIOGRAPHY

Benjamin, Walter *Illuminations*, trans. Harry Zohn, London, Collins, 1973.
Deleuze, Gilles (1962), *Nietzsche and Philosophy*, trans. Hugh Tomlinson, London, Athlone Press, 1983.
Derrida, Jacques (1982), *The Ear of the Other*, ed. Christie McDonald, Lincoln and London, University of Nebraska Press, 1988.
—— (1987), *Ulysse gramophone deux mots pour Joyce*, Paris, Editions Galilée, 1987.

—— (1987), *Of Spirit: Heidegger and the Question*, trans. Geoffrey Bennington and Rachel Bowlby, Chicago, Chicago University Press, 1989.

Heidegger, Martin (1950), 'The Anaximander Fragment' in *Early Greek Thinking*, trans. David Krell and Frank A. Capuzzi, San Fransisco, Harper & Row, 1984, 22.

—— (1954), *What is Called Thinking*, trans. J. Glenn Gray, New York, Harper & Row, 1968.

—— (1961), *Nietzsche I: The Will to Power as Art*, trans. David Farrell Krell, London, Routledge & Kegan Paul, 1979.

——, *Nietzsche II: The Eternal Recurrence of the Same*, trans. David Farrell Krell, New York, Harper & Row, 1984.

——, *Nietzsche III: The Will to Power as Knowledge and as Metaphysics*, trans. Joan Stambaugh *et al.*, San Francisco, Harper & Row, 1987.

——, *Nietzsche IV: Nihilism*, trans. Frank Capuzzi, San Francisco, Harper & Row, 1982.

Nietzsche, Friedrich (1878–80), *Human, All Too Human: A Book for Free Spirits*, trans. R. J. Hollingdale, Cambridge, Cambridge University Press, 1986.

—— (1881), *Daybreak: Thoughts on the Prejudices of Morality*, trans. R. J. Hollingdale, Cambridge, Cambridge University Press, 1982.

—— (1882), *The Gay Science*, trans. Walter Kaufmann, New York, Random House, 1974.

—— (1883–5), *Thus Spoke Zarathustra*, trans. R. J. Hollingdale, Harmondsworth, Penguin, 1975.

—— (1888), *Ecce Homo*, trans. Walter Kaufmann, New York, Random House, 1969.

Rosenzweig, Franz (1921), *Der Stern der Erlösung*, Frankfurt, Suhrkamp, 1988.

NOTES

My thanks to Greg Bright and Gillian Rose for their thorough criticisms of an earlier draft of this paper.

Works are cited in the text by abbreviation and by section number, unless the page is specified.

D   *Daybreak: Thoughts on the Prejudices of Morality*, trans. R. J. Hollingdale, Cambridge, Cambridge University Press, 1982.

EH   *Ecce Homo*, trans. Walter Kaufmann, New York, Random House, 1969.

GS   *The Gay Science*, trans. Walter Kaufmann, New York, Random House, 1974.

HH   *Human, All Too Human: A Book for Free Spirits*, trans. R. J. Hollingdale, Cambridge, Cambridge University Pres, 1986.

Z   *Thus Spoke Zarathustra*, trans. R. J. Hollingdale, Harmondsworth, Penguin, 1975.

1 As when Jürgen Habermas criticizes Nietzsche for positing will to power

as a 'solution' to the aporia of judgement: 'If all proper claims to validity are dissolved and if the underlying value judgements are mere expressions of claims to power rather than validity, according to what standards should critique differentiate? It must at least be able to discriminate between a power which *deserves* to be esteemed and a power which *deserves* to be disparaged. Nietzsche's *theory of power* is intended to provide a way out of this aporia' (Jürgen Habermas, 'The Entwinement of Myth and Enlightenment: Rereading *Dialectic of Enlightenment*', trans. Thomas Y. Levin, *New German Critique*, 1982, vol. 26, 13–30). This reading of Nietzsche, whose provenance lies in Bäumler's emphasis on will to power, has become an *idée reçue* of commentators and textbook writers: one example: 'Nietzsche pressed his case against both Kant *and* Hegel by arguing for a yet more radical scepticism, one that treated all the truth claims of philosophy as mere emanations of an arbitrary will-to-power.' Christopher Norris, *The Contest of the Faculties*, London, Methuen, 1985.

2 See David Farrell Krell's 'Analysis' of Heidegger, 1961, vol. II, p. 268. 'The very worst thing that could happen is that the *thinking* of eternal recurrence, a thinking which Nietzsche and Heidegger share, should get lost in the barren reaches of the philological debate'.

3 See below, section II.

4 In the Preface to *The Critique of Judgement-Power* (1790) Kant wrote 'Yet even here I venture to hope that the difficulty of unravelling a problem so involved in its nature may serve as an excuse for a certain amount of hardly avoidable obscurity in its solution, provided that the accuracy of our statement of the principle is proved with all requisite clearness'.

5 Heidegger's lectures were published in 1961, and are translated in four volumes: I *The Will to Power as Art*, II *The Eternal Recurrence of the Same*, III *Will to Power as Knowledge And Metaphysics*, IV *Nihilism*. The 'new' Nietzsche is largely the outcome of Heidegger's engagement. David B. Allison prefaces his collection *The New Nietzsche: Contemporary Styles of Interpretation* (Cambridge, Mass., MIT Press, 1985) with the claim that Heidegger was the first to recognize Nietzsche as 'one of the prodigious thinkers of the modern age' and to show that 'what remains to be considered within Nietzsche's own thought somehow stands as a model for the tasks and decisions of the present generation' (ix). The power of Heidegger's reading of Nietzsche is such that reading Nietzsche today is inseparable from reading Heidegger.

6 Heidegger situates his reading of eternal return in this way: 'No wonder commentators have felt it to be an obstacle and have tried all sorts of manoeuvres to get round it, only grudgingly making their peace with it. Either they strike it from Nietzsche's philosophy altogether or, compelled by the fact it obtrudes there and seeing no way out, they list it as a component part of that philosophy. In the latter case they explain the doctrine as an impossible eccentricity of Nietzsche's, something that can count only as a personal confession of faith and does not pertain to the system of Nietzsche's philosophy proper' (Heidegger, 1961, vol. II, 5).

7 The classic *loci* for the moment of eternal return are *The Gay Science*

section 341 'The Greatest Weight' and *Thus Spoke Zarathustra* 'Of the Vision and the Riddle' and 'The Second Dance Song'.

8 For a profound analysis of Heidegger's 'avoidance' see Jacques Derrida, *Of Spirit: Heidegger and the Question*, 1987.

9 *'Ja ist kein Satzteil, aber ebensowenig das kurzschriftliche Siegel eines Satzes, obwohl es als solches verwendet werden kann, sondern es ist der stille Begleiter aller Satzteile, die Bestätigung, das 'Sie', das 'Amen' hinter jedem Wort'* (1921, 29). Rosenzweig's discussion of the exteriority of the 'yes' beyond yes and no in the section *'Gott und sein Sein oder Metaphysik'* has been crucial for contemporary French thought, notably Emmanuel Levinas, *Totality and Infinity. An Essay in Exteriority* ([1961] trans. A. Lingis, Pittsburgh, Duquesne University Press, 1987), and Jacques Derrida, *Ulysse gramophone deux mots pour Joyce*, 1987, 122.

10 Nietzsche wrote four prefaces in 1886, one each for the two volumes of *Human, All Too Human* (1878–80), one for *Daybreak: Thoughts on the Prejudices of Morality* (1881) and one for *The Gay Science* (1882).

11 For an excellent discussion of the circumstances under which the Free-Spirit Trilogy was conceived and composed, see Peter Bergmann, *Nietzsche, The Last Antipolitical German*, Bloomington, Indiana University Press, 1987, esp. chapters 4 and 5.

12 Walter Benjamin's work is the most significant and rigorous deployment of Nietzsche's view of remembrance; see his *Theses on the Philosophy of History*, especially Thesis XVII on the 'messianic cessation of happening' which both preserves and destroys (trans. H. Zohn, London, Collins, 1973).

13 'All my writings, with a single though admittedly substantial exception, are to be *dated back* – they always speak of something "behind me" ' (HH, 209).

14 'Strange and at the same time terrible! It is our *alleviations* for which we have to atone the most!' (HH, 212).

15 It is of course by no means clear that Hegel is pronouncing a funeral oration, or if he is, for whom. The flight of Minerva's owl in the Roman dusk is seen by Gillian Rose as heralding a philosophy of the Greek morning: 'Minerva cannot impose herself. Her owl can only spread its wings at dusk and herald the return of Athena, freedom without domination' *Hegel contra Sociology*, London, Athlone Press, 1981, 91. What is indisputable though is that both Hegel and Nietzsche's prefaces are extremely questionable invitations.

16 In Franz Kafka, *Metamorphosis and other Stories*, tr. E. Muir, Harmondsworth, Penguin, 1975.

17 See my book *Art of Judgement* for details of the history of invention and judgement and Kant's diagnosis of the 'aporia of judgement'.

10 Art as insurrection: the question of aesthetics in Kant, Schopenhauer, and Nietzsche

Nick Land

Artists; those savage beasts that can't get enough of too much.

(Land)

Immanuel Kant's *Critique of Judgement* is the site where art irrupts into European philosophy with the force of trauma. The ferocious impetus of this irruption was only possible in an epoch attempting to rationalize itself as permanent metamorphosis, as growth. Which means that it is a trauma quite incommensurable with the sort of *difficulties* art has posed to western philosophy since Plato, for it is no longer a matter of irritation, but of catastrophe. Our own.

The consistency of Kant's critical philosophy throughout all three of the great *Critiques* rests in the attention to excess inherent in the conception of synthetic a priori judgements. The very inception of the critical project lay in Kant's decisive response to the voiding of logical metaphysics – the disintegration of the philosophical endeavour to reduce synthesis – that was consummated by Hume. Perhaps nothing was clearer to Kant than the radical untenability of the Leibnizian paradigm of metaphysics, still dominant in the (Wolfian) philosophy of the Prussian state. Logicism had been exposed, by the sceptical and empirical thought of a more advanced social system, as a sterile tautological stammering that belonged to the Middle Ages when positivity had been given in advance. It was with extraordinary resolve that Kant jettisoned the deductive systematization that had characterized the philosophies of immobilist societies – philosophies deeply and deliberately rooted in stagnant theism – and replaced it with the metaphysics of excess. He was even prepared to assist in the razing of all theoretical theology; because philosophy, too, had to become (at least a little) revolutionary. Nothing substantial was any longer to be presupposed.

Although the hazards of synthesis – of having to think – were clearly no longer eliminable, Kant still clung to the prospect that they could be traversed and definitively concluded. Philosophy would have to *take some ground*, but it could still anticipate a place of rest; an impregnable defensive line. If history could no longer be avoided, at least it could be brought swiftly and meticulously to its end. Time would have to be transcendentally determined, once and for all, by a new metaphysics. It would thenceforth just continue, without disruption, in an innocent confirmation of itself. For a while – a period some time between the early 1770s and 1790 – it is possible that Kant was as cheerful as any bourgeois philosopher has ever been. An ephemeral restabilization had been achieved. Then came disaster. Something was still shockingly out of control. A third *Critique* was necessary.

The terrifying insight that drove Kant into the labyrinthine labours of the *Critique of Judgement* was that utter chaos had still not been outlawed by an understanding whose pretension was to 'legislate for nature'. Kant's own words are these:

although this [the pure understanding] makes up a system according to transcendental laws, which contain the condition of possibility for experience as such, it would still be possible that there be an infinite multiplicity of empirical laws and such a great heterogeneity of natural forms belonging to the particular experience that the concept of a system according to these (empirical) laws must be totally alien to the understanding, and neither the possibility, even less the necessity of such a totality could be conceived.[1]

There are few horrors comparable to that of the master legislator who realizes that *anarchy is still permitted*. Far from having been domesticated by the transcendental forms of understanding, nature was still a freely flowing wound that needed to be staunched. This was going to be far more messy and frightening than anything yet undertaken, but Kant gritted his yellowing teeth, and began.

He found the resource for his new and final campaign in the precarious negative disorder which he called 'beauty'. When compared to the rigorous order of transcendental form, beauty was an altogether fragile and impermanent discipline. It was something the transcendental subject could not promise itself. Nevertheless, it seemed that something beyond reason, something that was prepared to get its hands dirty, was keeping nature down. 'Purposiveness without purpose', Kant's last name for excess, has all the extravagance of triumph. Even without trying, we win. History is written by the victors and ascendancy is presupposed as the condition of presentation, so that the submission of nature to exorbitant law is given with the objectivity of experience:

> It is thus a subjectively necessary transcendental presupposition that unlimited dissimilarity of empirical laws and heterogeneity of natural forms does not arise, but that it rather, through the affinity of the particular laws under more general ones, qualifies as an experience, as an empirical system.[2]

> All those martialled formulas: nature takes the shortest way – she does nothing in vain – there is no leap in the multiplicity of forms (*continuum formarum*) – she is rich in species, but yet thrifty in genuses, and so forth, are nothing other than just this transcendental expression of judgement, setting itself a principle for experience as a system and thus for its own needs.[3]

Experience is thought of in terms of an extravagant but explosive inheritance; an ungrounded adaptation of nature to the faculties of representation. The increasingly tortured and paradoxical formulations that Kant selects indicate the precarious character of the luxuriance (stocked and expended in the imagination as 'free-play'). Consider just one example: 'Purposiveness is a lawfulness of the accidental as such.'[4]

Like Marx's Ricardo, it is the extraordinary cynicism of Kantianism at the edge of its desperation that lends it a profound radicality. Kant's 'reason' is a reactive concept, negatively defined against the pathology with which it has been locked in perpetual and brutal war. In the third *Critique* all inhibition is lifted from this conflict; it becomes gritty, remorseless, cruel. His theory of the sublime, for instance, is sheer exultation in an insensate violence (*Gewalt*) against the pre-conceptual (animal) powers summarized under the faculty of the 'imagination'. In the experience of the sublime nature is affirmed as the trigger for a 'negative-pleasure', in so far as it humiliates and ruins that part of ourselves that we fail to share with the angels. To take one instance (out of innumerable possibilities) he says of the sublime that it is:

> something terrifying for sensibility . . . which for all that, has an attraction for us, arising from the fact of its being a violence which reason unleashes upon sensibility with a view to extending its own domain (the practical) and letting sensibility look out beyond itself into the infinite, which is an abyss for it.[5]

Kant is becoming remarkably indiscriminate about his allies, asking only that they be enemies of pathological inclination (*Neigung*), and know how to fight. If reason is so secure, legitimate, supersensibly guaranteed, why all the guns?

Irrational surplus, or the ineliminable and beautiful *danger* of unconscious creative energy: nature with fangs. How do we hold on to this thought? It is perpetually threatened by collapse; by a reversion to a depressive philosophy of work, whether theological or humanistic. The three great strands of post-Kantian exploration – marked by the names Hegel, Schelling, and Schopenhauer – are constantly tempted by the prospect of a reduction to forgotten or implicit labour; to the agency of God, spirit, or man, to anything that would return this ruthless artistic force of the generative unconscious to design, intention, project, teleology, Kant's word 'genius' is the immensely difficult and confused but emphatic resistance to such reductions; the thought of an utterly impersonal creativity that is historically registered as the radical discontinuity of the example, of irresponsible legislation, as 'order' without anyone giving the orders.

Kant is quite explicit that a generative theory of art requires a philosophy of genius – a re-admission of accursed pathology into its very heart – and one only has to read the second *Critique* alongside the third to notice the immense disruption that art inflicts upon transcendental philosophy. Kant only manages to control this disruption by maintaining art as an implicitly marginal problematic within a field mastered by philosophy. Even though he acknowledges that the autonomy of reason is to the heteronomy of genius what fidelity of representation is when compared to creation – poverty and wretchedness – the message scarcely seeps out. In addition, there is a perpetual and pathetic effort to subsume aesthetics under practical imperatives, 'beauty as the symbol of ethical life'[6] being one example, and the basic tendency of his theory of the sublime (the infinite privilege of transcendental ideas in comparison to nature) being another.

Despite superficial appearances it is not with the thought of noumenal subjectivity that the unconscious is announced within western philosophy, for this thought is still recuperable as a pre-reflexive consciousness, so innocuous that even Sartre is happy to accept it. It is rather out of an intertwining of two quite different strands of the Kantian text that the perturbing figure of the energetic unconscious emerges: first, the heteronomous pathological inclination whose repression is presupposed in the exercise of practical reason, and second, genius, or nature in its 'legislative' aspect. The genius 'cannot indicate how this fantastic and yet thoughtful ideas arise and come together in his head, because he himself does not know, and cannot, therefore, teach it to anyone'.[7]

It is no doubt comforting to speak of 'the genius' as if impersonal creative energy were commensurable with the order of autonomous individuality governed by reason, but such chatter is, in the end, absurd. Genius is nothing like a character trait, it does not belong to a psychological lexicon; far more appropriate is the language of seismic upheaval, inundation, disease, the onslaught of raw energy from without. One 'is' a genius only in the sense that one 'is' a syphilitic, in the sense that 'one' is violently problematized by a ferocious exteriority. One returns to the subject of which genius has been predicated to find it charred and devastated beyond recognition.

II

Schopenhauer reconstructed the critical philosophy in several very basic ways: by eliminating the dogmatic presupposition of a difference between subjective and objective noumena; by shifting, not in an idealist (phenomenological) direction, but towards unconscious will; by simplifying the transcendental understanding from the twelve categories and two forms of sensibility inherited from Kant to the integrated 'principle of sufficient reason'; by nipping Kant's proto-idealist logicism in the bud; by charging the critical philosophy with the furious energy of sexual torment, attacking its (at least) germinal academicism, and immeasurably improving its stylistic resources. Where Kant distorts, marginalizes, and obscures the thought of the unconscious, Schopenhauer emphasizes and develops it. He defies the pretensions of imperalistic idealism by describing reason as a derivative abstraction from the understanding, co-extensive with language, so that Kant's transcendental logic is rethought through a transcendental aesthetic organized in terms of the 'principle of sufficient reason', simplified, de-mystified, and pushed downwards towards pre-intellectual intuition. Reason is no longer thought of as an autonomous principle in reciprocal antagonism with nature, but as a film upon its surface. All these moves involve a massive shift in the term 'will' (*Wille*), the placeholder for the psychoanalytical comprehension of desire.

For Kant, the will is aligned with reason, as the principle of the investment of nature with intentional intelligibility, the resource from which teleological judgement must regulatively metaphorize all exorbitant natural order:

> The will, as the faculty of desire, is one of the many natural causes in the world, namely, that one which is effective through concepts, and everything that is represented as possible (or necessary) through a will is called practically possible (or necessary), in contradistinction from the physical possibility or necessity of an affect for which the ground is not determined in its causality through concepts (but rather, as with lifeless matter, through mechanism, and, with animals, through instinct).[8]

In contrast, Schopenhauer's great discovery is that of non-agentic will; the positivity of the death of God. Rather than thinking willing as the movement by which conceptually articulate decision is realized in nature, he understands the appearance of rational decisions as a derivative consequence of pre-intellectual – and ultimately pre-personal, even pre-organic – willing. Unconscious desire is not just desire that happens to be unconscious, as if a decisionistic lucidity is somehow natural or proper to desire, it is rather that consciousness can only be consequential upon a desire for which lucid thought is an instrumental requirement. For Schopenhauer the intellect is constituted by willing, rather than being constitutive for it. *We do not know what we want.*

There is an important sense in which Schopenhauer's will is the thought of genius taken towards its limit, subsuming the entire faculty of knowledge under that of exorbitant natural order, as a mere instance (although a privileged one) of purposiveness without purpose. But Schopenhauer's own usage of the thought of genius preserves it in its specificity, as a proportional exorbitance on the part of the intellect in relation to the will. Genius is the result of a positive overcoming of unconscious 'purpose', an excess of intellectual energy over that which can be absorbed by desire, thus redundancy, or dysfunction through superfluity:

> an entirely pure and objective picture of things is not reached in the normal mind, because its power of perception at once becomes tired and inactive, as soon as this is not spurred on and set in motion by the will. For it has not enough energy to apprehend the world purely objectively from its own elasticity and *without a purpose*. On the other hand, where this happens, where the brain's power of forming representations has such a surplus that a pure, distinct, objective picture of the external

world exhibits itself *without a purpose* as something useless for the intentions of the will, which is even disturbing in the higher degrees, and can even become injurious to them – then there already exists at least the natural disposition for that abnormality. This is denoted by the name of *genius*, which indicates that something foreign to the will, i.e., to the I or ego proper, a *genius* added from outside so to speak, seems to become active here.[9]

The mother of the useful arts is necessity; that of the fine arts superfluity and abundance. As their father, the former have understanding, the latter genius, which in itself a kind of superfluity, that of the power of knowledge beyond the measure required for the service of the will.[10]

For Schopenhauer the body is the objectification of the will, the intellect is a function of a particular organ of the body, and genius is the surplus of that functioning in relation to the individual organism in question. Genius is thus an assault on the individualized will that erupts from out of the reservoir of archaic pre-organized willing. It is a site of particular tension in his thinking, caught between a vision of progressive redemption, achieved through humanity as perfected individuality in which the will is able to renounce itself, and regressive unleashing of the pre-individual will from the torture chamber of organic specificity, ego-interests, and personality. Schopenhauer's attachment to the first of these options is well known, but the possibility of an alternative escape from individualization – by way of dissolution into archaic inundating desire – constantly strains for utterance within his text.

This tension generates a terminological fission that can be easily detected along the jagged fault lines separating sexuality from art. One example is 'beauty'; a word that is driven by Schopenhauer's overt (metaphysical) policy into an uneasy alignment with renunciation. He interprets it as the negative affect – relief or release – associated with disengagement from interested thought, attained through contemplative submergence in the pure universal 'ideas' of natural species as they exist outside space, time, and causality, and manifest to a radicalized Kantian disinterestedness that is greatly facilitated by artistic representation.[11]

If in the end Derrida's *Spurs* is an absurd book, it is because it is tapping into Nietzsche's negotation with Schopenhauer's discourse on woman and the aesthetic without knowing what it is listening to, because it is too busy perpetuating the Heideggerian mutilation of libidinal post-Kantianism. Nietzsche's recovery and affirmation of the fictive power of art (in his later writings) is a response to the violent denigration of this power in Schopenhauer's thought, a denigration that is programmed by a complex of interlocking factors that are evidenced with particular intensity in his discussion of sexual difference. Schopenhauer founds the modern thought of excitement as suffering, a thought which survives into the twentieth century in a variety of guises, and most importantly in Freud's libidinal economy. In order to perpetuate a rhythm of desire and its tranquillization, in which there is no space for positive pleasure, but only variable degrees of pain, it is necessary to be profoundly *misled*. This is why Schopenhauer refers to the principle of sufficient reason, which is associated with the pure form of material reality, and is the transcendental condition of individuated appearance, as the veil of *Maya*, or illusion. Art, as the escape from individuation and desire, is thus the very negative of fiction. Beauty is an experience of truth.

But there is also another troubling, enticing, arousing, and captivating type of beauty (Nietzsche will come to say it is the only one), the beauty that is exemplified – in post-Hellenic western history at least – in the female body. For Schopenhauer this is an immense problem, as is the domain of the erotic in its entirety. The anegoic disinterestedness of resignation is echoed and parodied by an indifference to ego-interests that leads in a quite opposite direction; *deeper into the inferno of willing*. After acknowledging with his usual raw honesty that 'all amorousness is rooted in the sexual impulse alone',[12] Schopenhauer is forced to accept that 'it is precisely this not seeking *one's own* interest, everywhere the stamp of greatness, which gives even to passionate love a touch of the sublime, and makes it a worthy subject of poetry'.[13]

There is thus both a renunciatory and a libidinous sublime, each with its associated objects and aesthetic 'perfections' or intensities. And it is not only beauty that is torn in separate directions, fiction too is split; on the one hand as the condition of individualization, and on the other as an appeal to constituted individuality. Either the ego is a dream of desire, or desire has to creep up on the ego as a dream. In sexuality,

> nature can attain her end only by implanting in the individual a certain *delusion*, and by virtue of this, that which in truth is merely a good thing for the species seems to him to be a good thing for himself, so that he serves the species, whereas he is

under the delusion that he is serving himself. In this process a mere chimera, which vanishes immediately afterwards, floats before him, and, as motive, takes the place of a reality. This *delusion is instinct*. In the great majority of cases, instinct is to be regarded as the sense of the *species* which presents to the will what is useful to *it*.[4]

Woman is matter, formless and unpresentable, arousing and thus tormenting; everything about her is pretence, deception, alteration, unlocalizable irrational attraction, *Verstellung*. Schopenhauer's notorious essay *On Woman* is mapped by the movement of this word, as it organizes the play of seduction, of indirect action, of non-ideal beauty, disrupting the seriousness and responsible self-legislation of the male subject through an 'art of dissimulation'.[15] Woman is wicked art, art that intensifies life, art whose only truth is a whispered intimation that negation, too, is only a dream, the figment of an overflowing positivity that deceives through excess. Could the dream of redemption be nothing but a bangle upon the arms of exuberant life? Schopenhauer reels in horror:

> Only the male intellect, clouded by the sexual impulse, could call the undersized, narrow-shouldered, broad-hipped, and short-legged sex the fair sex; for in this impulse is to be found its whole beauty. The female sex could be more aptly called the *unaesthetic*.[16]

Women are so terribly non-Platonic, so outrageously vital and real, so excessive in relation to the cold sterile perfections of the ideas. With infallible instinctive power they propagate the dangerous delusion that there is something about life that we want. Pessimism has to be misogyny, because woman refuses to repel.

III

A few of the things that Nietzsche learnt – at least in part – from Schopenhauer were the elementary tenets of libidinal materialism or the philosophy of the energetic unconscious (the unrestricted development of the theory of genius), the primacy of the body and its medical condition, pragmatism (asking not how we know but why we know), effervescent literary brilliance, aestheticism (with a musical focus), an 'aristocratic' concern for hierarchy and gradation (which he turned into an implement for overcoming Aristotelian logic), antihumanism, a construction of the history of philosophy as dominated by Plato and Kant and the problematic of reality and appearance, virulent anti-academicism, misogyny, and the distrust of mathematical thinking. Schopenhauer even wrote that:

> The genuine symbol of nature is universally and everywhere the circle, because it is the schema or form of recurrence; in fact, this is the most general form in nature. She carries it through in everything from the course of the constellations down to the death and birth of organic beings. In this way alone, in the restless stream of time and its content, a continued existence, i.e., a nature, becomes possible.[17]

But the shifts Nietzsche had brought to the Schopenhauerian philosophy by the end of his creative life were at least as immense as this inheritance, involving, amongst other elements, a displacement from the will to life to the will to power, so that survival is thought of as a tool or resource for creation, a displacement of antihumanism from the ascetic ideal to overman (non-terminal overcoming), the completion of a post-Aristotelian 'logic' of gradation without negativity or limits, a 'critique of philosophy' that diagnosed Plato and Kant as symptoms of libidinal disaster, a return of historical thinking freed from the untenable time/timelessness opposition of bankrupt logicism, and a displacement from the principle of sufficient reason to 'equalization' (*Ausgleichung*), which – since differentiation was no longer thought of as an imposition of the subject – implied a shift from primordial unity to irreducible pluralism, and from the disinterested 'world-eye' to perspectivism.

Nietzsche's intricate, profound, and explosive response to the provocation of Schopenhauer resists hasty summarization. It is helpful to start with the transitional movements of *The Birth of Tragedy*, in which the Schopenhauerian will is re-baptized as 'Dionysus'. Like the undifferentiated will, it is only in the dream of Apollonian appearance that Dionysus can be individualized. As Walter Otto remarks (about the mythological, not just the specifically Nietzschean god): 'He is clearly thought of on the oriental pattern as the divine or infinite in general, in which the individual soul longs so much to lose itself' (p. 115). The tragic chorus is the focus of a delirious fusion, in which the personality is liquidated by the collective artistic process. Otto says some other very important things about Dionysus, the twice born:

> The one so born is not merely the exultant one and joy-bringer, he is also the suffering and dying god, the god of tragic

contradiction. And the inner power of this dual nature is so great, that he steps amongst humanity as a storm, quaking them and subduing their resistance with the whip of madness. Everything habitual and ordered must be scattered. Existence suddenly becomes an intoxication – an introduction of blessedness, but no less one of terror.[18]

To this female world the Apollonian stands opposed, as the decidedly masculine. The mystery of life of blood and of terrestrial force does not rule in it, but rather clarity and breadth of spirit. But the Apollonian world cannot persist without the other.[19]

Doric civilization, the hard Apollonian spine of western culture, vaunting the defiant erectness of its architecture, is fundamentally defensive in nature. Already in this, Nietzsche's most 'Schopenhauerian' book, the minor register of the pessimistic quandary prevails without compromise; the overcoming of wretched individuality is to be referred in the direction of the reservoir of insurgent desire, not in that of a metaphysical renunciation. One does not build fortifications against saints:

to me the *Doric* state and Doric art are explicable only as a permanent military encampment of the Apollonian. Only incessant resistance to the titanic-barbaric nature of the Dionysian could account for the long survival of an art so defiantly prim and so encompassed with bulwarks, a training so warlike and rigorous, and a political structure so cruel and relentless.[20]

The difference between Dionysus and Apollo is that between music and the plastic arts (Schopenhauer's differentiation that Nietzsche describes as 'the most important insight of aesthetics'[21]), will and representation (primary and secondary process), chaos and form. In the tragic fusion of music and theatrical spectacle desire is delivered upon the order of representation in a delirious collective affirmation of insurgent alterity (nature, impulse, oracular insight, woman, barbarism, Asia). Greek tragedy is the last instance of the occident being radically permeable to its outside. The Socratic death of tragedy is the beginning of the ethnic solipsism and imperialistic dogmatism that has characterized western politics ever since, the brutal domestication process with which the repressive instance in *man* ('reason') has afflicted the impersonal insurrectionary energies of creativity, until they became the whimpering, sentimental, and psychologized 'genius' of the romantics. With Socrates began the passionate quest of European humanity to become the *ugly animal*.

In his later, more fragmentary writings on art, Nietzsche perhaps says something a little like the following. The aesthetic *operation* is simplification; the movement of abstraction, logicization, unification, the resolution of problematic. It is this operation which, when understood in terms of the logical principles formulated by Aristotle – in terms, that is, of its own product – seems like a negation of the enigmatic, the re-distribution of alterity to the same within a zero-sum exchange, the progressive 'improvement' and domestication of life. But simplification is not a teleologically regulated approximation to simplicity, to the decadent terminus we call 'truth', it is an inexhaustibly open-ended creative process whose only limits are fictions fabricated out of itself. Nothing is more complex than simplification; what art takes from enigma it more than replenishes in the instantiation of itself, in the labyrinthine puzzle it plants in history. The intensification of enigma. The luxuriantly problematic loam of existence is built out of the sedimented aeons of residues deposited by the will to power, the impulse to create, 'The world as a work of art that gives birth to itself'.[22]

Enigma, positive confusion (delirium), problematic, pain, whatever we want to call it; the torment of the philosophers in any case, is the stimulus to ecstatic creation, to an interminable 'resolution' into the enhanced provocations of art. What the philosophers have never understood is this: *it is the unintelligibility of the world alone that gives it worth*. 'Inertia needs unity (monism); plurality of interpretations a sign of strength. Not to desire to deprive the world of its disturbing and enigmatic character'.[23] Not, then, to oppose pain to the absence of pain as metaphysical pessimism does, but, rather, to differentiate the ecstatic overcoming of pain from weariness and inertia, to exult in new and more terrible agonies, fears, burning perplexities as the resourse of becoming, overcoming, triumph, the great libidinal oscillations that break up stabilized systems and intoxicate on intensity; that is Dionysian pessimism – 'refusal to be deprived of the stimulus of the enigmatic'[24]; 'the effect of the work of art is to *excite the state that creates art – intoxication*'.[25]

IV

After Nietzsche there is Freud, tapping into a reservoir of genius (the unconscious of late nineteenth-century Viennese women) that drives him to the point of idiocy, he pushes onwards without knowing what the fuck he's doing. Freud is a thinker of astounding richness and fertile complexity, but I shall merely touch upon his most disastrous confusion. When he writes on art, degenerating – despite his wealth of acuity – into banal psycho-biography, a terribly damaging loss of direction afflicts the psychoanalytic enterprise. The inherent connection between the irruptive primary process and artistic creativity, or the basis inextricability of psychoanalysis and aesthetics, slips Freud's grasp, and art is presented as a merely contingent terrain for the application of therapeutically honed concepts. The adaptation of the mutilated individual to its society, in which art is illegal except as a parasite of elite commodity production circuits, is the scandal of psychoanalysis. It becomes Kantian (bourgeois); a delicate police activity dedicated to the social management and containment of genius. As if 'therapy' could be anything other than the revolutionary unleashing of artistic creation!

The two basis directions in which the philosophy of genius can develop are exemplified by psychoanalysis and national socialism. Either rigorous anti-anthropomorphism, the steady constriction of the terrain of intentional explanation, and the rolling reduction of praxes to parapraxes, or the re-ascription of genius to intentional individuality, concentration of decision, and the paranoiac praxial interpretation of non-intentional processes (the Jewish conspiracy theory). The death of God is operative in both cases, either as the space of the generative unconscious, or as that of a triumphantly divinized and arbitrarily isolated secular subjectivity. It is easy to see that the role of discourse in these two cases is a very precise register for the difference at issue; on the one hand the talking cure, in which the texts of confession and rational theory are both displaced by the compression wave of a radically senseless energy process that defies the status of object in relation to an auto-nomously determinable agent language, and on the other, the interminable authoritative monologue of the dictator (politically instantiated ego-ideal), in which the will is returned to a quasi-Kantian acceptation to capitalize upon its libidinal detour, finding its true sense in the lucid decision of an individual who speaks on behalf of a racially specified unconscious clamour.

That part of twentieth-century philosophy resonant with the aesthetically oriented tendency outlined here has as its two great tasks the diagnosis of Nazism and the protraction of the psycho-analytic impulse, in other words the arming of desire with intellectual weapons that will allow it to evade the dead-end racist *Götterdämmerung* politics which capital deploys as a last ditch defence against the flood. No revolution without insurrectionary desire, no effective route for insurrectionary desire without integral anti-fascism. Wilhelm Reich, Georges Bataille, Gilles Deleuze, and Félix Guattari are perhaps the most important theoretical *loci* in this development. The latter three I shall say a little about.

It is not *simply* ridiculous to describe Bataille as Schopenhauer with enthusiasm, in so far as this might crudely characterize a certain variant of 'Nietzscheanism', or Dionysian pessimism. After all, Bataille too is concerned with value as the annihilation of life, challenging the utilitarianism that finds its only end in the preservation and expansion of existence. If this affirmation of loss is 'nihilistic', it is at least an 'active nihilism'; the promotion of a violently convulsive *expenditure* rather than a weary renunciation. Art as the wastage of life. And Bataille's involvement with art, above all with literature, is of an unparalleled intricacy and intensity. Philosopher and historian of art, literary theorist, in his 'philosophy' a stylist, dazzling as an essayist, a novelist and poet of both profundity and incandescent beauty, his is a writing oblivious to circumscription, spreading like an exotic fungus into the darkest recesses of aesthetic possibility. A rather tortured and incoherent leap? Come on now! A 'philosophy' of excess that draws out an inner connection between literature, eroticism, and revolt could hardly be irrelevant to our problematic here. As Bataille states, 'beauty alone . . . renders tolerable a need for disorder, violence, and indignity that is the root of love.'[26]

Bataille also has the peculiar honour, shared with Nietzsche and Reich, of beginning his assault on germinal national socialism before Hitler had exhibited its truth. His early essays sketch a vision of fascism as the most fanatical project for the elimination of excess, an attempt at the secular enforcement of the perfectly ordered city of God against the disorder, luxuriance, and mess of surplus production, as it sprawls into the voluptuary expenditure of eroticism and art. Assailing the fascist tendency is the disindividualized delirium of tragic sacrifice and revolution, when

> Being is given to us in an *intolerable* surpassing of being, no less intolerable than death. And because, in death, it is withdrawn from us at the same time it is given, we must search for it in the *feeling* of death, in those intolerable moments where it seems that we are dying, because the being in us is only there through excess, when the plenitude of horror and that of joy coincide.[27]

For there is no doubt that the fascists are right, the very incarnation of right, yes: 'Literature is even, like the transgression of moral law, a danger.'[28]

A theory of the real as art (primary production) that is melded seamlessly with an anti-fascist diagnostics characterizes the work of Gilles Deleuze and Félix Guattari. In their *Antioedipus* they indicate that the rational regulation or coding of creative process is derivative, sterile, and eliminable. Their name for genius is 'schizophrenia', a term that cannot be safely domesticated within psychology, any more than 'genius' can (and for the same reasons). If nature is psychotic it is simply because our psychoses are not in reality 'ours'.

Libido – as the raw energy of creation – is ungrounded, irreducibly multiple, yet it precipitates a real and unified 'principle' out of itself. The body without organs is its name; at once material abstraction, and the concretely hypostasized differential terrain which is nothing other than what is instantaneously shared by difference. The body without organs is pure surface, because it is the mere coherence of differential web, but it is also the source of depth, since it is the sole 'ontological' element of difference. It is produced transcendence. Paradox after paradox, spun like a disintegrating bandage upon the infected and deteriorating wound of Kant's aesthetics, teasing the philosophical domestication of art – the most gangrenous cultural appendage of capital – towards its utter disintegration.

How does desire come to desire its own repression? How does production come to rigidify itself in the social straitjacket *whose most dissolved form is capital*? It is with this problematic, inherited from Spinoza, Nietzsche, and Reich, that Deleuze and Guattari orient their work. In our terms here: how does art become (under-) compensated labour? Their answer involves a displacement of the problem into a philosophical affinity with Kant's paralogisms of the pure understanding, rethought in *Antioedipus* as materially instantiated traps for desire. A paralogism is the attempt to ground 'conditions of possibility' in the objectivity they permit, or creativity in what it creates. This is, to take the most pertinent example, to derive the forces of production from the socio-economic apparatus they generate. Sociological fundamentalism, state worship, totalitarian paranoia and fascism, they all exhibit the same basic impulse; hatred of art, (real) freedom, desire, everything that cannot be controlled, regulated, and administered. Fascism hates aliens, migrant workers, the homeless, rootless people of every kind and inclination, everything evocative of excitement and uncertainty, women, artists, lunatics, drifting sexual drives, liquids, impurity, and abandonment.

Philosophy, in its longing to rationalize, formalize, define, delimit, to terminate enigma and uncertainty, to co-operate wholeheartedly with the police, is nihilistic in the ultimate sense that it strives for the immobile perfection of death. But creativity cannot be brought to an end that is compatible with power, for unless life is extinguished, control must inevitably break down. We possess *art* lest *we perish of the truth*.[29]

To conclude is not merely erroneous, but ugly.

NOTES

Where both original texts and translation are given I have sometimes translated directly from the original, and sometimes cited the English version without modification.

1 Immanuel Kant, *Kritik der Urteilskraft*, Frankfurt am Main, Suhrkamp, 1974, 16.
2 Ibid., 22.
3 Ibid., 23.
4 Ibid., 30.
5 Ibid., 189–90 (*The Critique of Judgement*, trans. James Creed Meredith, Oxford, Oxford University Press, 1982, 115).
6 Ibid., 294–9 (English, 221–5).
7 Ibid., 244 (English, 170).
8 Ibid., 79 (English, 9).
9 Arthur Schopenhauer, *Die Welt als Wille und Vorstellung II, ii*, Diogenes, 1977, 446 (*The World as Will and Representation*, vol. II, trans. E. F. J. Payne, New York, Dover, 1966, 377).
10 Ibid., 484 (English, 410).
11 Of all the complex issues I have skimmed over recklessly this is perhaps the richest and most impacted. Schopenhauer, by referring exorbitant form back to a Platonic *eidos* is undoubtedly sacrificing a great deal of the fertile tension in Kant's thought of purposiveness without purpose, although he also reduces the risk of a slide back into teleological theology. The thought that was perhaps necessary in order to depart most radically from the possibility of theistic relapse was that of a divine unconscious, eliminating all possibility of agentic creation at any level. But this would be the image of a mad god. Dionysus?
12 Ibid., 624 (English, 555).
13 Ibid., 650–1 (English, 555).
14 Ibid., 630 (English, 538).
15 Schopenhauer, *Parerga und Paralipomena II, ii*, Diogenes, 1977, 671 (*Parerga and Paralipomena*, vol. II, trans. E. F. J. Payne, Oxford, Clarendon Press, 1974, 617).
16 Ibid., 673 (English, 619).

17 *Die Welt als Wille und Vorstellung II*, *ii*, 559 (*The World as Will and Representation*, vol. II, 477).
18 Walter F. Otto, *Dionysos, Mythos und Kultus*, Frankfurt am Main, Vittorio Klostermann, 1933, 74–5.
19 Ibid., 132.
20 Friedrich Nietzsche, *Die Geburt der Tragödie*, Frankfurt am Main, Ullstein Materialien, 1981, 35 (*The Birth of Tragedy*, trans. Walter Kaufmann, New York, Vintage Books, 1967, 47).
21 Ibid., 89 (English, 100).
22 Friedrich Nietzsche, selected and edited by Peter Gast and Elisabeth Förster-Nietzsche, *Der Wille zur Macht*, Alfred Kröner Verlag, 1964, 533 (*The Will to Power*, trans. Walter Kaufmann, New York, Vintage Books, 1968, 419).
23 Ibid., 413 (English, 326).
24 Ibid., 330 (English, 262).
25 Ibid., 553 (English, 434).
26 Georges Bataille, *Oeuvres Complètes*, Paris, Gallimard, 1976, III, 13.
27 Ibid., 11–12.
28 Ibid., IX, 182.
29 *Der Wille zur Macht*, 554 (English, 435).

11 Reading the future of genealogy: Kant, Nietzsche, Plato

Michael Newman

> From this moment forward all my writings are fish hooks:
> perhaps I know how to fish as well as anyone? – If nothing was
> caught, I am not to blame. *There were no fish.*[1]

I

Nietzsche closes the preface to *On the Genealogy of Morals* by
drawing attention to a difficulty in reading. To seek merely to
'understand' an aphorism is not to take it seriously enough as a form
'properly stamped and moulded'. It 'has not been "deciphered"
when it has simply been read; rather, one has to begin its *exegesis*
[*Auslegung*], for which is required an art of exegesis'. This 'art' has
been 'unlearnt' today and as a result it will be some time before
Nietzsche's writings are 'readable'. The conditions for reading as an
art is 'something for which one has almost to be a cow and in any
case *not* a "modern man" [*moderner Mensch*]: *rumination* [*das
Wiederkäuen*]'.

The aphorism is not in principle unreadable, but rather unreadable by a certain epochal type, the *moderner Mensch*. It is in
the second essay that Nietzsche gives an account of the formation of
'modern man': '[w]e modern men are the heirs of the conscience-
vivisection and self-torture of millennia' (OGM II, section 24).
Modern humanity is called upon by Nietzsche to engage in the task of
overcoming itself. What is to be overcome is not simply rejected by
Nietzsche: he writes of justice that 'it ends, as does every good thing
on earth, by *overcoming itself*' (OGM II, section 10). For Nietzsche:
'All *great* things bring about their own destruction through an act of
self-overcoming [*Selbstaufhebung*]' which is 'the law of the necessity of
"self-overcoming [*Selbstüberwindung*]"' in the nature of life' (OGM

III, 27).[2] Modern humanity will only be able to overcome itself when it acknowledges and assumes the history of its self-formation in terms of a slave revolt in morality as its own history, and indeed as the very basis for the possibility of its own self-destruction and translation to a higher level of existence. This 'self-overcoming' is to be achieved through the practices of writing and reading, hence the importance both of the account of reading in the preface, and the performative dimension of the *Genealogy of Morals*.

Reading as 'rumination' is to displace the self-reflection of consciousness of 'we knowers' which fails according to the little mock-sermon with which the preface begins.[3] Incomprehensibility in the epoch of modernity would take on a positive value, in so far as it might open the book to a future, the future of the reader, who will no longer be a *moderner Mensch*.[4] Thus if the reader were able to read the aphorism he would be transposed; and the *Schrift* itself, by prompting, through its difficulty, that reading which Nietzsche seems to be demanding, will have been party to the self-overcoming of modernity. The difficulty may thus be taken as a question of epochality: the epochal site from which the aphorism *would* be readable is not yet available to the 'present' reader: the difficulty is to intimate a future not determined by the present in a *telos*; yet a future which must also, in order not to be merely contingent, be in some sense 'in' the present and related to the past. In other words, the problem is that of the formation of a being who is historical – who is capable of having and making a history – yet who is not dominated and burdened by the past, and consequently who has a future. This will be the 'sovereign individual' who is not calculable (not wholly determined by the repetition of custom), and consequently for whom the future is open, yet who has the '*right to make promises*' (OGM II, 2): 'the right to stand security for oneself' is 'a *late* fruit' of the 'long history' of the formation of a conscience (OGM II, 3).

Connected with the difficulty of the projection of an epochal site of reading is the problem of the agency or effectivity of the book *On the Genealogy of Morals* itself. The book is not only to intimate the 'other future', but to be effective in its attainment. The *Genealogy* will have to be Janus-faced: to be both readable and unreadable. This is not so much a matter of two teachings, the exoteric and esoteric,[5] one behind the other like a 'true' meaning to be penetrated through a façade or narrative surface as the movement from 'understanding' to 'reading', the process of transformation as 'self-overcoming'.

Following the title page Nietzsche described the *Genealogy* as 'A Sequel to My Last Book, *Beyond Good and Evil*, Which it is Meant to Supplement and Clarify' (OGM, p. 3). Why did *Beyond Good and Evil* need supplementation and clarification? We might say, following the hint of the preface to the *Genealogy*, because *Beyond Good and Evil* is a book of aphorisms which are unreadable by 'modern man', hence the need for a repetition of the themes of *Beyond Good and Evil* in a more accessible form. But the problem of access is not so simple. Nietzsche writes in the preface to the *Genealogy*,

> If this book is incomprehensible to anyone and jars on his ears, the fault, it seems to me, is not necessarily mine. It is clear enough, assuming as I do assume, that one has first read my earlier writings and has not spared some trouble in doing so: for they are, indeed, not easy to penetrate.

If the *Genealogy* is incomprehensible, it is not because the earlier books have been penetrated, but it is because of the impenetrability of those books that the supplement, and 'fish hook', of the *Genealogy* is required. If, as Nietzsche writes in *Ecce Homo*, *Beyond Good and Evil* marks the turn from the 'yes-saying' to the 'no-saying' part of his task (EH, 'Beyond Good and Evil', 1), as a book of aphorisms – he seems to be suggesting in the preface to the *Genealogy* – it remains impenetrable. So, according to Nietzsche, to read the *Genealogy*, one will have to have read his earlier books, above all *Thus Spoke Zarathustra*, which the *Genealogy* is to aid in reading. Yet, if the essay is not a 'difficult' form, why should the *Genealogy* be incomprehensible? Does not Nietzsche turn to the essay form to provide a point of access to the circle of his texts?

In other books the problem is posed by the spaces, the silences, in between the aphorisms. In 'no-saying' books the 'yes' is the unsaid – 'the art of silence is in the foreground' (EH, 'Beyond Good and Evil', 2). During June–July 1885 Nietzsche wrote in a note:

> In aphorism books like mine many lengthy, forbidden things and chains of thought stand between and behind short aphorisms. And many among them that would be questionable enough for Oedipus and his Sphinx. I don't write essays – those are for asses and journal readers. No more do I write speeches.[6]

Essays and speeches are contrasted with the 'hermit's philosophy' which 'even were it written with a lion's claw, would still look like a philosophy of quotation marks', which is echoed in *Beyond Good and Evil* 289, where for the hermit every philosophy is a 'foreground' philosophy which '*conceals* a philosophy; every opinion is also a hideout, every word also a mask'.

A hermit does not write essays or speeches, and engage in public polemics (except, as the note suggests, 'in the most intimate dispute and dialogue with his soul'). Yet, two years later, this is precisely what Nietzsche did in the *Genealogy*, a book subtitled *Eine Streitschrift* (a polemic), and consisting of three essays written at many points in the performative style of a speech and even incorporating snatches of dialogue. The hermit ceases to be a hermit in writing which will be both a repetition ('a philosophy of quotation marks') and for 'another'. We could also say, conversely, that every writer and reader is a hermit, a solitary in the experience of writing and reading. This places the problem of 'self-overcoming' through a transformed reading in the context of the question, which goes back to Plato, of whether writing is an appropriate mode of philosophical teaching.

Nietzsche suggests at the end of the preface that the third essay of the *Genealogy* is a lesson in reading. He tells his reader that he will offer an 'example' of what he regards as 'exegesis': an aphorism is prefixed to the third essay, 'the essay itself is a commentary on it'. Let us, for the time being, assume that the aphorism to which Nietzsche refers is the epigram prefixed to the essay.

Unconcerned, mocking, violent – Thus wisdom wants *us*: she is a woman and always loves only a warrior.[7]

It is taken from one of Zarathustra's speeches, 'On Reading and Writing', in the first book of *Thus Spoke Zarathustra*. Nietzsche has claimed in the preface that the *Genealogy* 'is clear enough, assuming, as I do assume, that one has first read my earlier writings' – above all, '[m]y *Zarathustra*'. But this, again, assumes that the reader will have been able to read them, which is denied in the preface to the *Genealogy*, in so far as the latter presents itself as a response to the difficulty in reading. So the *Genealogy* could be read as an exegesis of *Zarathustra*, which will have to have been read for the exegesis to be readable. And the reading Nietzsche offers will be of an aphorism from a speech on reading and writing. So an 'essay' will be a reading of a 'speech', neither of which, Nietzsche claims, he writes: having condemned speeches, as opposed to aphorisms,

Nietzsche makes an aphorism out of a quotation from a speech by Zarathustra. Moreover, the essay which is supposedly a commentary on the aphorism nowhere cites or explicitly refers to it. The marginal position of the aphorism, neither, or both, inside and outside the book, marks the transitional role of the book itself, as a passage into the Nietzschean corpus. The passage is difficult in so far as it is not only 'personal', the passage into Nietzsche's authorship, but also epochal, the self-overcoming of nihilism into a historical condition in which the inscription of the Nietzschean corpus would become legible. This means that the passage into and through Nietzsche's authorship must be 'exemplary', while its destination is to be originality or singularity. What is certain is that the strategy of the *Genealogy* can only be understood in relation to a problem which arises in Zarathustra, in which the problem of authorship (who is Zarathustra?) is so sharply posed.

II

'On Reading and Writing' is the seventh of the twenty-two speeches Zarathustra makes in order to gather companions for the task of the creation of new values. This is his second attempt: his first, when he tried to teach the 'overman' (*Übermensch*), the being who is to follow the overcoming of 'man', has failed. If Zarathustra loves man (Z, p. 123), it is as 'a bridge and not an end': 'I love him who justifies future and redeems past generations: for he wants to perish of the present' (Z, p. 128). This justification is contrasted with contempt and pity. The overman, described as 'frenzy' and 'lightning' (p. 126), is 'the meaning of the earth' (p. 125). Those in the market-place laugh at Zarathustra's teaching, and he vows 'Never again shall I speak to the people: for the last time have I spoken to the dead' (p. 136). The speeches mark the attempt to address – perhaps even to constitute – another group: 'Fellow creators, the creator seeks – those who write new values on new tablets' (p. 136). These creators, 'celebrants' and 'harvesters', will also be called 'destroyers . . . and despisers of good and evil'. This second attempt must also fail: not this time because Zarathustra is rejected, but because for the follower to be a creator, Zarathustra himself must now be resisted: 'Now I go alone, my disciples. You too go now, alone . . . go away from me and resist Zarathustra!' (p. 190). He does not want 'believers': 'you had not sought yourselves: and you found me. . . . Now I bid you lose yourselves; and only when you have all denied me will I return to you' (p. 190). While

Zarathustra offers himself as exemplary, he rejects, with an ironic reference to Christ's resurrection, the relation to him which would take the form of a following, of the imitative repetition of the example. The third coming of Zarathustra will be 'the great noon' (p. 190).

These and other passages which precede and follow 'Zarathustra's speeches' are echoed in the first section of the preface to the *Genealogy*, which begins and ends with the question of self-knowledge: 'We are unknown to ourselves, we knowers, we ourselves to ourselves. . . . So we are necessarily strangers to ourselves, we do not comprehend ourselves, we *have* to misunderstand ourselves.' The knower, 'as one divinely preoccupied and immersed in himself', misses 'the twelve beats of noon'. Zarathustra's 'word of the great noon' is associated with the teaching which, if it were to free man from the revenge against time, would be his overcoming (*Überwindung*) (pp. 310–11). The 'knower' as the 'modern man' of the preface is not yet in a position to undergo the thought of the eternal recurrence of the same, Zarathustra's teaching which is to vanquish the revenge against time; a possibility which, however, might arise with the failure of self-reflection.

The problem posed in the preface of the *Genealogy* is the same as that in *Zarathustra*: the relation between teaching and creation or creative legislation. This affects the determination of the status of the three essays of the *Genealogy*. If Nietzsche, having repudiated 'essays' as 'for asses and journal readers', turns to the essay form in the *Genealogy*, might this indicate that it marks an attempt at the task in which Zarathustra failed – to teach in the market-place? The failure of Zarathustra to extend his affirmation beyond himself in *Thus Spoke Zarathustra* as a whole might be seen as following from this first failure, not least because it is never explained who the potential disciples to whom he addresses his speeches are; an indeterminacy which, however, permits the interpellation of the reader as listener. From the perspective of the later writings, especially the prefaces, the *Genealogy* and *Ecce Homo*, if nihilism is to be surpassed in a process of 'self-overcoming', where else can this begin but in the market-place where journals are read and books published? The problem which Nietzsche confronts in the *Genealogy*, and which determines its form, is analogous to the 'broken' transition from Zarathustra's first attempt to communicate his teaching of the overman, to the speeches by which he intends to gather and constitute the destroyer-creators.

That this epigram is from the speech 'On Reading and Writing', and is referred to as an example of the 'art of exegesis' in the preface, indicates the direction which Nietzsche's attempted solution to the problem has taken by the time of the *Genealogy*. The destroyer-creators are to be constituted through the process of reading. The text is offered to the 'knower', its initial addressee: yet in so far as this 'knower' is a 'modern man' Nietzsche's 'writings', he tells us (his readers who presumably, at this stage, are as yet untransformed 'knowers'), are not readable.

Nietzsche again draws attention to the problem of reading in his discussion of the *Genealogy* in *Ecce Homo*, where it is now shown to concern the relation between the 'no' and the 'yes', or destruction and affirmation: 'Regarding expression, intention, and the art of surprise, the three inquiries which constitute this *Genealogy* are perhaps uncannier than anything else written so far. Dionysus is, as is known, also the god of darkness.'

Why should a book of essays be more 'uncanny' than *Zarathustra* and the aphorism books? This uncanniness concerns the way in which it is peculiarly strategic. Dionysus is also the god of masks: the *Genealogy* is uncanny because it is more masked, and as such, more Dionysian than the more overtly Dionysian *Zarathustra*. This is confirmed by the next passage:

> Every time a beginning that is *calculated* to mislead: cool, scientific, even ironic, deliberately foreground, deliberately holding off. Gradually more unrest; sporadic lightning; very disagreeable truths are heard grumbling in the distance – until eventually a *tempo feroce* is attained in which everything rushes ahead in a tremendous tension [the tension required for 'self-overcoming']. In the end, in the midst of perfectly gruesome detonations, a *new* truth becomes visible every time among thick clouds.

The movement is from the deliberately misleading 'scientific' beginning of each essay to the 'new truth'. Note that the redetermination of truth, through truthfulness, as *will* to truth, in the third essay of the *Genealogy*, does not prevent Nietzsche from asserting that what is important about his book is the 'truth' that emerges from each essay: 'truth' is to be revalued rather than simply abolished. Each time the movement of the destruction of an ideal involves an implicit affirmation: Christianity, born out of *ressentiment*, is a 'countermovement' against 'the dominion of *noble* values'; conscience is not 'the voice of God in man' but the instinct, turned back against itself, of cruelty, 'the most ancient and basic substrata of culture that simply cannot be imagined away'; and the ascetic ideal derives its power not from God but from the fact that 'it was the only ideal so far'. If the 'ideal' is the goal for a will to power, and man is will to power, then Schopenhauer's negation of the will, which Nietzsche takes as the final form of the ascetic ideal – nihilism – must be redetermined as the *will* to nothingness, 'For man would rather will even nothingness than *not* will.' And Nietzsche concludes this summary, 'Above all, a *counterideal* was lacking – *until Zarathustra.*' Nietzsche goes on to answer the question ('Am I understood? . . . Have I been understood?) which ends the first section of the third essay, and compels the latter's continuation, with: 'I have been understood.' But the question remains whether he has been understood by anyone but himself – or, if he has been understood by someone other, what sort of understanding and otherness are involved. Specifically, what is the relation between understanding and the creation of values: 'the art of exegesis', and the 'reading and writing' of Zarathustra's speech?

The attempt to answer this question assumes, of course, that we already know the answer, since it must be based on a reading of *Zarathustra* and the *Genealogy*. Rather than attempting to explicate this hermeneutic circle I will venture a suggestion for a reading of 'On Reading and Writing' in the hope that it can be justified at least retrospectively. By treating Zarathustra's speech as a 'reply' to Socrates' condemnation of writing in Plato's *Phaedrus*, this reading will throw light on the way in which Nietzsche takes up the problem of philosophical teaching. My suggestion is that the *Genealogy*, as another response to this problem, draws on the logic of the Kantian genius as a possible model for the 'self-overcoming' transition.

III

The warrior of the aphorism loved *by* wisdom seems like an inversion of the Socratic philosopher's love of wisdom. Who, or what, then, does the warrior or noble love? An answer is suggested at the very beginning of Zarathustra's speech 'On Reading and Writing': 'Of all that is written I love only what a man has written with his blood. Write with blood, and you will experience that blood is spirit.' If the writer who writes with blood will experience that 'blood is spirit', what of the reader, assuming that there is a distinction to be made between reading and writing? 'It is not easy to understand the blood of another.'

The reader who seeks to understand is rejected: 'Whoever knows the reader will henceforth do nothing for the reader. Another century of readers – and the spirit itself will stink.' This reader, who presumably is the 'journal reader' who expects essays, is not, then, the addressee of Zarathustra's 'speeches'. This raises the problem of how Zarathustra's speeches, as written by Nietzsche, are to be read. So far a distinction has been made between love as the proper response to what is written with blood, and understanding, or the activity of the 'knower' with which the *Genealogy* begins. This latter kind of reader is a member of the 'rabble'. Love is then redetermined as a mode of reading: 'Whoever writes in blood and aphorisms does not want to be read but to be learned by heart.'

This is surprising: the philosopher of the will appears to be suggesting through Zarathustra that a noble response to the aphorism, a response requiring 'courage', involves a moment of submission, of the sheer repetition of the text. But this is less surprising if thought of as incorporation, the 'rumination' described in the preface to the *Genealogy*. The submission of 'learning by heart' is immediately contrasted by the metaphorical description of aphorisms as 'peaks – and those who are addressed, tall and lofty'. The link between reverence and loftiness is given in 'You look up when you feel the need for elevation. And I look down because I am elevated.'

The educative process of self-transformation begins in the need which seeks out the noble exemplar. It is this need – since Plato the starting point of philosophical education to self-knowledge – which is, rather than standing as 'reactive' in opposition to the 'active' will to power, to be transformed into the noble form of reverence.[8] Reading *Zarathustra* through the *Genealogy*, we can infer that this process of transformation will involve 'mnemotechnics' of pain by which a memory is created; the *'right to affirm oneself'* is 'a *late* fruit' of this formative history (OGM II, 3). Through 'learning by heart', what is written with blood will be 'burned' into the memory, and the aphorism is the form of writing which brands.

Aphorisms as a noble form of writing are peaks which jut above the 'cloud' of 'blackness and gravity'. The epigram might be thought of as a 'peak' above the third essay of the *Genealogy* – recall that Nietzsche described the 'new truth' of each essay becoming visible 'in the midst of perfectly gruesome detonations . . . every time among thick clouds' (EH). The 'blackness and gravity', which Zarathustra is above, is 'your thundercloud'. If the overman is earlier described as 'lightning' as well as 'frenzy' (p. 126), this is how he will appear to those still beneath the clouds, to 'you' the addressees. The clouds become 'tragic plays and tragic seriousness' at which those who are elevated to nobility and see from above are able to laugh, a laughter which will kill the 'spirit of gravity' (see Z III, 'On the Spirity of Gravity'). If, according to this spirit, 'all things fall' and life is a burden, Zarathustra 'would believe only in a god who could dance'. This dance may be associated with the 'frenzy' of the overman. The same word, *Wahnsinn*, is repeated in the following passage: 'True, we love life, not because we are used to living but because we are used to loving. There is always some madness [*Wahnsinn*] in love. But there is also always some reason [*Vernunft*] in madness.'

The suggestion here is that what is to overcome 'understanding' will not be simply the irrational as reason's other. The 'elevated' discourse would be assigned a position in the opposition of reason and madness from the perspective of the market-place or nihilism. But 'love' cannot be properly thought within this opposition as it contains both *Wahnsinn* and *Vernunft*. Love, in other words, is the medium of the elevation to nobility.

This is, of course, analogous to the role of love (*eros*) in Plato's dialogues; but different too since the Nietzschean elevation will not be to the supra-sensible forms. 'On Reading and Writing' can be seen as a reply, or reinscription, of the *Phaedrus*,[9] where Socrates praises the elevating effect of divine madness (249d–e).[10] It is a consideration of the role of love in philosophical education which motivates the need to distinguish between writing and speech, and the good and bad varieties of each. In the myth which Socrates recounts, King Thamos rejects Theuth's gift of writing.

> For your invention will produce forgetfulness in the souls of those who have learned it, through lack of practice at using their memory, as through reliance on writing they are reminded from outside by alien marks, but from inside, themselves by them-selves: you have discovered an elixir [*pharmakon*] not of memory but of reminding.[11]
>
> (275a)

Socrates claims that 'dead' discourse is a 'kind of image' (a mimesis) of the 'living speech'.[12] Speech is living when the dialectician plants it like a seed in the right type of soul who can be nurtured and benefit from the teaching (276e–277a), which will involve engaging in dialogue, by being brought to a memory (*anamnesis*) of the forms. By contrast, words written in 'black water' are 'incapable of adequately teaching what is true' (276c). While the drama of the dialogue begins by emphasizing the way in which Socrates adjusts his remarks according to his knowledge of Phaedrus' character, the problem with writing is that it cannot adjust itself to and assess the addressee. Thamos continues,

> To your students you give an appearance of wisdom, not the reality of it; having heard much, in the absence of teaching, they will appear to know much when for the most part they know nothing, and they will be difficult to get along with, because they have acquired the appearance of wisdom instead of wisdom itself.
>
> (275a–b)

Would this apply to writing with blood, and learning by heart?

The 'teaching relation' is at issue in Zarathustra's speeches both thematically and performatively, as it is in Plato's dialogue. My claim is that this is equally the case with the *Genealogy*, which also contains a number of echoes of the *Phaedrus*. Where these occur is significant. First, the preface, like the *Phaedrus*, begins by raising the question of self-knowledge and ends with a discussion of reading. Socrates dismisses the 'expert' who reduces the myths to probabilities 'with his boorish [i.e. ignoble] kind of expertise': 'For myself, in no way do I have leisure for these things, and the reason for it is this. I am not yet capable, in accordance with the Delphic inscription, of "knowing myself" ' (229e).

The myths, then, are justified as a means toward self-knowledge. Nietzsche begins by telling the 'knower' that he does not know himself, and identifying the authorial *persona* with that knower in a 'we': author and addressee are constituted 'internally' to the written text. The genealogical accounts in the first two essays take at least a quasi-scientific form. But the failure of reflection, when coupled with Nietzsche's critique of the Kantian transcendental validation of the possibility of objectivity, undermines the ground of science as objective knowledge. Thus these quasi-scientific accounts can also be read as myths for the purpose of the self-education of the reader: indeed for the transformation of the 'knower' into a 'reader' who 'ruminates'.

IV

While I have so far considered a few of the analogies between the *Genealogy* and the *Phaedrus*, it is important not to exaggerate this to the extent of implying an identity between Nietzsche and Plato.

In the *Genealogy* Nietzsche describes Plato as 'the greatest enemy of art Europe has yet produced', and sets him in opposition with the poet Homer, 'the instinctive deifier, the *golden* nature' (III, 25). This should not, however, be taken as a rejection of Plato (who should not be simply identified with 'Platonism'), but rather as implying that Plato is one of the worthy enemies in the 'agon'[13] of the 'polemic' – if not the most 'noble' of them.[14]

The *Phaedrus* concludes with a prophecy and a prayer. Socrates predicts that young Isocrates will surpass anything that Lysias the rhetorician has achieved, because of his 'natural powers' and his 'nobler composition' – his mind 'contains an innate tincture of philosophy' (279a). He then offers a prayer to Pan – like the Satyr half-beast half-god, and like Dionysus associated with intoxication and madness – which recapitulates the topics of the dialogue, 'that I may become fair within, and that such outward things as I have may not war against the spirit within me' (279b). The second essay of the *Genealogy* ends similarly, with what could be taken as a prophecy and a prayer, which immediately precede the question posed by the title of the third essay, 'What Is the Meaning of Ascetic Ideals?', and the epigram from *Zarathustra* with which we began our discussion.

In section 16 Nietzsche writes that 'the existence on earth of an animal soul turned against itself, taking sides against itself, was something so new, profound, unheard of, enigmatic, contradictory, *and pregnant with a future*, that the aspect of the earth was essentially altered' and suggests that by this fortuitous event man might become 'not a goal but only a way, an episode, a bridge, a great promise'. The question with which we are left as the second essay draws to a close is that of transition.

Let us for a moment imagine that Nietzsche had ended the *Genealogy* with section 23 of the second essay, as he could plausibly have done, since we appear to have been given all we need for a genealogy of morals. We would have an account of the origin of moral ideas and experience (above all guilt and conscience) based on philology, economics, physiology, and psychology, fundamentally grounded in the philosophy of life. The result of morality is shown to be a sickness, life turning against life culminating in nihilism as the will to nothingness. This is contrasted with the affirmative life of the nobles and the creators of states, and the ancient Greek health. However, whether based on historical truth or a device for the constitution of an hermeneutic horizon, any straightforward return to a Greek or noble beginning is precluded by Nietzsche's repeated assertions throughout the second essay that the history of the formation of 'modern man' is a necessary condition for 'self-overcoming'; and the oppositional contrasts give no indication of how nihilism might itself be overcome.

Nietzsche intimates just such an overcoming in the last two sections of the second essay, which could be taken to form the beginning of a transition into the third.

To the questions, 'What are your really doing, erecting an ideal or knocking one down?' Nietzsche replies, 'If a temple is to be erected *a temple must be destroyed*: that is the law.' Although, or perhaps, indeed, because '[w]e modern men are the heirs of the conscience-vivisection and self-torture of millennia' resulting in the repudiation of the natural instincts (will to power), '[a]n attempt at reverse would *in itself* be possible – but who is strong enough for it? . . . To whom should one turn today with *such* hopes and demands?' It would require 'a *different* kind of spirit from that likely to appear in this present age': a spirit of 'great health', a warrior with the noble virtues. Nietzsche appears to be calling for nothing less than a redeemer who 'may bring home the *redemption* of this reality' from the curse of the 'hitherto reigning ideal'.[15] After employing the rhetoric of prophecy in the final section,[16] Nietzsche cedes to Zarathustra with a trope of *aposiopesis*, falling silent. Does this mean that Zarathustra is to be the prophet of the redeemer, or the redeemer himself? Whichever is the case, the implication is that this negative prophecy of silence could be taken as an answer to the reactive attempt to determine the future by projection from the determinations of the past. Prophecy is not merely prediction.[17] If prediction, as a scientific procedure, seeks to anticipate the result through knowledge of the determinations which precede it and their causal relations to the probable outcome, the prophet may be conceived of as the medium of and open to determination *by* the future.[18] What, then, is the relation here between prophecy and redemption?

In *Ecce Homo* Nietzsche writes that what Zarathustra says as 'he returns again for the first time to his solitude' is '[p]recisely the opposite of everything that any "sage", "saint", "world-redeemer", or any other decadent would say in such a case. – Not only does he speak differently, he also *is* different' (Pref. 4). The call for a redeemer would imply that the agency for the overcoming of nihilism would be external to it. But this cannot be the case if it is to be a self-overcoming: the difference marked by Zarathustra would have to arise internally to nihilism, yet at the same time not be identical with it. It follows from Nietzsche's critique of what he interprets as the metaphysical dualism culminating in Kant and Schopenhauer that he requires the possibility of an *immanent* overcoming which would consequently be a *self*-overcoming. This is the problem which the third essay sets out to resolve through, I will argue, a reworking of the logic of exemplarity from Kant's account of genius in the third *Critique*.

V

The last words of the second essay are '*Zarathustra the godless* . . .' Nietzsche's falling silent is not the Platonic silent contemplation of the forms. Nietzsche's silence concerns not the transcendent status of the true and the good, but rather an immanent, yet other future. This silence, which measures the failure of reflection, is a silent answer to the questions of subjectivity, production and history which distinguish the modern age.[19] But just as Nietzsche is not simply inverting Plato, so he is not simply opposed to Kant and Hegel as *the* philosophers of modernity. His emphasis on the relation between will and legislation is Kantian, and his idea that the past will be justified by its goal is Hegelian, even if there are also crucial differences between Nietzsche and these philosphers. I cannot explore these topics here. Rather, I will continue to focus on the problem of philosophical communication. It is now time to consider why this problem arises in the way that it does specifically for Nietzsche, and what we may take as his solution. First, we must return to the question of creation and destruction, which we have encountered both in *Zarathustra* and in the *Genealogy*. I want to suggest that this problem arises as it does because of the modern conception of originality which finds its first philosophical articulation in Kant: the problem of teaching the true becomes the problem of teaching originality, or the activity of legisla*ting* rather than conformity to the extant law. The exemplarity of genius in Kant's *Critique of Judgement* provides a logic which answers to this difficulty by combining relation with non-relation. This complicates the agonistic doubling which we find throughout this *Streitschrift*, this polemic.[20]

Nietzsche begins the investigation of the meaning of ascetic ideals with the consideration of the meaning of an inversion: 'What does it mean when an artist leaps over into his opposite?' (III, 2). Note that, even if art is intended as a 'counterideal to nihilism', Nietzsche does not, in the *Genealogy*, define precisely what 'art' after nihilism would be. Since *The Birth of Tragedy* Nietzsche's project had been to undercut the category of the aesthetic as delimiting an autonomous sphere of art. Having broken with Wagner in *Human, All Too Human*, Nietzsche takes him as a lesson in how the attempt to make art pass over into life may be recouped by nihilism, specifically its forms of religion and nationalist politics. Wagner turned pious, making the 'nature boy Parsifal' into a Catholic (II, 3). In order to suggest what the self-overcoming of such ideals would involve, Nietzsche asks what *Parsifal* would be if viewed from the height of nobility: 'intended as a joke', it would be 'a kind of epilogue and satyr play' by which the artist would take leave 'of tragedy . . . with an extravagance of wanton parody of the tragic itself', thus overcoming at last 'the *crudest form* . . . of the anti-nature of the ascetic ideal'.

> This, to repeat, would have been worthy of a great tragedian, who, like every artist, arrives at the ultimate pinnacle of his greatness only when he comes to see himself and his art *beneath* him – when he knows how to *laugh* at himself.

The artist ennobles himself by parodying his own seriousness. Is this a clue to the intended effect of the *Genealogy* itself?

Behind the seriousness of the artist-turned-ascetic is the philosopher Schopenhauer, for whom music is sovereign, set apart from the other arts as 'not offering images of phenomenality . . . but speaking rather the language of the will itself, directly out of the "abyss" ' (III, 4). We should not forget that Nietzsche, himself leaning on Schopenhauer, had intended to be Wagner's philosopher; so the self-parody he advocates for Wagner is Nietzsche's own self-parody, of himself as the author of *The Birth of Tragedy out of the Spirit of Music* (its full title in the first edition of 1872). The desire to penetrate the veil of phenomenality to the authentic, non-derivative 'abyss' of will is now understood as an aesthetic of the spectator rather than the artist. While the Kantian disinterested spectator is supposedly the subject-correlate of the work of fine art as 'a production through freedom' (CJ 43), Schopenhauer was pleased by the beautiful out of the strongest, most personal interest; that of 'a tortured soul who gains release from a torture'. When a philosopher pays homage to the ascetic ideal, 'he wants *to gain release from a torture*' (III, 6).

This release is at the cost of further, self-inflicted torture. It might therefore be contrasted with the release – from seriousness, from tragedy, from the solemnity of disinterested 'truth' – to be gained not through hermeneutic 'penetration' but through laughter, and which is achieved through the acknowledgement of torture, of pain and suffering, as part of the process of noble self-formation. Laughter, for Nietzsche, elevates. This elevation to nobility should not be confused with the transcendental self-abstraction from the empirical (including the empirical ego) of irony,[21] as it is also a paradoxical elevation downwards into an affirmation of the 'nearest things'.[22] Elevation through laughter contrasts both the Platonic and the Kantian elevation beyond the sensible, as well as Schopenhauer's negation of the will – and therefore, in Nietzschean terms, negation of life – as the culmination of the metaphysical tradition in nihilism which as a whole is epitomized in the ascetic priest, 'this *life-inimical* species' (III, 11). As Adorno and Horkheimer write, 'Laughter is marked by the guilt of subjectivity, but in the suspension of law which it indicates it also points beyond thralldom.'[23]

VI

If art is the counterideal to nihilism, how is art to be determined in such a way that it will not be subsumed under the metaphysical category of the aesthetic? Once again, if the overcoming of nihilism is to be a self-overcoming, the possibility of the overcoming of aesthetics will need to be retrieved from aesthetics itself – which means, for Nietzsche, from Kant. Behind Wagner's betrayal of the affirmative possibility of art lies Schopenhauer's negation of the will, and behind Schopenhauer, 'Kant's version of the aesthetic problem':

> Kant, who like all philosophers, instead of envisaging the aesthetic problem from the point of view of the artist (the creator), considered art and the beautiful purely from that of the 'spectator', and unconsciously introduced the 'spectator' into the concept 'beautiful'.

> (III, 6)

The non-conceptual universality of the beautiful can only be determined through reflective judgement manifesting the *sensus communis* (CJ 20–2). Such universality will be contained in the judgement in so far as it is disinterested. In Nietzschean terms, such a conception of judgement, which we may contrast with noble laughter, belongs to the herd, and moreover is false. But is not

Nietzsche providing a travesty, and quite possibly a deliberately misleading one, of Kant's aesthetics? Kant is, after all, also the most rigorous philosopher of genius as originary creation. While Nietzsche attacks the myth of the inspired, Romantic genius (i.e. Wagner), especially in *Human, All Too Human*,[24] I will argue that he continues to draw upon the logic of the exemplarity of genius in the *Genealogy*.

According to Kant, the beautiful in art is a work of *production*, and more specifically, a *creation*, in so far as the production is *free* (CJ 43). However, the very freedom of creation poses a problem: how to distinguish the work of fine art from 'original nonsense'? The 'foremost property of the genius must be *originality*' because no concept or rule can be given which subsumes the particular work, and genius cannot be learned by following rules. How then are the products of genius to be distinguished from nonsense, which is also non-conceptual?

> Since nonsense too can be original, the products of genius must also be models, i.e. they must be *exemplary*; hence, though they do not themselves arise through imitation, still they must serve others for this, i.e. as a standard or rule by which to judge.
>
> (46)

Thus the distinction between works of genius and 'original nonsense' is to be made in so far as the former serve as a standard for judgement. It would seem so far that Nietzsche is correct in his criticism, in so far as the original products of the artist are confirmed *as* art rather than nonsense by the spectators through judgement. This would be confirmation by the generality – the 'herd' in Nietzschean terms: if the work of art is only to serve as a touchstone for judgement, then it is primarily for, and justified by, the spectator.

In his treatment of the relation of genius to genius in the following section (47), Kant suggests another mode of effectivity of the work, which is both prospective and retrospective:

> the rule must be abstracted from what the artist has done, i.e. from the product, which others may use to test their own talent, letting it serve as the model, not to be *copied* [*Nachmachung*] but to be *imitated* [*Nachahmung*].
>
> (p. 309)[25]

The exemplarity of the work consists not in its mere singularity, but in the creation of a rule, a rule constituted in its practical confirmation through, on the one hand, reflective judgement, and, on the other, the subsequent constitution of a tradition.[26] In so far as the work may be both original and universal, it could be said to destroy the 'rule' of its predecessors, thus figuring the fusion of freedom and violence Kant regarded in the French Revolution[27] (and which Nietzsche affirms, as we have seen, in *Zarathustra* and the *Genealogy*).[28] The suspicion of such a possibility may have impelled Kant to divide originality from universality, making the donation of the latter the role of 'spectator' judgement. On the other side of the division, however, the work of genius

> is an example that is not meant to be imitated but to be followed by another genius. (For in mere imitation the element of genius in the work – what constitutes its spirit – would be lost.) The other genius, who follows the example, is aroused by it to a feeling of his own originality, which allows him to exercise in art his freedom from the constraint of rules, and to do so in such a way that art itself acquires a new rule by this, thus showing that the talent is exemplary.

(p. 318)

And Kant goes on to write of genius as 'nature's favourite' – talent is, as he wrote earlier, a 'natural endowment' (p. 307), a gift of nature. On the other hand, he also claims that, since nature operates according to the law of causality – its products are effects – art is distinguished from nature as a free human 'work' (p. 303). Therefore, while on the one hand the art of genius is to be the site of the reconciliation of nature and freedom, on the other this reconciliation must remain limited to an autonomous sphere, and teleologically directed towards the rational 'aesthetic idea', if it is not to pose a threat to the identification of freedom with rational, autonomous self-determination.

In the logic of the exemplarity of works of genius for the successor genius, Kant figures the teaching relation which generates the paradoxical relation of Zarathustra's speeches to the audience who are to be formed into destroyer-creators, where what is to be taught is originality. In the *Genealogy* the entwinement of destruction and creation is figured in the 'blond beasts of prey' who forge the state, and begin the process of socialization which will lead to the necessity for and possibility of self-overcoming through the '*instinct for freedom* (in my language: the will to power)' (II, 18) made '*latent* under their hammer blows and artists' violence' (II,

17): '[t]heir work is an instinctive creation and imposition of forms; they are the most involuntary, unconscious artists there are'. For Kant, when extended outside the autonomous sphere of art the freedom of genius is, in so far as it is a natural rather than a rational moment, dangerous because of its destructiveness. The successor genius, by taking the predecessor as a model, confirms him as a genius, but by taking him as a model of original rule-giving, destroys him as well. By constructing the third essay of the *Streitschrift* as an agon with the ascetic priest, Nietzsche in effect sets him up as a predecessor genius to be at once imitated and destroyed – destroyed by exposing the content of the ascetic will to be 'the nothing', the very abyss of *Schein* of the noble artist who laughs, even at his own products. The structure of this agon as a mimetic doubling,[29] required for an immanent self-overcoming according to the logic of genius, threatens to recoil on Nietzsche's project: a recoil which may, however, be necessary to its success.[30]

I want to suggest – and I can do no more here – that the agonistic 'doubling' is broken by the introduction of the figure of woman in the epigram. This 'third' introduces an irreducible difference between the ascetic priest and the noble 'warrior'. The difference in their behaviour towards woman stands for the difference in their relation towards truth and wisdom, contrasting the 'noble' asceticism of the warrior with the pretended disinterest of the ascetic priest. However, it must be acknowledged that this leaves woman a mere signifier of the difference between masculine types, and a means to male creativity.[31] Nonetheless, to determine truth, or wisdom, as woman is at least to indicate the interest of avowed distinterestedness.

There does, however, seem to be a contradiction in Nietzsche's project. The question is whether it is to be considered a vicious one; or whether the work that this contradiction does is a part of the provocation to self-overcoming of 'we knowers', and is a continuation of the history of the problem of philosophical education since Plato. This contradiction may be taken as the legacy of the ascetic priest who has been rendered exemplary according to the Kantian logic of genius. The destruction of the universality of the ascetic priest's valuation must necessarily involve not only one legislating act amid a plurality of others, but the generalization of a principle: in other words, the same move as that ascribed to the asectic priest, even if the principle which is generalized is perspectivism as the non-universalization of interpretations (III, 12). The creative act, which is 'beyond' or prior to the law, is affirmed as value-creating legislation, which would not have the force of law if it were merely contingent. The doctrine of will to power universalizes the sovereign and particular legislat*ing* act, rendering its violence an ontological ground, which, as violence, is the abyss which underwrites life as the sheer creative production of the value-legislating will to power. If the *Genealogy* is to succeed, the reader would become a writer who, as a creator of works of genius, will destroy the 'rule' of the exemplar, that is, of the *Genealogy*, itself.

The *Genealogy*, then, offers a law of originality – the law of legislation indeed – which, as a law, must be generalizable. For Kant the talent of the genius is a 'gift' of nature which 'gives the rule to art' (CJ 56); Nietzschean will to power could be conceived as nature redetermined according to the generalization of its work through the genius as its highest product: a *physis* of self-exceeding legislation – the laughter of the god at his own creations, the Heraclitean child's play of creation and destruction, Zarathustra's 'gift-giving virtue' (see Z, pp. 186–8). And rather than being the example of a 'transcendental exemplified',[32] each instance of this engendering – this inscription of will to power – is exemplary of nothing but itself, in so far as it will return to all eternity. It is the thought of the eternal recurrence of the same, alluded to in the *Genealogy* as the trace of affirmation, which could be said to be the self-overcoming of the metaphysical exemplar. In the affirmation of eternal recurrence exemplarity becomes singularity through the originality of the legislating will.

The question, which must still remain an open one, is whether this thought can be taught, and if so, how? Can philosophical teaching, despite Socrates' condemnation, take place through writing and reading? Is it possible for reading as 'rumination' (*Wiederkäuen*) to lead to the affirmation of eternal recurrence (*die ewige Wiederkunft*) through a return (*Wiederkehr*) that is not – or through being willed is more than – the mere repetition of custom? In other words, beyond its deceptive approachability, is it possible to read the *Genealogy*, where the question of reading is concerned with the problem of teaching originality, which arises in the Kantian logic of the examplarity of the genius, as the condition for the self-overcoming of nihilism?

If the signatory of the preface to *Ecce Homo*, 'Friedrich Nietzsche', claims that, because of the greatness of his task and the '*smallness*' of his contemporaries, 'I live on my own credit; it is perhaps a mere prejudice that I live', this is not least because the abolition of the 'beyond' associated with the distinction between the 'real' and the 'apparent' worlds opens the possibility of another 'beyond', an 'eternity' which will be no longer the unity of Platonic being or Kantian reason. This 'beyond', which is to be heard in 'beyond good and evil', makes the *Genealogy* at once deceptively easy, and impossible to understand. The hinge of the turn from 'understanding' to reading and writing is nothingness or 'the nothing' (*das Nichts*). It is possible to take the 'aphorism' to which Nietzsche refers in the preface as not the epigram but rather the first section of the third essay which, since according to an interpolated dialogue it has not been understood, ends, 'let us start again, from the beginning'. The proposition of this section is, '*That* the ascetic ideal has meant so many things to man . . . is an expression of the basic fact of the human will, its *horror vacui: it needs a goal* – and it will rather will *nothingness* than *not* will.' If there is an ambivalence between the epigram and the first section as the object of the reading lesson of the third essay, this might imply that Schopenhauerian nihilism is identical with the abyss of Zarathustrian godlessness as the condition of possibility for a non-resentful, noble and creative affirmation. This turn would be the final transformation of sense, the transmutation of the nihilist's 'nothing' into the abyss of self-overcoming destruction and creation, whereby 'we' knowers and modern men become the noble 'us' of the epigram.[33] Zarathustra says that 'as creator, guesser of riddles, and redeemer of accidents, I taught them to work on the future and to redeem with their creation all that *has been*' (Z III, 'On Old and New Tablets', p. 310; cf. also II, 'On Redemption', p. 251). But such a redemption can be achieved neither by Zarathustra, nor in and by the *Genealogy* itself, but only by the reader as the 'beyond', the future of the text, in a reading which would confirm the *Genealogy* as exemplary according to the Kantian logic, and consequently destroy it as well.

Could it be that through this paradox the *Genealogy* may begin to serve as a medium of philosophical education, and venture to overcome the debility of which Socrates accuses writing? If so, it is in the very break between the text and its readers after the failure of self-reflection of 'we knowers', marked in the dialogic interpellations of incomprehension, that the noble future, the future of the other, is intimated. And if it is the future readers who may be the outcome of the 'self-overcoming' of the nihilism of the knower who Nietzsche addresses as 'my *unknown* friends (for as yet I *know* of no friend)' (III, 27), we are left 'once more' with the question whether such readers are possible.

REFERENCES

Nietzsche

BGE   'Beyond Good and Evil' in *Basic Writings of Nietzsche*, trans. Walter
      Kaufmann, Modern Library edn, New York, Random House, 1968.
EH   *Ecce Homo* in *Basic Writings of Nietzsche*.
GS   *The Gay Science*, trans. Walter Kaufmann, New York, Random
      House, 1974.
OGM   *On the Genealogy of Morals*, trans. Walter Kaufmann and R. J.
      Hollingdale, New York, Random House, 1969. Roman numerals
      refer to the number of the essay.
Z   *Thus Spoke Zarathustra* in *The Portable Nietzsche*, ed. and trans.
      Walter Kaufmann, New York, Penguin Books, 1959.

Other

CJ   Immanuel Kant, *Critique of Judgement*, trans. Werner S. Pluhar,
      Indianapolis, Hackett, 1987. Pagination refers to the *Academie*
      edition: *Kants gesammelte Schriften*, Berlin, Königlich Preussische
      Akademie der Wissenschaften, 1908–13.

Numbers after abbreviations without a 'p.' refer to the number of a
section or aphorism. When quotations following a citation come
from the same page, section or aphorism, references will not always
be repeated. Occasionally I have modified translations, usually to
make them more literal.

NOTES

I owe a particular debt to discussions and seminars on Nietzsche's
writings, including *On the Genealogy of Morals*, with Robert Rethy,
Visiting Reader at the University of Essex during 1989–90. I would
also like to thank Jay Bernstein, Peter Dews and Simon Critchley
for their criticisms of earlier drafts of this essay.

1 EH, 'Beyond Good and Evil', 1.
2 For the notion of 'overcoming' in Nietzsche, see Keith Ansell-
  Pearson, 'Nietzsche's Overcoming of Kant and Metaphysics: From
  Tragedy to Nihilism', *Nietzsche-Studien*, vol. 16, 1987, pp. 310–39,
  where it is pointed out that Nietzsche employs interchangeably the
  expressions *Selbstaufhebung* (self-annullment, lifting up, and suspension) and *Selbstüberwindung* (self-conquest, victory, and overcoming)
  (p. 312, fn. 7).
3 Coming after the announcement of the failure of the reflection of
  consciousness at the beginning of the preface, reading as 'rumination'

suggests an unconscious process. Nietzsche may have derived this application from Schopenhauer (who uses the term *die Rumination* rather than *Wiederkäuen*): see *The World as Will and Representation*, Vol. II, trans. E.F. Payne, New York, Dover, 1958, pp. 135–6. For a discussion of this passage, and of Schopenhauer's influence the role of the unconscious in Nietzsche's conception of language, see Claudia Crawford, *The Beginnings of Nietzsche's Theory of Language*, Berlin, Walter de Gruyter, 1988, pp. 54ff.

4 For a brilliant discussion of individuality, the future and indeterminacy in Nietzsche, see Werner Hamacher, ' "Disgregation of the Will": Nietzsche on the Individual and Individuality' in *Reconstructing Individualism*, ed. Thomas C. Heller *et al.*, Stanford, Stanford University Press, 1986, pp. 106–39.

5 Cf. BGE 30.

6 *Friedrich Nietzsche Sämtliche Werke, Kritische Studienausgabe* in 15 volumes, ed. Giorgio Colli and Mazzino Montinari, Berlin, Walter de Gruyter, 1980, vol. 11, p. 579, 37 [5]. I am grateful to Robert Rethy for drawing my attention to this passage; the translation is his.

7 An adequate discussion of the vexed question of 'Nietzsche and woman' would require a very detailed reading of the relevant passages throughout Nietzsche's writings and their context, and a consideration of commentaries and debates. Rather than deal with this topic inadequately, I have chosen to limit my remarks below to its relation to the theme of my essay in a way which I acknowledge is expedient rather than satisfactory.

8 Cf. BGE 260: 'It is the powerful who *understand* how to honour; this is their art, their realm of invention. The profound reverence for age and tradition – all laws rests on this double reverence – the faith and prejudice in favour of ancestors and disfavour of those yet to come are typical of the morality of the powerful; and when the men of "modern ideas", conversely, believe almost instinctively in "progress" and "the future" and more and more lack respect for age, this in itself would sufficiently betray the ignoble origin of these "ideas".'

9 Laurence Lampert in *Nietzsche's Teaching: An Interpretation of 'Thus Spoke Zarathustra'*, New Haven and London, Yale University Press, pp. 44–7, fn. 69, draws attention to the relation between 'On Reading and Writing' and Plato's *Phaedrus*.

10 References and given according to the pagination conventionally used in editions of Plato.

11 Plato, *Phaedrus*, trans. and commentary C. J. Rowe, Warminster, Aris & Phillips, 1986.

12 Cf. Jacques Derrida, 'Plato's Pharmacy' in *Dissemination*, trans. Barbara Johnson, Chicago, University of Chicago Press, 1981. I have preferred not to engage with Derrida's discussion of the question of speech and writing in the *Phaedrus*, as this could not have been done without considering the problematic of deconstruction in Derrida's work in general. Also Derrida does not consider the ostensible topic of the *Phaedrus*, the relation between teaching, writing and love, which I believe is the focus of Nietzsche's concern. For a criticism of Derrida's reading, see Stanley Rosen, 'Platonic Reconstruction', *Hermeneutics as Politics*, Odeon, New York, Oxford University Press, 1987.

13 See the extract from 'Homer's Contest' in *The Portable Nietzsche*, ed. and trans. Walter Kaufmann, New York, Penguin Books, 1959, 32–9.

14 See BGE, preface ('Christianity is Platonism for the people'), and 14, 28, 190 ('the Socratism for which [Plato] was really too noble'), 211.

15 Cf. preface: this is a reply to the knowers as 'the honey gatherers of the spirit' who only care about 'bringing something home' – a reference, in part, to Hegel, and the Christian basis of German idealism, but also to Dionysus who is supposed to have invented honey. Cf. also Z IV, 'The Honey Sacrifice', where honey is 'bait'.

16 In OGM Nietzsche frequently has recourse to the rhetoric of the sermon and the inquisition; one of the connotations of its subtitle, *Eine Streitschrift*, is of a pamphlet in a religious controversy.

17 Socrates in the *Phaedrus* claims that 'the prophecy of inspiration' is superior to 'omen reading' (244d).

18 Maurice Blanchot writes, 'the prophetic word announces an impossible future'. See 'La parole prophétique', *Le Livre à venir*, Paris, Gallimard, Folio/essais, 1959, pp. 109–19.

19 For the role of silence in Plato's *Phaedrus*, see Rosen, op. cit. p. 55. By contrast with Plato, Nietzsche's silence concerns not the contemplative vision of the atemporal ideas, but the otherness of the future.

20 Plato vs. Homer (III, 25), Kant vs. Stendhal (III, 6), the ascetic priest vs. the noble, and, possibly, Schopenhauer vs. Nietzsche.

21 See *Human, All Too Human*, I, 372.

22 Contrasting Kant, for whom laughter, like music, is a 'merely bodily' aid to the digestion: see CJ 54.

23 T. W. Adorno and M. Horkheimer, *Dialectic of Enlightenment*, London, Verso, 1979, 77–8.

24 See vol. 1, ch. 5, 'Tokens of Higher and Lower Culture'.

25 The distinction is a fine one, so fine, indeed, that Kant had written in his manuscript '*Nachmachung . . . Nachmachung*' which was subsequently corrected (according to Karl Vorländer, editor of CJ in the *Philosophische Bibliothek* edition: see Pluhar's note 43 to CJ 47, p. 309). Kant's 'slip' (if it was that) may be more radical than his final formulation (if it was his): the relation of genius to genius would be that of 'imitation without imitation', at once a relation (of the passivity of imitation) and a non-relation, an absolute separation or rupture.

26 For a different discussion of exemplarity in CJ, see Jacques Derrida, 'Parergon', *The Truth in Painting*, trans. Geoff Bennington and Ian McLeod, Chicago and London, University of Chicago Press, 1987, pp. 15–147.

27 See 'An Old Question Raised Again: Is the Human Race Constantly Progressing?', *Kant On History*, ed. Lewis Beck White, New York, Macmillan, 1985, pp. 143–6. The 'universal yet disinterested sympathy' of the spectators regarding the French Revolution for one side of the conflict is for Kant a 'historical sign' of progress in human history. This structure is analogous to that of reflective judgement to the work of art as a creation of genius.

28 For Nietzsche's interpretation of the French Revolution, see OGM I, 16: while '[w]ith the French Revolution, Judea triumphed once again over the classical ideal', it also gave rise to 'Napoleon, this synthesis of the

inhuman [*Unmensch*] and the *superhuman* [*Übermensch*]' i.e. the French Revolution overcame itself.

29 For mimetic doubling in Nietzsche, see René Girard, 'Strategies of Madness – Nietzsche, Wagner, and Dostoevski', '*To Double Business Bound*', Baltimore, Johns Hopkins University Press, 1978.

30 Cf. Charles E. Scott on 'A Discourse Overcoming Itself', *The Language of Difference*, Atlantic Highlands, Humanities Press, 1987, pp. 46–52.

31 Cf. Z, 'On the Way of the Creator', and 'On Little Old and Young Women', pp. 174–9.

32 I.e. the particular as example of the universal, as an imitation of a Platonic form, or of the love of God in Christ, or of God and the non-caused cause containing all possible particulars as in the scholastic conception of exemplarity. For the latter, see Etienne Gilson, *History of Christian Philosophy in the Middle Ages*, London, Sheed & Ward, 1980, 307.

33 The one change which Nietzsche made in the quotation from Z is that in OGM the 'us [*uns*]' is stressed in spaced type.

12 Nietzsche, Heidegger, and the metaphysics of modernity

Robert B. Pippin

I

Nietzsche has become a *fin-de-siècle* phenomenon again. It is a different century this time, and its intellectual wars are waged over such things as texts, discourses, logo-centrism, and gender, rather than Christian morality, the death of God, progress, and *l'art pour l'art*. But, in the last twenty years or so, Nietzsche has again come to occupy the centre of everything intellectually radical, even 'post-modern' or 'post-philosophical'.

However, such renewed attention has not much helped and has greatly complicated the vexing problem of 'categorizing' the nature of Nietzsche's contribution to the seemingly endless self-doubts and unmaskings and dissatisfactions of European high culture. What has allowed Nietzsche to become such a perennial lightning rod for intellectual discontent? Is he a 'psychologist', a bit like Freud in the sweep and ambition of his claims about the delusions of conscious life? Is he a littérateur, some self-created, non-fiction version of a Stendhal or a Dostoyevsky? Is he an 'irrationalist philosopher', finally deflating the western dream of 'emancipation through knowledge', unmasking that project as a mere strategy of the weak and resentful, ultimately 'inimical to life'? Is he basically a political reactionary, so disgusted by the hypocrisy and mediocrity of mass bourgeois society that he promotes a dangerous, pre-modern heroic overman? Or is he simply an interesting aphorist, a minor culture critic, and essayist, much like Voltaire and Heine, and hardly the 'master thinker' he is sometimes proclaimed to be by the French?

However Protean Nietzsche's thought, however much he intends to challenge the traditional distinctions between philosophy and psychology and politics and art, and so to experiment with any number of personae and masks, at some level such a categorization problem is *the* unavoidable, basic issue in understanding Nietzsche. It cannot be dismissed as merely academic, nor be undermined by a jejune acceptance of a polymorphous or 'nomad' Nietzsche who writes in a way that makes him available to all camps. The question of what, fundamentally, Nietzsche is doing is simply the question of how we ought to think about him, to assess him; what questions are appropriate to ask, what implications he must be committed to, what kinds of criticisms beg the questions he is raising. It is a question that must be asked with some caution, but, if we are ever to understand the strange hold Nietzsche seems to have over much of twentieth-century European thought, it must be asked.

It is in the context of this problem that one interpretation of Nietzsche has been both extremely influential and quite controversial, an interpretation that raises the stakes in Nietzsche studies about as high as they can be raised, making use of Nietzsche as a way of discussing nothing less than the entire western philosophical tradition. For Martin Heidegger, in his lectures on Nietzsche in the 1930s and 1940s, and in a couple of articles, the question of the correct way to read Nietzsche can be answered straightforwardly: Nietzsche is a metaphysician.[1] Indeed Nietzsche represents the completion of western metaphysics, the fulfilment of a kind of destiny fated for it since Plato's inauguration, a nihilistic fate that Heidegger also connects with contemporary 'technological' existence and its profound 'meaninglessness'.[2] Heidegger's extraordinarily ambitious, even often outrageous, claims about Nietzsche can provide a useful focus (if only often as a foil) for beginning to discuss a number of issues related to the categorization problem mentioned above, its current implications, and finally for the general issue involved in any comprehensive 'reading' of the 'tradition' and of its 'true fate' or 'real', hidden agenda. I shall be especially interested in issues raised by Nietzsche's own readings of his predecessors, and by Heidegger's complex re-reading of the narrative provided by Nietzsche.

II

I begin with some concessions to Heidegger's unusual approach to the history of philosophy. As with his many other controversial readings of great thinkers, Heidegger freely admits that his goal is not scholarly fidelity. His reading is not an interpretation, but a 'confrontation' (*Auseinandersetzung*) and the goal of such a 'genuine criticism' (*echte Kritik*) is not anything like understanding the author's intention or the text's meaning, but is ultimately our own preparation for the 'supreme exertion of thinking'. (WPA, pp. 4–5; N I, pp. 12–13). In a 1940 lecture, in his frankest statement of his hermeneutical procedure, he wrote.

> In the following text exposition and interpretation are interwoven in such a way that it is not always clear what has been taken from Nietzsche's words and what has been added to them. Of course, every interpretation must not only take things from the text, but must also, without forcing the matter, be able quietly to give something of its own. . . . This something extra is what the layman . . . deplores as interpolation and mere caprice.
>
> (N II, pp. 262–3)

Moreover, throughout the course of the Nietzsche lectures, Heidegger was beginning to formulate quite a complicated 'meta-history', it might be called,[3] an account of how the history of philosophy ought to be understood. According to this account, the history of thought is itself the 'history of Being'; it is not a history determined by individual thinkers influencing and criticizing each other's ideas. Instead, a thinker is said to be 'called' to his 'thought' by 'what there is to think' and, consequently, what determines the course of such a history of thought is the 'destiny' or fate of Being itself, a destiny Nietzsche is 'called on' to complete in announcing the advent of nihilism.

While it is important to note these dimensions of Heidegger's approach – that Heidegger openly admits he will stray, sometimes very far, from Nietzsche's self-understanding in characterizing Nietzsche's thought, and that Heidegger has bigger fish to fry than a confrontation with the individual thinker, Nietzsche – I do not propose to pursue these meta-level themes here. As we shall soon see, there is controversy enough in the detailed results of Heidegger's attempt to understand Nietzsche 'better than he understood himself'. I shall assume that, in a way relatively independent of his large-scale theory of historical interpretation, Heidegger simply proposes to tell us something that is, just of itself, of great potential importance in understanding Nietzsche, and it is that proposal, not its meta-philosophical presuppositions or meta-historical implications, that I want to assess.[4]

The basis issue can be put this way. Nietzsche himself claimed to have understood why, with the general characteristics of en-lightened, rationalized, 'humanistic' modernity taking shape before us, it turned out to be so fundamentally dissatisfying, so enervating and conformist, why it created the vapid creatures he called 'the last men', and promoted such mediocrity, *ressentiment*, purposelessness. For Nietzsche, contrary to Freud, Weber, even Rousseau, modernization is not a *necessary* Faustian bargain, clearly an anomic, spiritless moral disaster, but a historical project whose overwhelming utility simply could not be denied. Such a conception of an inevitable modernity is, for Nietzsche, a self-serving modern delusion, and he proposes to unmask its practical origins, and so to re-create a different sense of history and the future. It is this sweeping, apocalyptic claim about modernity, its nihilistic ending, and a possible 'transvaluation of its values', that Heidegger proposes to reconstruct as an attack on the implications of the *metaphysics of modernity*, especially the metaphysics of subjectivity. It is that confrontation I want to assess, conceding to Heidegger that we are not talking about 'what the individual, Nietzsche, understood himself to be doing' and that the stakes in such a confrontation are high. They are, perhaps, 'fundamentally ontological', or, at least, not limited to an academic controversy between two individual philosophers.

Here then is a general summary of Heidegger's claims about Nietzsche.

1 Nietzsche's thought is 'metaphysical'. This means that Nietzsche propounds a comprehensive teaching on the 'beings' or 'entities' as a whole, a view of what all entities are. For Heidegger, this doctrine also presupposes a more fundamental, much more elusive account of what he calls the 'meaning of Being qua Being'. Heidegger claims that this is so, even though much of the latter, genuinely ontological dimension of Nietzsche's metaphysics remains 'unthought' *by* him; it functions as a silent but decisive presupposition in his thought.

2 At the heart of that metaphysical teaching are two doctrines which somehow 'say the same thing', but in radically different ways: the will to power, and the eternal recurrence of the same. (Heidegger will often list 'five' central Nietzschean ideas, adding the overman, nihilism, and the transvaluation of all values, but these are clearly derivative from the supposedly central metaphysical account of will to power/eternal return.)

3 This metaphysical teaching is not only continuous with the western metaphysical tradition since Plato, it represents a decisive

moment in such a tradition: its 'completion' or 'ending' (*Vollendung*). There is something fundamentally common to the Platonic account of Being as form or *eidos*, and the Nietzschean account of Being as 'value' or *Werte*, although what is distinctive about Nietzsche's position is that a) he realizes that the tradition inaugurated by Plato has made it impossible to think Being (and this is the true meaning of Nietzsche's 'nihilism' charge, in Heidegger's extremely eccentric reading), and b) Nietzsche is wrong to think that his own account of transvaluation can escape such nihilism by promoting a notion of Being as 'value'. Being remains unthought in Nietzsche too, who is described as the 'last metaphysician of the west'. According to Heidegger, Nietzsche is propounding a metaphysical position that itself reveals the exhaustion, or ending, or even impossibility of metaphysics, once its traditional form has been radicalized, or 'thought through to its conclusion'.[5]

4 While Nietzsche's thought is in some way a consequence or result of the entire metaphysical tradition, it is especially representative of 'modern metaphysics'. Heidegger claims to see a deep affinity between Nietzsche and Leibniz, Schelling and Hegel on the will, and, especially in the later lectures, between Nietzsche and, remarkably, the 'father of modern rationalism', Descartes. Nietzsche's metaphysics is basically a metaphysics of subjectivity, and therein lies the basic reason why Nietzsche's thought 'remains nihilistic'.

III

Although Heidegger's Nietzsche lectures are presented in a way that is very much internal to Heidegger's own project, these claims about Nietzsche can be said to have quite a widespread significance. For one thing, Heidegger's assertion that Nietzsche, for all of his success in unmasking the pretensions of traditional and modern philosophy, remains wedded to modern assumptions about subjectivity, will, representation, humanism, and so forth, that Nietzsche remains a modern nihilist, deluded about the presuppositions of his own enterprise, could all stand as a kind of paradigm issue in the recent, often bewildering controversy about the possibility of a genuine 'postmodernism'. If the centre of the postmodern dissatisfaction with modern thought involves a suspicion about modern accounts of subjectivity, identity, and autonomy, then Heidegger can be said to represent one of the first 'postmodern' attempts to render suspicious the great modern masters of suspicion.[6] Nietzsche himself, one of the most eloquent critics of the thought and politics of modernity, on this account would be soiled by his own mud-slinging. Indeed, he is the culmination of modernity; a Cartesian, of all things. The break with modernity will have to be more radical still, extreme, Heideggerian, a break with philosophy itself.[7]

Heidegger's extensive confrontation with Nietzsche raises, however, an even broader question, one that is difficult to state briefly. As a first pass at the issue, consider the problem this way. Let us assume that there is something correct in the familiar but still controversial characterization of modern, especially post-Kantian, academic philosophy, as 'anti-' or non-metaphysical. In its empiricist, idealist, positivist and critical dimensions, modernity is characterized by some sort of opposition to metaphysical realism, by a denial that unaided human reason can obtain a priori knowledge of the 'true' or underlying substance of things, that there can be any knowledge of being as it is in itself.[8] Reason's traditional attempt to 'measure itself' by what there is, in itself, is to be replaced either by a certainty-producing methodology, asserted (or 'willed') to be the measure of what there is, or by some 'self-grounding subjectivity', historically achieving full self-consciousness about its 'absolute' status. Let us also assume that Nietzsche represents some sort of radicalization of such a modernist sensibility, either as an extremist, unaware of the subtleties and qualifications in the figures he crudely appropriates and exaggerates, or as the only 'honest' modern, the only thinker to see clearly the implications of modern subjectivity, and the only one to reject its timid, ineffective attempts at moderation and qualification. Then the claims made by Heidegger, summarized above, raise a large question.

Heidegger claims that this tradition, culminating in Nietzsche, is still, despite itself, a *metaphysical tradition*, that it does not reject any possible doctrine about Being, but that in fact it embodies, even while it 'forgets', an ontological doctrine, and that, since this hubristic self-assertion represents a forgetting of any authentic or genuine interrogation of Being, it must culminate in the nihilism and meaninglessness of modern life (since, for Heidegger, only genuine 'thought' about Being will yield some sense of human 'meaning' within the whole).[9] Then that large question is simply: *Is all of this true?* And the confrontation with Nietzsche is one of the best, initial ways to raise the issue. From Nietzsche's point of view, I want to suggest, modernity hasn't forgotten anything; it has, thankfully, destroyed the possibility of what Heidegger wants, even granting him his unique characterization of 'metaphysics';[10] has, finally, through Nietzsche, revealed the contingent, social and psychological origins for the 'religious' motives that inspire Heidegger's anti-humanism, his atavistic hope for an experience of Being that, in the context of contemporary existence, looks simply like pre-modern nostalgia. If there is to be a genuine 'confrontation' with Nietzsche, this is the Nietzschean counter-charge that needs to be considered, and, as we shall see, such a confrontation is best played out over the respective 'readings' of modernity given by both Nietzsche and Heidegger.[11]

But it cannot be considered properly until more of the details of Heidegger's position have been presented. Let us begin with the question of metaphysics, and with Heidegger's interpretation of Nietzsche's doctrines of the will to power and the eternal recurrence as metaphysical.

IV

Heidegger begins his first (1936) lecture on Nietzsche in a way that is doubly controversial. First he announces that the text will be Nietzsche's 'work', *The Will to Power* (the scare quotes are Heidegger's). This will mean that throughout the lectures, with the exception of *Thus Spoke Zarathustra*, Heidegger will completely ignore Nietzsche's extensive published works, and will instead concentrate on a patchwork compilation of Nietzsche's unpublished handwritten notes taken from the period of 1883–8, especially 1885–8.[12] Accordingly, Heidegger announces as a focus of interest a topic that is indeed prominent in the *Nachlass*, but is by no means a major theme in the published work, the 'will to power'.[13]

Such a use of the unpublished notes raises a number of very complicated issues, about both Heidegger and the status of the *Nachlass*, all of them too involved to discuss in this limited context. For purposes of this discussion, I shall simply assume here that at least a great deal of what Nietzsche says in these notes *is* represented in other works, even if formulated differently, often more cautiously, elliptically, and even ironically, and that Heidegger, for all the oddness of his approach, *is* addressing himself to topics that are of central importance in Nietzsche's project, in some cases whether explicitly acknowledged as such or not.

Second, and more important for my purposes, Heidegger immediately formulates Nietzsche's 'fundamental thought' in a way that seems foreign to Nietzsche's style and interests. According to

Heidegger, by 'the will to power' Nietzsche means to refer to the 'name for the basic character [*Grundcharakter*] of all entities [*Seiende*]' (WPA, p. 3; N I, p. 12).[14] This means that Nietzsche will not be treated as a 'poet philosopher' or essayist, but as a 'rigorous thinker' and as a 'metaphysician', although, predictably, Heidegger wants us to understand that characterization in a special sense.[15]

Towards the end of the 1937 lectures, on the eternal recurrence of the same, Heidegger spells out that special sense in a lecture called 'The Essence of a Fundamental Metaphysical Position'. Metaphysics, says Heidegger, seeks 'not for some isolated event, not for unusual and recondite facts and relationships, but purely and simply for the being [*das Seiende*]' (ERS, p. 187; N I, p. 452). Metaphysics is an inquiry into origins, in the sense of first principles; an inquiry into the '*arche*' of entities as such. The leading question (*Leitfrage*) of all metaphysics is 'what is Being', *to ti on*.

By itself, this would be a relatively non-controversial, if turgidly expressed, view of metaphysics. Heidegger does not here make the distinction between 'special' and 'general' metaphysics he often makes elsewhere, and instead provides a large overview of metaphysics, the inquiry into what could 'account' for all entities, could account for their 'being' and for their being as they are, questions that are answered by such theories as Plato's ideas, Aristotle's forms, Descartes' two substances, Leibniz's monads, Hegel's Absolute Idea, Wittgenstein's facts. But as he proceeds the unique features of Heidegger's position begin to emerge, particularly his critical treatment of *all* traditional metaphysics as *limited*, insufficiently radical in its 'search' for Being.

Heidegger mentions a point he says 'we will have to think about again and again', and indeed it is Heidegger's own 'fundamental thought'. This point is that 'inasmuch as Being is put in question with a view to the *arche*, Being itself is already determined [*ist das Seiende selbst schon bestimmt*]' (ERS, p. 188; N I, p. 453). Simply put, this means that the way in which metaphysics poses the question of the beings, as a question for which a 'principle' (*arche*) is the answer, already somehow prejudges the nature of the question, and so 'already determines' the character of the answer. (He often will call the original, western, metaphysical orientation towards the Being-question a 'decision', emphasizing even more its distinctness and contingency.) At this point in the lecture, Heidegger only hints at what he means by this 'prior determination', pointing to the Greek privileging of *physis*, or nature in their inquiry as an indication that Being is delimited for them as a kind of 'standing presence' (*ständige Anwesenheit*), as 'what holds sway and presences' in the 'upsurge' or 'rising' (*Aufgehend*) of beings. With this very limited, even cryptic account of the priority of *physis* and so of presence (*Anwesenheit*) for the Greeks, Heidegger defines metaphysics as 'knowledge and inquiry that posits (*ansetzt*) Being (*das Seiende*) as *physis*' (ibid., p. 189; p. 454).

Metaphysics, then, as the attempt to say what everything is, just *qua Being*, pursues its inquiry by developing this 'guiding question' (*Leitfrage*). And again Heidegger tries to point out the limitations of such a questioning by distinguishing this *Leitfrage* from what is not 'developed' in such a pursuit, from the 'grounding question', the *Grundfrage*. As the term implies, the grounding question raises issues presupposed in the 'guiding question'; in raising such a fundamental question we are not simply inquiring about the beings, but raising the possibility of a 'meaning of Being'; we are interrogating what Heidegger calls 'beingness' (*Seiendheit*) or *ousia*. The object of our inquiry is not a domain of beings (*Seiende*), or even all the beings considered as a whole, but 'the Being of beings' (*das Sein des Seienden*) (ibid., p. 195; p. 460). We would not, in such a grounding question, take for granted that the meaning of Being itself should be understood in a way that depends on some domain of the beings, as if it were some generalization, or highest genus, or on some particular way of addressing the beings, as in metaphysics (or what is, for Heidegger, its modern derivative, natural science). We would not, in pursuing such a 'grounding question', be deceived by the priority naturally given a conception of being as some sort of 'enduring presence'. In genuine 'thinking', while we are always 'guided' to an understanding of 'beingness' itself by reflection on the beings, our thought of Being is not determined by such reflection, and instead 'lets Being be'.

Although crucial to an understanding of Heidegger's criticism of Nietzsche (Nietzsche too will be guilty of not 'developing' the 'grounding question', of inheriting western, metaphysical pre-determinations of Being), Heidegger's brief lecture on the 'ontological difference' (between Being and the beings) raises more questions than it answers. Somewhat more simply stated, his basic position can be summarized this way.

For Heidegger, all our dealings with and claims about 'everything that is', entities, *Seiende*, presuppose an underlying 'sense' or familiarity with the 'meaning' of Being, a pre-ontological, non-thematic, but completely decisive, unique mode of 'fore-know-ledge'. Such a familarity is not an opinion or belief we have, but itself is a mode of being or existing. In *Being and Time*, Heidegger was very successful in showing how much of *Dasein*'s dealings with entities in the world presupposed this implicit familiarity, or always already 'thrown' involvement with the world, a 'Being-in-the-world' that was not itself an object of *Dasein*'s dealings and certainly not an object of its representings. This account, and many much more radical later treatments of this underlying, presupposed Being-orientation, is meant by Heidegger to be truer to the phenomenology of our experience of Being and to run counter to the standard ways in which our understanding of Being has been thematized by philosophy and science, and has thereby come to dominate and confuse this more original phenomenological experience. Normally, we now tend to think of our understanding of Being as simply the *result* of our encounter with beings 'out there', 'present' before us, whose sensible 'looks' we 'allow to encounter us' or which we 'represent to ourselves', determining Being by reckoning up which self-presentations will turn out to allow the greatest security and mastery. We think of truth as a matter of *Aussagen*, assertions *about* being, the true ones being the ones that match up with the way things are. What remains unthought according to Heidegger is what is pre-predicative in our experience, what allows Being to be originally present ('presencing', as he sometimes puts it),[16] always already 'illuminated' in some way or other, such that we can subsequently make assertions about the beings so already 'lit up'. Being itself should thus be interrogated *as* this illumination itself, even though when so interrogated, because all such interrogation always already seems to presuppose such an orientation, we end up formulating the meaning of being ontically, as if again we were formulating an *Aussage*, an assertion *about it*. As befits the elusive, non-representable, 'concealed' character of such Being, the best indications of what Heidegger is getting at are often aesthetic. It is as if Heidegger means to somehow address such 'non-objects' as the eternal, sourceless light in a Cézanne landscape, a light that isn't *in* the painting, or isn't an object painted, but is that by means of which the 'world of Cézanne' can possess its disturbing qualities of great stillness and great tension, as if at once supremely objective and weighty, and chaotic, threatening to come apart. In the Nietzsche lectures, Heidegger himself makes use of a small poem by Goethe to make such points, a poem about the 'rest', *Ruhe*, in a forest, a stillness that cannot itself be 'heard', and which suggests both death and an encounter with Being undistorted by 'noise' and chatter (EN, p. 189; N II, p. 248).

All of which must be trying the patience of anyone primarily interested in Nietzsche. What *does* all of this have to do with Nietzsche? In Lecture 26 of the 1937 series Heidegger summarizes his answer. Nietzsche, according to Heidegger, is, throughout his work, attempting to answer 'the question concerning the *constitution* of being and being's *way to be*' (*die Frage nach der Verfassung des Seienden und nach seiner Weise zu sein*) (ERS, p. 199; N I, p. 462). Or, stated in all its splendid obscurity, 'The determination "will to power" replies to the question of being with respect to the latter's constitution; the determination 'eternal recurrence of the same' replies to the question of being with respect to its way to be' (ERS, p. 199; N I, p. 464).

Very roughly, what Heidegger means is that a) Nietzsche is proposing, by his claims that 'everything' is 'will to power', a metaphysical thesis in the 'delimited' sense sketched by Heidegger. Nietzsche means to be playing in the 'major league' game of metaphysics, rejecting all standard essence/appearance distinctions, denying a 'true' stable world, beyond the sensible world, and asserting that what is *is* the fleeting, formless 'chaotic' apparent world, a world whose 'constitution', in a sense we have yet to see, can be said to be 'will to power'. And b) Nietzsche wants, consistent with his supposed metaphysical intentions, to say that 'all that is' *is* will to power *in a way* appropriate to the metaphysical dimensions of the claim; all that is 'recurs *eternally*' as what it is, as will to power. It is 'eternally', not contingently or 'from my point of view', will to power.

Throughout the lectures, this is the reading Heidegger gives to what is for him clearly the most important fragment of *The Will to Power*, 617, dated some time between 1883 and 1885.

> To impose [*aufzuprägen*] upon becoming the character of being – that is the supreme will to power.

> Twofold falsification on the part of the senses and of the spirit, to preserve a world of that which is, which abides, which is equivalent, etc.

> That *everything recurs is the closest approximation of a world of becoming to a world of being* – high point of the meditation.[17]

As we shall see in more detail Heidegger is struck both by the fact that Nietzsche construes his own theory of radical becoming as a 'world of *being*' and that he admits that it can be such a world only through an 'imposition' effected by the will to power. That there is such an imposition is the 'red flag' that Heidegger attends to again and again in the later lectures, the sign that Nietzsche is not 'thinking' Being but replacing such thinking with human self-assertion, with an attempt to achieve 'dominion over the earth'.[18]

None of which can be comprehensible until we know some more about Heidegger's view of the will to power doctrine itself but we can note, from the preponderance of the evidence in the lectures, what Heidegger is not saying with such a 'metaphysical reading'. Both Heidegger and Nietzsche can appear to assert, by saying that 'everything is will to power', some first-order, or *de re* assertion about the nature or essence of everything that exists.[19] On such a reading Heidegger would be ascribing to Nietzsche a 'metaphysical' view of 'present-at-hand' forces, or a kind of 'conatus' theory, according to which everything, from cold asteroids to mathematical sets, to one-celled animals, to nation-states, somehow constantly strives for self-enhancement and ascendancy, power, even at the risk of self-preservation. Such an ascription would not only be grossly inconsistent with Nietzsche's well-known rejection of 'metaphysical' attempts to discover 'reality as it is in itself' (the 'truth in itself'), but it is not borne out by the way Heidegger glosses his own metaphysical reading.[20]

First of all, in the remainder of lecture 26 in ERS, Heidegger virtually identifies the claim that all is will to power with the claim that all is radical becoming, or the *absence* of any stable, identifiable substance. Nietzsche's 'fundamental thought' is supposed to assert the *absence of substance*, not to propose a new theory of 'substantial forces'. As we shall see, it is the unavailability of any appeal to real identity, stable categories, enduring or underlying substances, etc. (or, said conversely, it is the affirmation of the totality of becoming), that makes everywhere *necessary* the interpretive activity Nietzsche so frequently insists on. To say that the world is will to power is then to say that there is 'nothing' to say about the world that is not already a result of competing *interpretations of the world*. To be sure, this affirmation of 'nothing' (*as* the affirmation of the will to power) is supposed to be asserted 'eternally'; Nietzsche wants to 'imprint the emblem of eternity on our life', (ERS, p. 201; N I, p. 466) and such an intention will turn out to be deeply problematic for Heidegger, but what is affirmed eternally is 'becoming'. This issue of a supposed Nietzschean 'metaphysics' of absence or of 'nullity' is one we shall return to in section V.

Second, when Heidegger gestures towards the complex historical context within which Nietzsche's account of becoming must be understood, he most often invokes the German idealist, or critical tradition, not the classical metaphysical tradition (something Jaspers also frequently does).[21] 'Being as will' is supposed to be understood 'in line with the best and greatest tradition of German philosophy' (WPA, p. 34; N I, p. 44) and Schelling's 1809 lectures on human freedom and Hegel's *Phenomenology* are cited as sources. 'We know', he pronounces, 'that German idealism thought Being as will', (WPA, p. 61; N I, p. 73) and Hegel especially is said to 'grasp the essence of Being as knowing, but grasps knowing as essentially identical to willing' (WPA, p. 35; N I, p. 45).

Such references, which are frequent throughout the lectures and essays, make finally a little clearer the Pickwickian sense of 'metaphysics' employed by Heidegger. For although Heidegger frequently speaks of the 'metaphysics' of German idealism he is also clear that such a metaphysics always considers the central problem of 'the beings' (*Seiende*) *from within the horizon* of, roughly, the human experience of being. This was Kant's great inauguration, a 'laying of the foundation' of a true metaphysics that would finally be completed in Heidegger's 1927 'fundamental ontology', in *Being and Time*. All of which is Heidegger's way of stating Kant's basic Copernican revolution or transcendental turn, his replacement of the classical inquiry into 'the beings' (*Seiende*) with an inquiry into the human conditions for an experience of beings. Heidegger only wishes to keep his historical focus fixed on the consequences of such a turn for the often forgotten question of Being (*Sein*). Kant's revolution is relevant in that context too, as Heidegger begins to argue in *Kant and the Problem of Metaphysics*.[22] It was, though, apparently the later idealists, especially Schelling and Hegel, who for Heidegger insisted with the greatest consistency and thoroughness that what there is *is* what appears within the 'horizon' of a subject's self-understanding and, finally, in endlessly complicated ways, within the human horizon of self-determination or free action. All beings, in the tradition within which Heidegger locates Nietzsche, can be said to have a 'meaning' as beings only within the horizon of, or 'for', an active, self-reflective being. The question is the nature of this self-relation within which beings can be 'illuminated' as they are. It is that question that Nietzsche wants to answer with his 'will to power' doctrine, and it is the details of his answer, his account of a creative self-willing, unconstrained (at the 'fundamental ontological' level) by transcendental conditions or empirical facts, that provides the horizon of significance for all that could be, that makes it possible to say, indirectly but in Heidegger's sense 'metaphysically', that 'everything *is* will to power'.

This post-Kantian reading of the 'metaphysics' of Nietzsche's will to power idea is much clearer in the first lecture series than anywhere else, particularly since, in the lectures after 1939 Heidegger's tone is often much more critical of the subjectivist intentions of modern metaphysics, and that tone can interfere with his exposition. In the 1936 lectures, when he first introduces the topic of the will to power, he does so exclusively in the context of the human act of willing, and only subsequently, through a connection with the Kantian strategy, to 'metaphysics'. Indeed, he often makes sympathetic use of the vocabulary of the fundamental ontology of *Being and Time*, of a *'Daseinanalytik'*, to interpret Nietzsche.

First, he denies that the will to power has anything to do with a striving for power, or 'any behaviour directed toward something' (WPA, p. 39; N, p. 49). Rather, the problem is introduced with the vocabulary of the Kantian 'autonomy' problem: 'willing is self-willing', (WPA, p. 37; N I, p. 46) or a 'submission of ourselves to our own command and the resoluteness of such self-command, which already implies our carrying out the command' (WPA, p. 40; N I, p. 50). This use of 'resoluteness' (*Entschlossenheit*), so important a term in *Being and Time*[23] is frequently invoked to explain Heidegger's reading of Nietzschean will, and its connections with metaphysics. Will is called a 'resolute openness to oneself' (WPA, p. 41; N, p. 51) and in such openness (the 'clearing' or 'lighting' mentioned earlier) 'he who wills stations himself abroad among beings in order to keep them firmly within his field of action' (WPA, p. 48; N, p. 59). It is by means of such resolute willing (here affirmed as a kind of 'openness'; later in the lectures described as a 'dominating' or 'obscuring' of Being)[24] that 'we find ourselves particularly attuned [*gestimmt*] to beings which we are not and to the being we ourselves are' (WPA, p. 51; N I, p. 62).[25] And it is in this sense, so similar to Heidegger's own work of the late 1920s and early 1930s, that the will to power can be said to be not 'the willing of a particular actual entity' but to 'involve the Being and essence of beings; it is this itself' (WPA, p. 61; N I, p. 73).

To be sure, this connection with the Kantian tradition itself depends on a highly controversial reading of Kant's legacy. The connection is clear in such passages as,

In that we know what is encountered as a thing, as thus and thus constituted, as related to others in this or that way, as thus and thus elaborated, thus and thus large, we have already in advance created thinghood, constitution, relation, effect, causality, and size for what is encountered.

(WPKM, p. 95; N I, p. 583)

The controversy is already clear in the use of the word 'created' and in such claims as,

This creative essence of reason [*dichtende Wesen der Vernunft*] was not first discovered by Nietzsche but only emphasized by him in some particularly blunt respects, and not always adequately. Kant first explicitly perceived and thought through the creative character of reason in his doctrine of the transcendental imagination.

(WPKM, pp. 95–6; N I, p. 584)

All of which brings us again to the basic question, whether Heidegger's reading of the tradition within which he locates Nietzsche is correct, identifies properly its concerns, and 'positions' Nietzsche properly within those concerns. The question is the appropriateness of the label 'metaphysics of subjectivity' and Heidegger's ultimate charge of superficiality, or at best, forgetfulness.[26] This is the charge that becomes so much more prominent in the lectures, until, in 1939, the language of attunement and openness is dropped and Heidegger now summarizes his position this way.

To think Being, the beingness of beings, as will to power means to conceive of Being as the unleashing of power to its essence; the unleashing transpires in such a way that unconditionally empowering power posits the exclusive pre-eminence of beings over Being. Whereas beings possess objective actuality, Being collapses into oblivion.

(WPKM, p. 164; N II, p. 10)

V

To assess such a charge we need to disentangle Heidegger's claims in still more detail. At issue are points 3 and 4 sketched above, Heidegger's claims about the nihilistic fate of the western tradition, and the role of 'subjectivity' in that fate. As we have seen, he is especially interested in what he identifies as the 'modern' metaphysics of subjectivity. According to Heidegger, the post-Cartesian tradition involves a claim about 'what all the beings are': they are what they are *thought, or represented or taken (or even 'willed') to be* by an essentially self-defining, or 'self-willing' free subject.[27] As we have seen, Heidegger then maintains, to summarize his position somewhat more concisely, that a) this 'self-assertion' of subjectivity also represents a 'forgetting' of Being, a kind of hubristic denial of the origins of subjectivity in something *beyond or other than*, its own self-definition. He claims b) that this characterization of metaphysical self-assertion is actually true of the tradition since Plato,[28] c) that it culminates in Nietzsche's account of Being as will to power, and d) that Nietzsche fails to escape nihilism, that the 'truth' of his position can be seen in the meaningless, or purposeless attempt to establish dominion over everything so characteristic of modern technological man.

Heidegger's interpretation of the tradition (c) is much too complicated to address here. I am mostly interested here in showing that, since Heidegger is wrong about (a), his position on Nietzsche (d) fails to establish the criticism of nihilism.

To address the issue raised by (a) we need to consider the relation between 'subjectivity' and 'nihilism', as Heidegger sees it. In his 1943 essay, 'The Word of Nietzsche: "God is Dead" ', Heidegger cites many of Nietzsche's well-known accounts of nihilism – 'that the highest values are devaluing themselves', and that 'God is dead', and construes the phenomenon of nihilism, so defined by Nietzsche, to be 'the fundamental event of western history' (WN, p. 67; H, p. 206), an event that Heidegger takes to be 'the metaphysical event of modernity'. Metaphysics is interpreted as

> history's open space wherein it becomes a destining that the suprasensory world, the Ideas, God, the moral law, the authority of reason, progress, the happiness of the greatest number, culture, civilization, suffer the loss of their constructive force and become void.
>
> (WN, p. 65; H, p. 204)

Heidegger realizes that Nietzsche intends for his own position to be a 'countermovement' to metaphysics, but, for Heidegger, such a counter fails, and Nietzsche is guilty of an 'inextricable entanglement [*Verstrickung*] in metaphysics' (WN, p. 61, and p. 75; H, pp. 200, 214), especially the metaphysics of subjectivity. Since, on Heidegger's interpretation, all of modern metaphysics 'as the metaphysics of subjectness, thinks the Being of that which is in the sense of will' (ibid., pp. 88, 225) then Nietzsche, by 'transforming' the question of Being into the question of 'values' *posited by a subject*, 'completes' this modern tradition, and especially makes clearer how 'value', so understood, 'does not let Being be Being' (ibid., pp. 104, 239), or even 'murderously' (pp. 108, 242) does away 'with that which *is* in itself',

> making secure the constant reserve by means of which man makes secure for himself material, bodily, psychic and spiritual resources, and this for the sake of his own security, which wills dominion over whatever is – as the potentially objective – in order to correspond to the Being of whatever is, to the will to power.
>
> (Ibid., pp. 107, 242)

In the 1939 lectures this leads to an account of Nietzsche on 'Knowing as Schematizing a Chaos in Accordance with a Practical Need', and on the 'Essence of Will to Power' as 'Permanentizing Becoming into Presence'. In the 1940 lectures on 'European Nihilism', Heidegger produces a 'secularization' thesis about the origins of this modern notion of subjectivity.

> To be free now means that, in place of the certitude of salvation, which was the standard of all truth, man posits the kind of certitude by virtue of which and in which he becomes certain of himself as the being that thus founds itself on itself.
>
> (EN, p. 97; N II, p. 143)

And he concludes,

> The securing of supreme and absolute self-development of all the capacities of mankind for absolute dominion over the entire earth is the secret goad that prods modern man again and again to new resurgences, a goad that forces him into commitments that secure for him the surety of his actions and certainty of his aims.
>
> (Ibid., pp. 99, 145)

It is in this context that Heidegger can make the sweeping claim in lecture 20 for an 'Inner Connection Between the Fundamental Positions of Descartes and Nietzsche', between Cartesian truth as 'secure conveyance of what is represented in self-representing representation' and Nietzschean truth as 'taking for true . . . defined by what man makes of the being and what he takes as being' (ibid., pp. 137, 190).

Heidegger's wide-ranging association of Nietzsche with so many different figures in the history of philosophy – Plato in the first series, then, more often, the transcendental project of German idealism, and finally the 'foundational' project of Descartes – makes it extremely difficult to assess his argument. In the first place, all the details of the historical precedents of the Nietzschean 'nihilism crisis' in the German tradition would have to be presented before Nietzsche's position *vis-à-vis* his predecessors could be understood. (Indeed, to anyone familiar with those origins in Jacobi's criticisms of Fichte, Heidegger's perorations against the 'killing of God', and his objections to any attempt at a 'self-defining' subjectivity can, without the details of such a larger context, sound somewhat like Jacobi's religiously inspired doubts about modern 'egoism', its claims to self-sufficiency.)[29]

For another thing, Heidegger simply ignores the innumerable passages in which Nietzsche caustically attacks the modern notion of a self-grounding, or even a stable, enduring, causally efficacious 'subject'.[30] This leaves Heidegger wide open to the pointed criticisms of commentators like Michel Haar who complain, with much textual justification, that i) Nietzsche's 'subject' is a 'plurality' of forces, not a self-defining ego, ii) Nietzsche rejects the 'priority of consciousness' typical of post-Cartesian thought, noting that 'thoughts come when they will, not when I will'. (To expand a bit on Haar's simile, consciousness for Nietzsche is like the political 'unity' effected by a Reagan presidency, by a monarch who *reigns*, but does not *govern*, who is unaware of the various conflicting forces responsible for the activity in his kingdom, preferring to see himself as the supremely responsible agency, but who, in his simple-minded *naïveté*, makes a grand mess of everything when he actually does try to assume the role of a conscious director.)[31] And iii) Nietzsche's very unusual account of subjectivity can be highlighted by noting Nietzsche's acceptance of a kind of 'authentic' subject who unhesitatingly plays many roles, adopts many masks, or rejects any (ironically, quasi-Heideggerian) notion of an 'authentic self', or authentic 'existence'.[32]

While these and many other qualifications could be pursued at great length, however, they do not seem to me to affect Heidegger's fundamental point. Even if the Nietzschean subject is itself an interpretation,[33] manifold, changing, even communal,[34] Heidegger's point about the continuity between Nietzsche's account of the origin of any possible 'determination' of *Being* and some sort of constitutive, interpreting human activity would have to be addressed. When it is addressed, the problems inherent in Heidegger's views are apparent only if his whole 'agenda' in reading the history of modern philosophy as he does is confronted.

That is, Heidegger, by seeing philosophic modernity as an attempt at a radical 'self-grounding', is working with what is essentially a Hegelian characterization, one in which all the problems of the post-Kantian tradition come to a head. This is transparent in such characterizations as: 'The essence of consciousness is self-consciousness. Everything that is, is therefore either the object of the subject or the subject of the subject. Everywhere the Being of whatever is lies in setting-itself-before-itself [*Sich-vor-sich-selbst-Stellen*] and thus in setting-itself-up [*Sich-auf-stellen*]' (WN, p. 100; H, p. 236).

Heidegger is well aware that post-Kantian philosophers understood such 'grounding activity' (thinking, synthesizing, 'setting-itself-up', representing, positing, or 'negating') as *constrained* by some sort of logical limits, by rules for what any subject must think or do in order to experience or represent anything, even its own thoughts, and that it was only by reference to some such claim for transcendental necessity that a connection between such activity and beings (or objectivity) could be defended.[35] What Heidegger is doing, I am suggesting, is making use of Nietzsche as a way of denying that there is any possible appeal to such metaphysically significant constraints or grounds. Once, that is, Kant has rejected any appeal to the immediate, the positive, the given, the other as 'ground', once he has argued that any such object could be a determinate object only as construed or determined or thought by me to be such an object, then, Heidegger clearly wants to maintain, such a construal or determining cannot 'ground' itself, as one supposedly can see in the 'culmination' of such an attempt in Nietzsche. Such a subjective origin will always have to be wholly contingent, 'human all too human'. The German idealists, and if Heidegger's eccentric interpretation is correct, even Descartes, introduce the idea of Being as 'pure possibility' and once they do, then the profound *insignificance* of any actualized possibility (equally as worthy as any other) cannot be redeemed by some human pride in our own power (or potentiality).[36] Nietzsche is thus being read as the 'truth' of modern philosophy, the revelation that there is no way to moderate or qualify the subjectivist turn, the turn to the subject as source or ground. Such a source grounds by itself standing on 'nothing'.

The problem with all this is simple: it begs the question. First, as noted throughout, the *question* of the possibility of the idealist

project, a '*self*-grounding', or in Kant's terms a 'critique' by reason
of itself, the question of whether this ever amounts to anything
more than an '*un*grounded' or 'illegitimate' legislation, cannot be
resolved simply by invoking the Nietzschean reading of the prior
tradition (in which *all* philosophy is such a contingent projection, or
'confession' by its author). It is, I would suggest, far more likely that
the deficiencies Heidegger finds in Nietzsche's account of the will to
power as an ontological doctrine result from Nietzsche's ignoring or
forgetting essential components of the post-Kantian problem of
subjectivity (the problems of the transcendental deduction, of
Fichte's 'nicht-Ich', Hegel's sceptical 'highway of despair' in the
Phenomenology); much more likely in any case, than that these
problems 'emerge' because Nietzsche can be said to 'complete' or
end such a project.

That is, Heidegger is correct to note that Nietzsche owes us, in
effect, what philosophic commentators have always demanded from
him: some argument or analysis that will show why a demonstration
of the contingent, historical, sociopolitical 'origins' of some
institution like morality or philosophy should *count* as an analysis of
the nature or possibility of such an institution, that morality *is* the
resentment of the weak, philosophy *only* an interpretation designed
to secure an ascetic version of the will to power, and so forth.
Heidegger proposes that the link between such genealogies and
Nietzsche's very strong claims about the possibility or nature of such
institutions (indeed all institutions and practices) should be
understood to depend on the most general, ambitious dimension of
Nietzsche's project, his account of the possibility of the significance
or meaning *of any* '*being*', and his demonstration of the 'conditioned' nature of any such significance, conditioned by some sort of
human self-assertion. Heidegger does not bother with the detailed
genealogies provided by Nietzsche which purport to show the
conditioned and so contingent nature of various particular institutions, rightly implying that unless Nietzsche has some general
account of the possibility of *being* (of the necessity of such a
'conditionedness') then such accounts would have to be characterized as merely 'cultural analyses' of the 'social appeal' or
'psychological attractiveness', etc. of various historical phenomena.

As we have seen, it is Heidegger's view that, since there is no
such 'fundamental' ontological account in Nietzsche, we get instead
a kind of profane, hubristic assertion of will by Nietzsche himself, a
demand that Being be measured by contingent, ever becoming,

protean man, a measuring Heidegger claims must end up meaningless because so 'ungrounded'. Heidegger's language sometimes suggests that modernity is some kind of (Greek) 'sin', a forgetting of place, now brought to its tragic end by the dreariness, rapacity and filth of technological life.

But all of this is relevant to the *pre-Nietzschean* tradition only by adopting a Nietzschean reading of that tradition, and this is what begs the question. Heidegger cannot *show* that this tradition itself 'culminates' in Nietzsche's nihilism because he begins his analysis with a Nietzschean version of, among others, Kant (with a purported 'creative essence of reason', a poetizing reason, etc.).

To be sure, such a counter-claim would be worth pursuing only if an alternate reading of at least the 'critical' tradition is possible, one that could counter in detail the Heideggerian suggestion of a 'slippery slope' in post-Cartesian philosophy, the slope that begins in making self-certainty the measure of Being, and ends up with such a subject itself 'measureless' and nihilistic. That clearly involves much more than can be discussed here, but the possibility and importance of such a reading can be defended simply by contrasting briefly the self-understanding of such a tradition with Heidegger's reconstruction of modernity.

That is, one way to assess the 'modernity culminates in Nietzschean nihilism' reading, the assertion that the critical insistence on the absence of metaphysics itself presupposes a metaphysics of absence (of the *nihil*) and so a practical nihilism, is to ask whether Heidegger successfully answers a crucial question about modernity that he poses for himself: 'We are asking, how do we arrive at an emphatic positing of the 'subject'? *Whence* does that dominance of the subjective come that guides modern humanity and its understanding of the world?' (EN, p. 96; N II, p. 141, my emphasis).

We have already seen that Heidegger's answer to this question involves asserting a 'secularized' salvation motive in a modernity; once religious certitude was lost, self-certitude 'filled the gap', the apparently unavoidable quest for security, reassurance (ibid., pp. 89, 99, 133, 143).

While there may be something to this account (although Blumenberg has demolished much of the idea of a 'secularization' theory of modernity),[37] Heidegger leaves out a crucial element in the 'self-assertion' of modernity, particularly obvious when one considers the contemporaneous development of modern philosophy and modern science.

In that context, while it is true that late medieval Christianity was burdened by ever more severe theological and social problems, and so could not serve as the sole 'means of salvation', it is also true that the modern scientific notion of security, the mastery of nature, the rejection of the classical ideal of contemplation in favour of technical control, did not simply emerge in a vacuum. One no longer hears the old positivist story about sudden great 'discoveries' that set the new science on its way but it is still true that early scientific and technical successes in astronomy and optics and physics raised a variety of new questions that could not be avoided. However one explains the great shift in sensibility and expectation that defines the origin of the modern, that vast shift itself made necessary a reconsideration of, especially, the problem of truth. Modernity's 'epistemology crisis', in other words, is better understood as provoked, rather than simply inaugurated, and *only thereby* was the Heideggerian problem of salvation or security raised. Very crudely, one can fairly say that the attempt to 'break free' from one's implicit, unreflected involvement with the world, and then to 're-establish' a connection with Being through a methodologically determined, mathematically certain procedure, or a critically self-conscious criterion of knowledge, can only be assessed in the light of the historical experience which required it, the uncertainty and doubt that prompted such reflection. The *need* for establishing a self-conscious relation to being (or the impossibility of anyone immediately 'being' in the world) would then look like a historically appropriate need; not a mask for subjective self-assertion, and so a forgetting of being, but *a way of avoiding a profound, two millennia-long self-forgetting*.

That is, while for Nietzsche himself 'Descartes was superficial',[38] whatever analysis or textual 'uncovering' might make plausible the idea of an 'inner connection between the fundamental positions of Descartes and Nietzsche' might also make plausible some sort of very appropriate, quite defensible 'Nietzschean' affirmation of this remark by Hegel, the greatest modern philosopher of self-consciousness. Hegel writes that, with Descartes,

> we are at home, and like the mariner after a long voyage in a tempestuous sea, we may now hail the sight of land. With Descartes, the culture of modern times, the thought of modern philosophy, really begins to appear, after a long and tedious journey.[39]

REFERENCES

EN   Martin Heidegger, *Nietzsche. Volume IV. Nihilism*, trans. David
        Krell, San Francisco, Harper & Row, 1982.
ERS   —— *Nietzsche. Volume II. The Eternal Recurrence of the Same*,
        trans. David Krell, San Francisco, Harper & Row, 1984.
H   —— *Holzwege*, Frankfurt am Main, Klostermann, 1972.
N   —— *Nietzsche*, 2 vols. Pfullingen, Neske, 1961.
VA   —— *Vorträge und Aufsätze*, Pfullingen, Neske, 1967.
WN   ——, 'The Word of Nietzsche: "God is Dead" ', in M. Heidegger
        (ed.), *The Question Concerning Technology and Other Essays*,
        trans. W. Lovitt, New York, Harper & Row, 1977.
WPA   —— *Nietzsche. Volume I. The Will to Power as Art*, trans. David
        Krell, San Francisco, Harper & Row, 1979.
WPKM   —— *Nietzsche. Volume III. The Will to Power as Knowledge and
        Metaphysics*, trans. David Krell, San Francisco, Harper & Row,
        1987.

NOTES

1 All references to Heidegger's Nietzsche lectures and articles are made in the text, first to the English translation and then to the German. The first reference makes use of abbreviations of the English titles.

2 The best short discussion by Heidegger of this connection between metaphysics and technology is in *Holzwege*, '*Die Zeit des Weltbildes*', Frankfurt am Main, Klostermann, 1972, 69–104, translated as 'The Age of the World Picture', in *The Question Concerning Technology and Other Essays*, New York, Harper & Row, 1977, 115–54. He claims there that 'modern technology' is 'identical with the essence of modern metaphysics', (p. 116), and that 'the fundamental event of the modern age is the conquest of the world as picture [*Bild*]', (p. 134).

3 As in Bernd Magnus's *Heidegger's Metahistory of Philosophy: Amor Fati, Being and Truth*, The Hague, Nijhoff, 1970.

4 For a discussion of some of the main aspects of Heidegger's claim that Nietzsche is a '*Vollendung*' of the tradition, see Lawrence Lampert, 'Heidegger's Nietzsche Interpretation', *Man and World*, 1974, vol. 7, 353–78.

5 Said somewhat more technically, in the language of Heidegger's 1943 essay, '*Nietzsches Wort: "Gott is tot"* ', in *Holzwege*, op. cit., translated as 'The word of Nietzsche: "God is dead"', in *The Question Concerning Technology*, op. cit., ' "nihilism" means that *nothing* is befalling Being [*dass es mit dem Sein nichts ist.*]. Being is not coming into the light of its own essence' (WN, 110; H, 244). Nietzsche is right to see that Being is 'no thing', not an available object of representation or manipulation, but he is so much under the sway of modern presuppositions that he concludes that Being is therefore 'nothing', a meaningless, religious projection. He is thus a nihilist. Or, as Heidegger, in the 1940 lectures, puts the basic question he wants to ask Nietzsche, 'What if in truth the nothing were indeed not a being but also were not simply null

[*Nichtige*]?' (EN, 22; N II, 54). Cf. the excellent discussion by Wolfgang Müller-Lauter, '*Nietzsches Lehre vom Willen zur Macht*', *Nietzsche-Studien*, 1974, vol. 3, 1–60.

6 Such an issue, of course, is only one of the many currently discussed as falling under the 'modern postmodern' controversy, a dispute that ranges over architecture and literary criticism as well as philosophy. See the summary article, followed by a useful bibliography, in ' "Modern", "Postmodern", and "Contemporary" as Criteria for the Analysis of 20th-Century Literature' by Gerhard Hoffmann, Alfred Hornung, and Rüdiger Kunow in *Amerikastudien*, 1977, vol. 1, 19–46 and the special issue of the *New German Critique*, 1981, vol. 22.

7 I do not mean to pass over the fact that such a 'labelling' issue is quite complicated. For many commentators, Nietzsche himself, contrary to what Heidegger says, is the quintessential '*post*modernist'. See J. Habermas, *Philosophical Discourse of Modernity*, trans. Frederick Lawrence, Cambridge, MIT Press, 1987, 83–105; Mark Warren, *Nietzsche and Political Thought*, Cambridge, MIT Press, 1988, and my 'Nietzsche's Farewell: Modernity, Pre-Modernity, Post-Modernity', in *Nietzsche* ed. B. Magnus, Cambridge, Cambridge University Press, 1991.

8 Obviously, modern, seventeenth-century rationalism is far more difficult to fit into such a characterization but I am mostly interested here in the post-Kantian modernity problem. However, I think there is something quite right in Heidegger's attention to the phenomena of will, method, and subject in Descartes and Leibniz, although nothing I say in what follows will depend on accepting Heidegger's reading of early modern philosophy.

9 The Heideggerian formula for this: '*Das Lichtung-lose des Seins ist die Sinnlosigkeit des Seienden im Ganzen*' (WPKM II, 180; N II, 26).

10 This point should be especially emphasized. On the surface this posing of such a 'confrontation' seems to involve conceptions of 'metaphysics' too different to allow much of anything interesting to emerge. As Magnus has pointed out, Nietzsche understood metaphysics to be an essentially religious phenomenon, a hope for an 'other world' of stability, self-identity, purpose, etc., and little of what Heidegger is interested in involves any necessary metaphysical dualism. Thus there is nothing Nietzsche would recognize in the characterization of his own position as 'metaphysical'. See Bernd Magnus, *Heidegger's Metahistory*, op. cit., 125, 131. My claim is that, once we note the different uses of the terms, there is still an important common issue between them over the significance of 'beings as a whole', a problem Heidegger quite rightly sees is connected to the implications of post-Cartesian, or modern 'subjectivity' (with Nietzsche roughly 'affirming' and Heidegger roughly 'rejecting'). My question will be whether either of them has formulated properly the question of subjectivity, or what is at issue in such affirmation or rejection.

11 Müller-Lauter, in the article cited above, accepts Heidegger's characterization of Nietzsche's project as metaphysical (in the broad sense defined by Heidegger) but rejects the 'metaphysics of subjectivity' label, and concludes '*Nietzsches Philosophie schliesst die Frage nach dem*

Grund des Seienden im Sinne überlieferter Metaphysik als eine für das wirkliche Geschehen relevante Frage aus', op. cit., 60. He does so, however, for reasons different from those presented below in section V.

12 The use of these notes has become quite a controversy over the last thirty years or so. A brief list of the relevant sources: Cf. Heidegger's confident remarks in the fifth lecture of WPA about the plan and organization of Nietzsche's 'major work', (WPA, 33; N I, 43) with the very different assessments of Bernd Magnus in 'Nietzsche's Philosophy in 1888: *The Will to Power* and the *Übermensch'*, *Journal of the History of Philosophy*, January 1986, vol. 24, no. 1, 79–98; Mazzino Montinari, *Nietzsche Lesen*, Berlin, Walter de Gruyter, 1982; and the original champion of the anti-*Nachlass* forces, K. Schlechta's *Der Fall Nietzsches*, Munich, C. Hanser, 1959. For counters to Schlechta and/or defences of Heidegger, see K. Löwith, *'Zu Schlechtas neuer Nietzsche-Legende'*, Merkur, 1958, vol. 12; E. Heftrich, *Nietzsches Philosophie. Identität von Welt und Nichts*, Frankfurt am Main, Klostermann, 1962, 291–5; and W. Müller-Lauter, op. cit., 6–12.

13 Cf. among the rare occurrences, *Beyond Good and Evil*, trans. Walter Kaufmann, New York, Vintage, 1966 (BGE, hereafter) #36, and *On the Genealogy of Morals*, trans. Walter Kaufmann, New York, Vintage, 1969 (OGM, hereafter) II, #12.

14 To facilitate reference I have tried to use Krell's translations of the lectures without emendation, but there is one feature of his rendering that cannot be accepted. For reasons we shall see in a moment, it is extremely important to know when Heidegger is referring to a theory or account of the 'beings' or entities, which he consistently refers to as *'Seiende'*, and when he means to refer to an account of Being, of *Sein*. This is a difficult problem (especially since Heidegger often refers to *das Seiende* as such, and it would be grossly inaccurate to translate that as 'the entity') but the English reader needs more of an indication of Heidegger's variation in the cognates of 'to be' than are provided by Krell's use of capitalization and plurals.

15 Heidegger, of course, is well aware that Nietzsche presents himself as an anti-metaphysical thinker and that, thus, Heidegger's classification will be controversial. Cf., *inter alia*, the beginning of the 1939 series, N II, 7).

16 For the best contemporary account of Heidegger's theory of Being as 'presence', and especially of the 'interdependence of existence and presence'. See Frederick A. Olafson, *Heidegger and the Philosophy of Mind*, New Haven, Yale University Press, 1987.

17 *The Will to Power*, trans. Walter Kaufmann and R. J. Hollingdale, New York, Vintage, 1968 (WP, hereafter), #617.

18 In the 1953 public lecture, *'Wer ist Nietzsches Zarathustra?'* published in *Vortäge und Aufsätze, Teil I*, Tübingen, Neske, 1967, and in translation as an appendix to the ERS lectures, 209–33, Heidegger poses this issue in terms of Zarathustra's account of human 'revenge' against time, and he tries to show that 'Zarathustra's doctrine does not bring redemption from revenge', ERS, 229; VA I, 114. Magnus discusses the slim textual basis for Heidegger's criticism in *Heidegger's Metahistory*, op. cit., 124ff.; and I have argued elsewhere that Zarathustra's account of

revenge cannot be extracted from the dramatic structure of the entire narrative. See my 'Irony and Affirmation in Nietzsche's *Thus Spoke Zarathustra*', in *Nietzsche's New Seas*, ed. Michael Gillespie and Tracy Strong, Chicago, University of Chicago Press, 1988, 45–71.

19 There are numerous examples in the *Nachlass* of passages that can be read this way. The clearest are from 1888: 'all driving force is will to power . . . there is no other physical, dynamic, or psychic force except this'. (WP, #688); life itself 'is merely a special case of the will to power' (WP, #692); or 'the innermost essence of Being is will to power' (WP, #693). The question is how Nietzsche means for us to understand the authority of these claims, on what they are based, given his famous denials not just of 'other worldly' but all '*true* worldly' metaphysics. In BGE he more cautiously notes that the world 'defined and determined according to its "intelligible character" is will to power and nothing else' (#36). That qualification will be important in answering such a question, as are his numerous claims in the *Nachlass*, such as those from #556–60 that 'The origin of "things" is the work of that which imagines, thinks, wills, feels'; that 'thingness has been invented by us owing to the requirements of logic'; and especially 'That things possess a constitution in themselves quite apart from interpretation and subjectivity, is a quite idle hypothesis.' For a discussion of these and other 'oppositions' in Nietzsche's thought , see Eckard Heftrich, op. cit., especially 257ff., and Wolfgang Müller-Lauter, *Nietzsche, Seine Philosophie der Gegensätze und die Gegensätze seiner Philosophie*, Berlin, Walter de Gruyter, 1971, 29, and his remark on Heidegger, 30.

20 It is also not clear that the appeal to the will to power as a comprehensive *explanation* can be defended against a charge of either triviality or incoherence. Cf. Maudmarie Clark, 'Nietzsche's Doctrines of the Will to Power', *Nietzsche-Studien*, 1983, vol. 12, 458–68.

21 Karl Jaspers, *Nietzsche, Einführung in das Verständnis seines Philosophierens*, Berlin, Walter de Gruyter, 1947, 290.

22 *Kant und das Problem der Metaphysik*, Frankfurt am Main, Klostermann, 1965; *Kant and the Problem of Metaphysics*, trans. James S. Churchill, Bloomington, Indiana University Press, 1968. See especially sections 36–45. Cf. also the last two-thirds of *Die Frage nach dem Ding*, Tübingen, Niemeyer, 1962; *What is a Thing?*, trans. W. B. Barton Jr, and Vera Deutsch, South Bend, Regnery, 1967.

23 *Sein und Zeit*, Tübingen, Niemeyer, 1972; *Being and Time*, trans. J. Macquarrie and E. Robinson, New York, Harper & Row, 1962, section 62.

24 This tendency to qualify the wholly 'subjective' character of the will to power is particularly evident in Heidegger's remarks on aesthetic experience, and the 'attunement' available in 'rapture' (*Rausch*). See WPA, 112, 113–14; N I, 132, 133–4.

25 Cf. *Being and Time*, op. cit., on 'Stimmung' and 'Gestimmtsein', #29ff.

26 I note that the characterization of Heidegger's position as a 'charge' or a 'criticism' is, while true to the polemical and even contemptuous tone of much of what he says (see especially the extraordinary fourth lecture in the second part of the 1939 WPKM series on '*das Zeitalter der vollendeten Sinnlosigkeit*, 174ff.; N II, 20ff.), nevertheless problematic.

This is nowhere more evident than in a strange emendation of the first part of the 1939 series. At the end of the third lecture Heidegger had written that the will to power doctrine represents a 'peculiar dominance [*Herrschaft*] of Being 'over' beings as a whole'. This is a curious expression since, as we have already seen, the 'metaphysical' nature of the will to power notion is supposed to involve the traditional 'dominance' of beings, *Seiende*, over our thought about Being, *Sein*. This formulation oddly suggests that this very confusion or forgetting is *itself* a manifestation of Beingness, that, somehow, it is its own 'forgetting'. When Heidegger emends the passage in 1961 he does not alter it to make it read more consistently with his usual charges of error and forgetting against metaphysics, but adds instead the phrase 'in the veiled form of Being's abandonment of beings [*Seinsverlassenheit des Seienden*]', WPKM, 21; N I, 495. This greatly adds to the confusion since it suggests that Heidegger's *own* characterization of Nietzsche's position as a *Seinsverlassenheit* is itself a 'veiled' (*verhüllten*) form of 'Being's dominance over beings'. See also his remarks in WN that metaphysics is not an 'error', that, even as the forgetting of Being, it 'would be, in its essence, the mystery of Being itself' (WN, 110; H, 224). If, as some have suggested, Heidegger's famous *Kehre* or turn can be detected occurring in the Nietzsche lectures, this would be a place where the pull of different elements of his emerging thought and the confusion that can create, is most evident. Cf. Hannah Arendt, *The Life of the Mind*, San Diego, Harcourt Brace Jovanovich, 1978, 172–95. See also the very interesting analysis by Philippe Lacoue-Labarthe, *L'imitation des modernes*, Paris, Galilee, 1986, 113–31, especially his attempt to show that, in the Nietzsche lectures 'Dans la déconstruction de l'esthétique se joue d'abord le différend de Heidegger avec le national-socialisme' (115).

27 *Modulo* all the usual qualifications assumed in the 'transcendental' tradition from Kant to Husserl: that this claim does not refer to an individual or empirical subject, but either to 'transcendental subjectivity' (what any subject, in order to experience at all, would have to represent beings to be, etc.) or to a collective, historical subjectivity for which the criteria of objectivity can be shown to possess some sort of historical necessity. As we shall soon see, these are important qualifications not attended to by Heidegger.

28 In 'Remarks on Nietzsche's "Platonism" ', in *The Quarrel between Philosophy and Poetry*, New York, Routledge, 1988, 183–203, Stanley Rosen has argued that neither Plato nor Nietzsche can be said to have an ontology, or a comprehensive teaching about Being, the former because of the fundamentally finite, or unsatisfiable character of human desire (the unknowability of the ideas), the latter because of perspectivism. This leads him to suggest that the 'genuine "Platonism" of Nietzsche' (p. 199) lies more in the common importance of rhetoric, or wholly political speech in both. For Plato, on this reading, human desire can still be said to be guided or regulated by what cannot be said; for Nietzsche there is nothing to say, and so all speech is fundamentally poetic. This all seems to me still to share a great deal with Heidegger's account, even though Rosen is more interested in Nietzsche's political

distinctions between the 'high' or noble, and the 'low' or base. As will be clear below, I disagree with both Rosen's and Heidegger's rejection of Nietzsche's modernism. For a different view of why there is, especially, a great *German* political issue at stake in the confrontation between Nietzsche and Heidegger, see Lacoue-Labarthe, op. cit.

29 Indispensable in such an account would be the articles by Otto Pöggeler, '*Hegel und die Anfänge der Nihilismus-Diskussion*', Man and World, 1970, vol. 3, 193–9, and Wolfgang Müller-Lauter, '*Nihilism als Konsequenz des Idealismus: F. H. Jacobis Kritik an der Transzendentalphilosophie und ihre philosophiegeschichtlichen Folge*', in *Denken im Schatten des Nihilismus*, ed. A. Schwan, Darmstadt, Wissenschaftliche Buchgesellschaft, 1975, 113–63.

30 It is true that Heidegger discusses the distinct importance of the body, or the sensible (passion, affect, etc.) in Nietzsche's account of the subject, and he occasionally lectures on Nietzsche's 'biological' notion of knowledge, but these notions are all interested in an 'existential' way, as 'the lived body', and so do not play a major role in Heidegger's account. Cf. WPA, lectures 6–11; N I, 44–81; WPKM, 101–10; N I, 590–602. See the remarks on this topic by Michel Haar, 'La Critique nietzschéenne de la subjectivité', *Nietzsche-Studien*, 1983, vol. 12, 86ff.

31 Michel Haar, op. cit., 87ff.

32 Ibid., 94ff. See also his remarks in this section on the similarities and differences between Heidegger's notion of *das Man*, and Nietzsche on 'the herd'.

33 CF. WP, 481.

34 Cf. the remark in *The Gay Science*, trans. Walter Kaufmann, New York, Vintage, 1974, bk. 5, 298: 'Consciousness is really about only a net of communication among human beings.'

35 That is, without such a notion of necessity, the proper 'master thinker' to interrogate about the great 'fate of modernity' issue is Hume, not the Germans. Without the transcendental dimension the subjective turn generates the unavoidable and unsolvable problem of scepticism, the suspicion that the required role of mental activity in all representation ends 'modern *metaphysics*', or any account of 'the beings', before it can get started.

36 Again Heidegger poses this 'escape from nihilism' issue in very general, theoretical terms, and does not deal much with the question of Nietzsche's practical, or even his political, transformative intentions. Stanley Rosen has argued in several places that, even if Nietzsche's rhetoric and the difference between his exoteric and esoteric teachings are taken into account, it is still true that the conditions for the possibility of Nietzschean creativity also ensure the impossibility of ascribing any significance or 'nobility' to that creativity. See 'Nietzsche's Revolution', in *The Ancients and the Moderns: Rethinking Modernity*, New Haven, Yale University Press, 1989, 189–208, and especially his treatment of Nietzsche, Heidegger, and the modernity issue in *Nihilism*, New Haven, Yale University Press, 1969, ch. 4, 'Historicity and Political Nihilism', 94–139. For all their differences, Rosen and Heidegger agree in reading Nietzsche as some sort of logical culmination (and *reductio*) of the Kantian revolution. I dispute such a reading in *Modernity as a*

Philosophical Problem: Remarks on the Dissatisfaction of European High Culture, London, Basil Blackwell, 1990.
37 Hans Blumenberg, *The Legitimacy of the Modern Age*, trans. Robert Wallace, Cambridge, MIT Press, 1983.
38 BGE, #191.
39 G. W. F. Hegel, *Lectures on the History of Philosophy*, trans. E. S. Haldane and F. H. Simson, vol. III, New York, Humanities Press, 1974, 217; *Vorlesungen über die Geschichte der Philosophie*, III, Frankfurt am Main, Suhrkamp, 1971, 120.

Index

06   39   3.4   71   87